Thomas G. Braga

THE
FORGOTTEN
PORTUGUESE

BY

MANUEL MIRA

Luso-Brazilian Books
Box 170286
Brooklyn, NY 11217
718-624-4000

Published by
The Portuguese-American Historical Research Foundation, Inc.
Printed in the United States of America

Library of Congress Catalog Card Number: 97-92675

The Forgotten Portuguese
The Melungeons and Other Groups
Series: The Portuguese Making of America
Early North-American History

Includes 100 illustrations, 1028 footnotes,
bibliographical references and index

ISBN 0-9658927-0-0

Proceeds of the sale of this book will be donated to the Portuguese-American Historical Research Foundation, a North Carolina non-profit corporation dedicated to the research of early American history and the Portuguese people's contribution to the making of America.

History and the subject of this book is an ongoing research. The author invites the reader to submit any corrections, omissions or suggestions to be inserted in the next edition. Contributions are welcome and authorship acknowledged.

Write to:
The Portuguese-American Historical
Research Foundation, Inc. (P.A.H.R.F., Inc.)
Franklin, NC 28734 - USA
email:portugal@dnet.net
http://www.dnet/nonproft/portugal

The paper used in this book meets the minimum requirements of American National Standard for Information Sciences–Permanence of Paper for Printed Library Materials, ANSI Z39.48–1984.

Dedication

To all authors whose books and papers have been quoted in this work. Without their prior research, this book would have been almost impossible.

Also to my wife Lurdes, my family, and friends who went without my company during my long hours of research.

Contents

Contents (Cont.)

Cont.

Contents (Cont.)

Table of Illustrations

Table of Illustrations (Cont.)

Table of Illustrations (Cont.)

Preface

Manuel Mira's research is as solid as his integrity. No one has brought more energy and expertise to the question of a Portuguese origin for the Melungeon people than has Manuel.

From his earliest conversations with me, to his prolific series of articles published in Luso Americano, he had always shown a welcomed attention to detail and, equally important, a sensitivity and compassion toward the people about which he was writing.

I was relatively sure before meeting Manuel that our people possessed at least a partial Portuguese heritage; after meeting him, watching his research and reading an early draft of this book, I am totally convinced that Portuguese genes do indeed play a significant role in who we are as a people.

I congratulate Manuel on a masterful job and encourage him to not stop at this juncture. We need him — and others like him — to keep us to continue the research for roots and the rebuilding of self-dignity.
Thank you, Manuel, for a job well done!

N. Brent Kennedy, Ph.D.
Vice Chancellor for Development
& College Relations

Clinch Valley College of the
University of Virginia

Author of
The Melungeons
The Resurrection of a Proud People

Acknowledgments and Credits

I am most grateful to the following people who furnished material, and permitted me to use and quote from it: N. Brent Kennedy, Ph.D., Clinch Valley Virginia University; Jean Patterson Bible, historian and author; Barbara McRae, Franklin, N.C. historian and author; Belmira Sardinha of Jupiter, Florida; César and Alexandra Gomes, Rute Ramalho, all from Portugal; Victor Marques of CNN; Antonio Matinho and Fernando dos Santos, of Newark, N.J.'s Luso-Americano newspaper; José Júlio Sousa, Carlos Veloso and Humberto Carvalho of Toronto; Benita Howell, Ph.D., anthropology professor, University of Tennessee-Knoxville; Manuel da Costa Fontes, Ph.D., professor of foreign languages, Kent State University, Ohio; Ruth Y. Wetmore and Dave Moore, North Carolina archaeologists; Manuel Luciano da Silva, M.D., Bristol. Rhode Island, historian and researcher; Douglas L. Wheeler, Ph.D., professor of modern history, University of New Hampshire, Durham; David J. Viera, Ph.D., professor of Spanish,Tennessee Technological University Cookeville ; Geoffrey L. Gomes, M.A., California State University, Hayward, language Lab Director; Leo Pap, Ph.D., State University of New York, New Paltz, linguistics professor; Joseph Judge, senior editor of the National Geographic Society; Luther J. Carter, journalist and Robert Mason, editor, both of the Virginian Pilot, Norfolk newspaper; Joseph Theriaga, Portuguese consul in Miami, for the use of his library; Helen Patton, Ph.D., of Franklin, N.C.; Richard Melvin, attorney, of Highlands, N.C.; Ruth Johnson of Kingsport, TN; Scott Collins, Ed.D., Hancock County, Tennessee, clerk master; Evelyn McKinley Orr, Melungeon Research Committee member of Omaha, Nebraska, and George Reis Jr. of New York.

Last but not least, to Adalino Cabral, Ph.D., Hispanic culture and language educator of the Greater Boston Area, for his careful, and detailed analysis of this work, his constructive criticism and suggestions.

Also, to the many participants who graciously provided personal interviews. To one and all, my sincere thanks.

Prologue

Why am I doing this research? The question may arise as to why this research has been undertaken. In his excellent, well written and well documented book, *The Portuguese Americans,* [1] Professor Emeritus Leo Pap, himself an immigrant from Switzerland, and a distinguished linguist of the State University of New York, at New Paltz, defends the Portuguese Community from an absurd remark made over 70 years ago. In Pap's preface, he cites a demeaning comment made by a bibliographer after a sociological study of the 1920's. It reads: *The study shows that the Portuguese are, by all accepted standards, a low grade people...* In response, Pap maintains that the Portuguese are neither high-grade or low-grade, but that *on their overwhelming majority* [they] *consist of ordinary laboring people with their distinct traditions.* [2] This research is in tune with Dr. Leo Pap's sense of justice to the Portuguese who have helped, and continue to help, build a strong America.

I have heard it said many times, *I don't know what my ancestors did for America*. Even one more reason to get involved. If I don't know, does anyone else care to know? I would like to call this project *We are America's Portuguese*. The Portuguese people are one of the oldest European groups of settlers, if not the oldest in the U.S., and its presence is recorded since Colonial times. However it is one of the most ignored, and the researcher M. Estellie Smith is absolutely correct when she classified them as the *invisible minority*.

The Portuguese saw what happened to the more militant Irish and Italians when they were discriminated against and signs read *No Irish need apply* and *No Micks, Dagos...* thus invisibility was their best protection. [3]

Douglas Wheeler in his *Historical Dictionary of Portugal* also writes: *For a small country perched on the edge of Western Europe but with an early history which began more than 2,000 years ago, there is a vast bibliography extant in many languages.* [4] Family unit is still the best survival means for mankind, and I believe that strong family ties account for the survival of the Melungeons and other groups. Unfortunately, the future is not so bright for families throughout the world. Doug Levy wrote in *USA Today* that families are declining worldwide. Developing nations are seeing the breakdown of traditional families in much the same way as the United States and other industrial nations. Rising divorce rates, childbirth outside of marriage, and migration are among the reasons cited. [5]

This book may not be able to prove that the Portuguese are the ancestors of the Melungeons and other groups, although it may come very close. Also, it does not criticize any of the research or work done in the past, by very qualified persons. By all means, they helped me and will help others who would like to pursue this subject any further.

I will try to focus on the fact that the *Melungeons and other groups* may have several genetic mixtures, with a possibility of one stronger component, and if it seems that I am placing a stronger emphasis on the Portuguese, it is mostly because I can relate to what has been written about them, and at the same time try to fill the ever present knowledge vacuum about the history of Portugal.

I have just compiled the facts as recorded by others. If they seem speculative, others have made them so. My work only asks questions that someone else with more expertise may be able to answer. In certain instances, I may also have doubts about fact authenticity. If so, it will be up to the reader to be the final judge based on the information presented.

Introduction

In today's age of easy transportation and communication, most of us believe that 1,000 or even 500 years ago, humans traveled very little or not at all. This is a misconception. Just because they did not have cars or airplanes does not mean that they did not go anywhere. By doing a surface history study, we quickly discover that people and goods moved from one place to another, carrying with them their culture in all its aspects.

During the reign of Portugal's King João II (1471-1495) the total distance traveled by the crew of the discovering vessels totaled fifty million miles. [6]

Wherever I go in my travels, I always wonder if the Portuguese were there or if they had any impact on the locale I happen to be visiting. The Appalachian Mountains had a special attraction for my wife and me. In 1987 when we visited western North Carolina, we liked it and decided to stay.

As time went on, I kept wondering if the Portuguese had been there or not. Near Franklin, N.C., I noticed a historical plaque honoring Juan Pardo for having passed through while commanding a Spanish expedition in 1567. Barbara McRae, a local writer and historian, told me about the Melungeons, other groups, and the Portuguese. That was the start of my research. Since then I have made contact with Mrs. Jean Patterson Bible and Dr. N. Brent Kennedy. These two fine persons have written and published books about the Melungeons. Since the start I was fascinated with their story, and so was Antonio Matinho, the editor of the the Luso-Americano of Newark, New Jersey, the largest Portuguese-American newspaper, published twice a week in the United States and distributed to all fifty states,. I wrote a series of seven articles for that newspaper, and publication started on March 14, 1995. The interest was overwhelming on the part of the readers, who made numerous calls and showed an interest in knowing more about the Melungeons who, like them, also emigrated, to this continent in search of a better life and freedom, and equally suffered discrimination in one form or other.

Finding myself living in the area where the Melungeons lived – and some still live – an opportunity presented itself to do research with a personal feeling and involvement with the local people.

Discrimination ? The Melungeons suffered discrimination and prejudice. I am no stranger to that; just like them, I have been a victim of it since I was born, and did not stop until much later. At 18, and tired of living in a country that was not offering the space and opportunity that I needed to build my future as a free person, I left Portugal and immigrated to Brazil where I lived for five years.

Although the language is the same, I was discriminated against and recognized that I was not one of them because I had lighter skin. Most Brazilians have a darker olive skin – and the natural treatment was derogatory.

My Portuguese accent gave me away. That prompted me to learn the local lingo and mimic their pronunciation, so much so that in two years, it was hard for anyone to detect my Portuguese ancestry through my daily speech.

Five years later when I visited Portugal, my own mother did not recognize my voice. Why did I learn to speak like the Brazilians? The answer is very simple. It was a means of survival, and when you are alone and many thousands of miles from the place you used to call home, you will do anything to survive and gain acceptance.

After five years in Brazil, I came to the United States in 1957 and then to Toronto, Canada, where I lived for the next 16 years.

Again, I felt discrimination because of the language difference and the color of my skin. I was not blonde; I had dark brown hair and brown eyes.

In Brazil, I stood out because I was lighter, and in Canada, I stood out because I was darker.

Discrimination does not choose places. Again, as a means of survival, I tried to learn the language and eliminate my foreign accent. Unfortunately I was not able to do it totally; I was already 24 years old.

In the process of learning the best way how to get accepted, I also learned quickly that if you are valuable and productive to the society and the system, discrimination slowly disappears. Still, many persons anglicized my name to Manny, which I did not mind, and shifted the pronunciation of my last name – Mira – from a Portuguese sound to an American sound, and in the process, misspelling it, as I I keep pointing out.

I also proved to myself that one can overcome discrimination, and that I did, when I was able to have my son admitted to Upper Canada College. That was a place one could not be admitted to if one's great-grandmother spoke broken English. That was a truly WASP type college (White Anglo-Saxon Protestant). Why am I expressing all this? The Melungeons had to do the same and more, as the reader will see after reading any of the books about these proud people.

As the reader will later read, the Melungeons did change their names, culture, religion, and language to survive in a strange and dangerous environment, where discrimination and prejudice were prevalent.

One thing they did not change, was their origin. When asked by John Sevier –] who attempted to organize the State of Franklin (1784), forerunner of Tennessee, later governor – and new settlers more than 200 years ago, who they were, they said with pride. We are Portuguese,they *proudly called themselves Portuguese.* [7]

Today they still know that their ancestors were *Portuguese,* although that word does not have the same meaning for them as it does for me.

Unfortunately, many of them avoid, and want to forget, the past, as well as the names Melungeon and Portuguese, because of the hardships that were brought upon them. My goal is to wipe that sad memory out of their minds and say, be proud of your ancestors no matter who they were. If this work can accomplish that in just a single Melungeon, the author's efforts were not in vain. It has been very difficult to trace the many Melungeon families. There are many who left their villages and went in search of a better life in the different parts of this country, which they did successfully. Many immigrants identify with their plight, as they also have been there before.

I bring up some points on the books written by Bonnie Ball, Jean Patterson Bible and Dr. N. Brent Kennedy, first to reenforce their theory on the Portuguese Melungeons, and second to question others.

Because this is a Portuguese point of view, I have to admit my own strong emphasis on anything connected with the Portuguese. However, I will also look into possibilities of other nationalities, races or ethnic groups, to compare, strengthen or weaken the Portuguese theory.

I acknowledge and emphasizes that I am not a professional writer or historian, therefore criticism or corrections that may help this book
to make this book's message better understood, are welcome. Also it is not the author's intention to criticize, glorify or villify any races or nationalities.The reader

Fig. 1 - The author, Manuel Mira, overlooking the Appalachian Mountains

must be warned beforehand that the events should be taken in the context of time or epoch in which they occurred. The reader must keep in mind that the world of the 15th and 16th centuries was a totally different one from that of the 20th century. What was accepted as normal behavior by the society then is unthinkable in terms of the last quarter of the 20th century.

Throughout the book, skin colors or races are mentioned, such as *Black, White, Negro, Mulatto*, etc. These words must be taken in the context of this research. There is no intended derogatory connotation whatsoever.

As far as the word *Negro* is concerned, it is a fact that in Portugal it is not derogatory. On the contrary, what is derogatory is using the name Black or *Preto* in Portuguese. Also what is common and politically correct in the USA, such as the usage of the name African-American to denote a *Black* person of African ancestry is not proper in Portugal where the term African-Portuguese describes not only a Black person of African ancestry, but also the many White persons born in Africa.

This book in many instances is arranged chronologically, and may have an appearance of a history of Portugal in certain chapters. This it is not intended to be, but I will focus heavily on the Portuguese during the 15th and 16th centuries and afterwards. Whenever a Portuguese or other nationality name is shown, the Portuguese or one of that particular nationality spelling is kept, or as known. I strongly object to the use of Portuguese names translated from Portuguese to Spanish and then using the Spanish name describing an original Portuguese name in an English book. I can also check the facts more easily from a dual cultural point of view, as a Portuguese and as an American, plus a good share of Appalachian Mountain feeling. In any event, it is believed that the Melungeons or other groups – Portuguese or not – should have their place in the historical making of America, and if this work can help accomplish that, then all the time spent will have been worth while.

The Spanish and the Portuguese

This is not a book about the governments of Portugal, Spain or any other country. It is about their people, who gave their contribution to the making of America. While most of the navigation and exploration done by the Portuguese in America was done under the Spanish flag and paid for by the Spanish crown, it was their individual work and pioneering spirit that contributed to the making of this nation. Eloy Gallegos, a historian and researcher at University of Tennessee in Knoxville, is writing a book soon to be published about the Spanish influence in the Southeast, which is ever present in Florida and most of the Southwest.

The Spaniards and Portuguese are like two brothers. They may look alike, however they are very different in many respects.The first Spanish discovery was made when the grandchildren of the first Portuguese navigators were already adults.

The Melungeons, an Endless Subject of Study and an Old Story

As soon as I started researching the Melungeon people, I found out that this was not something new. Their claim of being Portuguese as well as the name Melungeon was always there. Looking at the several books and articles already written on the subject, they have proven their existence in the 1700's in remote western regions, including Arkansas, as early as 1810.

For more than a century, much has been written about these people: theses, dissertations for masters' and Ph.D. degrees, articles in daily newspapers, magazines, historical reviews and books.

Fig. 2 - Bonnie Ball, author of the book **The Melungeons**.

Many authors, scientists, and scholars have studied the mystery of the Melungeons with varied results, but no definite conclusions.

Books about Melungeons

***The Melungeons* by Bonnie Ball.** Miss Bonnie was a teacher and historian, and taught elementary school in Virginia to the Melungeon offspring. She is the author of numerous articles, poems and small books. Her parents were well acquainted with the Melungeons from their generation.

She is author of the book *The Melungeons* – the first major work written about the Melungeons. It provides considerable information for anyone who intends to study this subject. While doing the research, Jean Patterson Bible provided me with one copy.

Fig. 3 - Jean Patterson Bible

It can be acquired from Over Mountain Press, Johnson City, Tennessee.

The Melungeons, Yesterday and Today by **Jean Patterson Bible,** is a historical, travel, and feature writer whose articles have been published in T*he New York Times, Baltimore Sun, Atlanta Journal, The American Home, Historical Review and Antique Digest.* She became interested in the Melungeons in the early 1970's. Her extensive research on their history in the Southeast culminated in the writing of *The Melungeons, Yesterday and Today.* A lecturer and former history, modern language, and English teacher, Mrs. Bible also writes historical articles for regional newspapers.

One of the first books I consulted was written in 1975 by Jean Patterson Bible, a very valuable resource. Additionally Jean loaned some photos and provided further important information. The title of her book is *The Melungeons, Yesterday and Today* and may be ordered through Jean Patterson Bible, P.O. Box 886, Dandridge, Tennessee 37725. It is a hardcover book, easy to read, and with many illustrations. Recently, Jean donated Brent Kennedy's book to the Macon County Regional Library. Dr. Kennedy did refer to these two books, as well as others, quite often, and the author will be doing the same.

Fig. 4 - Mike McGlothlen

Melungeons and other Mestee Groups by **Mike McGlothlen.** This book was originally prepared in 1993, then revised and enlarged in 1994, as a class handout for an anthropology course at the University of Florida in Gainesville. It contains much information about the different mixed race groups and their possible origins. It does not treat the Melungeons in detail as other books do. It has been distributed to university libraries, and may be requested through interlibrary loan. The text of the book in small print, without the reprinted articles, is being posted on the Internet. It also may be obtained by writing to Mike McGlothlen, 401 E. University Ave., Gainesville, FL 32601.

With his background as a geneticist working in cattle breeding, he believes strongly in heterosis (alteration) and that hybridization is advantageous. Thus he prefers to be viewed as mixed, and not a member of any one racial classification. The book dismisses the Portuguese origin, and does not present a logical explanation for many facts associated with the Melungeons. It provides another group of Melungeons that may or may not be connected with the Melungeons from the Appalachians. McGlothlen's book also contains copies of Melungeon related articles which make for a good research package for anyone interested in researching that or other groups. The book seems like some sort of personal crusade favoring the recognition of all un-officially recognized groups of mixed races into one class, the Mestee race. It also gives some of the data previously published by Pollitzer and Gilbert as well as a description of all separate groups and a table showing the Melungeon name frequency in northwest Florida.

McGlothlen's book ends with a postscript written in a July 1994 insert: *I now accept that it may be easier to be Indian and fit into one of the already established categories than it is to get a new category like Mestee recognized. This accords well with my preference to not proliferate human taxonomy any further.* [8]

It is commendable that Mr. McGlothlen thinks in that manner. People have enough labels as it is. Another one would not help make us better human beings.

As for the word Mestee, it does not matter how it is written. In the end it will always sound like mestizo. This word is not necessarily well accepted. As for the French word *mestis* or *mêtis*, it is not necessarily very well accepted in France since a large North-African population, mainly Algeria, emigrated into France. In Brazil, the word *mestiço* in Portuguese should not be used loosely. There, the word *mulatto* is well accepted and seldom used in a derogatory manner. However, *mulatos* refer to themselves as *caboclos*. In Brazil originally *criolo* meant a home-born slave; now it also means a native of Rio Grande do Sul, and, again it is not taken in a derogatory sense. The Portuguese word *caboclo* also is often used to describe in an affectionate manner a person from the countryside (*sertão, sertanejo*) which is usually a Brazilian of European, Indian and Black ancestry. The dictionary describes it as born of African and Indian. Gilberto Freyre, the Brazilian writer, teacher, politician, and great humanist wrote of the Portuguese: *God created the White and Black men, but the Portuguese made the mulatto.* [9]

Mr. McGlothlen points out that there are other groups which may call themselves Melungeons but are not connected with the Appalachian Melungeon community, such as the Dead Lake people from the Florida panhandle, the Redbones from Louisiana and others. [10] According to Brewton Berry, Dead Lake people of West Florida have no connection with the Melungeons of Tennessee, whereas the Redbones from Louisiana do. Let us keep in mind that there was a large community of Portuguese in Louisiana, of which there are still signs today, such as a tombstone marking with a Portuguese name in the early 1800's. See Portuguese in Louisiana.

The Melungeons' own explanation of their origin is that they descended from Portuguese sailors... Newman's Ridge on the Tennessee-Virginia border, is a long way from the sea-going people... [11] That did not stop the early Spanish and Portuguese explorers – Hernando de Soto, Juan Pardo and others before them –

Fig. 5 -The book by Dr. N.Brent Kennedy, published by Mercer University Press

from reaching the same area in the early 1500's, and later when our American pioneers went west. However Mike McGlothlen, in a reply to Brent Kennedy's objection to this statement, conceded that, after settling on the coast and mixed with the Indians, their descendants might well have moved to the mountains.

What has not yet been fully researched is other communities much closer to the coast that also call themselves Portuguese and have been there at least since the early 1800's. See Chapter VIII.

***The Melungeons - The Resurrection of a Proud People* by Dr. N. Brent Kennedy.** Kennedy's book was published in 1994, and is fascinating reading especially for Portuguese-Americans, as well as others who wish to appreciate the odyssey of early Spanish and Portuguese explorers who arrived in the New World long before other Europeans.

His book is very important for anyone interested in researching Melungeon family genealogy. It provides many names and their family trees. It is full of pictures of many Melungeons of the past. Brent Kennedy ends his book with the following invitation: *You are invited to participate in ongoing research regarding all aspects of Melungeon history.* The author not only accepted the invitation and reinforced some points in his book, but also added some comments on some of the possible theories presented.

Kennedy's book will be cited very often, to the point that it may look like a study, which is not the case. He is the first (Melungeon) writer to look into different aspects of the mystery and has taken a genuine interest to solving it.

Certain aspects presented in these books may not be relevant for the Portuguese point of view, but are still important enough for the reader to became familiar with the Melungeons and their odyssey. The reader is directed to their importance. By reading them, it will help in better understanding what follows in this book.

Fig. 6 -Brent Kennedy author of the book The Melungeons - **The Resurrection of a Proud People.** *Background shows a river where he used to play as a child.*

Who are they? - Where did they really come from? and... Why?

The following are the questions by those who have seen and observed the Melungeons. As a Portuguese-American, the author also has other questions to add:

1. What is the reason for their Mediterranean appearance?
2. Why did they choose the area in the states of North Carolina, Virginia, Tennessee and Kentucky?
3. Why did they live most of the time in the mountain ridges?
4. Why, in 1958, did another group classified as Portuguese have their children segregated, and not allowed in white schools?
5. Why did they use names with Portuguese roots?
6. Why did most of them always answer *We're Portuguese*?
7. Why was the classification of Portuguese able to survive to date (1997)?
8. Why was it necessary to enact specific laws for the Portuguese, the Melungeons and other groups?
9. Why is there evidence of Portuguese-style food and folklore in Melungeon locales?
10. Why do we find little houses over the graves in the cemeteries, much like those in Portugal?
11. Why have the Melungeon looks of an East Indian survived to this century and in the middle of the mountains, away from seaports? See Chapter VIII.
12. Why the name Canará was used by Melungeons, a name all the way from India? See Chapters II and IX.
13. Why were the Melungeons able to survive in the early beginnings of America, and the English only after several attempts much later?
14. Why is the Melungeon name so similar to the name of an Angolan province, a former Portuguese colony?
15. Why is the name Melungeon so similar to a name used by the Blacks in the African East Coast, where many Portuguese ships stopped on their way to India or returning to Portugal?
16. What people, besides the Portuguese would have the means to come to the Americas in those early days?
17. Why did the name Gois or Goa find so many derivatives used by countless numbers of Melungeon descendants?
    The Gowen Research Foundation out of Lubbock, Texas 79413 was created to research the Goins family genealogy.
    Email: gowen@llano.net. See Appendix B for common surnames.

Many more questions may arise as the reader proceeds.
Please feel free to forward them to the Foundation.

I will address these questions, or at least provide additional information in the attempt to decipher the Melungeon mystery, and other so-called Portuguese groups of unknown origin.

I have no intention of removing or demeaning other possible heritages that the Melungeons may have, nor it is my intention to criticize or judge the action or actions taken by previous individuals or Governments. Societies change, and facts taking place in a particular time frame must be judged in the context of that same period. Moreover it is clearly not his intention to demean any race, ethnic group or religion. It is a fact that the Portuguese people mixed with different races and ethnic groups in many different parts of the world, without a major problem.

To reiterate, this book will describe several coincidences and hypotheses that may or may not be related with the Portuguese. The reader will need to arrive at a conclusion. This book is an attempt to research some of the early settlers of America from the 15th to the 17th centuries. It may benefit those who are trying to trace their origins, in the same way that many are able to trace their family origins to England or Ireland. The descendants of the Melungeons or other groups should also be able to trace the origin of their ancestors with some logic.

Melungeons and Human Ethnic Heritage - *A human being can be of many ethnic heritage, and indeed all human beings are just such a mixture.* [12]

Fig. 7 - Scott Collins , Hancock County Clerk Master.
A Melungeon descendant.

The Melungeons may be another human vestige of the Portuguese presence in the Americas of the 15th and 16th centuries.

Each group, nationality or race should be proud of their past achievements. Whatever ethnic background one comes from, one should be able to find many contributions that their ancestors made for America.

Hancock and Sneedville the Last Stand

Fig. 8 - Hancock Court House in Sneedville Tennessee, and until recently was one of the areas with the most Melungeon population.

Notes

[1] The book still in print may be ordered from Luso-Americano newspaper in Newark, NJ.

[2] *The Portuguese-Americans* by Leo Pap, preface

[3] *Portuguese Enclaves: The Invisible Minority* by M. Estellie Smith, pp. 83, 88

[4] *Historical Dictionary of Portugal* by Douglas L. Wheeler, p. 184

[5] *USA Today* newspaper, 5/28/95

[6] *O Roteiro da Flandres e D. João II* by Joaquim Bensaude, p. 20

[7] Note on the Melungeons by Swan M. Burnett, p. 347 (*American Anthropologist*, V. II, 1889)

[8] *Melungeons and other Mestee Groups* by Mike McGlothlen, p. 167.

[9] *Os Pioneiros Portugueses* by Dr. Manuel Luciano da Silva, p. 159

[10] *Melungeons and other Mestee Groups* by Mike McGlothlen, p. 30

[11] Ibid, p. 38

[12] *The Melungeons* by Brent Kennedy, p.14

Chapter 3

Possibly the first European settlers of the USA

Melungeon - Melungo - Melunjão - Malungo - Mulango
Malange - Malanje - Mazungu- Muzungo
Melan - Mélange - Melun-cãn

Is the discovering of the Melungeons really necessary? The historian John Parker wrote about the four year cruise of the oceans in the late 1800's by H.M.S. *Challenger*, considered one of *the truly great discovery voyages of all time.*[1] Although no new lands were discovered, a broader and deeper knowledge was acquired. History should be a constant voyage of discovery.

Possible Origins of the Name Melungeon

The Melungeon name may not be a mystery as will be discussed later in this book. It is possible that the Melungeons knew the word, and used it among themselves to such an extent that others heard it and associated it with them. The name ...*had to do with the meaning of the term Melungeon itself: it had always been a mystery. Others had discovered the Afro-Portuguese word Melungo or Mulango, supposedly translated Shipmate or Comrade, but could draw no direct correlation to Melungeon.*[2] Malungo means comrade, companion or friend.[3a]

Two Portuguese dictionaries – recent editions available at the (Biblioteca Nacional) Portuguese National Library in Lisbon, Portugal – confirm that the name Melungo means *white person* insofar as the Blacks are concerned. It is a title given to Europeans by the natives of East Africa on the Indian Ocean. It is also the same as Mazungo or Mazungu.[3] Melungo was also a term used by the Changane tribe, a branch of the Zulus in Mozambique and South Africa, with the meanings of *white* or *boss.*[3a] Mike McGlothlen, who spent six and a half years teaching Bantu-speaking people in Zambia, notes a possible Bantu origin of the word Melungeon, later changed to Melungo in Portuguese. *Hence the word for white person is Muzungu but the Swahili word is Mzungu.*[4]

The first nine names shown above are connected to the Portuguese people. There are several explanations for the name Melungeon; they derive from the last three. One of them is *mélange* given to them by the French. Why would the French name the Melungeons from the French word *mélange?* Because they were darker? The French are not on the average fair skinned or blonde people. Also the name is spelled with an a, not u, as in *Melungeon.* Although it has been misspelled many times, the letter u, always remained.

That Melungeon originates from *mélange* is mentioned by some writers. *The word Melungeon probably derives from melange and was the name given to these people by French traders...*[5] This statement is being perpetuated by other authors. However, the chronology does not seem right, since it has been said that the Melungeons came in the late 1700's to the mountains already inhabited by people other than the French. They were fur traders passing through, and did not stay long enough to coin a name. There were no French settlements in the Appalachians to speak of, and the few that were present would hardly give them a name that would stick for a long period. One other question comes to mind: Why did the French apply the name *mélange* to a certain group of people only in the U.S.? The name could also have been applied in Brazil, because the French arrived in Rio de Janeiro in 1555. The mixture of races in Rio was similar to that in the British Colonies in North America. There were Indians, Blacks, and Whites in Brazil, at about the same time. No record of such a name has been found or attributed to the French.

The French activity started with the project of establishing colonies of French Protestants (Huguenots) in 1555. [6] However, they arrived in Florida in 1562, with Jean Ribaut as their leader, but stayed only until 1565. After the French civil wars in 1598 colonizing efforts were renewed, mostly in Acadia (Nova Scotia), Canada. Fur traders had earlier reached Lake Superior, traveled the Fox and Wisconsin rivers to the Mississippi in 1673, and descended to Arkansas. In Louisiana, the French explorer Robert Cavelier de La Salle descended the Mississippi River in 1682, and claimed the entire river basin for France. A later consequence was the founding of New Orleans (Nouvelle-Orléans) in 1718 by Jean-Baptiste Lemoyne. Although in Louisiana the French left considerable influence – with most of the people there having darker skin – the name Melungeon was never used. It has been said that the French named the *Redbones* of Louisiana, apparently derived from the French *Os Rouge* which was used to describe persons of mixed Indian blood. We have to question that, because it appears that the *Redbones* name went with the groups. Maybe the name *Os Rouge* was applied to descendants of the *Redbones*. [7] Redsticks, Sabines and the Natchitoches are also important. McDonald Furman's late 1800 work on the Redbones and *The Cherry Winche Country* written in the 1930's by Webster Talmadge Crawford where he concludes: *They appear to bear the stamp of Mediterranean stock.* [8] Red Stick or Baton Rouge in French was first recorded by the French, and can be traced back to 1686. [9]

Another term, *Cane River Mulattos,* was also applied to dark skinned people in Louisiana. In that part of the country, where the French stayed for quite some time, they did not call the *mixed* or *mélange* people *Melungeon.* Why, would they do so in Tennessee where the French just passed through mostly as fur traders ? Dr. Celestine Pierre Cambiaire, an *Officer d'Academie* in France makes a good case for the French word *mélange* in his 1933 book about East Tennessee and West Virginia. He even changes the word Melungeons to *Melangeons.* Bonnie Ball, repeated it by quoting the same name out of his book. Cambiaire also justifies the French connection by stating that *in 1714, Charleville had already a store where Nashville stands now.* Also that *some French traders or trappers must have given the name Melangeons.* [10]

Nashville is almost 400 miles away from the Appalachian Mountains and even farther from Charleston, West Virginia. Cambiaire writes that the Melungeons arrived in Tennessee between 1810 and 1815, – which is not correct – established dates that connects them with John Sevier in the late 1700's. The established *store* in 1714 and the French in Nashville could not have had anything to do with the name Melungeon. When the first settlers arrived they found the Melungeons, but there are no reports of finding any French settlement, except in 1699 where a Colony of French Huguenots settled in Virginia in the Indian Town of Monacan. [11]

By then there were communications between the English, and the French and no report of the name Melungeon to anyone with dark skin or mixed ancestry. By late 16th century and early 17th century, the Southeast was heavily traveled.

Finally, a French document written in 1699 was found, with the word *CHARAQUI* (Cherokee), and to date no French document was found with the name Melungeon or any other similar. The name Cherokee was first written in 1708 as the English name for that Indian nation. The Portuguese chronicler with Hernando de Soto in 1540 wrote *CHALAQUE* naming the Cherokee as shown on the book published in Portugal in 1557. [12]

Another possible origin for the name Melungeon, is the Greek word *Melan*. However Dr. Edward T. Price wrote in 1951 that the possibility of the word deriving from the French *mélange* or even the Greek *Melan* seems remote. [13] But, these groups of settlers probably knew no Greek, and why would they choose a Greek derived term to coin such a name.

The last term is *Melun-cãn*, a Turkish word from the old Ottoman language, which when pronounced, sounds the same way as Melungeon. It means *cursed soul or one whose luck has run out.* [14] It is possible to consider that origin, but harder to justify, unless there was a small group of Turkish slaves – not necessarily from Turkey but from areas under the Ottoman Empire – that may have been left by Sir Francis Drake in the coast of North Carolina or Virginia. It is also possible that the word Melungeon and the word *Melun-cãn* may have been accepted by both Portuguese and Turks due to the similarity of sounds. Later in this book there will be discussion on that aspect of the Melungeons. The modern expression of Melungeon may be derived from the time of discoveries by the Portuguese to mean shipmate or companion, that in old Portuguese was pronounced *Melunjão*. *A clever suggestion is that it is derived from the Afro-Portuguese melungo (melõongo), meaning shipmate, the term by which Portuguese sailors were said to call one another.* [15] It may also have derived from the Portuguese word Melungo, which has two meanings, depending on the area where it is used. For the present, we may accept the definition of white man. And, according to officials at the Embassy of Portugal, in sixteenth-century Portuguese mulango probably was pronounced very similarly, if not identically, to our present-day word Melungeon.

These people later resented the name Melungeon, when it started to be used in a discriminatory manner. Eventually the same happened when they considered themselves Portuguese, which meant the same as Melungeon. What they really wanted was to erase from their memories anything that would not look like English or British origin; they just wanted to assure their survival. Similar situations occurred with other groups that were not necessarily identified as Melungeons but as Portuguese. This did not help either. Discrimination was there because of skin color.

Melungo or Melungeon, Possibly Brought by English Explorers in Africa

In an interview with Portuguese from Mozambique (East Africa), the author was told that the name Melungo is still being used today. The letter "G" , has the sound of J, as in JET and also the sound as in GET. In Portugal during the early 1940's children were taught in the early grades of school to pronounce the letter G, as in JET, however, later generations were taught to pronounce it as in GET. Also the pronunciation varies. It is either *melon Jon* or *melon go*. The English had a great influence in this former Portuguese colony.

Both British and Dutch traders followed in the wake of 15th century Portuguese explorers. English navigator Frobisher went on voyages to the Guinea coast of Africa in 1553 and 1554. It is possible that when the English arrived in Africa, they were also called Melungos by the natives in the same manner that they were calling the Portuguese already living there. The English naturally carried the name to England, and later when they found the same looking people (the Portuguese) in America, naturally they called them Melungos or Melungeons.

It is a fact that the English had a great influence in Mozambique. Some tribes still pronounce English words ending with a Portuguese sound or vowel, e.g., spoon as "spoona", fork as "forka", etc. They also drive on the left as in England, contrary to the other former Portuguese West Africa colony, Angola, where driving is on the right. Recently (1995) Mozambique joined the British Commonwealth, and they are talking about the possibility of changing the national language from Portuguese to English to which a government official replied, "not so", but it is considered a second language.

There is another fact which is very often ignored. Quite a number of people from India and Asia settled on the East Coast of Africa, due to the stopover by the navigators going to or returning from India. It is not unusual to see a person born in Mozambique with an Asian appearance.

The expedition of Diogo Cão, ordered by King João II, discovered the major part of Angola in 1482-83 including the area of Malange. [16] This name may be connected with the Melungeons. The other possibility is the contact with the Portuguese people living in the Angolan province of Melange, and/or the city of Melange. Portuguese navigators reached the Kongo kingdom in the northwest and parts of the Malanje highlands by the 1480's and converted the king of Kongo, together with many Bakongo, to Christianity.

They could have associated the name with the Portuguese people already living there. Malanje, also spelled Malange is a town on the country's principal plateau, and also a name of a province in north-central Angola, West Africa.

This may be one of the reasons why the Melungeons accepted this name in the beginning, as it had a familiar and dear sound, although they did not like it later as it would be mentioned in a derogatory manner.

Geographical Regions

The Melungeon people and their descendants have lived for many years in the Appalachian mountain region, particularly in the Blue Ridge and the Smoky Mountains.

The Melungeons were sometimes considered a an Indian group.*Indian, White, and specially Portuguese blood are said to be* prominent, according to Gilbert. [17]

Most of them have left the security of the mountain ridges for the valleys and cities to take advantage of the progress that has bypassed them. The Melungeons and other groups lived in the

Fig. 9 - Map of the States, showing where the Portuguese and Spanish explored in the 1500's and where the Melungeons and other groups settled.

following sizable communities: Counties in North Carolina - Jackson, Swain, Robeson, Allegheny, Surry, Macon, Cherokee, Northampton, Buford. In South Carolina, Lancaster. In Tennessee: Hancock, Ashe, Yancey, Hawkins, Tazewell, Claiborne, Hamblen, Rhea, Roane, Loudon, Cocke, Davidson, Franklin, Grundy, Hamilton, Knox, Marion, Meigs, Morgan, Overton, Rhea, Roane, Sullivan, White, Wilson, Bledsoe, and Van Buren. In Virginia Lee, Blackwater, Scott, Wise, Dickenson. In KY; Letcher, Dickerson, Magoffin. In southwestern Virginia: Giles, Russell, and Washington. [18]

These were the safe places known, but they were not the only ones. Thousands of Melungeons migrated to the West, most to Arkansas, Oklahoma, Indiana, Texas and California. Still others went to Rockville, Maryland, Ohio, and to Blounstown, Florida, just west of Tallahassee. Generally, the ones that stayed were the ones with fair skin, who were able to prosper and did not feel the – FPC free persons of color – discriminatory laws as much. These were put into place by the English settlers in the mountains.

Melungeons before Roanoke and Jamestown

There are enough reasons to believe that the Melungeons arrived in America before the English settlers of Roanoke and Jamestown, Virginia. One fact no one can dispute is that they were able to establish a colony and survive on their own to date, probably since the early 1500's. Therefore, by the time the English settlers arrived in Jamestown, there were already at least one or more generations of Melungeons established. So far, all the research points to that.

Portuguese and Spanish Inquisition 1391-1492

Jane Gerber in her book *The Jews of Spain* writes that after the Black Death in 1348, which wiped out almost a fifth of Europe's population, many German towns had expelled Jews or destroyed their communities... – expulsion from Germany began earlier after the 12th century [19] – the Spanish Jews were refused entry in many countries... *in 1391 the Spanish persecution overwhelmed the Sephardim,* [20] and, prior to that Portuguese kings, (1325-1383) protected the Jews. Apparently they had a relevant position in the public finances. [21] King João I (1385-1433) pursued the same policy after winning the war against Castile. Professor Viera stated that the 1391 pogrom in Spain was not motivated by kings, who often protected the Jews. It was motivated by a Spanish preacher, Ferran Martinez. For further research in this time period and related with the Inquisition, Professor Viera also suggests studies by Henry Kamen and Phillippe Wolff. *The Inquisition was just established in Castile when Columbus arrived in Spain (1484)* – Cecil Roth gives 1482 – [22] and the Inquisition was instituted in Portugal in 1536 for no apparent reason, except for the pressure put on João III of Portugal by Spanish monarchs who wanted his son to marry one of their daughters. Since the Jews and Moors not converted were practically non-existent and the Muslims had already been absorbed by the Christian community, they did not constitute a major problem. The Portuguese King João III used it as an excuse to exercise more power and terror. The Jews were a relatively small group - just before the 1500's probably 30,000 - and the Moors were a much smaller minority. [23] As for anti-Moor activities in Portugal, we must again make a separation between what was happening in Spain and Portugal, which would be to similar events in Northern Spain, where the Berbers and Moors had already assimilated with the Spaniards, after they had been there for almost eight centuries. The expulsion of the free Muslims was more a hypothetical measure than anything else, as most had been absorbed by the Christian community. [24] Also in Portugal, the Moors and Berbers in the 15th and 16th centuries were integrated into the culture and language of the Portuguese since the 1200's. There were not many genuine Moors or Berbers at that time in Portugal, with the exception of the ones captured in the conquest of some Northwest African Moorish towns, and who were used mainly for prisoner exchanges.

The monarchs of Spain expelled the Moors and Jews from Spain after conquering Granada, the last stronghold of the Arabs in the Iberian Peninsula. That caused many people to find a way out of Spain, and, later on, out of Portugal. It has been suggested that the Melungeons may be part of that group.

Kennedy quotes Major Arthur Griffiths (inspector of prisons in Great Britain): *...the Portuguese Kings João III, Sebastião, and Felipe II were engaging in the same anti-Moor activities in Portugal. In fact, Portugal's Inquisition was far more vicious than Spain's.* [25] Major Griffiths does maintain that: *Autos de Fé* (Acts of Faith) *were frequent, and on a scale hardly known in Spain, though the records are fragmentary.* [26] Out of well over 200 pages, the author dedicates only 12 pages to the Inquisition in Portugal, and a few about an execution of an Englishman who attacked the cardinal archbishop while he was raising the host during a mass celebration.

A serious study after the first quarter of the 16th century in Portugal shows that the economic situation, famine and disease, more than the Inquisition, prompted many people to look elsewhere for survival at any risk.

That part of the Portuguese history was bad, and no matter how small or large its actions were, it should not be considered unimportant. On the other hand, records show that it was not nearly as terrible as Spain's.

Now, as for Portugal's Inquisition being *far more vicious than Spain's*, let us look at the statistics. In the Inquisition Courts of Lisbon, Évora and Coimbra, 50 persons were condemned to death and executed in a public square between the years 1540 and 1609, according to Antonio Joaquim Moreira and described in his book *Historia dos Principais Actos e Procedimentos da Inquisição em Portugal.* [27] During the same period, 5,000 persons were executed in Spain, 70% of them having been Moors and Jews. *Between 1530 and 1609, the Inquisition in Valencia had dealt with more than five thousand cases, an average of sixty a year.* [28] Portugal at the end of the 16th century had a population of about 1.5 million compared to Spain's 8 million, or less than 20%. That means while Portugal executed one for every 30,000 population, Spain executed almost twenty as many for the same population ratio. To have some idea of European population at that time, England's population was between three and four million. [29]

Although Spain's numbers were higher than Portugal's, those were dark years in the Iberian Peninsula. Professor Manuel Fontes of Kent State University in Ohio wrote: *Without minimizing the horror, these sordid activities must be evaluated within the context of the time. To a great extent, Portugal and Spain avoided the witch hunts and the religious wars that brought death to many thousands in Europe… A couple of examples of what was happening elsewhere will suffice to place the two Iberian Inquisitions in perspective. In England, nearly 1,000 individuals were executed for witchcraft between the reign of Elizabeth I (1558) and the Act of 1736. In Southwestern Germany, at least 3,229 persons were executed as witches between 1561 and 1670. Concerning religious conflict during the same period, one only has to remember the numerous victims of the Reformation. A good example is the massacre of St. Bartholomew on August 24, 1572, when Catholics put to death at least 2,000 Huguenots in Paris alone. Thousands more were butchered as the massacre spread throughout the country. Other examples could be brought forth, but these are more than enough to show that the times were at least as cruel elsewhere in Europe.* [30]

The Inquisition not only persecuted Moors and Jews but also the Lutherans. On September 14, 1559, 23 were executed, and 13 more on April 24, 1562. [31]

Santa Elena and the Carolina coast - 1526

There are many theories about the origin of the Melungeons, but the most plusible one is the Santa Elena theory. This Colony was inhabited by thousands of men,

Fig. 10 - Sign near Franklin, N.C honoring Juan Pardo.

women and children from the Iberian Peninsula. That gave the Spaniards a base of operations for their explorations of the Carolinas, Georgia, Alabama and Tennessee.

In July 1526, a fleet with 500 men, women and children, soldiers and priests, along with the first Black slaves, sailed from Spain to American shores. Later in that year, after disease, Indian attacks and many other problems, the Colony was abandoned, and only 150 made it back home.

That was the first attempt to establish a colonial town in the territory of the United States, with the first landings in the south Santee river and the second in the Sapelo Sound area of Georgia. [32] Joseph Judge wrote in the *National Geographic Magazine*: *From Santo Domingo –* Dominican Republic – *a wealthy lawyer, Lucas Vasquez de Ayllon, led the first settlement attempt to the Carolina coast in 1526.* And in the west coast of Florida near *Tampa Bay was also the site of Hernando de Soto's landing with 600 men in ten ships.* Among them were many Portuguese noblemen along with the writer of the first book about the Southeast, Alvaro Fernandes, a native of Elvas. *He wandered for three years through the Southeast, discovering the Mississippi River, in which he was buried.*

[Again on the east coast of Florida] *Pedro Menéndez de Aviles founded St.*

Fig. 11 - Juan Pardo, explorer reaches the Tennessee Valley and meets the ancestors of the creek and Cherokee Indians [34]

*Augustine in 1565 along with a town on modern Parris Island – Santa Elena –
from which expeditions reached the Tennessee Valley and Chesapeake Bay.
...Excavations at Santa Elena, St. Augustine, and St. Catherines – South Carolina
– along with recent scholarly work on 16ᵗʰ century documents in Spain, have shed
light on this long-neglected epoch.* [33]

Lost Followers of Hernando de Soto - 1540

Louisa Davis writes about a letter that was post marked 1907 and had been sent
to Miss Collins of Sneedville, Tennessee by J. H. Rhea, one of her uncles. The
letter mentions *a legend that persists to explain the presence of the dark/skinned
people in the area; they are descendants of the Spaniards and Portuguese men in*
Hernando *de Soto's party who ventured from Florida into parts of North Carolina
and Tennessee in search of gold in 1540... were captured or befriended by the
Cherokees.* After reading it, Davis made the following remarks: *There is nothing
of the backwardness of the traditional mountaineer in the letter, and it is obvious
that Hancock County has – and for generations has had – its aristocracy, some of
whom take pride in their Spanish and Portuguese ancestry...*[35]

That legend talks only of men. If the Mediterranean European looks were to
survive for 400 years, complete families from Southern Europe would be needed.
The Hernando de Soto exploratory trip was narrated in a book by a Portuguese
member of the expedition, the Gentleman of Elvas. There is no mention of any lost
soldiers, except for the many deaths – including Hernando de Soto himself – that
occurred during the expedition due to the extreme harsh living conditions.

(See Chapter VII for more on Hernando de Soto and the Elvas book.)

Pardo and Caravels with Emigrants - 1566

In July (1566) *a troop of 250 men under Capt. Juan Pardo arrived from Spain
and built a more substantial fort and a number of houses.* [36] Later in the year he
reached the Tennessee Valley, after having passed near Asheville and Franklin,
where there is an historic plaque commemorating his passage in the area. *On his
way home – to Santa Elena – drove in a series of manned forts across the Southeast
from Tennessee to South Carolina, and on March 2, 1568, he reached Santa Elena,
bringing sacks filled with corn and tales of the wild west. Pardo describes the
interior as good for bread and wine and all kinds of livestock.* [37]

This same good news most likely would have arrived in Portugal, even if Pardo
was not Portuguese. In either case, it would not have been difficult to recruit some
or most of the emigrants from Portugal, which at the time was suffering a serious
economic and social crisis, due to famine and plagues, as well as religious
persecution from the recently installed Inquisition, and if that was not enough,
also the perspective of Portugal's crown being united with that of Spain. All that
made it easier for many families to leave and look for a better life or just a means
to survive in a promised land.

That hope soon brought settlers to Santa Elena. Two caravels unloaded 193 immigrants, farmers and their families, who formed a town government... By October 1569, the little capital numbered 327 souls. Around the fort clustered 40 houses... [38] If some of these families survived together with other earlier arrivals a population of just 200 could very well be the Melungeon's ancestors, according to Kennedy: *...given a known Melungeon population in the late 1700's of a minimum of 1,000 people, possibly as high as 2,000, coupled with a possible arrival date during the Elizabethan period, an average of four surviving children per couple, and the death of older members, I backtracked to an original population in the range of minimally 200 people, including both men and women.* [39] This is very interesting, but research has shown that they also had other physical traits besides Mediterranean.

Possibly this may be new information about America's lost century. *In 1566, Captain Juan Pardo, a Spanish officer most likely of Portuguese origin, recruited some two hundred soldiers, probably from the mountains of northern Spain and Portugal that is, the Galician Mountains, and brought them to the Santa Elena Colony... What is of great interest here is that if these soldiers were indeed recruited from either the Galician Mountains or southern Spain, then there is every likelihood that they and their families were of mixed Berber, Jewish, and Basque heritage.* [40]

The mixture of these three heritages is likely but with the Berber element in a much smaller proportion, since they settled in the north of the Iberian Peninsula during the 8th century. Let us keep in mind that Galicia and the Basque region were later overwhelmed by the Visigoths, a Germanic people. If so, they should not be darker. The people of the northeast Iberian Peninsula are usually of a fair complexion, and those found in America in the 18th century are of darker skin. It is easier to find fair skin and blond haired people on the north of Portugal, than in the South, where the Moorish influence was greatest.

Pardo's Forgotten Soldiers - 1567

Another theory is that Juan Pardo, while setting up forts as a means of support for the explorers during their expeditions, the soldiers and the forts would have been forgotten. The theory about the origin of the Melungeons may be connected with Juan Pardo. *The historian and writer Eloy Gallegos, when doing research in the Archives of Seville for his upcoming book about the American Southeast, discovered that Juan Pardo's name was signed as Joao Pardo as it was written in Portuguese according to original records of the XVI century.* [41] This explorer, who may be the key of the Melungeon mystery, had working for him Portuguese men.

David J. Weber, in his book *The Spanish Frontier* poses a question: *Unlike Hernando de Soto, Pardo planted settlements along the way. He built a chain of five small fortifications with a detachment assigned to each one. Pardo returned safely to Santa Elena, but his path of garrisons disappeared, their few defenders either killed by Indians or absorbed into Indian tribes.* [42] If they were absorbed by the Indians, the group would be too small to make any noticeable difference, and the Melungeons kept their physical characteristics to the present.

Historian J. G. Hollingsworth writes an account of Pardo who, in 1566, left *Spaniards at Joara, but soon after his departure the Indians became hostile and forced the Spanish force... to flee to the lands of the Creeks.* [43] Another story states: *the soldiers in the interior forts became reckless and unruly... the red men revolted and drove them out.* The name Joara is also called Xula or Cofitachequi, and is located near Marion in North Carolina, near present McDowell Bottom. Archaeological excavations are planned for that site, according to the archaeologist David More.

Pardo went on to the foothills of the Appalachians... he built a fort and left behind a company under Sgt. Hernando Moyano de Morales. ...During the spring of 1567 a letter from Sergeant Moyano in the faraway foothills reached Santa Elena. He was up to his neck in Indian trouble. [44] After we read Joseph Judge's article, *letter from Sergeant Moyano... reached Santa Elena,* and Pardo received *news of the French.* We know that they had communications, so they could not be lost or forgotten.

It is also a fact that the policy of King Felipe I of Spain, in order to colonize the vast American territories of the Southeast – known then as La Florida – was to recruit only married men to go to the New World. But in the same fleet of which Pardo was part, in total were sent *1200 soldiers, 500 sailors and 14 women.* [45] The proportion of man/woman is somewhat unexplainable.

The Arrival of the Melungeons - Before 1558 or 1584?

Sir Walter Raleigh's first expedition departed England on April 27, 1584 and arrived at the Carolina coast on July 4. Included in this expedition were Captain Master Philip Amadas, Master Arthur Barlowe, and as Master Pilot, the Portuguese Simão Fernandes from Terceira Island, Azores, who discovered the inlet that later would be called Port Ferdinand. Master Arthur Barlow, who discovered part of the country now called Virginia, gave to Sir Walter Raleigh a narrative of the voyage. After having had contact with the natives, he writes the following description: *They are of colour yellowish, and their haire blacke for the most part, and yet we sawe children that had very fine auburn and chestnut colour haire. ...and few early descriptions mention hair of other colours, except with the assumption that it represents admixture with the Europeans. ...reddish hair is often found in children whose hair later becomes, to all appearances, black.* [46]

If in 1584 the English found European looking children, we have to assume that their ancestors must have arrived long before that. You can easily find brown and auburn hair among the Portuguese, from the center to the North of Portugal. They could not be English, as that was their first trip there.

Also worth considering is the story told by the Indians about a shipwreck 20 years before ... *it seems they had twentie yeers since, which as those two men declared, was out of a wracke which happened upon their coast of some Christian shippe, being beaten that way by some storme, and outrageous weather, whereof none of the people saved.* [47] That date would be about 1564, making it possible for the ship to be French, Spanish or Portuguese indeed.

A similar story is told after Master Barlowe traveled inland near a town called Sequotan where Wingina appears to be the chief of all the villages from the Pamlico River to Roanoke Island *...neere unto which, sixe and twentie yeers past, (1558) there was a shippe castaway, whereof some of the people were saved, and those were white people, whom the Countrey people preserved. After ten daies, remaining in and out Island uninhabited, called Wococan,* (an island in the Carolina Outer Banks) *they with the help of some of the dwellers of Sequotan , fastened two boates of the Countrey together, and made mastes unto them, and sailes of their shirtes, and having taken into them such victuals as the Countrey yeelded, they departed after they had remained in this out Island three weeks: but shortly after, it seemed they were cast away, for the boates were found upon the coast, cast aland in another Island adioyning:* These shipwrecks prove that they were common in these parts of the east coast. They may not have survived but why not others? *...other than these, there was never any people apparelled, or white of colour, either seen, or heard amongst these people.* [48] These natives in particular may not have seen any other white men, but it is known that other explorers and navigators were traveling along the east coast since the early 1500's, starting with the Portuguese, and the Spaniards with their early settlement in South Carolina as well as the French in Port Royal (all prior to the English). However, it was important for England to justify to the world that taking possession of the land in the name of Her Majesty Queen Elizabeth was right since no other country had claimed it.

Santa Elena Settlers Left Behind and the End of the Colony - 1587

For twenty years Spanish and Portuguese settlers and their families lived intermittently in Santa Elena. During that time, there were Indian attacks and hungry soldiers. Then, in 1587, *a year after Drake's attack, orders were issued* by King of Spain Felipe II *to the 33 families at Santa Elena to tear down their fort and move to St. Augustine, where defenses would be concentrated.* The *English freebooter, Sir Francis Drake,* had sacked and burned it in the previous year. *Despite their vigorous protests, it was done, and Santa Elena was no more.* [49] *All of the Santa Elena colonists, however, did not make this last journey. There is strong evidence that large numbers of the settlers abandoned the Colony and escaped into the hinterland.* [50] This is possible, but again they could not be the main element of the Melungeons, since most of the 33 families must have made it to Florida. Did they all go to St. Augustine ? *The American History* – written by the English – states that there were no survivors, which is not possible. The same historians did not have any problem in accepting the survival of the English settlers when attacked by the Indians, then why not the settlers of Santa Elena. *I contend that the remnants of João "Juan" Pardo's forts, joined by refugees from Santa Elena, and possibly a few stray Dominicans and Jesuits, exiled Moorish French Huguenots, and escaped*

Acadians, along with Drake's and perhaps other freed Moorish and Iberian captives, survived on these shores, combined forces over the ensuing years, moved to the hinterlands, intermarried with various Carolina and Virginia Native Americans, and eventually became the reclusive Melungeons. [51]

These conclusions may be valid; however a strong component is needed to complete the equation. Although it may be possible, it does not explain the Asian features and skin color darker than the average Portuguese.

The greatest conflicts in Melungeon research have resulted from those well-meaning individuals who have latched onto a single component of our multifaceted origins and incorrectly pushed that lone "explanation" as the only one. Such narrow interpretations are not only in serious error, but damaging to the credibility of all those seeking to establish our true roots. [52]

Although sometimes it may appear that this book is latching on to the Portuguese origin theory, this is not the case. However, it is difficult to believe that so many different races, nationalities and cultures would have been able to live together for a long period of time under stressful conditions. What may be possible is that if all these different groups of people landed on this continent, they would have gone on their separate ways and formed separate groups; but staying together and calling themselves Portuguese, would not have been logical.

Meanwhile, further north, the English were trying to establish a settlement at Roanoke. Is it a coincidence that both Santa Elena and Roanoke were lost colonies, or did some of the settlers survive? Apparently John White was confident the settlers were alive, and had gone to live with the Hatteras Tribe of Manteo. [53] (See Chapter IV for more on Roanoke and Sir Francis Drake.)

New England in 1602 and Jamestown Colony - 1607

After the Roanoke Colony failed, an effort was made by 32 Englishmen to establish another colony in 1602. They reached Cape Cod about May 15. A letter to Sir Walter Raleigh describes their encounters with the natives. *These people, as they are exceeding courteous, gentle of disposition…of complexion or colour much like a dark olive…black hair…Some of them are black, thin bearded…They pronounce our language with great facility…* [54]

Is it possible that they could have been descendants of early 16th century arrivals on the U.S. east coast? No colony was established in New England, but as soon as Jamestown was founded, attempts were made to find the missing settlers of Roanoke Island. *Captain John Smith records… information obtained from Indians in the Jamestown vicinity told about men… who dressed like Englishmen.* [55] It is unlikely that the Indians could tell the difference between English dressing and other Europeans, since there were Germans and Poles beside English, according to John Smith.

In 1700, John Lawson wrote: *…some Indians, that are more civilized than the rest, which wear Hats, Shooes, Stockings, and Breeches…will often buy the English-made coats, which they wear on Festivals and other days of visiting.* [56]

It did not take long for different Indian nations to acquire the dressing habits of the English, which was already happening for some time in 1700.

In the October 30, 1966, issue of the *Baltimore Sun*, Mary Conelly wrote about the Lumbees and quoted one of the original settlers George Percy: *a savage boy about the age of ten years, which had a head of perfect yellow hair and a reasonable white skin, which is a miracle amongst the savages.* [57] The Lumbees have just recently been recognized as an Indian tribe, and the same encounters with white people have been attributed to them and the Melungeons as a sign of their presence in the early days of English settlement. The Lumbees claim to be direct descendants of the Lost Roanoke Colony settlers; however, their complexions vary from very dark to very fair, which leads us to believe that they intermixed with others beside the English and the Indians. In any case George Percy's statement indicates a presence of white people, beside the English, in the early 1600's.

Portuguese Sephardim Jews and Ethnic Diversity - 1643

With the expelling of all non-Catholics from the Iberian Peninsula, once again the Jews went to other parts of the world such as North Africa, Middle East and Holland. Many of the Jews who left possibly emigrated to North Africa, bringing with them Hebrew and other languages they picked up. Bernard Weisberger wrote *A Nation of Immigrants* and remarked on the variety of peoples that came to America and helped bring on the revolution. [58]

John Smith wrote of the presence of other nationalities in subsequent British settlements, as the 1608 colony with people who came from Poland and Germany. *...as for hiring the Poles and Dutchmen...*[59] By 1643 a lot of traveling was done all along the east coast and it is possible that some of the people found in New Amsterdam – Novum Belgium, Nieuw Netherland, later New York City – may have come from the Carolinas and Virginia. Isaac Jogues, a French Jesuit missionary visiting in New Amsterdam wrote in 1643: *On the Island of Manhatte, and in its environs, there may well be 400 or 500 men of different sects and nations: the director general told me that there were men of eighteen different languages.* [60] Bernard Weisberger adds... *which probably included Mediterranean and North African dialects and the Hebrew of a small settlement of Sephardic Jews.* [61] In 1700, Lawson wrote a rather strange piece of information about Indian customs found in some families: *...two Families of the Machapunga Indians, use the Jewish Custom of Circumcision, and the rest do not .* [62] Why such a custom among the Indians? Did some Jews actually arrive at an early period and settle with the Indians? The English established the first colony in 1607 – Jamestown, not too far away – and 36 years later, there were that amount and variety of people. Is it possible that in such a short period, so many and different people settled in New York? Or were they a result of groups of people moving there from other parts of the country, groups that arrived in North America much earlier?

Search in 1624 - First Encounters in 1654

The earliest encounter by Europeans with non-native people is registered in Spanish archives which show that several unsuccessful expeditions to the Georgia-Carolina interior, were sent to find *Gente Blanca* (White People) in 1624. Apparently there was a belief in Spain that white people were already in the southeast before Spanish forces arrived. These rumors continued as late as 1661. This has been one of the arguments used by Welsh people advocates. The lack of success of the Spanish expeditions may mean one of two things: either the search party did not go sufficiently north and west, or they were looking for fair skinned people only. [63]

If they *(gente blanca)* were the ancestors of the Melungeons or other groups of early settlers, most likely they would be darker, having blended with the Indian population in similar settlements. Later in 1654, Cole adds a footnote to Abraham Wood's letter ...*Spaniards were in intercourse with the Cherokees from an early date. They were in the gold regions of the southern Alleghenies in 1654.* [64] It is not logical that a settlement of Spaniards would live in the midst of the English, unless they were not Spanish but Portuguese, a common error by many historians, due to the fact that Portugal was governed by Spanish kings from 1580 to 1640. It is also possible that some of the settlers brought in by the Spaniards may have survived. However, non-Spanish could be the main element. In order not to sound overwhelming on the Portuguese side, here is what Yeardley wrote: ...*he told them was one Spaniard residing, who had been seven years with them, a man very rich, having about thirty in family, seven whereof are negroes...* [65]

This was in Tuskarorawes Indian country, and may not prove much but it tells us something about Spanish living with Indians and having slaves.

...*[B]efore the year 1700 French explorers reported finding them...One theory of their origin is that a band of ship wrecked Portuguese sailors wandered from the North Carolina coast.* [66]

Why Portuguese? Why not the French, English or the Spaniards? They all sailed along the east coast. There is no record of any other nation sailing on the open Atlantic Ocean. The only other power in the 15th and 16th centuries was the Ottoman Empire, and they were confined to the east Mediterranean Sea or the Indian Ocean. Therefore we have to assume that they must have been people of one of these four nationalities, and that it should have happened in the early part of the 1500's or not much later than the middle of the 1500's. By the late 1500's there was much activity by the Spaniards, the English, and the French, who attempted to colonize the Southeast coast.

With the exception of the English Roanoke lost colony, neither Spain nor France claimed having lost any colony. It is also known that there was trading activity according to the following account from Francis Yeardley, in South Virginia and Carolina: *In September last, (1653) a young man, a trader for beavers...with three more...went to Rhoanoke Island...found the great commander of those parts with his Indians... who received them civilly, and shewed them the ruins of Sir Walter*

Ralegh's fort... [67] There is no mention of the English colonists or the survivors 66 years later.

Yeardley, a minister, was shown the ruins of the fort in Roanoke Island by local Indians, and met an Indian trader who upon seeing children reading and writing, gave up his son in order that he be taught how to read and write:

... [H]earing and seeing the children read and write...he asked me...whether I would take his only son...and teach him to do as our children, namely in his terms, to speak out of the book, and to make a writing. [68] This did not turn out so simple since the rest of the colonists were not ready to accept Indians in their community. Yeardley later describes their attitude in his narrative when the Indian brought in his child: *...and carried themselves* (the colonists) *uncivilly towards them, forbidding their* (Indian and his child) *coming in any more.* [69]

Rev. Morgan Jones - Welsh Speaking Indians and Fables - 1669

Admiral and historian Samuel Elliot Morison describes the following encounters as tales. *When Rev. Morgan Jones, traveling through the Carolinas in 1669, fell with the Tuscaroran tribe called the Doeg, who understood his native Cymric, and among them he happily lived for months, preaching the Gospel in Welsh. There are several eighteenth century travelers' tales to the same effect, only it is always a different Indian tribe who speaks Welsh, exhibits a relatively fair complexion, and cherishes Welsh relics such as a printed Bible in that language.* Morison also describes John Evans' trip in search of Welsh-speaking Indians. During one year of living with Indians from latitude N 35° to N 49° (North Carolina to Newfoundland) he responded to the London Literary Society that: *I think you may with safety inform my friends that they* (Welsh Indians) *have no existence.* Morison ends the Madoc Welsh story with *We may dismiss the Welsh Indians myth with the authoritative words of the Bureau of American Ethnology: "There is no provable trace of Welsh, Gaelic or any other European language in any native American language."* [70]

Morison also wrote that when Columbus sailed, he already knew that the only way to cross the Atlantic was by way of the Canary Islands, to find the westerly winds and currents. Did Madoc know? What school of navigation did he attend? What scientific information was available at that time? Admiral Morison also writes: *fable that...despite all proofs that it is not and could not be true.* [71] Then the question of why they would be called Welsh re-appears after 400/500 years. A language with a few people amongst strangers would not survive, and if they were many, why did they practically disappear?

In Europe during this same period, entire nations were born out of very small counties and in 400 years, even with plagues and wars, their population grew. John Sevier's letter dated October 9, 1810, states that according to his source: *...they are no more white people; they are now all become Indians, and look like other red people of the country.* [72] This letter is kept in the Newberry Library in Chicago, that also holds the Greenlee collection of more than 10,000 Portuguese history works and rare maps. [73]

What population growth can Madoc and the Welsh account for, even with the help of the Indians? Surely in the same period in Wales, the growth was phenomenal compared to the size of a small kingdom. Much more is needed even to consider such a possibility.

While doing research about the Welsh, the author came across a story that adds more confusion. Captain Wynne wrote a letter in 1608 to Sir John Egerton from Jamestown that: *The people of Monacan speak a far differing language from the subjects of Powatan, their pronunciation being very like Welsh, so that the gentlemen in our company desired me to be their interpreter.* [74]

Was it really Welsh or did it just sounded similar? Did he really become their interpreter? Cambiaire, a French writer, points out on other possible confusion about French Bretons that sounds like Welsh... *in 1622 when some English settlers attacked by the Indians fled from Virginia into Carolina, they met some French Bretons, descendants of French people left in the vicinity of Fort Caroline in 1565. As these Bretons were still speaking their native language, which resembles that of the Welsh, those among English settlers who had come from Wales thought that these Frenchmen were the descendants of an ancient Welsh Colony.* [75] With all the Spanish activity, it is hard to believe that many French would still be around, and if so that would be another lost colony, this time the Fort Caroline lost colony.

There is still a letter written by John Sevier in 1810, replying to a request for information about the Welsh. It relied heavily on oral information by the Indian Chief Oconostota, but it is rather confusing. It connects the supposedly Welsh with the French and the chronology does not seem to fit. [76]

There is still the Irish fable of the sea-going monks. St. Brendan the Navigator who was born in the last quarter of the 5th century, set out to search for an island of monks with 17 others, called the Promised Island of Saints. The medieval conception of St. Brendan's isles also shows a western Antilla Island.

The Portuguese also have a story of seven bishops and other Christians – men and women from Porto, Portugal – who sailed with cattle, provisions and goods when the Iberian peninsula was conquered by the Moors and Rodrigo was the last Visigothic king. These people from Porto occupied the same Antilla island, also called seven cities. [77] This land or group of islands was located far to the west of Portugal, supposedly Newfoundland. At the time of Henry the Navigator, a Portuguese storm-driven ship landed at this place and was welcomed in Portuguese and urged to remain but declined. When the sailors returned, they told the story to Henry. He told them to return, but they refused to go.

According to Dr. Luciano da Silva, author of *The True Antilles* that describes his discoveries about the proper location of the Antilles, the Portuguese name for this island is *Antilhas* and was perpetuated as the Antilles, which is the name for the West Indies. [78] Did Madoc, Brendan's monks, Portuguese Christian arrive in America hundreds of years before Columbus? Nothing was ever found. What is left are fables. Morison also writes about the early boats: *This type could not sail to windward like the Portuguese caravels.* [79]

Spanish Fort and a Mine after Santa Elena - 1670

Historian Hollingsworth wrote that *1670 is the earliest date of which there is any probability of a trader from the English settlements traversing this section of the state* (Surry County, VA), *although the Spaniards seeking gold… on some expedition from their fort and mine near Lincolnton, N. Carolina.* [80] Were they really Spanish? This is in the western portion of North Carolina and the Spaniards were in Florida by then. Kennedy mentions the possibility of these being *new arrivals or Pardo's descendants.* [81]

It is rather difficult to believe that the Spaniards would forget or leave their men, after all, they were in St. Augustine, which is not too far away, and stayed there for a long time. According to Juan de Ribas, a soldier, *by 1600 the only Spaniards left in the Indian Fields were a* fifer with his wife and children. [82]

We just have to remember that Hernando de Soto's men had found their way to Mexico more than 20 years before. If so, why not Florida, which is much closer? The other possibility is that the Spaniards did not care, because these settlers were not Spanish but instead were descendants of Pardo's original settlers, either Portuguese or another nationality.

John Lederer in 1670

On May 20, 1670, there was another German adventurer named John Lederer, who wrote the following based on information given to him by local Indians (Santee and Cheraw): *…that two days journey and half from hence to the Southwest, a powerful nation of bearded men were seated, which I suppose to be Spaniards, because the Indians never have any…* [83] This is definitely a sign that either the Portuguese or the Spaniards were there in some form at those early times. Again the question, why would the Spaniards stay so far away from their secure settlement in Florida? This also may make a case for these people being the ancestors of the lost Roanoke Colony. More than 50 years had passed since Jamestown settlement, and its existence would be known, mainly to anyone who spoke English. As John Lederer traveled to this area, so had other people. John Watson also mentions the Keyauwee Indians, *who wore beards and mustaches, an unprecedent custom among Indians.* [84] This narration is from 1700, and it is possible that these Indians mixed with Europeans who arrived in the early 1500's.

A Man Named Portugal - 1671

The following story may indicate Portuguese ancestry and others. In September 1671, *Thomas Batts, Thomas Wood, and Robert Fallows …accompanied with Penecute* [85] *a great man of the Apomatack Indians and Jack Weson, formerly a servant to Major General Wood with five horses… who served as their guide…We hence sent back a horse belonging to Mr. Thomas Wood, which was tired, by a Portugal.* [86]

Why the name Portugal? The author knows several Portuguese with the surname Portugal, however he does not know anyone of any other nationality with that surname. Was he employed by the explorers?

Abraham Wood Letter, James Needham and Gabriel Artheur - 1673
Catholic Mass and the Bell

Samuel Cole Williams, a historian from Tennessee, transcribed from the letter of Abraham Wood to John Richards in London what could be considered a religious ceremony of a Catholic nature: *that ye white people have a bell which is six foot over which they ring morning and evening and att that time a great number of people congregate together and talkes he knowes not what...*[87] The ringing of church bells, called the *Trindade or* Trinity hour at sundown, was, and probably still is, a common occurrence in the villages in Portugal as well as the use of beads of the rosary for praying. The usage of beads for religious purposes is still present today. The archeological finds of any beads could be related to this. This is also a Catholic ritual in Portugal and one which the author can remember in the little village where he was born. The local church would ring the bell at sundown, which they called in Portuguese *toque da Avé Maria* or Holy Mary toll, to remind everyone to pause and pray on the beads of the Rosary – *terço* or *rosário* in Portuguese – which most older women did and still do on their knees. By the 15th century the Moors had for the most part been converted to Catholicism. The bell ringing – and bow – is part of the Catholic mass ritual, during the Eucharistic Prayer and the Breaking of the Bread.

The author remembers a young boy being told that when the bell rang, it was extremely important to be silent and bow; failure to do so would be considered a sin.

Wood's letter also mentions what we can safely assume, that they were not English and spoke a foreign language *and talkes he knowes not what*. If they could not understand, what language was it? The Catholic church always celebrated mass in Latin, and not until recently authorized the use of vernacular languages. Is it possible that the language they could not understand was Latin? Recently the author spoke with an old lady living in the mountains, and she mentioned that a friend of hers was a Melungeon, and that her friend's grandmother said her prayers in a strange or unknown language.

Kennedy writes that *The mere existence of a bell at that time period would seem to indicate a Catholic origin. And the fact that these English-speaking Indians did not understand the language of these mysterious, apparent Europeans is also an intriguing piece of evidence. These "hairy people" worshipping at a bell were obviously not English.* [88]

They could not be Spanish either, since the english speaking Indians, could recognize Spaniards and had mentioned them in other writings of the same period. As for *hairy people,* the Portuguese have that dubious honor.

On the same note, we should not overlook the possibility of elements of the lost

Roanoke Colony, having joined an already established colony of Europeans that may have arrived there much earlier and later taught them the English language. John Lawson, considered the first North Carolinian historian, writes in his journal in 1700 as he approaches the coast of North Carolina, ...*he was given two chickens by friendly Indians, a clear indication of contact with Europeans because the eastern Indians had no domestic fowl prior to the coming of whites.* [89]

There is also another claim: *they frequently communicate with spirit world.* [90] This is true, not only in Portugal but also in Brazil in a larger scale, where spiritual sessions called "Macumba" are practiced.

April 1673 Journey-White, Long Beards and Whiskers

Some chroniclers left an account of what they saw back in the 17th century. The following are some of what has been recorded: ...*Eight dayes journy down this river, lives a white people which have long beardes and whiskers and weares clothing, and on some of ye other rivers lives a hairy people.* [91] Chapman J. Milling wrote about old chronicles that described the Indians, ...*To appearance the men* (Carolina Indians) *have no beards nor hair on their head except a round turf on its crown.* [92] Gilbert confirms in his thesis in 1934 that beards and mustaches in the Cherokee were rare. [93]

This early report indicates that they were not Indians wearing clothing. They were white to the Indians and had hair on their bodies, besides the head or the face. An interesting fact, if they were Moors or Turks – Muslims – the clothing would be different from traditional European, and if they were different, the Indians would have mentioned that. Another much earlier report comes from Hernando de Soto's expedition in 1540 ...*The natives were a friendly people, appearing well dressed and more civilized than any people seen in all the territories of Florida, wearing clothes and shoes.* [94] Based on the above, it is possible that they might be referring to people that may be connected in some way with the Portuguese.

Blacks and Whites Living Together in Virginia

When discussing the first several groups that populated America after its discovery by the Europeans in the 15th century, we must note the presence of black people at an early period. In Abraham Wood's letter there is a story told by an Indian who was able to escape the white people after killing ten of them. These people had a bell and spoke in an unknown language. *They have many blacks among them...many swine and cattle...they have two mulatto women.* The letter adds that the Indians, since their men were killed, ...*all ye white and black people they take they put to death.* Wood's letter adds, ...*all this I presented to ye Grand Assembly of Virginia.* [95]

The letter goes on to describe Gabriel Arthur's travels ...*they travelled eight days west and by south, as he guest, and came to a town of negroes, spatious and great, but all wooden buildings...they marched... and about five or six miles...came within sight of a Spanish town...brick buildings.... Hung ye bell which Mr. Needham gives relation of and harde it ring in ye evening.* [96]

We have learned of a bell ringing and some sort of praying in a language the English could not understand. Now we are told of the same bell in the evening which is when Catholics pause to pray. What is puzzling is the Spanish town. Is it really Spanish or possibly Portuguese that look and dress like them? The letter further reads that *...Ye 7ᵗʰ day a Spaniard in a gentille habitt, accoutered with gunn, sword and pistol...one of the Tomahittans...shot him to death... In his pockets were two pieces of gold and a small gold chain...* Notice that the writer does not say that he was a soldier *...they hasted to ye negro town.* [97] After that they went to Port Royal in what is today South Carolina, which in earlier years was the Santa Elena of the Spaniards.

We could safely conclude that the town was not Spanish, or at least not controlled by the Spanish government. The Spaniards had left the area almost one hundred years before.

The fact that nearby was a town of *negros* hardly demonstrates that the Spaniards would let *negros* live free when in Florida and in the Caribbean they were importing and holding black slaves.

If they were Black and apparently living free, what would they have in common with the *white bearded men*? Is it possible that not all Black people that came to this country were slaves, but came on their own free will? It is doubtful, unless they were not aware of slavery in America.

David Beers Quinn wrote about Drake's captured slaves: *when free coloured labour was Drake's intended gift...it is curious and ironic commentary on the later history of this and other plantation colonies.* [98]

In 1564, John Sparke, who accompanied John Hawkins, wrote a description of Florida's natives: *There is one thing to be marveled at, for the making of their* (Indians) *fire, and not only they but also the Negroes do the same...* [99] Are these *Negroes* slaves? if so to whom do they belong? Or are they free Blacks living with the Indians from whom they learned their ways, having arrived before the Spaniards? Let us keep in mind that the Portuguese knew the location and existence of Florida prior to 1502.

There is still another question. When *Black* or *Negro* was mentioned in the 17ᵗʰ century, did they know the difference between Blacks from Arabia or the dark skinned Moors from North Africa (Berbers) and the Blacks from West Africa ?

As this book was just about ready to go to press, Victor Marques, President of the Portuguese-American Southeast Chamber of Commerce, uncovered additional information about the presence of blacks in Virginia, within the time frame of the early settlement of Jamestown. Bill Hendrick of the Atlanta Journal tells the story: *The four set of bones, first unearthed 5o years ago, are thought to date between 1620 and 1680... One of the skeletons was that of a Black man thought to be age 26...The four are among 21 sets of skeletons dug up on the coast of southeastern Virginia at the site of historic Jamestown, the first permanent English settlement in the New World.* [100]

History is constantly changing, so it is always a good idea to keep an open mind. The above information was based on declarations by Smithsonian forensic anthropologist Douglas W. Owsley. Prior to that discovery, scientists knew of only one other native of Africa who lived and died in the early colonial period.

This also proves that Africans came to America very early, and also that they were free. Whatever Blacks the Spaniards brought were slaves. What other nation was trading in both coasts of Africa, and had the capability of transporting people to the New World, both slave and free? At that time not all Blacks were slaves, and not all Whites – mainly from the Far East – were free.

Shipwrecked Sailors, Pirates - 1685

Bonnie Ball in her book presents another story: *James Aswell, a Tennessee history expert...possible explanation for the Melungeons is an old story that Portuguese ships were plying the Caribbean as pirates at the time of the Portuguese revolt against Spain in 1685.* [101]

That paragraph has to be imaginative, as the revolt against Spain was in 1640 and not in 1685. By 1685, if there were any spare Portuguese sailors or ships, they would have been better recompensed if they chased the Spaniards, near the Portuguese coast, when they would be returning home from the Caribbean loaded with gold and silver. King João IV of Portugal was the Duke of Braganza before he led the restoration of the independence of his country in 1640. When he took over the government, the Portuguese treasury was depleted, and when he died in 1656, there was a war still going on. In 1665, his son Afonso VI was the king. [102]

While Portugal's crown was united with Spain, Portugal lost many overseas colonies and trade facilities. It does not make sense that Portugal would embark on such an expensive venture at a time when the national defense interests demanded all resources and attention. [103]

Not until 1668, did Spain only signed the peace treaty with Portugal. Most of the overseas time and resources after the separation from Spain were spent in removing the Dutch from Brazil, [104] and Cuba was of little interest to Portugal. In none of the Portuguese sources consulted, are there any references to such an expedition to capture Cuba from Spain.

Also, there is the tradition of a Portuguese ship and a mutiny. *A letter... from Mr. L. Gibson, a resident of Scotland County... refers to a dark skinned people... The old man who told me about their ancestry more than fifty years ago... called them something to me like Mongolians... No doubt the name he called was Melungeons... in another paragraph... local legend that the people were descendants of Portuguese pirates or sailors... and anglicized their Portuguese names... whether they were pirates or shipwrecked sailors would have made little difference – their safety lay in changing their names. With the passage in 1699 of the stringent anti-piracy laws, rope happy citizens were apt to act first and think afterwards.* [105] Piracy was common in the 16th century. Even countries at peace with each other allowed piracy for their own benefit.

As for there being Portuguese pirates or pirates of any other nationality, it is unlikely. The presence of families or women aboard pirate ships could hardly be considered. This again points to a presence of Portuguese before the 17th century. As for the Mongolian name, let us keep our mind open, remembering that it has been written that the Melungeons had an occasional Asiatic appearance.

Pirates, shipwrecked sailors... it is possible, but most likely they would all be men and with no provisions and plans for a long stay. That does not explain the surviving of the Melungeons to this century as a group. Perhaps they were part of a boat full of would-be settlers, bound for another part of the world, with complete families, provisions and plans for a long stay.

French Theory - 1690

A fairly large English community was already in place in South Virginia and North Carolina, and the only French settlement reported in 1700 was near the Santee River. Lawson writes that *...The first Place we design'd for, was Santee River, on which there is a Colony of French Protestants.* [106] Bonnie Ball also writes: *Some of the Indians of Robin County have stated that the French immigrants settled the area as early as 1690, and they (French) came in contact with a mixed race they named "Mero" (Melungeons).* [107] The name *Mero* certainly does not sound much like Melungeon, and this is quite far from East Tennessee. However, the name *Mero* pops up once in a while.

Dr. Celestine Pierre Cambiare wrote in 1933 about the Melungeons: *They have dark complexion, black hair, brown eyes... their English is the English of two centuries ago.* The author did not provide the source for this information. *Their names are typically English, they claim Portuguese ancestry...there is nothing to justify that claim...The French came into Tennessee a long time before the English. Some French traders or trappers must have given the name* Melangeon. [108]

In the 1930's the Melungeons spoke just like most mountain people and to a French person that would naturally sound like the English of the 1700's, which by then was no longer Elizabethan English. The Melungeons may not be able to prove their Portuguese ancestry, but did Dr. Cambiare do enough research to prove otherwise? There was no large French settlement in Tennessee and traders or trappers did not stay long enough to put such a long lasting label on a group of people. It is also strange to find that Dr. Cambiare is the only writer that spelled the word *Melungeon* in a French way -*Melangeon*- to justify the French origin *Mélange*. As for the French theory of the Melungeons being French Huguenots, there is no such indication. If there were, they would follow the various French settlements all the way up to Canada or Louisiana, which were claimed by French explorer Robert Cavalier for France in 1682. However, we should not discard the fact that many fleeing the Inquisition were received by the Huguenots in France. The Moors were included, and later emigrated to South Carolina with the French Huguenots.

The Huguenots Found White People in 1708

Bonnie Ball writes: *There is also a legend of a white people found on the Lumber River in Robeson County in North Carolina, by the French Huguenots in 1708, and were said to have owned farms and living like Europeans. They also reputed to have spoken an older form of English.* [109] The author has not been able to find the source for that information. Is it possible that the French Huguenots would be traveling so close to the English when they were at war? Is it possible that an older form of English would be recognized by French speaking people?

After all, only 100 years had passed since Elizabethan English was spoken in England. The language did not change that much to be considered an old form of English. If these white people were the survivors of the Lost Roanoke Colony, would there be that many who would be able to keep the language for 120 years, while living with the natives? If there were just a few, that would not be possible. If there were many, and knew the language and English culture, why not look for them? Lawson writes in 1700 that a second settlement was made in 1650. *A second settlement of this Country was made about fifty years ago...by several substantial Planters, from Virginia and other Plantations.* This is about 60 years after the settlers were left in Roanoke. The first two European children – Virginia Dare and Harvie – born in the United States (1587) shortly after their arrival, would have a good chance of still being alive and had received from their parents or other English survivors some culture they could remember.

In the same manner as we today are able to get some information of what was happening then, I am sure that they or any other group of people would know that the English were in Jamestown with a growing settlement and ships coming or going to and from England. ...[T]*he Fame of this new discovery Summer-Country spread thro' the neighbouring Colonies, and in a few Years, drew a considerable Number of Families thereto, who all found Land enough to settle themselves in...* [110] Even then it was hard to keep a secret.

Let us not forget the Indian traders who traveled over long distances for as long as one year or more. The traders and the Indians would move often and carry with them information found along the way. *...and to this day, they are a shifting wandering people; for I know some Indian Nations, that have chang'd their settlements, many hundred miles; sometimes no less than a thousand...* [111] Also, *they are expert Travelers, and they have not the use of...our Compass.* [112]

Dress and language, may be a characteristic of more than one group, not to just any one in particular. Is it possible that the Huguenots did not recognize the language and assumed that it was an older form of English?

John Lawson in 1700/45 and the Hatteras Indians

On December 28, 1700, John Lawson began a voyage to Carolina from Charles Town and wrote about the Hatteras while describing the first colony of Carolina: *A farther Confirmation of this we have from the Hatteras Indians, who either then lived on Roanoke-Island, or much frequented it. These tell us that several of their Ancestors were white People, and could talk in a book, as we do; the Truth of which is confirm'd by gray Eyes being found frequently amongst these Indians, and no others.* [113]

Just before Lawson arrived in Virginia, a law was passed providing for the offense of stealing or setting adrift a boat or canoe. *Whereas white persons violating this law were only fined, Indians received 39 lashes on their naked backs for the first offense and suffered the amputation of an ear for the second. Many years before these acts were passed by the white colonist the Cusabo* (Indians) *had been forced to sell their best lands to the invading race.* [114]

With this type of discrimination and justice – only one of many instances – the Melungeons, Indians or any other group not readily identified with whites would seek a safer place away from the English colonies near the coast. Chapman also tells us that *Here and there...are small groups of people who are plainly not of pure white ancestry...The hereditary prejudice of these people is demonstrated by the fact that...their children are not allowed to attend white schools, they habitually refuse to send them to colored schools.* [115]

Rich, Dark and Portuguese - 1745

Sometimes a wrong impression is given that the Melungeons, just because they stayed in the mountains, had never amounted to anything. It is not true because many left the mountains. Just as many emigrants left their countries and succeeded, so did the Melungeons.

The following may be just one example with a possible connection between a Robinson from Robeson County – home of the Lumbees and Melungeons – and another Robinson from Virginia.

A public records Office in London states that on *Apr. 26, 1745, to John Robinson et al 100,000 acres on Green Briar N.W. & West of Cow Pasture [river] and new foundling (partly surveyed).* [116] In 1942 a 93 year old neighbor of the Robinson family also stated, *The Robinsons were rich people who lived at Castlewood. They were dark and said to be Portuguese.* [117]

Possible Route to the Mountains - 1740-50

The early history of the pioneers is a long way from being completed. Swanton gave us a very good glimpse of what North Carolina was like in the early colonial days. Many documents are still to be uncovered. Samuel Cole Williams, in his *Early Travels in the Tennessee Country,* may give us a clue to which direction the early unknown group of settlers was traveling.

Pioneers trading with Indians passed through the area as early as 1740, and in 1747 Dr. Thomas Walker led an expedition. On March 31, 1750, Walker made a puzzling entry into the journal: *In the Fork between Holston's and the North River, are five Indian Houses built with logs and covered with bark.* [118]

Allegedly, Indians did not have log cabins in 1750. If these log cabins were not made by Indians, who built them? Another entry on April 9: *We travelled to a river...hunters call Clinch's River...*near what is now Sneedville in Hancock County. *...we rode four miles to Beargrass River.* This river was later renamed Powell for Ambrose Powell of Walker's party. [119]

...On the top of the Ridge are Laurel Trees marked with Crosses, and other blazed figures on them. ...in 1779...going to the spot they found it as related. [120] Since the natural gateway from north to south was through this gap, and it was one of the routes followed by later Melungeons to the East Tennessee mountains, it is possible that the crosses and the figures may have been made by a group of them on their way to Clinch Mountain, as they traditionally used the cross as a religious symbol. However, it is more probable that the crosses were made by trappers or explorers in the vicinity. Pollitzer and Brown's 1969 survey *strongly suggests that they migrated west* (from Virginia and North Carolina) *to form the nucleus of the present Melungeons.* [121] For a complete text of Thomas Walker expedition see *Annals of SW Virginia.*

The North Carolina Tax Lists of 1755

Jean Patterson Bible brings to our attention that most of the Melungeons may have originated in North Carolina.

The Orange County tax lists and censuses of 1755 shows a number of Melungeon family names, including John Collins, Samuel Colens... all noted as "mulatto". Since Negroes are recorded as such, it is probable that the tax officials simply used the word "mulatto" to indicate darker coloring...and then enumerators knew of no other way to classify them. [122]

Henry Price also mentions: *The dark complexion characteristics among Melungeon family names...records a settlement of mullatoes including Thomas Gibson...Thomas Collins...* [123]

See Chapter VIII of this book for the findings of other groups that claim Portuguese ancestry but may not be connected with the Melungeons.

John Sevier in 1782-84

Prior to 1769, and according to John Stuart in a letter to Governor Botecourt *none of his majesty's subjects were settled westward of the point where the Virginia-North Carolina line intersects the Holston River.* [124] John Sevier stated in a letter presumably to Major Stoddard, [125] about a conversation he had with the great warrior, Oconostota and related to the Welsh while on his campaign against the Indians in 1782: *...Sevier observed traces of ancient though regular fortifications...inquired of Oconostota...the reply was that it had been handed down by the forefathers... a period when the Cherokees resided in the South Carolina region, a race of white people had inhabited the country... were called Welsh.* [126] If Madoc had arrived in 1100, more than 600 years would have passed.

Could the Indians have kept this information for that long? If so, there should be plenty of other information about this continent, which apparently has yet to surface. Let us keep in mind, that was almost 300 years after a possible arrival of the first Europeans on the coast of South Carolina.

No one really knows when the Melungeons were first discovered, although by the time Tennessee Governor John Sevier encountered them in August 1784, their numbers were apparently substantial.

Sevier's original family name was *Xavier,* a very common name in Spain and Portugal. St. Francis of Xavier is an example, however the French writer Cambiaire claims that the name is French.

About the Melungeons and the State of Franklin, Louise Davies wrote: *When* (1784) *John Sevier attempted to organize the State of Franklin* (forerunner of Tennessee)*, there was living in the mountains of Eastern Tennessee a Colony of dark-skinned, reddish-brown complexioned people, supposedly of Moorish descent, who called themselves Malungeons, and claimed to be of Portuguese descent. They lived to themselves exclusively, and were looked upon neither as negroes or Indians.* [127] Why Moorish descent? By then the Moors had been in Portugal for over 800 years, 400 of those as Portuguese citizens. Naturally we inherit some of their appearance. There is, however, *the reddish brown complexion* puzzle. The Portuguese from Portugal do not have a reddish brown complexion, (must be a connection.) ...[O]*lder Melungeons always claimed positively that they were Portuguese.* [128]

Louise Davies adds that John Sevier *found, in the high ridges of Hancock and Rhea counties...Colony of... people...who... had fine European features and claimed to be Portuguese.* [129]

It is therefore assumed that at least a few generations have already been living there. *A yellowish document addressed to the Governor of North Carolina locked in a box in the State Archives, which contain the first official notice taken of the Melungeons. The report written with a quill on now-brittle foolscap by John Sevier, later the first Governor of Tennessee, described the large, mysterious Colony of bronze-skinned people he found in northeastern Tennessee. Sevier crossed the Appalachians in 1774, and 5 years before settlers discovered the Melungeons who had been there for 200 years, according to the estimate of Mary Sue Going of the Watauga Association of Genealogists.* [130] Sevier's reports written about 1782-84, describe some of the mysterious dark-skinned people as having straight black hair and dark blue eyes.

Pioneers of Pure English Strain - 1769

Cambiaire writes about the early settlers in East Tennessee and Western Virginia: *we find, almost exclusively, descendants of pioneers of pure English strain, who in 1769 began to settle this part of the country, then peopled by Indians, and almost inaccessible. These mountaineers have a distinct physical type, speak the English of the 18th century without any slang and modernisms.* [131] This situation may also be applied to the Melungeons living in the same inaccessible area, their language may have remain unchanged for long periods. Therefore, the Elizabethan English which no longer was spoken in the 18th century might not apply. Dromgoole describes their speech or dialect as *a cross between mountaineer and the negro...Their dialect is difficult to write.* [132] *...They spoke in broken English, a dialect distinct from anything ever heard...* in the area. [133] Could we consider this anything close to Elizabethan English?

The Indians of Robeson County have been connected with the lost Roanoke Colony, and in 1769 James Lowrie settled in Robeson. Among the family names was found an Allen Lowrie, son of William, married to Polly Cumba, or Cumbo, said to be of Portuguese extraction. [134]

Moors in South Carolina and FPC - 1790-95

In her book *The Arabs in America,* Beverlee Mehdi wrote that in 1790, The House of Representatives in South Carolina provided that *sundry Moors, Subjects of the Emperor of Morocco be tried in court according to the laws for South Carolina and not under Negro codes.* [135] Also, the South Carolina State Statute V1431 of 1792 banned Moors from entering the state for a period of two years. [136] This time period is much later than the one expected to be the time that the Melungeons arrived in North America. By the late 1700's it would have been possible for written records to survive to our days. Moors could be considered recent arrivals. Let us keep in mind that by then, there was more communication between settlers and natives. It is logic to assume that the original Melungeons did not have any contact with other people except the natives for at least a generation, and by the time they made contact, they were out of step with the rest of the world.

As we shall see later in this book, the term Moor is generic and applied mostly to Muslims and others from North Africa to the Indian Ocean, except the Turks. Also the term *Moor* was not used by the Moors themselves. Should we consider all subjects of the Emperor of Morocco as Moors? I do not think so. Many Jews and other nationals fleeing political and religious persecution went to Morocco and other North African regions.

Moors living in late 18th century America may have originated in southern Europe, Mediterranean North African countries or others, bordering the Indian Ocean half way around the world.

These sundry Moors most likely may have joined people that would have something in common, such as skin color or appearance, or even discrimination.

These possible connections with the Melungeons or any other group may not be too difficult to research as census records were already in place.

Anyone interested in pursuing genealogy roots on *"sundry Moors, subjects of the Emperor of Morocco"* should be encouraged to do so, and may establish a possible connection. However, if the research goes before the 1700's, then it is an enormous task.

In this same year (1790) a guide for census takers orders them to identify all free whites over the age of 16 and Blacks. This may have been the beginning of the term FPC – Free Persons of Color – as they tried to identify people like the Melungeons and other groups not seen as White Anglo-Saxon. [137]

It seems that whenever a person could not be classified as Black, Indian or White the term FPC was used. Naturally, the term was not designed to describe any one particular group of people, such as the Melungeons, although Kennedy does state that... *North Carolina declared Melungeons to be free persons of color.* [138] However it does not say that applied exclusively to the Melungeons.

Dr. Virginia DeMarce, in her review essay on the National Genealogical Society, does not think the same way. *North Carolina never "declared Melungeons" to be free persons of color; nor did a Tennessee statute single out Melungeons for persecution.* [139] North Carolina did, however, pass laws applicable to a specific group, the Portuguese, in this century.

Discriminatory laws may have been made in the past, but were always disguised or justifiable by the makers of such laws.

It is remarkable that Tennessee history is silent on the subject since by the census taken in 1795 the Melungeons must have been numbered with the 973 "free persons" other than whites. There could hardly have been so many free negroes within the bounds of the present state only about 25 years after the first settlement.[140] This may be due to the coming of the Melungeon population, which did not happen until later, and/or may not have been so obvious.

According to Kennedy, the book by Dr. Horace R. Rice, *The Buffalo Ridge Cherokee*, shares that, because some people had a black component in their gene pool, they could not be Indian. [141] If one converses with some old timers still living in the western mountains of North Carolina, near Cherokee, they will say that in the beginning of this century, many claims were denied to people – who would like to be considered Cherokee – on the basis of even the slightest chance of being Black, Mulatto or dark skinned.

Elizabethan and Broken English - Anglo Surnames

Is a manner of speaking, a clue?...*They reportedly spoke an Elizabethan English ...since their English was broken and not fluent as one would expect for a "mother tongue," I assumed they were not English, but instead had picked up the language and the surnames for survival's sake.* [142]

The Melungeons must have arrived in the early 1500's. The English spoken by them was of that time frame, and had to be learned from someone speaking a similar language from that period. By the time they were found, a few generations could have passed. The English were already settling in Virginia and other parts of the East Coast. Let us not forget that some Indians had been to England, learned the language and returned to America, spreading their knowledge among the different tribes.

Finally, these encounters with a people that spoke old English were reported by a Frenchman, not necessarily an authority on the language. These people, living in isolation, neither necessarily keep up with the language change nor with the colloquial speech patterns of country and mountain people.

This is not surprising, and surely many Americans' surnames were not necessarily written the same way, as when their ancestors first arrived in America. There are a number of stories – sometimes more like anecdotes – of immigrants arriving at the immigration officer's desk in New York's Ellis Island. Before they left the desk, they would unwittingly allow their names to be changed forever due to their illiteracy or unable to speak English.

This is not the case with the Melungeons. There were no immigration officers to greet them, but once they established that the English were in charge, they did whatever was necessary to get along. (See Chapter XI for the most famous name change in the world, which remains a mystery.)

Many immigrants change their names today, to make their lives easier. Others spend the rest of their lives correcting the spelling. On the other hand, there was the possibility of some of them already having English names.

As for speaking broken English, it is quite natural. By the time the first English settlers met them, and put it on record, it is possible that they might have had contact with other English-speaking people, thereby picking up the language from them, but not necessarily writing it down in such a way as to reach our present day. Again Kennedy's analyses are correct on the survival conclusion.

...[B]y the 1750s – when the first great waves of English and Scot-Irish settlers came down the Valley of Virginia – the Melungeons were speaking a broken form of Elizabethan (that is, sixteenth-century) English and carrying English surnames as well. ...and given England's heavy trade with Portuguese during the Elizabethan period, we would expect many Portuguese to speak at least some English. [143] A language can disappear in just one generation, and with no books, it would probably happen more quickly. Illiteracy was quite common in those days. However, in 1850, 40% of the Goinses Melungeons were registered in the census as literate. That was remarkable for that time. [144]

An explanation from a Portuguese point of view is easy, due to the fact that Portugal had at that time, and still has, very close ties with England. Edmund of Langley, the first Duke of York, and son of King Edward III of England, headed the Lisbon expedition of 1381-82 to aid King Fernando of Portugal against Castille, which unfortunately was a failure. However, this points out the early ties that Portugal had with England, and with the English language. ... *as far back as there are records, an English dialect has been spoken by the Melungeons, and they have been Christians.... they are similar to mountaineers in dialect...*[145] The term Elizabethan and/or broken English created some questions, and to clear them, further research was done to find out when these terms were first mentioned in connection with the Melungeons - also, interviews with local and long time residents of the Appalachian Mountains.

In Western North-Carolina, a more logical explanation was discovered. During an interview with several of the older folks, it was learned that it was common for mountain people to speak older English. This was confirmed by Benita Howell,

Ph.D., anthropology professor at the University of Tennessee in Knoxville, who stated: *"I've never heard this said of Melungeons in particular; rather of all "isolated" Appalachians. It turns up in the local color travel literature of the late 19th century and was related to WASPs obsession with British racial purity at a time when non-British immigration to the Northeast was increasing dramatically. Sometimes it is Elizabethan English, sometimes Anglo-Saxon even is referenced. The speech contains some archaic forms but certainly isn't and never has been frozen into Elizabethan or any other earlier form; that would be an impossibility from the standpoint of everything that is known about languages and language generally.*

It is well known that the southeastern states constitute the Bible belt, where religion is a very important facet of daily life. It is also common to hear the pastors in church quoting Bible passages from the original King James version, which is closer to Elizabethan English. It was learned through a local minister that the Pilgrims and the Puritans, when they first arrived in New England, preferred the German version of Martin Luther's Bible. Bonnie Ball writes about their speech, *Old Jack Bowling was the progenitor of the Scott County Bollings, and his people were strong, and spoke broken English* (1820). [146] Dromgoole also mentions that they *spoke a broken English, a dialect distinct from anything I ever heard* (1890).[147] Had Miss Dromgoole visited some Indian town or reservation in the same area, it would have been interesting to learn what she would have said about the Indian's speech.

Anglo-Norman and speaking 18th Century English

Dr. Cambiaire in 1933 writes about the mountaineers of East Tennessee and West Virginia as *a race of people who represent what is left of the pure ... Anglo-Norman race in America.* A Norman is a native of Normandy in the north of France, *...descendants of pioneers of pure English strain, who in 1769, began to settle this part of the country...These mountaineers have a distinct physical type, speak the English of the 18th century without any slang or modernisms...* [148] It is not known exactly what Dr. Cambiaire meant by *distinct physical type.* Anglo-Saxons or Anglo-Normans have the looks of most English. He could have actually been referring to the Melungeons. The description of their life style (Anglo-Normans) is the same as described by other writers about the Melungeons, and when describing the Melungeons, he states that *Their language is the English of two centuries ago* which makes it also the 18th century as the rest of the mountaineers.

The Indian Tribes of Croatoan, Hatteras and Lumbees

There is a strong belief that some of the Roanoke colonists may have joined these tribes and passed along the English language as spoken in 1587. In his 1971 book *European Discovery of America* Morison writes the following: *... and the existence of blue-eyed and fair haired types among them, as well as the* *incorporation of Elizabethan words in their language and their using surnames from John White's colonists bears this out.* [149]

This may be possible, but the incorporation of some Elizabethan words may also indicate that the number of colonists was extremely small. Let us not forget the Indians that have been to England.

Lawson also writes about the type of English spoken in 1700: *...yet those that speak English, learn to swear the first thing they talk of.* [150] As for the surnames, some of them were also common in the later English colonies. They, like the slaves and many other people in this country, used the most common names of the time. It is important to keep in mind that the information about these tribes was not found until much later. It was not until 1891 – with Alexander Brown's publication of *Genesis of the United States* – that a general interest was shown.

The blue-eyes and fair hair could have come from some other early settlers. *The Croatan Indians, was the legal description in North Carolina for a people of a mixed Indian and white blood, found in various E.[eastern] sections of the state, chiefly in Robeson County, and numbering approximately 5,000... Across the line in South Carolina are found a people, evidently of similar origin, designated the "Redbones". In portions of w. [western] N.C. and E.[east] Tenn. Are found the so-called "Melungeons"...or Portuguese.* [151] This was written in 1912, and Robeson County was traditionally also a Melungeon place.

When Scottish immigrants began to settle the upper reaches of North Carolina's Cape Fear Valley in the early 1730's, they were amazed to find a group of English-speaking people already living near the Lumbee River. [152]

This area is less than 100 miles from the coast, where shipwrecks were common. Weather patterns were not known, and no warnings of any kind existed. As a result, many vessels, when going to or coming from Europe or South America, would most likely meet with tragedy in the sea coast of North Carolina.

The fact that they spoke English for more than 100 years with continuous English settlement is hardly surprising. *... mid-twentieth century... spoke a pure Old English.* [153] This is a similar situation with the mountain people of Western North Carolina and East Tennessee. Is there a connection? *...the oral tradition of Cherokee blood is so strong among the Lumbees...that it is impossible to dismiss the claim.* [154]

In the beginning of this century, many Melungeons applied to be classified as Cherokee Indians, in western North Carolina and wrote on their application, describing themselves, as being part Cherokee and part Portuguese.

Notes

[1] Original Sources... Historiography... by John Parker, p. 31
(Terrae Incognitae 13, 1981)

[2] The Melungeons by N. Brent Kennedy, p. 94

[3] Antonio Morais Silva (1954), Vol. VI, p. 666,
José Pedro Machado (1981), Vol. VII - p.157

[3a] Dicionario da Lingua Portuguesa by Candido de Figueiredo, p. 1611,
Bertrand,1996

[4] Mike McGlothlen letter to author of March 1997

[5] Melungeons and other Mestee Groups by Mike McGlothlen, p. 36

[6] History of Huguenot Emigration to America, by Charles W. Baird DD, p. 21

[7] Gowens Research Foundation December 1996 Newsletter
by Evelyn McKinley Orr.

[8] Ibid

[9] Ibid, February 1997

[10] East Tennessee and Western Virginia by Celestin Pierre Cambiaire, p. ix

[11] Virginia Frontier by F. B. Kegley, p. 15

[12] Annals of Northwest North Carolina by J.G. Hollingsworth, p. 4

[13] The Melungeons... by Edward T. Price, p. 269

[14] The Melungeons by Brent Kennedy, p. xviii

[15] Ibid

[16] Historia de Portugal - Oliveira Marques, p.5,Vol. II.

[17] Surviving Indian Groups by William Harlen Gilbert, Jr. p. 426

[18] The Melungens by Bonnie Ball, p.61

[19] David Viera 2/26/97 document

[20] The Jews of Spain by Jane Gerber, p. xii., 138, 139

[21] Historia de Portugal by Oliveira Marques, V.I p. 222

[22] The Jews of Spain by Jane Gerber, p. xvi

[23] Historia de Portugal by Oliveira Marques, p.p. 289-290

[24] Ibid, p.367

[25] The Melungeons by Brent Kennedy, p. 102
(In Spanish Prisons by Arthur Griffiths)

[26] In Spanish Prisons by Arthur Griffiths, p. 113

[27] Historia de Portugal by Joaquim Verissimo Serrão, p. 267

[28] Ecclesia Miltans by Miroslav Hroch / Anna Skýbová, p.126

[29] Historia de España, Historia 16, p.507

[30] O Sacrificio de Isaac by Manuel da Costa Fontes, pp. 59,60

[31] Ecclesia Miltans by Miroslav Hroch / Anna Skýbová, p.110

[32] The Forgotten Centuries, by Charles Hudson, p.4

[33] National Geographic Magazine, March 1988, p.335

[34] National Geographic Society, March 1988 Issue, p. 330
(Painting by John Berkey)

[35] The Mystery of the Melungeons by Louise Davis, p. 11
(Nashville Tennesseean 9/29/1963)
[36] National Geographic Magazine, March 1988, p.351
[37] Ibid, March 1988, p.354
[38] Ibid, p. 354
[39] The Melungeons by N. Brent Kennedy, p. 94
[40] Ibid, pp. 104, 105
[41] Ibid p. 133
[42] Spanish Frontier by David J. Weber, p. 71
[43] History of Surry Country by J.G. Hollingsworth, p.5
[44] National Geographic Magazine, March 1988, p.353
[45] Catholic Historical Review, Vol.LI, No. 3, by Michael V. Gannon, p. 340
[46] The Roanoke Voyages by David Beers Quinn, Vol. I, pp. 102,103
[47] Ibid, p. 104
[48] Ibid, p. 111
[49] National Geographic Magazine by Joseph Judge, p. 362
[50] The Melungeons by Brent Kennedy, p.108
[51] Ibid p.119
[52] Ibid p.125
[53] The only land I know by Adolph Dial, p. 4
[54] The Elizabethan's America by Louis B. Wright, p. 143
[55] The only land I know by Adolph Dial, p. 4
[56] A New Voyage to Carolina by John Lawson (Hugh Lefler), p. 200
[57] The Melungeons by Bonnie Ball, p. 38
[58] A Nation of Immigrants by Bernard A. Weisberger (American Heritage)
[59] Makers of America by Wayne Moquin, p. 73 (The True Travels by John Smith)
[60] Ibid, p. 85
[61] A Nation of Immigrants by Bernard A. Weisberger (American Heritage)
[62] A New Voyage to Carolina by John Lawson (Hugh T. Lefler), p. 219
[63] Who Discovered…by Zella Armstrong, p. 94-95
(Herbert E. Bolton, Spain's Title to Georgia)
[64] Early Travels in Tennessee Country by Samuel C. Williams, p. 28-29
[65] Narratives of Early Carolina by Alexander S. Salley, Jr. , p.27
[66] The Melungeons by Bonnie Ball, p. vi (Knoxville News Sentinel Oct.10/1958)
[67] Narratives of Early Carolina by Alexander S. Salley, Jr. , p. 25-26
[68] Ibid, p.26
[69] Ibid
[70] The European Discovery of America by Samuel Eliot Morison, pp. 85-6
[71] Ibid, p. 85
[72] Who Discovered America by Zella Armstrong, p. 169-170
[73] Luso-Americano by Henrique Mano, April 2nd 1997
[74] The Elizabethan's America by Louis B. Wright, p. 186
[75] East Tennessee and West Virginia by Celestine Pierre Cambiaire, p. xiv
[76] The Melungeons by Jean Patterson Bible, p. 83,85

[77] La Busqueda del Paraiso y las Legendarias islas del Atlantico by Louis-Andre Vigneras, p. 45

[78] The True Antilles by Dr. Manuel Luciano da Silva (1987)

[79] European Discovery of America by Samuel Eliot Morison, pp. 16

[80] History of Surry County by J.G. Hollingsworth, p.12

[81] The Melungeons by Brent Kennedy, p. 105

[82] Catholic Historical Review, Vol. LI, No..3, By Michael V. Gannon, p. 352

[83] The Discoveries of John Lederer by William P. Cumming, pp. 31-32

[84] Red Carolinians by Chapman J. Milling, p. 218

[85] This name is also spelled as *Perachute*. See History of SW Virginia, p. 36

[86] Annals of Virginia 1746-1786 by Lewis Preston Summers, pp. 1-2

[87] Early Travels in the Tennessee Country by Samuel Cole Williams, 28-29

[88] The Melungeons by N. Brent Kennedy p.11

[89] The Only Land I Know by Adolph L. Dial, p. 6

[90] The Mystery of the Melungeons by Louise Davis p. 11 (Nashville Tennesseean 9/29/1963)

[91] Early Travels in the Tennessee Country by Samuel Cole Williams, 28-29

[92] Red Carolinians by Chapman J. Milling, p. 5

[93] The Eastern Cherokees by William Harlen Gilbert Jr., p. 196

[94] Ibid, p. 66

[95] Early Travels in the Tennessee Country by Samuel Cole Williams, 29-30

[96] Ibid, p. 34

[97] Ibid

[98] The Roanoke Voyages by David Beers Quinn, Vol. 1, p. 255

[99] Makers of America by Wayne Moquin, p. 67

[100] Native Africans' bones by Bill Hendrick, Atlanta Journal, p. C7, May 11th 1997

[101] The Melungeons by Bonnie Ball, p.73

[102] Historia de Portugal by José Mattoso, Vol. 8, p. 320

[103] Ibid

[104] Ibid, pp. 320-321

[105] Arkansas Gazette, January 14, 1914 by Eliza N. Heiskell

[106] A New Voyage to Carolina by John Lawson (Hugh Lefler), p. 14

[107] The Melungeons by Bonnie Ball p. 55

[108] East Tennessee...Ballads by Celestin Pierre Cambiare, p. ix

[109] The Melungeons by Bonnie Ball, p. 37

[110] A New Voyage to Carolina by John Lawson (Hugh Lefler), p. 70

[111] Ibid, p. 173

[112] Ibid, p. 200

[113] Ibid, p. 69

[114] Red Carolinians by Chapman J. Milling, pp. 56-58

[115] Ibid, p. 64

[116] Greenbrier Pioneers... by Ruth Woods Dayton, p. 16

[117] Pioneer Recolections of Virginia by Elihu Jasper Sutherland, p. 167-9

[118] Early Travels in the Tennessee Country by Samuel Cole Williams, p.171
[119] Ibid, pp. 172-173
[120] Ibid, p.174
[121] Survey of Demography... by Pollitzer and Brown, pp. 389-399 (Human Biology, Sept. 1969)
[122] The Melungeons by Jean Patterson Bible, p.20-The North Carolinian, Vol.1,1955-56, pp.107-8
[123] Melungeons: The Vanishing Colonoy of Newman's Ridge by Henry R. Price, p. 10
[124] Ibid, p. 6
[125] The Melungeons by Jean P. Bible, p. 83 (Who Discovered America by Zella Armstrong, p. 8)
[126] Tennessee Valley and Tennessee History by Samuel Cole Williams, pp. 1-2
[127] The Malungeons by Will Allen Dromgoole p. 469 (Arena 1891)
[128] Early Travels in the Tennessee Country by Samuel Cole Williams, p. viii
[129] The Mystery of the Melungeons by Louise Davis p. 11 (Nashville Tennesseean 9/29/1963)
[130] The Gowen Research Foundation newsletter, Vol.I, 4, December 1989
[131] East Tennessee and Western Virginia Ballads by Celestin Cambiaire, p. v
[132] The Malungeons by Will Allen Dromgoole, p. 475 (Boston Arena, 1891)
[133] Ibid, p. 745
[134] The American India in North Carolina byDouglas L. Rights, p. 146
[135] Arabs in America by Beverlee Mehdi, p. 1
[136] Gowens Research Foundation, letter from Evelyn McKinley Orr
[137] Letter by Evelyn Orr of the Melungeon Research Committee
[138] The Melungeons by N. Brent Kennedy, p. 46
[139] The Melungeons, Review Essay by Dr. Virginia DeMarce, p. 138 (N. Gen. Soc. June 1996)
[140] History of Tennessee and the Tennesseeans Hale and Merritt, p. 180
[141] The Melungeons by N. Brent Kennedy, p. 14
[142] Ibid, p. 94
[143] Ibid, p.121
[144] The Melungeons by Jean Patterson Bible p.57
[145] The Treatment of the Melungeon by Jacqueline Daniel Burks, p. 15 (Zuber p.2, 4)
[146] The Melungeons by Bonnie Ball, p.76
[147] The Malungeons by Will Allen Dromgoole p. 745 (Arena, 1891)
[148] East Tennessee and Western Virginia by Celestin Pierre Cambiaire, p. v
[149] The European Discovery of America by Samuel Eliot Morison, p. 677
[150] A New Voyage to Carolina by John Lawson (Hugh Lefler), p. 240
[151] Ibid
[152] The Only Land I Know by Adolph Dial, P. 1
[153] Ibid, p. 11
[154] Ibid, p. 16

Chapter II

The Portuguese Ancestry Follows - 1801
Portuguese - "Portyghee" or "Portoogais"

Just like Kennedy, the author faces the task of proving that the Melungeons were or were not of Portuguese ancestry. There are many claims but... *Believing the claim and proving it, however, were two different matters. I was faced with the daunting and unavoidable requirement of solving a three-hundred-year-old mystery in order to know my family's ethnic roots... Did we indeed have Portuguese roots? If we didn't, why in the world would our people have come up with such a strange heritage? Why not English? Or Irish? Or even Spanish? Why Portuguese, arguably the least believable of all? No, there had to be a basis for the claim .* [1]

Again, it has been documented that...*the Melungeons claim Portuguese ancestry.* [2] The name *Portyghee* has been popularized by English speaking people in several forms and may be connected with the Melungeons. ...*the earliest encountered Melungeons, regardless of their geographical dispersion, invariably claimed to be "Portyghee." Not "Portuguese" but "Portyghee," the way native Iberians or captured Moors would have pronounced it.* [3] Kennedy also writes ...*some of whom were born in the eighteenth century – claiming a Portuguese ancestry. Why such a consistent clamor over the years to be Portuguese if there was indeed no Portuguese ancestry?* [4] The name is known world wide as written in a November 1927 article by the National Geographic Magazine. *All over the world one finds the Portygee sailor and fishermmen.*

In every English speaking country, Portuguese immigrants are called *Portyghee,* short for Portuguese, and it is very often misspelled as *Portugee* or *Portugese.* Any name that distorts the original one can often be considered derogatory in nature for any group. The same applies to the Portuguese when they are called *Portygee* or similar sounding name. [5] The Portuguese ethnic group is not the only one. Every nationality or race has a derogatory connotation in its name, no matter how intelligent, rich or poor it is.

The way Iberian or captive Moors pronounce Portuguese is *Portoogais* and not *Portyghee,* which is how an English speaking person pronounces it today in every Portuguese-American community in the United States. On the other hand, Kennedy is correct that if the Portuguese are talking to an English speaking person, then they will say *Portyghee.*

Legend or reality - Bonnie Ball wrote: *One son, Andy Brown, also lived in Ab County* (Virginia) *; he married in 1794 and died in 1801, leaving five children. Three of these were married in Ab County after 1822. Later the entire family went west, and the only trace of them ever found was in a County in Illinois in 1848, where a son was recognized as "prominent citizen and grocer." ...There was legend that the Browns were Portuguese but the researchers failed to uncover any factual supporting information.* [6]

They may or may not have been Portuguese, but this proves that not all the

Melungeons stayed in the mountains and many of them, left in search of better opportunities, as soon as it was safe. *...those who stuck with it* (school) *... they often became successful business or professional people.*

He cited one in particular who is in charge of the city water department in a large town in Florida with over a hundred workers under his supervision-Dungannon, Virginia resident. [7] Insofar as the Portuguese are concerned, many are in the grocery business, some of them with supermarket chains, not only in America, but also in Brazil, Venezuela and other countries.

Lungeons Silver Smelters and Brandy - 1810

According to Melungeon names on Hawkins County tax list: *By 1810 it was certain that a Colony of dark skinned people inhabited the ridgeland near the Clinch River.* [8] In the same year... simple coincidences may point to directions that could result in the solving of a mystery. For example, genealogist Delores Sanders of Houston, Texas, informed Kennedy of the Melungeons' involvement with silver in Baxter County, Arkansas. *...Major Jacob Wolf... Father of Baxter County... established his famous trading post... in 1810... In search of fortune and adventure... Jacob Mooney... of McMinnville, Tennessee... four slaves and four other men.... The four other men who had come with Mooney were men of mystery – referred by old-timers as "Lungeons". They were neither Negro or Indian and in later years Jacob Mooney was ostracized for living with those "foreigners."* [Notice that there was a difference-four men were slaves.] *Could these men have been Melungeons – the mysterious people of the hills of Tennessee who have recently been identified as being Mediterranean possibly of Jewish lineage, and who lived in America prior to Columbus' discovery of the "new world"?... improvised a smelter to convert the silver ore into bars... Mooney... started down river ... They carried silver.* [9]

Working with precious metals is a tradition inherited from the Moors and it is important to note that in 1554, Lisbon had 430 jewelry stores, selling gold and silver artifacts, and they must have had plenty of craftsmen to supply the demand.[10] Not only did they have silver, but also *...lead, furs, wild honey and brandy*. Brandy? Brandy is a southern European alcoholic beverage... *It seems that Ned, the colored overseer, had discovered that a refreshing brandy could be distilled from the paw-paw fruit.* [11] Hale & Merrit also wrote: *In time they* [Melungeons] *became, almost to a man, distillers of brandy.* [12] It is known that Portuguese immigrants in North America also had their own home made brandy distilleries for personal consumption. (See following pages under the heading *Saturday Evening Post 1947* for more on brandy.)

The *Guineas* and other Groups - 1815

In the northern counties of West Virginia, there existed (1946) a people of mixed race, whose ancestry is shrouded in mystery. They are known locally as *Guineas* although they resent being called that name by outsiders. The area they populated was northern Barbour County and southern Taylor County as well as Garret County. In those counties, the Guinea family names began to appear in 1815. There was the mistaken notion that they were *Guinea Negroes.*

They claimed for many years to descend from one of the Guineas, British, French or Portuguese. The term *Guineas* may stem from the English *pennies, also* called *Guineas which* circulated in early American history. Also, during the 19th century the term was applied to things or persons of foreign, and uncertain origin. (Regarding terms and names, reference is made in another chapter, where the name *Turk* was applied in a similar manner.) The Guineas worked in both agriculture and mining.

The family names of the *Guineas* are interestingly close enough to those of the Melungeon population, such as Collins, Kennedy, Male, Miner, Newman etc. *The Guineas varied in color from white to black, often possessing blue eyes and gray hair, sometimes brother and sisters may range from the blackest Negro to a blonde, blue-eyed, fair skinned person with all the shades in between.* [13] During the World War II draft: *The Guineas of Taylor County have gone for the most part into the army as whites. Apparently there was some sort of prior agreement among them to register as white.* It was known then that in certain counties, military draft registration was refused based on skin color. Like one other group described as Portuguese, later in this book, they also had similar problems during WW II.

In addition to the Guineas, there are also the Wesorts of southern Maryland, and the Croatans of North Carolina who later became the Lumbees. Also there were the West Hills that were rather heavily into bootlegging. In the early census records, the Guinea family names were registered under the *free colored* or *mulatto* categories. Interestingly, there were *one or two cases of Portuguese inter-marriage with the Males,* [there is the theory that] *Guinea origins traces them back to lost followers of Hernando de Soto.* [14]

Pure Portuguese and Melongos - 1820

When written records are not available, writers very often rely on oral information. Bonnie Ball provides some interesting details about an interview: *A few years ago Mr. G. M. French Jr. A native of southwestern Virginia who lives in Cheverly, Maryland, sent me his notes from an interview he had with one of the oldest residents of the Dunganon area of Scott County, Virginia, who lived on Copper Ridge. The old timer was also known as "Uncle Washington Osborn." In the interview, he said that the Melungeons began their migration to that part of Scott County, Virginia, and neighboring Wise County, about 1820... "Uncle Washington Osborne also said that the first Collinses that came to his community were white. He mention one Melungeon "Uncle Poke Gibson" who came from Letcher County, about 1820, and claimed to be "Portuguese Indian"... Mr. Osborne referred to the Melungeons as "Melongo" which he defined as pure Portuguese... "The Bollings, who are numerous in Scott and Wise County...Another name associated with the "Melungo tribe was Lucas... He thought they were descended from the "Portuguese-Indians"...Another name Mr. Osborne connected to*

Melungeons was Moore. ...they came... as early as 1807 ...He claimed Ethan was one-third Portuguese Indian. [15] It is possible that some may have mixed with the Indians. Others simply took advantage of the special treatment and advantages that were being given to the Indians, thus claiming ancestry. Insofar as the word Melongo is concerned, it is definitely Portuguese. The correct spelling is "Melungo".

Education and Wilson County - 1827-30

It was believed that, in fact, most Melungeons were illiterate, and that their children did not like to attend school. In the 19th century that was common all over the world, not because the children did not like it, but because there were not enough schools and teachers. *Not only did many Melungeons grow up to be illiterate but their Scotch-Irish neighbors as well.* [16] In fact, if we consider the period of the early 1800's it is not surprising. Andrew Johnson, the 17th president, could neither read nor write. His wife taught him after their marriage in 1827. He was the only president who never spent a single day in a schoolroom. [17]

Furthering the issue of schooling, *...another problem that has made the Melungeon path a thorny one is that, until desegregation was legally decreed, they have almost consistently, refused to attend any school except those of the white children... authorities often tried to force them to attend Negro schools because of their dark coloring. For the most part, when this happened, the parents either refused to let their children attend school at all, or whole communities would move to towns or counties where they would be accepted without question in the white schools.* [18] Illiteracy may have played a part in the beginning, leaving people speaking broken or Elizabethan English when found by the first explorers. Isolation may be the explanation, but it is likely to be the case of colloquial speech.

Later and according to Dixon Merritt, one of the authors of A History of Tennessee and Tennesseans, *said recently that a Colony of Melungeons was imported to Wilson County about 1830 to work for a lumber mill...* [19]

According to personal interviews and local records, a similar situation may have occurred in Gaston, North Carolina when a Portuguese group was hired to work on the Roanoke canal, during the early 1800's.

Also the year 1830 was an *active time for Melungeon families acquiring land in the Newman's Ridge area,* [20] according to Hawkins County Registrar's Office.

Among the early Melungeon settlers... *were at least ten persons who saw service in the America Revolution,* [21] according to the list which constituted only a fraction of names.

Indian or Melungeon came from Portugal - 1834

From the following, it is evident that the Melungeons would not easily give up their heritage.

Even at a high cost, they kept their pride. *...the Lumbees embraced the official designation of "Indian"... Most of the Melungeons held out, never taking advantage of this classification. Instead, they continued in their struggle to preserve their*

Old World customs while insisting on their southern Europeanism. [22]

There is one factor of which many persons are aware: Portuguese immigrants are known to be hard workers, and do not necessarily look for welfare. *But hints at the truth come from changing "facts" surrounding certain ancestors, sometimes reflected in a single individual who was "Portuguese at birth, "Portuguese-Indian" as an adult, and, at death, simply "Indian".* [23]

The theory of Portuguese ancestry persists. *His wife Betty Reeves was possibly a full Melungeon, the daughter of Ashe Countians George Reeves, Sr. and Jane Burton. As Mary Killen Hollyfield, a descendant of Betty Reeves recalled in 1929: The Reeves are said to have come from Portugal. They had brown eyes and black hair. I've heard it said they were part Indian too. Betty Reeves herself claimed to be "Portuguese Indian," a term used by many Melungeons to explain their heritage*
.

The Portuguese portion of the term was eventually dropped, most likely because (1) no one believed it, (2) the Melungeons had no proof to back it up, and (3) it had become synonymous with Melungeon "anyway. Being "Indian" was increasingly considered preferable to "Melungeon" or Portuguese." [24]

Although this situation may make researching into the past difficult, there are still numerous documents awaiting expert eyes.

The Trail of Tears and President Andrew Jackson, a Spanish Citizen

Like the Melungeons, the Cherokees have suffered tremendously. One example is the Trail of Tears engineered by President Andrew Jackson. [25] It was part of the Great Removal, in 1838, when most Indian tribes in the east were taken to what is now northeastern Oklahoma, there they formed the Western Cherokees of Oklahoma. Before the 20th century this was one of the most massive and historical relocations of human population. [26] President Jackson was retaliating against the Indians for their service to Great Britain during the war of 1812. As part of that relocation, a large number of Melungeons may have gone west.

At the time of removal in 1838, a few hundred Cherokees escaped to the mountains, thereby serving as the nucleus for the 3,000 who in the 20th century lived in western North Carolina. Most still live there. It is believed that some Melungeons and others may have joined them and gone west to Tennessee.

In his book, Kennedy discusses a possible relation between the Melungeons and President Jackson, [27] an issue which may deserve further study for the interested reader. His life was very interesting, especially when searching the archives of the Indias in Seville. There, one of the archivists shared that some research had recently been done regarding President Andrew Jackson's biography. Some documents were found proving that he pledged the oath of allegiance to Spain. This was rather strange, and further research in the Library of Congress under the author Robert Remini, Jackson's biographer, proved that the archivist was right. Remini had already published a lengthy article in the 1995 Spring issue of the magazine *Tennessee Historical Quarterly.* [28]

Apparently, and in order to establish his law practice, he needed fast money. The quickest way was to become a Spanish citizen, thereby enabling him to trade, use the Mississippi and other rivers, own land and do business in Natchez. On July 15, 1789, Andrew Jackson and 17 other prominent Americans signed a three-page oath of allegiance to Spain. Later, he forgot about the document and went on to become a national hero in several battles.

Remini's story is fascinating, and gives us an insight into what life was like at the turn of the 18th century when the Melungeons first started to become visible. Jackson, just *like hundreds of others before him who took the oath, did what necessity dictated.* [29]

When discussing early settlers such as the Melungeons, one needs to be mindful that, at about the same time, North Carolina was reluctant to give up the western lands. During a discussion in the Senate, the characteristics of these western settlers were mentioned in a very descriptive manner: *...And these westerners were a tough, mean, and independent breed. Some of them were later described as "North Carolina blue beards, who are rugged, dirty, brawling, browbeating monsters, six feet high, whose vocation is robbing, drinking, fighting and terrifying every peaceable man in the community.* [30] Some of those characteristics sound familiar to Melungeons but also to frontier mountain men.

Discriminatory Laws and Free Persons of Color

The history of Tennessee records Miss Dromgoole's question to John A. McKinney, past chairman of the committee of the Constitutional Convention of 1834. Did he know the meaning of "Free Persons of Color", to which he replied: *...if it meant anything it meant Melungeon.* [31] In the same year a discriminatory law was passed that made life much harder for the Melungeons or other groups in the same circumstances. In the following year North Carolina amended its 1776 constitution. *No free Negro, free mulatto, or free person of mixed blood descending from Negro ancestors to the 4th generation shall vote for the Senate or the House of Commons.* From this wording a vote was denied to all people considered FPC. At the time, much was written, and according to Jean Patterson Bible, James Aswell was the author of the following passage: *The fact that the Melungeons occupied rich farmlands which God had clearly intended as a reward for Scotch-Irish righteousness and enterprise called the newcomers. They made up their minds to oust the squatters on the Promised Land. Of course the Melungeons could have been picked off one by one from ambush, but that method was far too slow. An added disadvantage lay in the fact that the Melungeons would have been more than their match at bushwhacking. So, with fine Scotch-Irish canniness, the settlers passed the law. It stated, this law, that in the State of Tennessee no free persons of color – meaning Melungeon – could vote or hold public office. Furthermore, no free person of color could bear witness in court against a white man. In a word, the Melungeons were made legally helpless in any legal dispute involving a white man. If a white man claimed a Melungeon's property, the victim had no* *recourse...Suddenly found that the strangers they had allowed to settle among them in overwhelming numbers were, cowbird like, pushing them out. Nevertheless, they fought tooth and nail to hold what they had. It was useless. They were driven up the ridges to land too high and poor to arouse the cupidity of the victors...*[32] Then came the Civil War, which presented an opportunity for the Melungeon revenge, and causing terror to the whites. They served honorably also in the Revolutionary War, some with distinction, and in every war in which the U.S. has been involved.

Kennedy describes this classification imposed on the Melungeons, in the following statements: *They and we were "free persons of color," or simply "FPC"... Neither White, Black, Mulatto, nor Indian,... as numerous writers have so often stated, "nobody at all."* [33] It can be understood as applicable to his own family. ...*Melungeons into any of the then four available legal categories (White, Indian, Negro, or Mulatto), the Scotch-Irish cleverly deployed a new term: "free persons of color", and used it to strip the Melungeons of their lands, their right to be represented in court, their right to vote, and their right to public education. One sweep of the judicial pen, the simple arbitrary assignment of the letters "FPC" (or "FC" to which it was sometimes shortened) alongside one's name in the federal census...*[34]

The white settlers in those days would take advantage of minorities, perhaps something still alive in current America. *When the Melungeons countered that they were Portyghee, and thus fellow Europeans who should be immune to such a law... "FPC" soon gave way to "Mulatto" as census takers lost patience with those Melungeons seeking to hold on to their lands. On several of the old census records one can see the term "Port." crossed through and "mulatto" written in its stead. In any event, census takers eventually settled in on the terms "FPC," "FC," or "mulatto" to describe any person of darker complexion, regardless of their ethnic origin.* [35]

We should not discount the fact that by the 18th and 19th centuries, miscegenation occurred between free Blacks or slaves and Indians as well as other races, thereby producing the Mulatto and Mestizo. It is possible that some groups may be darker than others with the natural gravitation towards the Blacks, Indians or other minority. However the Melungeons claim that they were *never slaves, and until 1834 enjoyed all the rights of citizenship...*[36]

Just like other groups, the Melungeons tried to maintain social boundaries between themselves and the blacks, due to discriminatory practices, according to Professor Paredes, in the case of the Creeks of Alabama. [37] Dromgoole in a very poetic manner adds: *Unenviable as is the condition of the slave, unlovely as slavery in all its aspects, bitter as is the draught the slave is doomed to drink, nevertheless, his condition is better than that of the 'free man of color' in the midst of a community of white men with whom he has no interest, no fellow-feeling and no equality."* [38]

Still, the Melungeons were able to endure all that and survive.

The Mulatto Class, Two Races and the National Census - 1850

Kennedy describes the census taker ... *"white," which meant only "pure" northern Europeans, or black," which meant Blacks, Mulattos, Indians, Jews, Arabs, Asians, and so forth, or anyone with as much as one-sixteenth so-called "nonwhite" blood. Intended to make the Appalachian census taker's task a simpler one.* [39] *From that point onward, the Melungeons became officially a mixture of White, Indian, and Black, or in the reputed words of one nineteenth century Tennessee senator, a "Portuguese nigger".*[40] While research was being done on the Melungeons, a reporter of a small southeast town newspaper was interviewed, and, in discussing discrimination, he mentioned that it is still very much alive, but in a subtle manner. In another instance, while in Florida, a typical looking Scotsman was asked if he knew what a Melungeon was. His answer: *Blue eyed nigger.* This was in 1995.

One of the reasons that may have caused the eventual disintegration of the Melungeon group as Portuguese – if they were, in fact, Portuguese – was, and still is, the easy acceptance of other peoples and races by the Portuguese. Mrs. Bible adds *...From 1850 on, national census includes state of birth... None of the Melungeons listed was born in Tennessee before 1800...* That meant the Melungeon families were already established in North Carolina and Virginia in the 1700's before they were pushed out by discriminatory laws. ... *No one listed was born in Tennessee before 1799... One Gipson wife, 70 years of age, was born in South Carolina – 1729.* [41]

That may also prove that the Melungeons came to the mountains much later and originated on the East Coast.

John Netherland of Tennessee - 1859

The Melungeons also had friends in high places... *Col. John Netherland of Hawkins County, Tennessee...1859... restored the right of citizenship for the Melungeons...and their gratitude was manifested towards him in every way as long as he lived.* [42] His daughter Eliza N. Heiskell wrote an affectionate article about the Melungeons later in 1914. The contents were totally different from the unfair and generalized description by Will Allen Dromgoole in 1891.

Melungeons from Portugal and Judge Shepherd in 1872

This story is so fascinating that it merits full reproduction from Jean Patterson Bible's book. It certainly would make a first-class story for a Hollywood movie. It tells how a young attorney, Lewis Shepherd, won a case based on the theory that the Melungeons were of Carthaginian or Phoenician origin, having emigrated from Portugal. (See Appendix G for the full story)

Portuguese, Phoenicians and Carthaginians are definitely people with common ancestors.

Coincidence of Typical Portuguese Names and Roots - 1888

Names are difficult to prove ancestry, but as Bonnie Ball tells us in her book: *in 1888...two of their children, Antonio and Dean, were later listed as "white" ...in 1902, Ulysses and Helena Jones — he Indian and black —, she Indian and white were both given a marriage license as white...*[43] She (Dromgoole) *added that a Portuguese named Denham arrived "from somewhere" and married another Collins daughter... common surnames as Gorven, Gibbens, Bragans or Brogan...*[44] The name Bragans is a derivative of Braganza or Bragança, to be exact, same as the Portuguese royal family and Antonio or Helena is a very common first name, but then the same happens with other Latin nations, except that the Portuguese write Helena with an H, as opposed to the Spanish *Elena*.

Swan Burnett - Note on the Melungeons in 1889 - Portuguese and Proud

Swan Burnett, a medical doctor in Washington, D.C., born in 1847, wrote that he heard the name *Melungeon* as a child, which had *a ponderous and inhuman sound as to associate them...with giants and ogres ...They resented the appellation Melungeon, given to them by common consent by the whites, and proudly called themselves Portuguese.*[45] The phrase *proud and Portuguese* was also mentioned in an article published in the *Boston Traveler* on June 13, 1889. *They have not recently married with Negroes or Indians... the "more thoughtful" people there was a "disposition" to give credence to the Melungeons' claim that they were a distinct race. A few inclined toward the Portuguese theory...*[46] One of the reasons that they may not have married Negroes or Indians was because they had plenty of women within their group.

The Portuguese, scattered all over the world since the 1500's, have intermarried with other races. They did not have Portuguese women with them, and were encouraged to marry the local natives in order to establish a better Portuguese hold. This point may also serve as an indication that the Melungeons arrived here with their wives, and children of perhaps mixed races. Further discussion on the topic appears later in this book.

It is likely that since the 1800's, or even prior to that date, Melungeons have mixed with Blacks. It is not uncommon to see a person with a black appearance claiming Melungeon ancestry.

It is reasonable to accept why the Melungeons did not want to be classified as Blacks: probably they were not, and if they already had Black ancestry, they had nothing to gain. Just like the Creeks of Alabama, they did whatever they could to distance themselves from the Blacks, not to be identified with a minority that was being discriminated against.

Will Allen Dromgoole *Boston Arena* articles in 1891

Judging from her articles, it appears that Dromgoole – a novelist and poet – knew little of life outside the big cities. Her description of people living in the mountains in 1890 does not take into account all the amenities that she took for granted. Dromgoole was originally from Nashville and had worked in New York when she came to Sneedville to work on her articles. Sixty years later, (1950) Edward T. Price wrote: *...The County* (Hancock) *has no telephone exchange, but one or two long-distance lines have been recently installed...Thus the inaccessibility of this area.* [47] What would Miss Dromgoole have said if she had visited them in 1950? Would she have blamed the Melungeons for the lack of progress in the county? After all, they were a minority.

On the positive side, her report possibly brought to the public's attention one of the very few documents that describe the life of the Melungeons in the 1890's, as well as their possible beginnings.

Her comments were derogatory, and were meant for headlines in the *Boston Arena*. She did not take into consideration that life was not so kind to the Melungeons. In her article, Miss Dromgoole wrote: *"The Malungeon Tree..."* adding to the Portuguese claim of ancestry: *The tree at last began to put forth branches, or rather...English (white), Portuguese, and African ...by claiming to have married Portuguese, there really being a Portuguese branch among the tribes. ... The Portuguese branch was for a long time a riddle... It has at last been... traced to one Denham, a Portuguese who married a Collins woman.* [48]

The name Denham as written is not Portuguese; however it may derive from *Dinho* a short form of *Godinho*. The combination of the letters **nh** is very common in Portuguese. It produces the same sound as the English word *onions*.

What is rather strange in her articles is that, Dromgoole mentions the Portuguese quite often and does not establish a parallel with the Portuguese community in New England, which by 1890 was quite noticeable, especially in the fishing industry. By that time also, the first Cape Verdeans, black Portuguese, employed by the whaling industry had arrived, a factor which may have caused the Melungeons to start dropping their Portuguese denomination.

Small, Shapely Hands and Feet, *She* (Dromgoole) *calls the hands of the Melungeon women "shapely" and adds that their feet were likewise, despite the fact they often travel barefoot over rough mountain paths.* [49] (See note a at the end of this chapter.)

The author's grandmother in Portugal also had small and shapely feet, except for the open skin cracks – sometimes bleeding – on her heels from walking barefoot all day on the not so smooth paths and ways in the 1940's.

Dromgoole also mentions: *They follow the body to the grave, sometimes for miles, afoot, in single file.* [50] As for walking single file to the cemetery, that was true in Portugal quite some years ago. Most of the times it was because the path was so narrow that only one person at a time could follow the path without getting scratched by the thorny briars.

Going Barefoot, Single File, to the Cemetery

Jean Patterson Bible quoted a letter by Mr. Grohse: *I have seen some women go barefooted with a good pair of shoes hanging over their shoulders... walking single file all the way to the cemetery.* [51]
During the early 1940's in Portugal it was common to see women in the countryside doing exactly that, mostly on Sundays, which was quite natural within the Portuguese culture.(See note b at the end of this Chapter.)
During the week, they would go barefoot, but with their legs covered from the ankles to the knees by a wool woven sleeve.

Fig. 12 - A funeral in the countryside of Portugal in the early 1960's

This protected them from both the thorns of the briars and from the cold. The reason they went barefoot most of the time was to divert water irrigation through small channels in the fields using hoes and their feet to better distribute the water. Being barefoot all week, they had a hard time wearing shoes on Sunday, as they felt very uncomfortable. Consequently, they just took them off, and hung them around their neck or over their shoulders. As a custom, the Melungeons follow *the casket to the cemetery and observe a year's mourning.* [52] It is still a custom in some villages in Portugal to do exactly that. Another aspect associated with their dead is the fact the Melungeons never cremated the body. They always buried it. Cremation is not readily accepted in Portugal.

Cemeteries, Little Houses over the Graves

Miss Dromgoole also mentioned a strange custom when she visited their cemetery. *...they build a kind of floorless house above each separate grave...The graveyard presents the appearance of a diminutive town, or settlement, and is kept with great nicety and care.* [53] The present day cemeteries in Portugal still show some graves with a cupola above, mostly in marble as a Portuguese tradition with very elaborate mausoleums. Kennedy's comments are worth quoting: *One can*

Fig. 13 - Old Cemetery in New Orleans

only imagine the Scot-Irish as they encountered these improbably dark-skinned mountaineers speaking broken English, claiming a Mediterranean heritage, placing southern European cupolas over the graves of their dead, sporting English surnames, practicing Christianity...[54] Melungeon burial customs also seem to have a remarkable fascination... Today there are few remaining... paint their house or their grave shelter, the latter always took precedence. [55] [See picture below] ...and their cemeteries look like miniature villages. [56] This is certainly a

Fig. 14 - Melungeon Cemetery in Sneedville (1996 Photo by the author)

tradition with the Portuguese, and sometimes the little house turns into a marble mausoleum. That is an equally common practice in the South Mediterranean region. Also interesting is the fact that in New Orleans, where the water level is high, a similar type of graves is used. Therefore, the logical reason for burying the cadavers above ground is to protect them from water or to prevent them from coming out of the ground from the water pressure.

The Christian Cross as a Religious Symbol and Indian Religion

Bonnie Ball writes about Dromgoole's experience with the Melungeons: *She*

Fig. 15 - Cemetery in Portugal showing similar cupolas or little houses

described many facets of Melungeon life, some of which she thought might have indicated a Latin origin... was puzzled by an unusual veneration for the Christian cross in view of the fact that most other people who lived in the area, if religious at all, were more inclined toward the "shouting", emotional type of Protestantism, seldom using the cross as a symbol in their *services.*[57] The veneration of the cross is also true with the Portuguese. In the small villages in Portugal during the early 1940's, it was common to see the cross in every pathway at a crossroads – and some still do – in a niche, or sometimes with a religious icon. Parents, as a matter of course, would get some kind of a cross made out of wood – or gold if they could afford it – and put it around the neck of their children to protect them from evil. *The Melungeons were never adherents of the Indian religion and rites, but adhered to the Christian religion. The cross was ever held by them* (Melungeons) *to be a sacred symbol.* [58] This fact would rule out Muslim or Jewish ancestry, however, they may already have been Christianized prior to coming to America. If so, they would have been free to practice whatever faith they had. We could also speculate that only Christian groups were found, which does not preclude the presence of Jewish, Muslim or Hindu groups.

History of Tennessee and the Tennesseans - 1912

Mrs. Eliza N. Eiskell of Memphis wrote in an article published in the Arkansas Gazette: *...They have had no poet or seer to preserve their history...*[59] This was very unfortunate but, when fighting to survive, keeping track of your ancestry is not necessarily the first priority.

The following description was furnished in 1912 by Col. W. A. Henderson, president of the Tennessee Historical Society, to be included in the history of Tennessee and Tennesseans as a description of the Melungeons in the 19th century: *The Melungeons are a peculiar people living in the mountains of east Tennessee, western North Carolina, southwest Virginia and eastern Kentucky... They have swarthy complexion, straight black hair, black or gray eyes... and are not tall but heavy set...*[60] The description certainly matches a large body of the Portuguese population. When the Melungeons faced hard times and discrimination, and their name was derogatory, their only key to survival was the family as well as joining others with similar problems. *...they wrote to a prominent citizen of upper East Tennessee, asking for information on the Melungeons. The answer to their letter came promptly with the statement that "We have no such a race. Our citizens are civilized people and believe in earning their living by the sweat of their brow, and are far superior to those who try to disgrace them by placing the fictitious name of 'Melungeon' upon them."* [61] Although that was back in the 19th century, this is still happening in this century.

The *Handbook of American Indians* speaking of the Croatan Indians: *Across the South Carolina are found a people evidently of similar origin, designated "Redbones." In portions of North Carolina and East Tennessee are found the so-called Melungeons or "Portuguese," apparently an offshoot of the Croatan proper, and in Delaware are found the "Moors."* [62]

This just reinforces the fact that the Melungeons were widespread, with the possible conclusion that some went west to the mountains and others stayed closer to the East Coast. As for the Moors, they form a part of the Portuguese ancestry.

Later in this book, the author will discuss his experiences as a stranger trying to research the Melungeons. There are still many people, government officials, that do not want to talk about or cooperate with the research. Also, the descendants of the Melungeon people avoid interviews or get very nervous.

School, Only with the Blacks, and Migration to Better Life

Bonnie Ball on schools: *After the Civil War the Wins were given a chance to attend the schools for blacks, but not for whites.* [63]

The Portuguese are generally not known as a racist people. As a minority they surely would not have survived around the world if they were.

In a racist and segregated society, if they were Portuguese, why should their children be forced to attend the black schools? They were a little darker, and were refused schooling in white schools then, and also in this century, as will be described later in this book. *The Melungeons... migrated... to southeastern Kentucky and Blounstown, Florida, just West of Tallahassee. It is also possible that some went westward to the Ozarks. Their numbers are estimated to be between five and ten thousand, and they have a high birth rate.* [64]

That is the reason for them to come to this continent in the first place. They did migrate, and most of them had success. Their success helped to build this great country. Should the spirit of adventure, ambition and a desire for a better life disappear, we would be sensing the eve of destruction.

Fig. 16 - George Farragut, father of David Farragut from the portrait by William Swain in the Smithsonian Institution, Washington DC.

Ability to Survive and Make a Living on Water

Means of livelihood: *...In earlier years riverboat carriage... Physique:... Their stoic endurance of out-of-doors life is notable... History:... Some believe they are derived from the Croatans; others say they come from the Portuguese...*

They appeared in Tennessee after the American Revolution. [65]*... There are also indications that some of these qualities* – The unusual endurance to a hardy, outdoor existence – *may have come from Portuguese and Moorish ancestors...* [66]

Portugal does not have many natural resources, the landscape is mountainous and not very fertile, and the plains of the South rely on rain, which is very irregular. The water was always a provider, and since remote times they looked to the sea.

The riverboat carriage was just another way for their subsistence. As for endurance, the Portuguese immigrants had to endure situations in the early 1950's that even today the poorest do not have to endure.

A true story has been told about Portuguese lumberjacks working in the cold Canadian north, who stayed up all night around a fire to keep warm. The ones that went to sleep found themselves with frost bite in their fingers, toes and nose and eventually lost them. At one time, one of them thought something was biting his ear, and slapped it with his hand. Part of the ear lobe fell to ground.

As for the women, they took care of the house, children, cooked the meals, while working the fields. Some still do. This is slowly disappearing, but if one visits the interior small villages of Portugal, one will find a semi-primitive but healthy life still existing, and the women play a big part in it.

Admiral David Farragut, a Possible Melungeon

Eliza Heiskell, the daughter of John Letherland also wrote about the Melungeons: *Rankin's Ferry at Chattanooga, Tennessee, was once operated by a family of Melungeons, and that Admiral Farragut, of naval fame during the Civil War, was a Melungeon... The Portuguese tradition seems to persist in connection with the Melungeons much more stronger than even that of the Lost Colony.* [67]

Like the Portuguese, the Melungeons seem to find a way of making a living on or near the water. Worthy of note is the fact that Admiral David Glasgow Farragut was born near the Holston River, 15 miles southwest of Knoxville, Tennessee. [68] This was a traditional Melungeon area. This is again repeated by Jean Patterson Bible, who maintains that Admiral Farragut was possibly of a Portuguese strain. *It is said on good authority that the brave Admiral*

Fig. 17 - Lieutenant David Glasgow Farragut, U.S. Navy ,from the portrait by William Swain in the Smithsonian Institution, Washington, DC.

Farragut was a descendant of a Portuguese of that name who married a poor North Carolina girl. [69] If he is not a Portuguese descendant, he is not far from it. Aragon was an ally of Portugal against Castille, and Portugal's army fought side by side with Aragon against the Moors. Farragut's biography states that his father was a swarthy man named George Anthony Magen Farragut, born in the island of Minorca of fighting blood. Farragut was directly descended from Don Pedro Farragut, who assisted James I of Aragon in driving the Moors from the Balearic Islands in the 13th century. [70]

Portugee Indian Tribe - 1926

A book by Arthur H. Estabrook and Ivan E. McDougle, published in 1926, discusses several tribes, such as the Wins, and also the so called Portuguese Indian tribe. *Geraldine Hall, a sister of Andrew, dark in color… considered herself a Portugee Indian.* [71] This book goes into detail describing the possible problems of marrying within their own group, which may have caused mental retardation. However it also explains the Virginia law at the time whereby marriages between races were forbidden by statute, and goes on to explain the need for recording the color of the persons. The Wins were also classified as *free persons of color* by the federal census. [72] It is also interesting that Virginia passed a law in 1924 describing the term *white person shall apply only to the person who has no trace of blood other than Caucasian.* [73]

Since we are looking into other groups, it is worthwhile noting that there was a group of *red skinned people* living in the Blue Ridge Mountains, who considered themselves white folks. *The general light color of the skin indicates the presence of some white blood.* [74] Why do we find isolated groups that clearly show white ancestry, who were also moonshiners?

In Robin County, North Carolina, another group called the Rivers is mentioned. They also claim to be descended from the Roanoke Lost Colony.

Interestingly, the author mention that *French emigrants, as early as 1690, had settled in Licking County, where they came in contact with the mixed race to whom they gave the name "Mero".* [75] Why not Melungeon, since early writers mention that the name originated with the French word *mélange*?

One more reason to question the French naming of the Melungeons.

Racially Distinct - 1934

As for being distinct, Bonnie Ball states in a newspaper article: *Roanoke News, February 25, 1934, Dr. Goodridge Wilson wrote the following: "They are socially and racially distinct from the blacks and white around them, and are not classified as Indians… cabins of Melungeons and their ancestors lived since 'time immemorial'…" … "They, themselves, disliked the term 'Melungeon.' The Newman's Ridge contingent prefer to be called 'Portuguese,' claiming descent from a band of Portuguese immigrants who, they say settled Newman's Ridge about the time of the Revolution…"* [76]

One major difference that makes the Portuguese racially distinct from others is that our sea border on the Atlantic was much easier to invade from Northern Europe. The Northwest African people, when going away from the Mediterranean, would also find the Portuguese southern and west coast, easy to reach. The other is the fact that while the Portuguese chose Lisbon as their capital, being by the sea and on a magnificent harbor of the Tagus River, able to receive very large vessels, the Spaniards chose Madrid as their capital, much against the Castilians that still today consider Burgos the rightful capital of Spain. Today this may not be important, but in the 15th and 16th century, the ocean was the gateway to the world, and the Portuguese had such a gateway in Lisbon. As for being in North-America before the American Revolution, it is correct, but possibly much before, and the Melungeons served in the army, thus taking an active part in it.

In chapter V the reader will discover more about the Portuguese, and their ancestry.

Fig. 18 - Mrs. Hazel Keith (left), former Graysville teacher, with Mrs. Carrie Goins and grandchildren. Nothing mysterious about them. Photo courtesy of Jean Patterson Bible.

Fig. 19 - Tammy Goins, a Melungeon girl. Photo Courtesy Jean Patterson Bible.

Shy and Mysterious People - 1937

The persistent Portuguese ancestry tradition is noted in 1937 by James Aswell, in the *Nashville Banner*, when he writes about the East Tennessee mountaineers… *"When the first Scotch-Irish settlers from Virginia and North Carolina came pushing over the mountains… they found… settlements of shy, mysterious people. They were not Indians … When asked who they were and whence they came, they said they were Portuguese.* [77]

The Portuguese people of today may not be mysterious, but they are shy on the average, when put into an unfamiliar and hostile environment. The Melungeons may have mixed with the Indians, but as studies have shown, not on a regular basis.

Childbirth a Minor Event - 1940

The Melungeon women's endurance is described thusly: *As a rule childbirth was a minor event with Melungeon women. The day that Marindy discovered she was in labor, she rushed outside and called a neighbor who in turn called my mother… with neither a physician nor mid-wife available, the child was borne before my mother reached the shack… By the time Marindy's husband arrived from work that day, Marindy and her baby were sleeping comfortably…The young mother, likely as not, resumed her household chores the following morning.* [78]

This probably happened in the 1940's. A story has been told in a small Portuguese village of a woman giving birth all alone, while working out in the fields, and bringing her baby home, carrying the baby on one arm and the sickle hanging on the shoulder.

Another story happened in Rio de Janeiro, Brazil, in the early 1950's which was common with Portuguese women. Right after giving birth, only a couple of days later, the mother came home. She not only did her normal house chores, cooked the meals, bought the groceries – without any means of transportation – took care of the baby, but also worked as a seamstress, to supplement the husband's income. Water was a problem in Rio de Janeiro, and very often the mother had to carry it in pails, and in those days, not only for household consumption, but also to wash the baby diapers. This is what it takes to survive, with the Portuguese or the Melungeons, and they knew how to do it.

Eating Habits

The culture of a people is often identified by their food, as written by Bonnie Ball: *...while the men were logging or clearing new ground, the women and children were often seen gathering a fuzzy green plant that grew along clear streams. They called it "bear's lettuce", and ate it raw with salt. They also picked pails full of wild "sallet" (greens). This consisted of poke, narrow dock, crow's foot, cress, lamb's quarter, and many other plants that were known to be edible. They cooked them with a piece of salt bacon, and ate them with a hard corn pone usually baked in a Dutch oven in the open fireplace, or in a small step stove. Corn meal mush was one of their favorite cold weather foods. ...watched Jassie preparing their evening meal. This consisted of stirring mush in a big black metal pot, using a wooden spade.* [79]

In Portuguese villages, women Customarily gather various greens from their garden. Also they may go to the nearby creek and collect greens that grow near the water for the family meal. It is also interesting to note the usage of a black pot and wooden spade by the author's grandmother.

The wooden spade had another purpose, and that was to discipline the less behaved children by a not so gentle strike on their behind. Finally, the corn meal or stirring mush – *papas de milho* in Portuguese – certainly was one of the children's favorites, with a spoon of sugar in the center of the plate, which would melt caramel-like.

Garlic and Spicy

Another example of a food connection: *It is strong and hot. This sort of ties them to the Latin people, who are fond of onions, garlic, and red peppers.* [80]

The Portuguese are fond of spices. They discovered the sea-route to India just to get them. The Azoreans are especially fond of spicy foods, this may be a possible connection between the Melungeon and the Portuguese. These Atlantic islands played an important role during the age of discoveries, to include later navigation to, and from, the Americas. Of course the Portuguese Azoreans are not the only ones that appreciate spicy foods.

Portuguese Ancestry and Record Keeping

Jean Patterson Bible mentions in her book an interview with an important citizen who has lived for many years in Hancock County and has known Melungeons all her life. She shares the following:

I have reached the conclusion that, if they once knew where they came from, after the discrimination practices started, they just didn't talk about it, didn't use the word, Melungeon;... thus did not pass the information on to heir offspring... It is only when one's bell is full and the chill is turned away that one can turn to thoughts of other things... Hence, in my opinion, no one traced ancestry or kept records. [81]

This has not changed today with many nations of the world, where starvation and disease are a daily occurrence.

First, people must survive in a society where they have to compete for jobs. Next is the education for their children, and later for themselves, as well as other less important matters such as keeping genealogical records.

Who cares about ancestry, if one is hungry, cold and sick? Record keeping in most of Europe did not start until the 15th or 16th century, when the churches were given the task of recording all births and deaths in a book. The royalty, nobility and wealthy could do it. They had their own chapels and priests that did all the writing and record keeping.

The common people were not even allowed to learn how to read and write, unless one was a monk, a priest or seminarian.

Bonnie Ball ends her book with the following conclusion related to the Melungeon ancestry: *It is reasonable almost beyond doubt that the Melungeons had English ancestry... According to historians, the Croatans, had some previous white mixture, which would likely have been Spanish or Portuguese... Blue Ridge and Piedmont tribes... They could have been extensions of the Maryland and Delaware groups, who, in some instances, also claim Portuguese ancestry. Is there a Portuguese ancestry? As I see it, Portuguese ancestry is likely; all the older Melungeons have claimed it. Nevertheless, the Portuguese theory has been too long-standing and consistent to ignore.* [82]

Mildred Haun tells of a Melungeon who lived in a smoke house near her grandmother's Hamblen County farm in 1942 and *claimed they* [the Melungeons] *were in this country before any other race.* [83]

Discrimination well into the 20ᵗʰ Century - 1912-46
Most Present day Portuguese have Negro Characteristics?

Between 1912 and 1946, Dr. Walker Ashley Plecker was Virginia's Registrar of vital statistics, and very instrumental in creating a two-class people, White or Black. The following did happen not long ago: *Dr. Walker Ashley ("W. A.") Plecker, as late as 20 August 1942 in a letter from the state of Virginia's medical registrar, to the Tennessee state librarian and archivist, Mrs. John Trotman Moore... Plecker was upholding Virginia's anti-miscegenation laws which prohibited marriages between Melungeons and "whites." ...Melungeons who... are now causing trouble in Virginia by their claims of Indian descent, with the privilege of intermarrying into the white race...In that class we include the Melungeons of Tennessee.* [84] Just recently Kennedy made available a copy of a letter dated August 5, 1930, addressed to Mr. J. P. Kelly in Virginia. The contents show clearly Plecker's problem in accepting the Melungeons. [85]

Shirley McLeRoy described Dr. Plecker as the most outspoken proponent of the anti-miscegenation law of 1942. He became a one-man campaign. *Plecker undertook to erase the state's contemporary Indian heritage, which he felt had been so substantially diluted with negro blood that few Indians still existed...those of Indian blood were described officially as free negros or free coloreds.* [86]

Mrs. John Trotwod Moore, Virginia state librarian and archivist, wrote a letter to Dr. W. A. Plecker that refers to early settlers in South Carolina who migrated from Portugal and later moved to Tennessee about the time of the Revolutionary war. [87] The Virginia doctor went as far as comparing the physical appearance of the Portuguese to the African Blacks. He wrote that: *It is a historical fact, well known to those who have investigated, that at one time there were many African slaves in Portugal.* [Here's what Dr. Plecker wrote about Portugal:] *Today there are no true negroes there but their blood shows in the color and racial characteristics of a large part of the Portuguese population of the present day. That mixture, even if it could be shown, would be far from constituting these people white.* [88] According to Plecker therefore, being of Portuguese heritage was meaningless because the Portuguese population had the color and racial characteristics of the Negro. [89]

Dr. Plecker most likely has never been to Portugal and his knowledge of the Portuguese people was obviously quite limited. It is possible that the Portuguese have Negroid blood. After all, they interacted much with Africans. Many Portuguese who went to the previous Portuguese-African colonies married black women and some of their offspring came to Portugal. Still, that did not alter the appearance of the majority of the Portuguese population.

Saturday Evening Post - 1947

In William L. Worden's article titled *Sons of the Legend* on October 18, 1947, there are many photographs of the Melungeon people of that time. The writer

*Fig. - 20 - Modern home-made
brandy distillery*

spells Melungeon with an **a** as *Malungeon*, the same as written by Dromgoole at the end of the 19th century. He also notes Dromgolole's remarks. He describes them as *thin-lipped, rather like Indians, but not quite like them ...they have some Latin characteristics ...the daughters of these people are very often lovely, soft and feminine, in striking contrast to the bony appearance of most mountain women.* [90] The Melungeons were already settled when *the first yankee and Scotch-Irish mountain men drifted down the Clinch River ...they found in the rich farmland of the Clinch Valley a strange people already settled. They were dark, tall, not exactly like Indians, certainly not at all like the escaped Negroes... There are in Rogersville a few tall, olive skinned people ...the young women often remarkably beautiful.* [91]

Worden also quotes Dromgoole as describing a common factor with the Portuguese: *...the Malungeons commonly made and drank brandy rather than whisky.* [92] Worden challenges several of Dromgoole's theories, and declarations. The Portuguese in general appreciate brandy, or what they call *água ardente* (fire water). Most commonly they make it out of grapes, as well as any fruits, such as plums, figs, berries, etc. Some Portuguese immigrants in Canada made brandy in their basement, and had their own homemade distillery. The brandy was a by-product of their annual wine-making routine which was and still is illegal. Presently they still do it every year during the fall. After making wine in their cellars at home, they proceed with making brandy from *grape-bagasse,* the pulp left over from the wine making process. Bonnie Ball also writes: *...In time they became, almost to a man, distillers of brandy.* [93] Is this a coincidence?

Edward T. Price Investigation - 1950

Dr. Price presented a paper on racially mixed blood groups. One of them is the Carmel Indians, perhaps the only ones found in Ohio. Their surnames, and life style characteristics are similar to the Melungeons'. *Few, if any, really look like Indians...The country people are quick to point out their differences in language.* [94] He considers the presence of both Indian and Negro, and draws a connection between this group and the Melungeons of Eastern Tennessee. [95]

The writer discounts the *persistent rumor* of Portuguese descent and name

Fig. 21 - Portuguese 16th century Caravel crafted in solid gold filigree

derivation, but does not present a plausible explanation for what he calls a rumor and the resemblance of many Portuguese names. Dr. Price also says that the word *Melunge*, deriving from the French *mélange, seems equally unlikely.* [96]

Louise Davis - 1963: Precious Metal Craftsman and Claim to Be Portuguese

Louise Davis wrote an article in the *Nashville Tennessean*, quoting the late Mildred Haun *as saying that she had always heard of Melungeon skill with gold and silver... and accepted as a fact, that they were especially good at making jewelry from gold, and they were the best silver-bullet makers when there were witches in the country.* [97]

It is still an accepted fact that the Portuguese are very skilled with jewelry. Anyone visiting downtown Lisbon will see many jewelry stores with the elaborate jewelry. In fact, the two most famous streets in Lisbon are called *Rua do Ouro* (Gold Street) and *Rua da Prata* (Silver Street).

Their skill is also very visible in a popular souvenir made out of gold wire in filigree in the form of a 15th century Portuguese caravel. This is one of the most popular souvenirs sold in Portugal. No one knows for certain of its beginnings.

They are available in pure gold, but most are just plated. This type of work, and other jewelry craftsmanship, is common in Portugal today but long ago was only used by the aristocracy. Kennedy adds a very interesting and more recent finding related to precious metals: *...the colonists at Santa Elena included metallurgists and others whose primary tasks was to reconnoiter for precious metals, and to refine and work them once found. The Moors of Spain, Portugal, and North Africa were known for their metalworking, having in fact taught the art to the Iberians in the first place. The Melungeons have long been known for their silver-smelting abilities, as well as metalworking in general.* [98]

The Jews were skilled in this art, and Gil Vicente (ca.1465-1536), a noted Portuguese lyric poet, was also a famous goldsmith.

Pollitzer and Brown - 1969

The *Human Biology* issue of September 1969 published a study done by the Department of Anatomy and Anthropology at the University of North Carolina in

Chapel Hill. While the study is not conclusive as to the ancestry of the Melungeon people, it does not rule it out either.

This survey of demography and genetics was conducted by Drs. William S. Pollitzer and William H. Brown. The article starts out by describing what was known about the Melungeons at that time. It cites Dr. Price's research in 1950 and affirms that the older people living in Hancock County in 1850 were born chiefly in North Carolina and Virginia.

The description of the Melungeon population is *moderately tall...within the Caucasoid range...The general closer similarity of the Melungeons...to the White population is evident.* [a comparative gene frequencies table shows that.] *...When English and Portuguese frequencies are used, along with Negro and Indian, the methods agree that Portuguese are the more likely of the two European ancestors and contributed the majority of the genes. The data are well fitted by a 90% Portuguese component, with slight Negro and Indian admixture; they are also fitted by a 94% Portuguese and 6% Indian.* [99]

However, the survey also cautions that due to the similarity in English and Portuguese gene frequencies, no clear resolution is possible as to certain contribution of one or the other. *But all methods do agree that a European element predominates.*[100] The English never recognized them as their own, and if this study points to one or the other, which one is the other?

Fig. 22 - Martha Collins, a Melungeon descendant and ex-president of the Sneedville Citizen's Bank. Photo courtesy of Jean P. Bible

Portuguese from Nazaré, a Village in Portugal - 1970

While in the process of gathering information for her book, Jean Patterson Bible interviewed a president of a local bank. In a photo comparison between the peoples of Tangier, Morocco, and Nazaré, Portugal, the people of Nazaré were chosen as the ones that would most resemble the Melungeons. *Back in Sneedville, seated at her desk in the Citizen's Bank... gray-haired and blue eyed Miss Martha Collins, its 74 year old President, said thoughtfully, "Yes, some of my ancestors were Melungeons. We don't know but we think possibly they were descended from Portuguese or Spanish from Navarre. Some months later at my home, we looked at slides made in Nazaré, a Portuguese fishing village, and others of scenes and people in Tangier, Morocco. Miss Martha studied*

Fig. 23 - Maria Antonia Sousa, born in Nazaré, Portugal. Photo courtesy of Antonio Sousa

Fig.24 - Nancy Kennedy Melungeon descendant. Photo courtesy of Dr. N. Brent Kennedy's mother.

the pictures carefully. Then, with typical banker's caution, she said slowly, "They might be, but I just don't know. If anything, the Portuguese look more like the Melungeons I've always known all my life than the people in Tangier" [101]

The people of Nazaré are wed to the sea; this is the reason they claim descent from the Phoenician mariners.[102] Note the similarity of the faces, forehead, eyes and nose in the photos as shown on Fig. 23 and 24.

A Portuguese government official accepts the possibility of Portuguese ancestry. *... in the words of Press Officer Luis de Sousa at the Portuguese Embassy in Washington, is "quite credible" and "quite convincing."* [103] *...the old Melungeon photos. They would look at home on the wall of working-class household in Beira, the central region of Portugal.* [104]

Tradition Dies Hard

This story may or may not have anything to do with the Portuguese, but it is very tragic and at the same time interesting. It was narrated by Mildred Haun in her book *The Hawk's Done Gone*. The story was told by a grandmother acting as midwife to her daughter, who died of childbirth. In her dying breath she asked her

Fig. 25 - Ruth Johnson, Melungeon descendant from Sneedville.

mother to raise her daughter as if she were parentless.

Granny raised the illegitimate grand-daughter. Her name was Cordia Owens, born June 1, 1902. She was never told that her father was a Melungeon. Cordia was kept mostly around the house and Granny never let her go anywhere. One day, she ran away and got married to a white man. The young couple settled down on a farm. One winter, a Melungeon man stayed over at their farm as a helper. Cordia became pregnant, and when the child was born, Granny's worst fears had been realized – it was Melungeon colored. The jealous husband took one look and yelled, *"That is why the devil wanted to stay here!" thinking that the wife had betrayed him with the Melungeon helper. In a fit of anger, he beat the weakened young wife to death with a stick of wood. Later, as she lay in the makeshift coffin, he seized the whimpering baby, crammed it into the coffin alive with the dead mother and nailed down the lid.* [105]

Melungeon Itinerary to the Mountains

It has been established that the Melungeons did not originate in Tennessee. However, no one knows for certain from where they came. Edward T. Price studied the Melungeons in 1950. From the maps and description of what he found, it seems that they crossed into Tennessee from Virginia and North Carolina in the late 1700's. He also tells us that Newman's Ridge in Tennessee was not very good land and possibly the only place where they could settle, since no one else wanted it. *...Though much of the ridge land is unused, the poor pastures and second-growth woods on nearly bare limestone attest the futility of cultivating more of it in the same manner.* [106] That certainly indicates that they originated from the east coast of the Carolinas much before the 1700's, where Portuguese, Spanish, English and French navigators were very active in the 16th century.

Skillful in the Trades - Jean Patterson Bible who has known Melungeons for many years, writes *...They go to Michigan and Ohio mostly, and some of them are very skillful in trades of carpentry and bricklaying. Of the Magoffin County Melungeons, a friend from Gifford, Kentucky, writes...They are clannish through necessity but warm up to anyone who will treat them fairly and without prejudice... most of them are very skillful in trades of carpentry and bricklaying.* [107]

In Portugal, during the 1940's, education past grade four was available only to the wealthier people. There was the option of being accepted in a catholic seminary, and dropping out before taking the final vows. But even that was limited to a chosen few. The only other choice was to learn a trade, which they started doing at a very young age. That was the only way parents were able to give their offspring a means for making a living.

This resulted in the Portuguese being skillful in the trades and sought after all over the world as good prospective immigrants. Not all immigrants were skilled workers, but most of them were hard-working people of the land and sea.

Navarrah, Varr, Vardy and Irish Wake

Based on a letter written by J.G. Rhea, Louise Davis wrote : *Navarrah* [a Melungeon common name] *opened a mineral springs resort long ago...health resort...* [108] One of the favorite vacations for the older Portuguese in Portugal is to spend a few weeks or months at a health resort, usually near a spring called *Termas de Verão.* Later Jean Patterson Bible wrote a story she heard from someone who made a study of Appalachian folkways: *The wakes, in particular the gathering of the "clan" in the home to sit up with the dead for several nights before the burial, are definitely Irish in origin rather than Melungeon.* [109]

This may have an Irish origin, but it is also a Portuguese tradition that is slowly dying out. In the rural areas, it is still customary to sit up all night with relatives and friends of the dead, doing what the Portuguese call a *velorio*, or in other words, sit up with the defunct. Also we should not forget that the Portuguese also descend from the Celts, and some of their culture may have been appropriated by the people living in what is today Portugal.

Navarrah or *Navarro* in Portuguese is an important name among the Melungeon history. It should be noted that Moses Navarro, a Portuguese Jew, arrived in Pernambuco, Brazil, in a fleet of Jews from Portugal. [110]

European Looking and a Group Too Large to Ignore

European looking people who were Christian to boot, a new heritage had to be invented. Never mind that from the earliest encounters the Melungeons seemed to know who they were that their claim of origin was a non exotic, easily verifiable one. [111] Why would the English be interested in verifying the origin of the Melungeons? If they were Portuguese or any other nationality, it would be embarrassing, since it was assumed that whoever got there first claimed the land for their king or nation. This is unfortunately true, and while research for this book was being done on a small southeast town's history where the Portuguese – or people officially registered as Portuguese – were part of the town's history, but were simply classified as ...*and others*. Adalino Cabral, Ph.D. shared a known fact. *There is the case of the Cape Verdeans in Massachusetts (in the 1970's) being classified as "Others", when racial status was officially (requested from public schools) for State purposes. Today, the minority classification includes, Black, Hispanic, Asian... Cape Verdean...*[112]

It is very interesting what just a few people can accomplish in a matter of human reproduction. Kennedy wrote: ...*professional historians have generally ignored them, even though they numbered in the thousands. Today their descendants undoubtedly exceed 200,000 individuals, perhaps far more, but most are unaware that they carry Melungeon blood.* [113]

McGlothlen, a geneticist stated: *One European, African or mulatto...could leave a very disproportionate number of descendants...So if five shipwrecked sailors were adopted by a village of a hundred Indians, in two generations the village would probably be 25 or 30% European rather than 5%.* [114]

Sarcoidosis and Thalassemia

Kennedy, before he wrote his book, contracted a disease called erythema nodosum sarcoidosis. Its causes are unknown, but it can be debilitating, crippling, suffocating, and even blinding to its victims. A sizable percentage of the cases result in death.

Because of this event in his life, Kennedy was compelled to take up the quest for his origins and the very essence of who his people were and are. Sarcoidosis is also a common disease with the Portuguese immigrants in New England as well as in California. It is also known as Machado's or Joseph's disease. A doctor presently practicing medicine in Portugal stated that the disease is known in Portugal, and found more often in the Portuguese southern province of Alentejo.

The author was just recently made aware of a case of Joseph's disease contracted by a Portuguese born in Flores island (Azores).

Melungeon descendants show a heavy propensity toward such Mediterranean diseases as thalassemia, familiar Mediterranean fever, and sarcoidosis. [115] Sarcoidosis and thalassemia, also called Mediterranean anemia, are common in Portugal, Italy, and Greece. According to Adalino Cabral of Boston, it has also been found in Japan and elsewhere. It has been referred to as Azorean disease.

The cause is unknown...genetic factors are important...occurs predominantly between the ages of 20 and 40...and Sephardic Jewish ancestry and is rare in other ethnic backgrounds. [116]

While in Lisbon, Portugal doing research for this book at the *Instituto Nacional de Saude* or The National Health Institute, information was obtained about the Portuguese population genetic diseases. Doctor Odete Rodrigues was kind enough to offer a copy of an article published in the *Medical Journal of Genetics* in 1993. This article deals with hereditary anemias in Portugal and was the result of a study made by five Portuguese doctors and three Portuguese institutions, and shows the relevant historical events related to thalassemia.

The prevalence of carriers of thalassemia is in the southern province of Alto Alentejo, which agrees with the information given above. *In fact the four commonest Mediterranean β thalassemia mutations are found in the Portuguese.* [117] It also connects this disease with African slaves brought in the 15th century and later, as well as Phoenicians, Romans and Moslems (Moors).

Skin Darker than the Portuguese

Traditionally Melungeons were not accepted as Portuguese, because of the color of their skin.

...But a skin darker than the English perceived the Portuguese should possess, as well as the use of both English surnames and Elizabethan English language, have historically been cited as evidence against this theory. [118]

That may be possible, but the English knew that the Portuguese were darker than themselves. On May 31, 1662, Charles II of England married Catherine of Braganza, a Portuguese princess. After the royal marriage, John Evelyn, a 17th century author, wrote in a diary he has kept since he was 6 years old of the Portuguese ladies-in-waiting for Queen Catherine, *they are swarthy and olive skinned.* [119] These same words were used later to describe the Melungeons.

The women from Alentejo – a southern Portuguese province – are affectionately called *trigueirinhas* or *trigueiras*, which means swarthy, brown, brunette. It is a derivative of the Portuguese word *trigo* for wheat.

Portuguese Presence in the East Coast and the Same Portuguese Origin

Kennedy also presents one possibility of shipwrecked Portuguese sailors and mentions what is mostly accepted in North America as a limited Portuguese presence. *Furthermore, it has generally been thought that there was only a minimal Portuguese presence along our southeastern coast, yet another factor arguing against a Portuguese heritage.*[120] The presence of the Portuguese may not have been as numerous as the Spaniards, but certainly was larger than the English or any other European nation in the first half of the 16th century. *...the individual pockets of these people dwelled, the same Portuguese origin was consistently offered to explain their existence.*[121] *Nevertheless, even the skeptics have admitted the difficulty in dismissing outright the possible Portuguese link, primarily due to the early, widespread nature of these claims among even the most widely separated Melungeon settlements, and seeming cultural and linguistic evidences.* [122]

With no easy means of communication, this is quite an accomplishment. With Portugal having the oceans full of caravels, you may also have different groups from various parts of the world being discovered and explored by the Portuguese. Some of these people may or may not be from continental Portugal and may be the result of miscegenation with natives from the most diverse regions. That may also explain why some groups may be different from the others, and claiming to be Portuguese. (See Chapter VII for a detailed description of the Portuguese presence in North America)

Spoke Arabic or Berber at Home and Moor Mass Immigration

A language survives for a while as long as it is spoken at home. Experience has shown that after just two or three generations, it disappears when the people are exposed to another language in every day life. Kennedy explains a possible Arabic connection with the Melungeons: *Following the Reconquest about 1200 AD, an uneasy truce was observed, during which time the Spanish and Portuguese Moors did their best to blend in with their Hispanic neighbors. In greater numbers they intermarried, converted to Christianity, adopted Spanish and Portuguese names, kept a low profile, and generally spoke Arabic or Berber only in the home.* [123] This could be true in southern Spain, but not in Portugal. The end of the reconquest for Portugal was in the 1200's, and by the 1500's the Moors had been absorbed by the Portuguese population.

It only takes as little as one generation to lose the language of your ancestors. This can be proven today, by the most recent immigrant arrivals in America. *Portugal had no Moors on its soil in the 15th century... and at that time, Spain still had to reduce the Moslem remnant in Granada.* [124]

Mass immigration took place after the *...first five years after the fall of Granada...large numbers of its inhabitants...emigrate an settled in ...Tunis, Alexandria and elsewhere in North Africa...*[125] Kennedy mentions the Canary

Islands ...*Large numbers of Christianized Moriscoes were permitted to emigrate to the Canary Islands,*[126] which happened much later in the 16th century. This mass emigration, again may be true with southern Spain, but not with Portugal, as there was no such mass immigration of the Moors in the 15th or 16th century. That could point to the Spanish Moors, but how did they get to America? Why the name Portuguese? By the time the English met them, there was no war with Spain, and no reason to be afraid of telling the truth to the English. That happened one or two generations later at least. On the other hand, there was a large movement of the Portuguese population in the 16th century, due to the establishing of settlements in Africa, Brazil and India.

Portuguese Name Used by the Jews

Jane S. Gerber, in her well written book *The Jews of Spain*, describes in detail the Sephardic experience of mostly Spanish Jews. The Portuguese Jews are also described. The amalgamation of Portuguese and Spanish Jews into one may not reflect the reality as it was known then. *Even among themselves, the conversos in Lisbon, Madrid, or Seville referred to each other as "Portuguese," or "Men of the Nation" and the term "Portuguese" became synonymous with Jew" or "Judaizer" not only in Spain but wherever these Portuguese New Christians went in western Europe.*[127]
Even after they moved to other countries such as Holland and later to America, they carried their nationality and the Portuguese name with them. According to the same author: [The Jews]...*even as dutifully continued to keep the minute books of their congregation in Portuguese well into 18th century.* [128] *In western Europe, the smaller branch of the Sephardic family was primarily crypto-Jewish and Portuguese speaking.* [129]
There is another fact to which the writer may be referring. It relates to a period after 1580, when King Felipe II of Spain was also King Filipe I of Portugal. Many of the Jews who were forced to Christian conversion in Portugal, began to settle in Spain, its colonies and elsewhere. *There were enough in number for the word "Portuguese" to become almost synonymous with "Jew" in Spain as well as Spanish America.* [130] If that were the case, they were actually Portuguese Jews emigrating to Spain.
The hypothetical time frame for the Melungeons' arrival points to the early 1500's. During the middle and late 1600's it is unlikely that a group of people would arrive and go unnoticed for more than one hundred years.
As for the term *Men of the Nation*, it is believed that was applied to Jews of all nations, not just of Portugal. Men of the Nation probably meant *The Jewish Nation* within the country or nation in which they settled. It appears to be like that throughout the world.
Their petition to the Dutch West India Company to be accepted by the governor of New Amsterdam states: *Your Honors... Should also please consider that many of the Jewish Nation are principal shareholders...and many of their Nation have*

also lost immense and great capital in its shares and obligations. [131]

Leo Pap also mentions: *The term "gente da nação" or "men of the nation" in portuguese, was also used by emigrants from the Azores, referring to other Portuguese from continental Portugal or others that had returned from America.* [132] It is obvious that the term does not necessarily apply only to Jews. When the crowns of Portugal and Spain united in 1580, many Portuguese Jews fled to Spain to escape the Portuguese Inquisition, and for a while they were ignored by the Spanish Inquisition. Also, it was much easier to travel to Spain then. In that group were also the descendants of the Spanish Jews who were expelled from Spain in 1492. By then, they considered themselves Portuguese whenever they went to Europe and the Americas.

The term *Portuguese* is not accepted by some historians to mean what it actually says. If people of the Jewish faith in America considered themselves Americans, then why not consider those from Portugal to be Portuguese?

Isaac Amoreiras Bitton, a native of Portugal, himself a Jew, emigrated to America in 1959. He was recently interviewed for a Spielberg documentary about the Nazi Holocaust. He is now a successful businessman in Chicago, and an American. He is proud of his Portuguese roots. His success and recognition will raise the esteem level of all Portuguese spread throughout the United States.

As far as the possible relationship with the Melungeons or any other early group of settlers, it is known that the Portuguese Jews arrived at a very early time and also participated in the making of America. [133] (See note c)

Fig. 26 - Grape arbor in Patton Valley, N.C Helen Patton, one of the descendants of early pioneers in the area, is a lively and active octogenarian who has answered many questions about the mountains, their people and culture.

Grape Arbor

Kennedy remembers his youth: *She raised chickens, and grapes, and blackberries which I can still see hanging from the long demolished grape arbors. In the summer, the thick growth of vines made Granny's little vineyard a jungle fantasy land.* [134] The grape arbor – *latada* in Portuguese – is very common in northern of Portugal. It is there that most grapes that produce the famous *vinho verde* are grown.

They form huge grape arbors, which are also seen in Madeira and Azores Islands beside steep hills and seem to be present in mostlry mountainous areas. Portuguese from the Azores living in southern New England use the grape arbor method to adorn their houses.

Names that may indicate Portuguese Origin

...Melungeon given names from the earliest known encounters are strikingly Mediterranean when compared to the Scotch-Irish neighbors: Louisa, Helena,

Navarrh, Salena, Salvadore, Mahala, Alonso, Sylvester, Eulalia, Elvas, and Canara were names present among the earliest-known Melungeon. "Canara," unknown among other Anglo Appalachian families, is especially intriguing. [136]

Fig. 27 - A typical Grape Arbor in Portugal in the Mountain area

The name Canara will be studied further, as it may provide a very important clue to solve the Melungeon mystery. As a result of the ongoing research, a logical and acceptable explanation will eventually be found.

The name "Canaira" (pronounced the same as Canara) has been in my family at least since the 1700's. It is the name of village in northern Portugal, ... and Canara was a family tradition well before any of our family could have read about the Santa Elena Colony or even randomly selected "Canaira" from a map of Portugal). [137]

It would be much harder if the name originated from another part of the world.

By the 17th century the Portuguese had originated an empire upon which the sun did not set.

Fig, 28 - Canara Nash, ca. 1910 Dr. N. Brent Kennedy's great-uncle.

Elvas is the name of a town located in the province of Alentejo in southeastern Portugal.

*Fig. 29, 30, 31 - On the left and the right are Portuguese soldiers ca.1900.
The one in the center is Canara Nash, Kennedy's Melungeon great-uncle
Note the similarity of the young men's noses, eyes and cheeks.* [135]

*Portugal. (Yes, Elvis Presley had North Carolina roots; his family left western
North Carolina in the early 1800's.)... We have access to many of the surnames of
the Santa Elena colonists, and the resemblance of these names to the most-common*

Fig. 32 - Family Portrait taken in Portugal ca. 1900.

and best-known Melungeon surnames is astonishing. [138] In Appendix C, see more
details about the Portuguese and Melungeon names that may have some connection.

Blood Analysis and Melungeon Comparison - 1990

The Pollitzer and Brown survey of 1969 was widespread news. More recently,
in 1990, James L. Guthrie made a comparison of gene distribution of the
Melungeons and those of worldwide populations. The results were published in

the *Tennessee Anthropologist*, spring of 1990, and the following are some of the conclusions: *Worldwide gene frequency distributions in five major blood group systems were searched for similarity to those of the Melungeons. Calculations of the Mean Measure of Divergence (MMD) identified populations from the Mediterranean region and those of coastal Europe that do not differ significantly from the Melungeons. All others, including Amerindians, differ widely...* Guthrie adds, *These results are consistent with the Melungeon tradition that they are Portuguese, and are in substantial agreement with the findings of Pollitzer and Brown, whose 1969 data provided the basis for the present calculations...*[139] [and concludes]...*their overall findings caused them to favor a predominantly Portuguese ancestry over English ancestry for the Melungeons... The Portuguese match closely by themselves, probably because of early incorporation of a Black component into Mediterranean populations.*[140]

It is known that it did happen in the 15th century. Also, the comparison mentions some other countries with which the Portuguese had contact, such as Arabia, India and Turkey. [141]

Notes

a. I remember my grandmother's feet, so small and shapely, except for the open skin cracks – sometimes bleeding – on her heels from walking barefoot all day on the not so smooth paths and ways. My mother used to send me every summer to my grandparents, and one of the first things I did was to get rid of the shoes, and go barefoot. The main reason was that my mother could not afford to buy me shoes as I was growing, with the result that sometimes I had to wear the same shoes for two years, and after one year, they were tight, so tight that my two toes in both feet grew on top of each other. But it certainly was confortable to go barefoot. The only problem was that my feet were not used to it, and by the end of the summer, my toes and nails were in pretty bad shape. My cousins used to go barefoot all the time, and would laugh at me when I carelessly hit a protruding root of a pine tree on the narrow path that we walked. They somehow were able to detect with their toes anything on the ground, before walking over it.

b. Among my recollections as a child, when spending the summers with my grandparents at the small village where I was born, was seeing women going barefooted with a good pair of shoes hanging over their shoulders, mostly on Sundays, which was quite natural.

c. Mr. Bitton and I were raised in the same area of Lisbon - Amoreiras - but never met. Despite the fact that he is a Jew and I am a Catholic, we still have our common roots in Portugal.

[1] Ibid, p.93
[2] The Melungeons by Byron Stinson, American History Illustrated, Nov.1973, p.41
[3] The Melungeons by N. Brent Kennedy, p.121
[4] Ibid, pp. 106,107
[5] Portuguese Enclaves, The Invisible Minority by M. Estellie Smith, p. 83

[6] The Melungeons by Bonnie Ball p.45

[7] The Melungeons by Jean Bible, pp.59,60

[8] Melungeons: The Vanishing Colony of Newman's Ridge by Henry R.Price, p. 11

[9] The History of Baxter County, Arkansas,
   (Mountain Home AR, 1972), pp. 5-6

[10] Dicionario da Historia de Portugal by Joel Serrão,V.6, p. 687

[11] The History of Baxter County, Arkansas, (Mountain Home AR, 1972), pp. 6

[12] History of Tennessee and Tennesseans by W. T. Hale and
   Dixon L. Merritt, p. 182

[13] Mixed Bloods of the Upper Monongahela, WV by William H. Gilbert Jr., p. 5

[14] Ibid, p. 11

[15] The Melungeons by Bonnie Ball, p.76-77

[16] The Melungeons by Jean Patterson Bible, p. 57

[17] The Presidents of the United States by John & Alice Durant, p. 137

[18] The Melungeons by Jean Patterson Bible, p.59

[19] The Mystery of the Melungeons by Louise Davies, p. 11
   (Nashville Tennessean, Sept.23, 1963)

[20] Melungeons: The Vanishing Colonoy of Newman's Ridge by
   Henry R.Price, p. 16

[21] Ibid, p. 17

[22] The Melungeons by N. Brent Kennedy p.15

[23] Ibid p. 20

[24] Ibid pp.56-57

[25] The Red Carolinians by Chapman J. Milling, p. 332

[26] Indians of the Southeastern U.S. by J. Anthony Paredes, pp. 2, 30

[27] The Melungeons by N. Brent Kennedy, p. 27

[28] Andrew Jackson takes an Oath of Allegiance to Spain by Robert V. Remini

[29] Tennessee Historical Quarterly by Robert V. Remini, p. 10
   (Spring 1995 issue)

[30] Ibid, p. 4

[31] History of Tennessee and the Tennesseeans Hale and Merritt, p. 182

[32] The Melungeons by Jean Patterson Bible, p.38,
   (James Aswell, Lost Tribes of Tennessee)

[33] The Melungeons by N. Brent Kennedy p. 5

[34] Ibid p.12

[35] Ibid p.13

[36] The Malungeons by Will Allen Dromgoole p. 469 (Arena 1891)

[37] Eastern Creek Indian Identity by J. Anthony Paredes, p. 65

[38] Ibid, p. 471 (Arena 1891)

[39] The Melungeons by N. Brent Kennedy, p. 13

[40] Ibid, p.15

[41] The Melungeons by Jean Patterson Bible, p.26-28

[42] History of Tennessee and Tennesseans by Hale & Merrit, p. 180, Vol. 1

[43] The Melungeons by Bonnie Ball, p.52

[44] Ibid, p.72

[45] Note on the Melungeons by Swan M. Burnett, p. 347
   (American Anthropologist, V. II, 1889)

[46] The Melungeons by Bonnie Ball, p.67-8

[47] The Melungeons: a mixed blood-strain... by Edward T. Price, p. 259

[48] The Malungeon Tree... by Will Allen Dromgoole, pp. 748-749
   (Arena, June 1891)

[49] Ibid, (Arena, March 1891) p. 473

[50] The Malungeons by Will Allen Dromgoole, p. 478 (Arena, 1891)

[51] Ibid, p. 106

[52] The Mystery of the Melungeons by Louise Davis, p.11
(Tennessean Magazine, Sept. 22,1963)
[53] The Malungeons by Will Allen Dromgoole, p. 478 (Arena,1891)
[54] The Melungeons by Brent Kennedy , p.12
[55] The Melungeons by Jean Patterson Bible, p. 107
[56] The Mystery of the Melungeons by Louise Davis, p. 11
(Nashville Tennesseean 9/29/1963)
[57] The Melungeons by Bonnie Ball, p.69
[58] History of Tennessee and the Tennesseeans Hale and Merritt, p. 180
[59] Strange People of East Tennessee by Eliza N. Eiskel,
Arkansas Gazette, Jan.14, 1914
[60] History of Tennessee and Tennesseans by Hale and Merritt, Vol. 1, p. 184
[61] Ibid, p.6
[62] Handbook of the American Indians by Frederick Webb Hodge, Part 1, p. 365
[63] The Melungeons by Bonnie Ball,p.51
[64] Ibid, p.61
[65] Ibid p.62-3
[66] Ibid p.96
[67] Arkansas Gazette, January 14, 1914 by Eliza N. Heiskel
[68] David Farragut by Charles Lee Lewis, V.1 p. 1
[69] The Melungeons by Bonnie Ball , p.111, Hale & Merritt, p. 185
[70] David Farragut by Charles Lee Lewis, V.1, p.1
[71] The Mongrel Virginias by Arthur Estabrook, p.132
[72] Ibid, pp.174, 175
[73] Ibid, p. 180
[74] Ibid, p. 182
[75] Ibid, p. 189
[76] The Melungeons by Bonnie Ball, p.74-5
[77] Ibid, pp.8-9 (James Aswell, "Lost Tribes of Tennessee...")
[78] The Melungeons by Bonnie Ball, p.89
[79] Ibid, pp. 84-85
[80] Ibid, p.93
[81] The Melungeons by Jean Patterson Bible, p.5
[82] The Melungeons by Bonnie Ball, pp. 95,96
[83] The Mystery of the Melungeons by Louise Davis, p. 11
(Nashville Tennesseean 9/29/1963)
[84] Ibid
[85] Letter dated August 5th 1930 from Dr. W.A. Plecker to J. P. Kelly
[86] Strangers in Their Midst by Shirley McLeRoy, p. 14
[87] Letter by Evelyn Orr of the Melungeon Research Committee
[88] The Melungeons by N. Brent Kennedy, pp.86-87
[89] The Melungeons by N. Brent Kennedy, p.87
[90] Sons of the Legend by William L. Worden, p. 29
(Saturday Evening Post, Oct.18, 1947)
[91] Ibid
[92] Ibid, p. 130
[93] The Melungeons by Bonnie Ball, p. 70
[94] Mixed-Blood Strain... by Edward T. Price, p. 281
(Ohio Journal of Science, No. 6)
[95] Ibid, p. 288
[96] Ibid, p. 269
[97] The Mystery of the Melungeons by Louise Davis, p. 11
(Nashville Tennesseean 9/29/1963)
[98] The Melungeons by N. Brent Kennedy, p.128

[99] Survey of Demography... by Pollitzer and Brown, pp. 389-399 (Human Biology, Sept. 1969)

[100] Ibid

[101] The Melungeons, by Jean Patterson Bible, p.2

[102] National Geographic Magazine by Howard La Fay, October 1965, p. 477

[103] The Melungeons by N. Brent Kennedy, p.119

[104] Charlotte Observer by Bruce Henderson, 15 Aug. 1993, p. 8a

[105] The Hawk's Done Gone by Mildred Haun, p. 97, 111

[106] The Melungeons: a mixed-blood strain... by Edward T. Price, p. 259

[107] The Melungeons, by Jean Patterson Bible, p.31

[108] Ibid

[109] The Melungeons by Jean Patterson Bible, p. 106

[110] Farewell España by Haward M. Sachar, p. 352

[111] The Melungeons by Brent Kennedy, p. xiv

[112] Document with author, p. 94

[113] Ibid, p. xv

[114] Mike McGlothlen, document dated March 1997

[115] Ibid, p.128

[116] Merck Manual of Diagnosis and Therapy by Robert Berkow, MD, p. 260

[117] Medical Journal of Genetics in 1993; 30:235-239

[118] The Melungeons by Brent Kennedy, p.83

[119] Catherine of Braganza by Manuel Andrade e Sousa, p.50

[120] The Melungeons by Brent Kennedy, p.83

[121] Ibid, p.10

[122] Ibid, p.83

[123] The Melungeons by Brent Kennedy, p.101

[124] The Spanish, Portuguese language by William J. Entwistle, p. 2

[125] Moors in Spain and Portugal by Jan Read,p. 220

[126] The Melungeons by Brent Kennedy, p.103

[127] The Jews of Spain by Jane S. Gerber, p. 188

[128] Ibid, p. 209

[129] Ibid, p. 146

[130] O Sacrifício de Isaac by Manuel da Costa Fontes, p. 58

[131] The Jews in America, by Max I. Dimont, p. 38-9

[132] The Portuguese-Americans by Leo Pap, p. 157

[133] Mundo Português pp. 28-29, September 1996

[134] The Portuguese-Americans by Leo Pap, p.51

[135] See notes at the end of Chapter XI

[136] The Melungeons by Brent Kennedy, p.121

[137] Ibid

[138] Ibid, p. 122

[139] Melungeons...Gene Distributions by James L. Guthrie, p. 13 (TN Anthropologist)

[140] Ibid, p. 17

[141] Ibid, p. 18

Chapter IIII

Besides Portuguese, Other Possible Origins

Besides being Mediterranean looking, there are other origins discussed. However, if the Mediterranean looks survived 400 years, even with miscegenation, other origins should also have been able to survive and better, because the inter-race marriages would have been minimal. Kennedy, with importance, maintains that *...given the surviving Mediterranean characteristics, further hypothesized that both genders of the original settling group must have possessed Melungeon genes, whatever their ethnic nature.*

Otherwise, over a four-hundred-year period the Melungeon's dominating Mediterranean physical characteristics would have most likely been "bred out" through successive inter-marriage with Native Americans. [1]

Armando Cortesão, a Portuguese historian, on assignment at *UNESCO in the early 1950's, said he was convinced that ancient peoples, Phoenicians and Greeks sailed far into the Atlantic.* [2]

The Melungeons and the Saponi-Tutelo Indians

McGlothlen writes that the Melungeons were founded by free mulattos and mestees (Indian/Black mix with or without white) from North Carolina. Also, they were in Hancock County before whites arrived there. From the time and location of their origin, the Indian element is probably Saponi and Tutelo, but it *is usually incorrectly thought to be Cherokee by the Melungeons.* On the other hand*, approximately 2,000 Saponi and Haliwa Indians still live in the Warren and Halifax Counties in Northeast North Carolina,* [3] the same area where until recently a group claiming Portuguese descent also lived. Another report revealing the Saponi and Tutelo Indians is the one from *Governor Spotswood in 1715, in which he states that the Indians of Fort Christanna, including the Tutelo, Saponi...numbered 300.*[4] Also, Mooney mentions in his book *Siouan Tribes of the East: Evidently the tribe...was in decline, as it was about to join the Saponi and Tutelo.* [5]

At that time, these Indians were still an identifiable group, and in order to survive until the 20th century the Melungeons would also be a group in itself. The Melungeons are not likely to be a creation of the 19th century! All immigrant groups arriving in the 19th century are traceable.

The Indian component of the Melungeons was identified by Jack Forbes as Saponi, which may be possible, but in J. Anthony Paredes' latest book *Indians of the Southeastern United States in the late 20th Century,* there does not seem to be any connection cited.

The Southern range includes the Redbones, Brass Ankles, and Turks. This last group is speculated by some outsiders as having Indian ancestry, such as the Sumter Turks. These, however, have said that they do not concur that they are Indians. They consider themselves to be *white Turk Americans.* [6] They also have common

Melungeon surnames. According to a story, the name Turk was given to them by General Sumter, who presented an affidavit to the authorities stating that they were indeed Turks imported personally from the Ottoman Empire as contract labor.[7] Turk groups may play an interesting part in the mystery of the Melungeons.

Kennedy seems to believe that the decimated Indian tribes in Virginia would present a *legitimate source of Moorish-Indian-European...*[8] to form the Melungeons. That it is doubtful. If they were Turks from the Ottoman Empire, how did they get here? Also, the blacks as a fourth element for being a part of some Melungeons cannot be ignored.

Both the Melungeons and the Redbones have spoken only English since they were first noted, even though the Redbones are surrounded by French. [9] Why would the French name them *mélange* if they were speaking English?

Henry Price questions the disenfranchising of the Melungeons in 1834 and states that the Melungeons arrived from North Carolina along with the whites, not long before them: *some of their leaders, got good land and quite a lot of it.*[10] Could it be that they left, or were pushed out of, North Carolina and some acquired large tracts of land, which were no good for agriculture? As for arriving there in 1834, it is likely to have been a much earlier date. One needs to be mindful of the ongoing problems that the Government had with the Indians, and the eventual removal in 1838.

Melungeon graves sometimes have small wooden houses built over them, which has reminded some observers of a similar trait among Eskimo members of the Russian Orthodox Church. [11] This was mentioned by Louise Davis in 1963 and again by Saundra Keyes Ivey in her dissertation of 1976.

Why look for the Russian Orthodox Church or the Eskimos? Such an exotic comparison when there are closer comparisons much closer at home. One needs only to visit a New Orleans cemetery. McGlothlen gives a table showing the frequency of Melungeon names in Northwest Florida to a total of 362, which is interesting. [12] *Some Indians groups absorbed so many Blacks that some of them became a separate entity, like the Black Seminoles in Florida.* [13]

This author who also comments about a community of Portuguese and Spanish ancestry being in the Appalachians before the 1700's, probably refers to a very small part of the Melungeon ancestry at best. It does not take many to grow into a large community if they started in the 1500's. It is understood, however, that they went into the mountains only after being pushed out by the other English-speaking immigrants. The writer also accepts the possibility of Moors, and Iberians having been incorporated into the Indians and others.

This is a start. Although it may not have happened, it is a positive note to look into other possibilities beside a mixed race of Indians, Blacks and English speaking Europeans. In Florida there is plenty of material to be researched if one keeps an open mind. What has been found so far is that many scholars are ready to accept any exotic explanation of the origin of the Melungeon ancestry and discount immediately the possibility of their having Portuguese ancestors.

This could be correct. Again, an open mind is necessary, however.

Native Iberians

Kennedy states: ... *simply because one considered himself or herself to be Spanish or Portuguese, this did not in any way translate to being truly native Iberian (whatever that would mean, since the native Iberians were themselves a mixture of Phoenician, Sea Peoples, Roman, Celt, and so on).*[14] Spain was made up of many small kingdoms. It originated with Leon, and later Castile – the strongest kingdom – which gave its people the Castilian or Spanish language. Some Spanish provinces still have their own languages and use them, e.g. Basques, Catalonians, Galicians. Because of the importance of Spain as a much larger country and population, the tendency is to amalgamate Spain and Portugal into a single nation. However, Portugal is a separate and totally different country, in language and culture. A misconception by many people is that the Spanish and Portuguese languages are one and the same. This is not so. William J. Entwistle, an Oxford University professor, wrote that the difference in the Portuguese and Spanish languages may be appreciated by reading the Lord's prayer in these two languages. [15]

The name Iberian is not commonly used in Portugal. One is either Spanish or Portuguese. Also, the name Iberian is used exclusively by Spain. Even their national airlines is called Iberian Air Lines. There's a possibility that some of the Melungeon ancestry originated in Spain, but only a very small number. Even that is questionable.

Why would the Spaniards remain in Virginia and the Carolinas when they had all the protection in their own province, Florida, which remained in their possession until the 19th century? Most Spaniards went to the Caribbean, Central and South America, because they heard that everyone was getting rich with gold and silver. Also, immigration from Spain to the United States has always been extremely low except between the 16th and 17th centuries. By 1650, a total of 440,000 Spaniards emigrated to the New World, mostly to Mexico and South America, unlike the English and French. North America was the only option in the New World.

Spaniards had the opportunity to make their fortunes in the fabulous mining regions of Mexico, Central America, and in the Andean regions of South America. Taking into consideration that Spain had four times the population, [16] Spaniards emigrated much less than the Portuguese. They were either Portuguese or Spanish, but not Iberians, as a race or nationality.

Lost Tribe of Israel, Phoenicians, Vikings, Welsh

The theories of ancient people being the direct ancestors of the Melungeons are difficult to consider due mainly to the span of time in which they may have occurred. In a period of only 500 years civilizations are created and destroyed, and if any of these people did indeed arrive in America, then a civilization would have been created in the same manner as in Europe. As for the Lost Tribe of Israel, Kennedy writes: ...*And although there may be a Jewish ethnic component within the Melungeon population, there is scant evidence to suggest that this component arrived on these shores thousands of years ago.* [17] Cyrus Gordon, professor of

Mediterranean studies, said that fleeing Jews discovered America 1,000 years before Columbus, based on evidence found in a burial mound at Bat Creek, Tennessee, in 1885.[18] That may be possible, but connecting them to the Melungeons or another group is a rather difficult task. It is hardly possible that a group would survive thousands of years and vanish as a group in a mere 400 years. A Jewish community would not live in isolation, and signs of their faith would not disappear.

Descendants of early Carthaginian, or perhaps Phoenician, seamen who may have discovered the New World some 2,000 years before the birth of Christ. [19]
...Melungeons look Mediterranean...John Fetterman...paints a graphic... image ... great ship, such as ...Phoenician used, shipwreck on Carolina coast... [20]

Although it may be somewhat difficult, it is not impossible to cross the ocean with the right wind and currents. But what about supplies for at least a month of crossing, and the return trip? How would they survive as a group for more than 2000 years? Even at a very slow population increase rate, one single couple alone would evolve an enormous population during such a long period. It is difficult to imagine galley slaves rowing across the Atlantic, (square sails spread). Conceivably, one would question what happened to the Phoenicians and Carthaginians that stayed in the Mediterranean. Is it probable that half of the Mediterranean population descended from them?

...Phoenicians were in the Western Hemisphere hundreds of years before Christ... a stone found in Brazil in 1872... The Instituto Historico do Rio de Janeiro... letter signed by Joaquim Alves da Costa... Ladislau Netto... Bernardo da Silva Ramos... Armando Cortesão... they are all partial to the Phoenician discovery of America. [21] However, Samuel Eliot Morison states that *...There are still advocates for this...* [Phoenician discovery of America] *before 146 B.C... Investigation failed to locate either the stone or Senhor da Costa.* [22]

Barry Fell, in his book *America B.C.*, shows the possibilities of Iberian Phoenicians coming to America, but his detractors state that the *common rat did not reach America until the time of Columbus*. This would prove *that there was no settlement from the ancient Mediterranean, since any decked ships must have carried rats.* [23]

What about the Portuguese? What is today Portugal was once home to the Phoenicians. There are many vestiges in the different Phoenician ruins which provide solid proof that they lived there for a long time. It is also possible that the Portuguese may have brought the Phoenician inscribed stone to Brazil, since so many are available in Portugal.

As for the Welsh theory, it has been subjected to study, and those who favor Welsh-Melungeon link, would benefit from the letter written by John Sevier. It reports a meeting with Chief Oconostota in 1782 about a possible Welsh people. However, Sevier wrote another report two years later about the finding of *reddish-brown complexion people* who were neither Negro nor Indian, but claimed to be Portuguese. If there were any connection between the Welsh and his finding, most likely he would have mentioned it.[24]

Tri-Racial, a Melungeon Orthodox View

Kennedy mentions in his book ... *the theory that the Melungeons are a simple "Tri-racial isolate," in this particular case the progeny of a few eighteenth-century whites, escaped slaves, and Native Americans. While there is undoubtedly some Native American and African influence in at least some, if not all, Melungeon populations, it is far more complex....* [25]

With their appearance remaining Mediterranean, their claim of origin, coupled with the small number of black slaves living in the Appalachians at that time, it is most difficult to accept that they would add up to a tri-racial. Complex indeed... *Burnett (1889) apparently originated this view which describes the Melungeons as a Tri-racial hybrid of Europeans, Blacks and Indians. Dromgoole in 1891 claimed to recognize Cherokee, African, English, and Portuguese surnames in the group.* [26] Again the anthropologists Pollitzer and Brown (1969) stated: *...Their findings were in line with those expected of a Caucasoid population, with little evidence of Negroid or Amerindian influence.* [27]

There are a small number of Melungeons with black and/or Indian appearance, but the majority are Mediterranean looking. The latter agrees with these findings. Also, the occasional Asiatic or Oriental appearance does not add up to a tri-racial group.

Portuguese Gypsy

Another possible origin is the Indian Gypsy. Due to political and social upheaval in the Kashmiri region about A.D. 1,000 , a large group left India. They traveled to Europe and later to America. Their population throughout the world is believed to be about 15 million with an estimated two million in the U.S., eight million in India and five million in Europe. In Portugal there are no exact numbers, but it is estimated at 80,000.

They arrived in Portugal in the 1500's after having been in Romania, Hungary, Bulgaria and Greece. Prior to their arrival in Portugal, the Gypsies came to the Iberian Peninsula and settled in Andalucia, Spain. They were also subjected to the Inquisition persecution, just like the Moors and Jews. In 1526 they were expelled from Portugal, and reentry was forbidden. In the 19th century the Portuguese government arrested them or any who led a nomadic life style. At the end of the 20th century they are still marginalized by the society in which they live, and accused of many crimes. [28]

Did they come to America at an early period? If so, when? There are no signs of any connection with the Melungeons, except for their Mediterranean and East Indian appearance. It is unlikely that there is a relation, mainly due to the type of life that the Gypsy people lead. They are mostly merchants who work in outdoor markets. They are a nomadic people and seldom establish roots in the area where they live temporarily. The Melungeons and other groups of people that settled early on the North America continent do not necessarily possess these characteristics.

Portuguese Sephardim Jews

There is an interesting theory that was brought to light as early as January 1971. Because of its potential, it would shed greater light if developed further. [29] It could have been possible that the enterprising Jews organized some form of transportation to America. *The role of the Jews in the slave trade is confirmed in Cape Verde, but it is essential to realize that they were only brokers* [30] It is known that during the 1600's they went to Holland, Brazil, and then from Brazil to the U.S. They may not be the ancestors of the Melungeons, but Portuguese Jews were in this country in the 1600's and may have played a role in the coming of some people that the English would later call Melungeons. Dixon Merritt does a comparison between the Jews and the Melungeons!...*as a body they were as concrete as the Jews, and their descendants are still to be found.* [31]

Another possible way for the Portuguese Jews to have left Portugal, was on one or more of the many vessels that sailed to India. This presented a way of escaping the Inquisition. Were they part of a group that wound up on the shores of America, later separated and spread to more populated areas? Legally they could not leave Portugal for India, but... *Officials of the India House in Lisbon and in Goa accepted bribes in return for allocating places on vessels.* [32]

Richard Lobban presented a paper at the University of Massachusetts-Dartmouth on February 11, 1996, about the Jews in Cape Verde and on the Guinea Coast. It reads that *King Manuel I made reference to a group of lançados – to throw out – on the Senegambian coast; most of these were Portuguese Jews who had been deported...They were usually fugitive Portuguese settlers... following conviction for some political crime as was the case for the Jews following the full scale Portuguese Inquisition in 1536.* [33]

This confirms that Portuguese Jews and others did leave Portugal for different areas of the world in ships that may or may not have arrived at their planned destinations.

Moor/Muslim Slaves Called Mulangos Sent to Madeira and Brazil

There is yet other possibility presented by Kennedy: *Of even greater significance than the "pardo" question, is the little-known fact that the sixteenth-century South American Portuguese employed large numbers of Muslim/Moorish laborers who called themselves "mulangos."* [34]

Regarding the use of the term *mulangos*, as a rule that name is not known in Brazil, unless it is connected with the African name given to the whites – *Melungo*. Furthermore, there are no records of Portuguese employing large numbers of North African Moors there. It is, however, possible that the Spaniards may have had Moors in other countries of South America.

The name mulango is the name of a plant from which a reddish oil is extracted. This name is used in East Africa as well as in India. However there is another similar word, *mulambo*, that means a piece of cloth or rag with which the natives dress themselves below the waist. It may be used in a derogatory manner, as *someone that stopped being a man and became a human thing.* [35] I don't think there is a connection with the name Mulango. *Mucamba* means young black girl, and *Mucambo* meaning fugitive slave settlement.[36] *Mulamba* is a fruit in East Africa, and *Mulambe* is a tree in West Africa. *Mazombo* is a child born in Brazil of European parents. [37]

The article quoted by Kennedy refers mainly to black Muslims seeking to escape enslavement in Brazil.

T. B. Irving of the Mother Mosque Foundation in Cedar Rapids, Iowa, does an excellent job in portraying the life of the Muslim Black slaves. However, the word *mulango* must have been of limited use in the *quilombos* or fugitive slave settlements, because it does not appear in any of the Brazilian dictionaries or encyclopedias consulted.

The book *The Master and Slaves* by Freyre, that goes into a deep study of the slaves in Brazil, is also a good source of information on this subject.

It is important to note that the article in question refers to a later time frame *...This African styled community lasted from approximately 1630 to 1697 ...The Mali movement bears the focal date of 1835.* [38] This almost certainly rules out any connection with the Melungeons or other groups that may have shown up in the Southeast. After the 17th century it would have been difficult.

Irving confirms that some Portuguese words have their roots in Arabic. Such words may start with **al** and end with **la**. As for being *Muslim/Moorish* laborers, the writer refers to Bartolomeu Las Casas, a Spanish bishop in Mexico, when he *suggested the importation of enslaved Africans to the new* (Spanish South America) *colonies... specially the Muslims, who he called "Moors".* [39] The Portuguese never called the Blacks from west or east Africa Moors, except the ones from the Arabian area and the Far East. Again, it is important to differentiate between Spain and Portugal in South America.

These were often West Africans but also Berbers/Moors captured during battle in the Mediterranean. [40] As mentioned elsewhere in this book, the Portuguese did not battle the Berbers/Moors in the Mediterranean. Most battles were inland, in the 15th century. Although no specific origin of Black or Muslim slaves seems to be on record, most of the slaves came from West Africa.

There were limited wars involving the Portuguese and the Turks in the Mediterranean. If any were captured, the number must have been small. The battle of 1501 against the Turks in Mers-el-Quibir failed. [41] Another was in 1535, as part of Carlos V's fleet in the Tunes operation.

What about Berber slaves in Madeira? ... *Since 1432, the Portuguese had regularly used captured Berbers as slave labor for the sugar plantations on the island of Madeira.* [42] These were replaced before 1500 by black slaves from Africa, and other slaves from the Canary Islands. The Madeirans eventually asked the Portuguese king to send them to other colonies. *Following the first contact with the Americas, there was a voluntary emigration of Moors from Spain, Portugal and North Africa to the Canaries.* [43] These Portuguese and Spaniards settled there and, probably later on, emigrated again to the Caribbean islands where their descendants still remain today. Most whites in the former Spanish Caribbean islands trace their ancestry to the Canary Islands. Also, it has been said that the Canary Islands were a source of indentured servants in colonial America.

Captured Berber slaves were used only in the early 15th century on Madeira sugar plantations, and by the 1500's there were very few. The earlier slaves were from the Canary Islands, as in 1439 when a priest owned a female slave. [44]

However, in the 15th century João Esmeraldo had 80 slaves and, among them, men and women Moors, Mulattos, Negros and others also from the Canaries. Esmeraldo's sugar plantation produced 20,000 *arrobas* [45] per year, being one of the largest farms at the time. [46]

In the 15th century there were white and Black slaves. Even a Jew by the name Mordofay was given to the queen as a slave, but the Jewish community in Évora raised enough funds to pay for his freedom. [47]

Is it too much to suppose that as the Portuguese developed [Madeira sugar plantations] *similar plantations in Brazil they also imported captured Berber laborers to accomplish the same tasks there?* [48] During the early 16th century, most immigrants in Brazil were too poor to afford slaves, the record shows. Only in the late 16th and 17th century were slaves brought in large quantities. [49]

One other possibility is the freeing of Moors by the Portuguese and Spanish in North America. According to Kennedy: *These people, usually captured in skirmishes with the Portuguese or Spanish in the Mediterranean, had been transported to South America for forced labor purposes...One can easily understand the Portuguese and Spanish rationale for freeing such unwanted "settlers" on North American shores, as opposed to their own territories: it was one more headache for their English adversaries to deal with.* [50]

As slaves they were a valuable commodity. Why let them go then? If the intention was to cause headaches to the English, did that happen?

Indeed, history records that these South American "Melungeons" almost invariably Portuguese and on more than one occasion were freed on distant, uninviting shores by their Portuguese captors. In these cases they were generally referred to as emancipados (that is, freed captives). [51]

It would hardly be possible for the Portuguese to free any Moor or Turk slaves captured in the Mediterranean wars, first because they did not have them, and second, if they had, they were too valuable to let go without compensation. However the Spaniards may have had some, but again, the same rule applies in regard to their value.

Pardos in the Spanish Military? To Brazil?

The connection made by Kennedy with South America warrants further study: *Although it may be pure coincidence, the darker-skinned Spanish and Portuguese recruits assigned to Brazil and the Caribbean during this same time period were known as "Pardos," a different classification from either "Negroes" or "Mulattos," both categories utilized by the Spanish military.* [52]

The name *Pardo* was used from the 17ᵗʰ century until recently to describe the Brazilian soldiers. Today that is no longer the case. *Pardo* in Portuguese means someone with a darker skin or a color that blends with darkness.

There is a Portuguese proverb *à noite todos os gatos são pardos* or, "at night all cats are *Pardos*", meaning that you can't distinguish their color. The Spanish were confined mostly to the Caribbean, central and southwest America. No significant number of Spaniards is known to have gone to Brazil. The Spanish military did not go to Brazil, not even during the early 1600's when the crowns of Spain and Portugal were united. They were occupied with the American southeast, Mexico and Peru.

Across the Atlantic before Columbus

Kennedy suggests in his book that others before Columbus may have been in the West Indies. *Are we, then, to assume that the seafaring Moors and Berbers could not have also made such navigational "errors," ending up by accident or design in the New World? Historians have generally discounted the notion, but I suspect the same old North European prejudices have influenced such dogmatically rigid thinking.* [53] He also quotes the following: *...and according to historian John Dyson, in 1504, during his fourth voyage, Columbus himself ...made an extraordinary find on the island of Guadeloupe. In a native hut was an iron pot and the stern post of a European ship, too heavy and distant to be that of the wrecked Santa Maria. All who saw it thought it could only have come from the Canaries, proof that at least one ship had made it across the Atlantic before Columbus.* [54]

This may be disputed, as Columbus and his son Fernando repeated that the natives from the Antilles *did not have any kind of iron objects*...Fernando writes what his father's men – *not Columbus himself* – found so marvelous was the finding of a *cassuelo de hierro*, some kind of frying pan with handle.

He further explains that, *must have been caused by the pebbles and silex being of a shine iron color...and only some one with little common sense would think it was iron... and since then no one has found anything made out of iron, among those people.* [55]

The preceding is what Mascarenhas Barreto found on the original documents by Fernando Colón, Columbus' son.

The same author does not mention the stern post. There is no evidence that the Moors or Berbers had the knowledge or the navigational capabilities of long voyages in the 15ᵗʰ or 16ᵗʰ century. However, it is indeed possible that a vessel may be pushed by the winds and currents to the U.S. East Coast. Would the people have survived? Would they have had the provisions for such an ocean crossing? If so did they bring their women on board? Muslims?

South Carolina Moors - Dark Genes - French Huguenots

Henry Coppee's book, *Conquest of Spain by the Arab-Moors,* alludes to another possible source for the Melungeons *...It has been asserted that, when the Moors were driven out, thousands took refuge in the south of France, who, afterwards abhorring the Roman Catholic persecutions, became Huguenots* (Lutherans) *and that of these many emigrated at a later day to South Carolina...and the great tide rushed in from Protestant Europe...* [56]

This is possible of course. Many other groups who emigrated to the New World may have mixed with groups already here in the 17th or 18th century. However, the Moors of southern Spain would not have anything to do with the Portuguese.

Columbus had Moor Sailors, Arabs, Jews and Portuguese

Henry Coppee brings to our attention a little known fact: *Christopher Columbus' fleet was fitted out in the little port of Palos, which had lately been a Moorish port; his sailors many of them with Moorish blood in their veins.* [57] It was learned in 1989, through Boris Feinman of Palm Beach County Community College in Florida, that Columbus had also six Jews – *conversos* – aboard his first voyage. Feinman created a visual display that documents the contributions of Jews to American history from 1492 to 1865 – from the voyage of Columbus to the end of the Civil War – which has been displayed all over the U.S. [58] Also Jane Gerber, in her book *The Jews of Spain,* provides six identifiable Jews as part of Columbus's expedition.[59]

Fig. 33 - Evelyn Orr

Rabbi Levinger's book *History of the Jews in the U.S.* teaches that five or six Jews were part of the 120 men on Columbus' first voyage. [60] He also states that Columbus was of Jewish blood, and claimed to be Christian. Although the name Colombo was common in northern Italy, in Spain he was always and still is known as *Colon.* There was in fact a family by that name of Jewish blood.

To bolster that theory, we should note that he always wrote in Spanish or Latin, but never in Italian or Genoese. Mascarenhas Barreto wrote a book about Columbus that describes him as being a Jewish descendant, and that may explain the secrecy that shrouded his early life. [61]

On the other hand, and according to Spanish history, the sailors in Columbus's first trip were mostly from Andalucia. [62] From the original crew list, there is at least one member from Portugal, João Areias, native of Tavira, Algarve, Portugal.

The list also shows many names with Portuguese characteristics, but translated to Spanish with no birthplace shown. [63]

According to recent discoveries, Evelyn Orr – a Melungeon research member – informs that Arabs were also part of the crew, according to Beverlee Mehdi. [64]In this same book, the author writes that *the Arab geographer al-Sherif, eight adventurers sailed from Lisbon, Portugal, trying to discover what was beyond the "Sea of Darkness' the Arab name for the Atlantic. It is said that they landed in South America.* These Arabs were probably the ancestors of the Portuguese Navigators.

Notes

[1] The Melungeons by N. Brent Kennedy, pp.94-95

[2] Atlantis Dwelling place of the Gods by Henriette Mertz, p. 54

[3] The Indians of the Southeastern U.S., by J. Anthony Paredes, pp. 46, 73

[4] Indians in 17th century Virginia by Ben McCary, p. 78

[5] Red Carolinians by Chapman J. Milling, p. 218

[6] The Indians of Southeastern U.S. by J. Anthony Paredes, p. 73

[7] Melungeons and Other Mestee Groups by Mike McGlothlen, p. 62

[8] The Melungeons by N. Brent Kennedy, p. 137

[9] The Melungeons and Mestee Groups by Mike McGlothlen, p. 40

[10] Ibid, p. 41

[11] Ibid, p.44

[12] Ibid, p. 64

[13] Ibid, p. 9

[14] The Melungeons by N. Brent Kennedy, p. 124

[15] The Spanish, Portuguese Languages by William J. Entwistle, p. 61-62

[16] Fomento Rural e Emigração by Oliveira Martins, p.34

[17] The Melungeons by N. Brent Kennedy, p. 82

[18] Fleeing Jews… by Cyrus H. Gordon, Arkansas Gazette, Oct. 19, 1970

[19] The Melungeons by N. Brent Kennedy, p. 82

[20] The Melungeons by Bonnie Ball, p.67

[21] Ibid , p.69

[22] European Discovery of America by Samuel Elliot Morison, p. 11

[23] The Melungeons and Other Mestee Groups by Mike McGlothlen, p. 171

[24] The Melungeons by Jean Patterson Bible, p. 86

[25] The Melungeons by N. Brent Kennedy , pp.81-84

[26] Ibid , p.127

[27] Ibid

[28] RTP TV Program Reporter, 1996

[29] Theory…Melungeons… from Jewish origin by
Cyrus H. Gordon, Argosy Magazine,1/1971

[30] Jews in Cape Verde and on the Guinea Coast by Richard Lobban
[31] History of Tennessee and Tennesseans by Hale & Merrit, p. 180, V.1
[32] Men under Stress: The Social Environment ...
     Carreira da India by A.J.R. Russell-Wood, p. 25
[33] Jews in Cape Verde and on the Guinea Coast by Richard Lobban
[34] The Melungeons by N. Brent Kennedy, p.106
[35] Dicionario da Lingua Portuguesa by Antonio Morais e Silva, Vol. 7, p.84
[36] The Masters and the Slaves by Gilberto Freyre, p. 491
[37] Dicionario Brasileiro da Lingua Portuguesa, Vol. 2, P. 30
[38] King Zumbi... by T.B. Irving, p. 404
     (Amer. J. Islamic S.Sciences, 9:3 Fall 1992)
[39] Ibid, p. 399 (Amer. J. Islamic S.Sciences, 9:3 Fall 1992)
[40] The Melungeons by N. Brent Kennedy, p.106
[41] Portugal nos Mares by Oliveira Martins, p. 72
[42] The Melungeons by N. Brent Kennedy, p.113
[43] The Worlds of Columbus by William D. Phillips, p. 60
[44] Economia Mundial by Vitorino Magalhães Godinho, p. 521
[45] *Arroba* is a metric measure of weight equal to 33 lbs.
     20,000 *arrobas* equals 660,000 lbs.
[46] Saudades da Terra by Gaspar Frutuoso, p. 124
[47] Economia Mundial by Vitorino Magalhães Godinho, p. 521
[48] The Melungeons by N. Brent Kennedy, p.113,
     King Zumbi... Irving 9/3 Fall 1992,399
[49] Portuguese settlement... by William Freitas, Portuguese Heritage,
     December 1993, p. 22
[50] The Melungeons by N. Brent Kennedy , p.111
[51] Ibid
[52] Ibid p.106
[53] Ibid, p.114
[54] Columbus: For Gold, God, and Glory by John Dyson, p. 188
[55] Cristovão Colombo by Mascarenhas Barreto, p. 576
[56] History of the Conquest of Spain by the Arab-Moors by
     Henry Coppee, vol. 2, pp. 445-46.)
[57] History of the Conquest of Spain by the Arab-Moors, by
     Henry Coppee, vol. 2 ,1881, 445-46
[58] Letter by John Townsend, Center for Multi-Cultural Affairs
[59] The Jews of Spain by Jane Gerber, p. xix
[60] History of the Jews in the U.S., by Rabbi Lee J. Levinger, p. 28-34
[61] The Portuguese Columbus by Mascarenhas Barreto
[62] Historia de España, Historia 16, p. 492
[63] The Log of Christopher Columbus by Robert H. Fuson, p. 225
[64] Arabs in America by Beverly Mehdi, p.1

Chapter IV

Drake and the Lost Roanoke Colony
Sir Francis Drake the Knight, Privateer and Pirate

This chapter is largely dedicated to bringing together the important details of Sir Francis Drake's voyages that may be connected with the Lost Roanoke Colony, and/or the possibility of Drake having left Moors, Turks or South American Indians in South Carolina.

Drake, was born between 1540 and 1543 in Devonshire, England. He became an admiral in the English navy and circumnavigated the globe (1577-80), playing an important role in defeating the Spanish Armada (1588). He was one of the most famous seamen of the Elizabethan Age. In 1572 – having obtained from the Queen a privateering commission, which amounted to a license to plunder in the King of Spain's lands – Drake set sail for America in command of two small ships, the *Pasha*, of 70 tons, and the *Swan*, of 25 tons. In 1577, he was chosen as the leader of an expedition intended to pass around South America through the Strait of Magellan, and to explore the South American east coast. He set sail in December with five small ships, manned by fewer than 200 men, and reached the Brazilian coast in the spring of 1578. Two years later, Drake and his ship *The Golden Hind* came back into the Atlantic with only 56 of the original crew of 100. On Sept. 26, 1580, Drake brought his ship into Plymouth Harbor. She was laden with treasure and spices, and Drake's fortune was permanently made. Despite Spanish protests about his piratical conduct in their imperial waters, Queen Elizabeth herself came aboard *The Golden Hind*, which was lying at Deptford in the Thames Estuary, and personally bestowed knighthood on Drake.

The queen's trust in him was shown in 1585, when Elizabeth placed him in command of a fleet of 25 ships. Hostilities with Spain had broken out once more, and he was ordered to cause as much damage as possible to the Spaniards' overseas empire. Drake fulfilled his commission, capturing Santiago in the Portuguese Cape Verde Islands, taking and plundering the cities of Cartagena in Colombia, St. Augustine in Florida, and San Domingo (Santo Domingo, Hispaniola). The effect of his triumph in the West Indies was cataclysmic. Spanish credit, both moral and material, almost foundered under the losses. The Bank of Spain broke, the Bank of Venice (to which Felipe II was principal debtor) nearly collapsed, and the great German Bank of Augsburg refused to extend the Spanish monarch any further credit. Even Lord Burghley, Elizabeth's principal minister, who had never approved of Drake or his methods, was forced to concede that *Sir Francis Drake is a fearful man to the King of Spain*. Drake's later years were not happy, however. An expedition that he led against Portugal proved abortive, and his last voyage, in 1596, against the Spanish possessions in the West Indies was a failure, largely because the fleet was decimated by fever, killing Drake, who was buried at sea off the town of Puerto Bello (modern Portobelo, Panama). [1]

English Navigation and the Portuguese

Official piracy was by no means an English monopoly. Already in the 15th century it had reached large proportions. During France's King Louis XI reign, French pirates and corsairs attacked Portuguese caravels to the point that, in 1458, Portuguese King Afonso V, prepared a fleet to exterminate the pirates near the coast. [2] *There was a strong feeling, which Drake shared, that English navigation lagged behind that of Spain and Portugal in that there were no training institutions for pilots and masters.* [3]

Drake used the Portuguese chronicler Lopes Vaz, a native of Elvas, to write about the voyage to Nombre de Dios, on the Gulf of Darien in 1572. He also wrote the account of John Oxnam of Plymouth to the West Indies, and the South Seas in 1575. [4] Nuno da Silva, another Portuguese from Oporto, was taken by Drake in the Cape Verde Islands during his famous voyage around the world in 1577, when he captured a Portuguese cargo boat. As a pilot he guided Drake to Brazil and [5] later he was released in Acapulco, Mexico.

Before Drake set off across the world he acquired a map in Lisbon, the best he could find. Thomas Cavendish, following Drake's courses, captured a Portuguese by the name of Diogo (last name unknown) on the coast of Mexico and another, Nicolas Rodrigo, off the California coast. Nicolas had been in Canton and Japan.

On that same trip Drake picked up useful information ...*from a Portuguese pilot, faithless to the Spaniards as were so many of his kind.* [6] Certainly the writer reflects here the difference between Portuguese and Spaniards.

Drake in Brazil and the Mulangos

Kennedy dedicates a number of pages to other Melungeons and alludes to the possibility of Muslim or Christian converts transported to South America in the 16th century. ...*They referred to themselves as "mulango", or, as pronounced in Portuguese "Muh-lun-zhawn". However, connecting these South American "Mulangos," or Melungeons, with their possible North American counterparts seemed a daunting if not impossible task.* [7]

As earlier discussed, the word *mulango* does not seem to be connected with South America or the Portuguese in Brazil. In chapter I, the meaning of *mulango* was presented. It is the name of a plant from which a reddish oil is extracted, and used in East Africa as well as in India. Dr. Bob Gilmer, a Melungeon research committee member, brought to Kennedy's attention that Sir Francis Drake may have dropped off *South American Muslims on Roanoke Island, just off the coast of present-day North Carolina* . [8] That story is repeated throughout David Quinn's books and is based on Irene Wright's translation of the original documents, written as a result of depositions taken by a Spanish official. ...*and a number of Negros, and Central American Indians he had rescued from the Spaniards with Lane. Lane had been involved in fighting with the Indians.*[9] (See other pages in this same chapter for more on these depositions.)

Kennedy cites Thomson: *...Drake's numerous excursions into Portuguese Brazil as well as other parts of South America, and of his collusion* (conspiracy) *with the Portuguese and the "Cimarrons" (a South American mixed-race people) against the Spanish.* [10] Cimarrón is a Spanish name and means runaway slave or domestic animal, and also lazy sailor. [11]

There are no references in the Portuguese-Brazilian dictionary or the *Grande Enciclopedia Luso-Brasileira*. In English it means wild and unruly. It is also the name of a river flowing from northeast New Mexico to the Arkansas River near Tulsa, Oklahoma. The connection between Cimarrón and the Portuguese does not seem to be there. Drake's brother John made contact with Cimarrons, but it seems that this people lived in the Caribbean islands occupied by the Spaniards. [12]

It did not make sense that they would try to colonize Brazil with Muslims – converted or not to Catholicism. Also, history records show that Portugal did not need any labor, forced or voluntary, in Brazil during the early 16th century. The slave trade to Brazil did not start until the 17th century.

It is also important to consider the fact that in April 1569, the English captured 11 ships of a Portuguese fleet going to Antwerp. How many seamen did they take as prisoners to England or elsewhere? Prior to that the city of Funchal, on Madeira Island, was raided by a fleet of Frenchmen led by the corsair Pierre de Monluc.

For a detailed story of this raid that killed hundreds of Madeirans, sacked all churches, and captured 300 black slaves, read *Saudades da Terra* by Gaspar Frutuoso.

Claim Portuguese Heritage to Be Safe

The usage of the name Portyghee as a possible ancestry is mentioned by Kennedy, but... *And here is yet another, more political reason for the Melungeons to claim a Portuguese heritage: the Portuguese, unlike the Spanish, were at least occasional allies with the English. Drake himself made use of a Portuguese navigator. It would not take a genius to recognize the wisdom of claiming to be "Portyghee" rather than "Spanish" when encountering Englishmen in the Appalachians...* [13] *Portuguese or not, it would have been the smartest "politically correct" heritage for either group to claim given the circumstances of the times.* [14]

That may be possible, but can a lie survive 400 years? Possibly, or even more. On the other hand, Drake was not sparing Portugal, or the Portuguese either, when he attacked Algarve. There was no love lost between Drake and the Portuguese, and that is why when he attacked Portugal after the Invincible Armada in 1589, he was defeated. As far as the English were concerned, being Portuguese was just the same as being Spanish, both being considered the enemy. They had not forgotten that the Invincible Armada was made up of many of Portuguese ships, and soldiers, who departed from Lisbon, Portugal, to attack England.

Drake Deposited Moorish Slaves and Indians in Roanoke

Boxer stated in his book *Portuguese Seaborne Empire* that *People engaged in oceanic trade did not travel with their families, least of all the Muslim men with rigorous ideas about the seclusion of women.* [15] This agrees with Kennedy's assumption of the Moors men only with the possible exception of Indian women also released by Drake.

Certainly if Drake's Moors were primarily men, as we know they were, the tendency for their children to adopt the father's heritage would be (1) strong, given the patrilineal tradition of the Moors, and (2) as a result of this tendency, would better explain the widespread dissemination of the so-called "Melungeon" heritage. Several hundred Moorish men could leave quite a genetic and cultural heritage after but one generation, to say nothing of the estimated fourteen generations since their arrival. Additionally, the accompanying claim to be "Portyghee" fits with both the South American Moors and the Pardo Santa Elena components as well. [16]

For only the male population to survive and be accepted by the Indian community is rather difficult, if not impossible. Surely the Indians were very protective of their women. The Indians, seeing only males coming to their villages to take their women, would be them in a very welcoming mood, to say the least. However, the possibility that a very small number could be accepted, if they did not pose any danger, should not be ruled out.

Kennedy presents an explanation: *He* (Drake) *arrived at Roanoke Island, just off the North Carolina shores, where large numbers of English soldiers implored him to take them home to England. In order to make room on his ships for the English garrison on Roanoke Island, it is believed that Drake may (and I emphasize the word may) have deposited most of these captives on the island or the nearby coast.* [17] This is a very important possibility, and particular attention should be given since it would answer some of the questions related to the Melungeons. However, records do not confirm Drake's passenger dropoff.

Preliminaries of the 1584 Voyage

The following is a summary of the voyages made by the English to establish a base of operations on the east coast closer to the West Indies. There are some controversies about what Drake did or did not do, depending on which writings one believes. Therefore both narrations are being presented, one by the English and the other by the Spanish. If one were to take what follows into consideration, Kennedy's possible assumption above is rather weak. But he does say *may*.

Drake, a few years earlier, was in the slave business with John Hawkins, and doing raids off the coast of Africa, capturing or buying slaves. Would he give up such a valuable cargo?

In 1584, Sir Walter Raleigh obtained a charter from Queen Elizabeth I giving him the right to possess lands in the New World not already under Christian control. A voyage was planned with Arthur Barlowe and Philip Amadas in charge, and the Portuguese Simão Fernandes was the pilot. They departed on April 27 and arrived on July 13 at Roanoke, Virginia. [18]

Irene Wright's book describes Simão Fernandes as having been in Florida in

1576. He is also described by Quinn as having *ambiguities in an obscure text* in reference to the Spanish narration.[19] Also, *the deponent says that when the Portuguese (Fernandes) discovered this port he wished to land on one promontory, but the wild Indians ate 38 Englishman... The Portuguese (Fernandes) took with him to England two wild Indians, leaving two Englishmen as hostages* to make sure *that he would return later.* [20]

The 1584 voyage was just to discover or to look for a base where the English could raid the Spaniards returning from the Caribbean.

Lumbees, Lost Roanoke Colony Mystery and the Portuguese

Fig. 34 - The "Lost Colony" replays the tale of the Roanoke Island Colony [22]

According to an English story, Roanoke is an interesting traditional name. Apparently, when an Englishman saw an Indian rowing his canoe with oaken oars on the Moratuck River (original name of the Roanoke River, and an Algonquin Indian name), he asked him: *What are you doing there?* The Indian replied in ill-tutored English, *Rowin' Oak.* [21]

The Indian tribe *The Lumbees... were found by the Huguenots* [Lutherans] *in 1708, and were said to have owned farms and lived in a "civilized manner" (like Europeans). They are also reputed to have spoken an older form of English... Their complexions vary from dark to very fair; it is not unusual to see blue eyes and blond hair among them.*[23]

If they were English, why did not they look for their countrymen? A permanent English settlement was already in place by the early 1600's.

The "Mediterranean appearance" of so many Melungeons, as well as their original denial of either an English or Indian heritage argue against a purely Lost Colony and/or English hypothesis [24]

After so many years and mixed marriages, their Mediterranean appearance is still present. ... *Captain John Smith, is giving an account of a conversation he had with the Powatan Indians. Apparently the Lost Colony was massacred, but some escaped.* [25] That report may shed light on some later findings. It is possible that some Melungeons, mixed with different Indian tribes, may have brought with them some names.

Among the more common names of the Lumbees are Berry, Brooks, Chavis, Cumbo (according to family legend to be of "Portuguese extraction". [26] However, Lumbee historian Adolph L. Dial, professor at Pembroke State University, N.C., does not mention any possible connection with the Portuguese in the books he wrote about the Lumbees. *He does not explain why the Lumbees have a dark-mixed population who, in the mid 1800's were also called Melungeons.* [27] If they had a strong component of the white English settlers, they would be lighter-skinned rather than dark, unless part of the English settlers were southern European. The Senate and the House of Representatives enacted a law designating this group of Indians as Lumbees in 1956, stating also that they may be connected with the Lost Roanoke Colony, and found by the first white settlers on the Lumber River and Robeson County. [28] They were also called the Cherokee Indians of Robeson County.

This same writer asserts that *parts of this book are based on logical supposition and oral history.* [29] Although historians generally do not accept oral history, many history books are partly based on written memoirs or edited documents. The surnames found among the Melungeon families are also found in the *Association Regional Lumbee Development*, such as Moore, Bell, etc. [30]

Many books have been written about this mystery, and no verifiable explanation has been found.

Since there is a strong possibility of Drake dropping Moors, South American Indians and black slaves at Roanoke – when he rescued the English colonists – research on several books and documents available has been undertaken, in an effort to analyze the trips made by the English who journeyed to America. These findings follow in chronological order.

First Trip - 1585

This trip was under Grenville and departed England on April 9 arriving in Port Ferdinand – Carolina Outer Banks – on July 21. The building of a fort, and houses was started later. On August 25, Grenville returned to England after capturing a Spanish ship off Bermuda. Aboard was Henrique Lopes, a Portuguese merchant who said that according to the ship's manifest, at least was 40,000 ducats in gold, silver and pearls was on board. All of that was handed over to Grenville, and more treasure was obtained from the passengers. Grenville denied that there *was any treasure registered at all.* [31] He proceeded to the Azores where he arrived in early October, landed the captured Spaniards, took in supplies and sailed home, arriving at Plymouth on October 18, and met Sir Walter Raleigh later. Lane was left with 108 men in August 1585. They stayed until the spring of 1586, and were later picked up by Drake. [32] With Grenville in charge, the second trip departed England on April 9, arrived at the Canaries on April 14 and Dominica on May 7. They finally arrived at Port Ferdinand on July 21.

Drake's Voyage of 1585-86 as Narrated by the English

Drake departed England on September 14, and headed to Spanish America with an armada of 25 vessels and 2,300 men. He started out by plundering some vessels at the Vigo River, sailed to the West Indies via the Canaries and the Portuguese

Cape Verde Islands, plundered and burned the town of São Tiago, crossed the Atlantic in 18 days and landed in Española or Hispaniola – what is today Haiti and the Dominican Republic – on New Year's Day, 1586. There is no account of capturing any slaves. Before arriving in the West Indies, two or three hundred men became sick and died. The following is part of Captain Walter Biggs' narrative while sailing with Drake. Biggs died before completion, but someone else completed it for him.

...Somewhat after midnight, they who had guard of the Castle, abandoned same; **some being taken prisoners**, *...and some fleeing away. After burning some of the houses, ransomed the town for 25,000 ducats, ransom for 110,000 ducats and burned Cartagena,... we do therefore consider, since all these cities, with their goods and prisoners taken in them, and the ransoms of the said cities , being all put together, are found far short to satisfy that expectation which by the generality of the enterprises was first conceived;*[33] *...slenderness of our strength...small number of able bodies... 28 May, sacked and burned St. Augustine... we came thwart St. Helena, the shoals appearing dangerous, and we having no pilot to undertake the entry, it was thought meetest to go hence alongst. ... We passed thus along the coast hard aboard the shore...The ninth of June upon sight of a special great fire... found some of our English countrymen that had been sent by thiter the year before by Sir Walter Raleigh... choice of two offers... leave a ship with... month's victual...being 103 persons... or return into England... desirous to stay... there arose a great storm... brake many cables, and lost many anchors... Master Lane and his company were driven to put to sea in great danger, in avoiding the coast, and could never see us until we met in England. Many also of our small pinnaces and boats were lost in this storm. ... after all this, the General offered them... passage into England, although he knew he should perform it with greater difficulty than he might have done before... the which being granted, and the rest sent for out of the country and shipped, we departed from that coast 18 June.* [The first account of prisoners was described by Biggs] *Somewhat after midnight, they who had the guard of the Castle, abandoned same;* **some being taken prisoners**, [author's emphasis] *and some fleeing away.*[34] The next account was when the Spaniards killed a Negro messenger boy sent by the general. In revenge a couple of friar prisoners were hanged. Drake burnt most of the town and took 25,000 ducats ransom for sparing the rest of it.

After spending a month in Santo Domingo Drake went to Cartagena, where he stayed for six weeks. There, some of Drake's men were attacked and killed by Indians – fighting alongside the Spaniards – armed with poison arrows. Still plagued with sickness, Drake gave up the idea of going to Panama. He decided to meet with his captains and leave Cartagena with the goods, ransom, and the prisoners.

No quantity or kind of prisoners were mentioned in this rather detailed and lengthy narrative by Captain Walter Biggs.

After leaving Cartagena, Drake went to Florida, burned and ransacked St. Augustine, and planned to attack Santa Elena, which he was unable to do as the shoals appeared dangerous.

On June 9, near Roanoke, Drake's men saw a great fire, went ashore and found some Englishmen, who showed them where Ralph Lane and the rest of his men were.

After a storm, and the loss of a few vessels, Drake departed from Roanoke with Ralph Lane and his men on June 18, arriving in Portsmouth on July 28 with a loss of 750 men. Three men were left behind, either by desertion or because they could not find their way back to the ship in time. Walter Spearman, in the American History Illustrated, [34a] attests that Drake left Roanoke in 1586 with Governor Lane, his group and the entire fleet of ships laden with spoils from the Spanish West Indians. There is no mention of slaves or captives, Indians or blacks, but if Drake in fact took the slaves from Santo Domingo and Carthagena, what did he do with them? Did he leave them ashore on Roanoke Island? Did he take them to England? How many? Biggs mentions that they took *some* in Santo Domingo. He was already hard pressed for space and provisions for his own men, which he already had to share with Lane and his men. [35, 36]

Irene Wright describes Pedro Diaz' answers to a questioning session realized in Cuba. Who was he? We came across him when he was in custody in Bidford after his return with Grenville in 1856. *His name appears to be Pedro (Pero) Diaz but also Franco or Pimenta, and he was the pilot of the Santa Maria when captured by Grenville in 1585 off Bermuda.* [37]

It is necessary to proceed with caution regarding Pedro Díaz' narration. He at one point says that he was taken – while with the English – twice to an English settlement, and that at that time there were some 320 men, and as many women there. [38] That would make a total of 640 people. The number was nowhere close to that. At some other point he also states that 210 people were recruited in London for the settlement in Virginia. [39] According to White the number is 150. The number who remained in Virginia was 110. [40]

Drake in the West Indies, as Narrated by David B. Quinn

Among others, Quinn uses Irene Wright's translation of the Spanish papers in the Archives of Seville.

Arrived in S. Domingo Jan. 1, 1586 ...*Sir Francis Drake, ...a major fleet under Drake... terrorized... Vigo, Santiago in the Cape Verde Islands...* [41] also written is: ...*he carried off 150 negroes and Negroes from Santo Domingo and Cape Verde.* [42] This could not be confirmed by Portuguese sources as Cape Verde had many Portuguese officials on the islands at the time. In *Santo Domingo...Cartagena Drake had released many European and Turkish galley slaves at these two last ports and at one point was said to have been carrying with him some three hundred of South American Indians who helped him at Cartagena as well as a number of black, predial slaves.* [43] If they were Indians from Cartagena, they could not be South American Indians. Quinn quotes Mary Frear Keeler as writing, *Indians of Cartagena* [44] ...*he also captured several vulnerable Portuguese "sugarmen" coming from Brazil. The Portuguese were forced to pay heavily for having been invaded by Spain in 1580.* [45] *...Sir Francis Drake, it was very different in 1586. Sir Francis Drake in his sweep through the West Indies, had released from the galleys at Santo Domingo and Cartagena hundreds of slaves of many nationalities – French blacks, a large number of subjects of the Turkish sultan, and members of other European nations ... Whether any of them got ashore on the Outer Banks and were deserted when Drake sailed away we cannot say, but it is not unlikely that a few saved their lives that way, though nothing has been heard of what became of any who may have done so. We know only that Drake brought Europeans and Moors back to England and, perhaps, a handful of blacks but no considerable number.* [46] *At Santo Domingo and Carthagena he had also been collecting men – galley slaves (mainly Moors, but including some Europeans), a few soldiers (again mainly Moors), Negro domestic slaves to whom he promised their freedom, and a substantial number of South American Indians (about 300 including women).* [47]

David Quinn also wrote: *We have no confirmation of this one report about the removal of the Indians from Cartagena.* [48] And adds a footnote that: *An early report to reach England said he had rescued no less than 1200 English, French, Flemings and Dutch from the galleys at Santo Domingo and took, besides 800 –* other English sources state only 80 [49] *– people of the country with him ...the numbers being, of course,* **exaggerated**. [50] (author's emphasis) England was trying to win European allies against Spain, and that would be good propaganda. The numbers are certainly exaggerated. They could add up to more than 2,000. With his original crew of 2,300, how would Drake feed and house them? The only French mentioned was the one they met in St. Augustine.

As counter propaganda, the English Ambassador in Paris wrote that there was a Negro in that town who ran away from Drake after he landed in England. He confessed that Drake brought home little or nothing, and the taking of Cartagena as well as the rest was false. [51]

During the same time frame there was much speculation about the English activity in Virginia. A deposition document of a Spanish sailor was translated by Irene Wright, which reads that:

No less than forty English vessels had set out for the settlement of Virginia by way of the Indies. Four of them were bringing women settlers...And in 1591 a grand assault by 150 vessels would be made on the Indies. [Quinn adds his own remarks] *This picture of the Virginia settlement, painted to illustrate English hopes and to colour Spanish fears, had little relation to reality, and raises suspicion that the information was 'planted' for Spanish consumption.* [52]

Quinn continues: *Whether these motley passengers were responsible for the outbreaks of sickness and disease among his own men we cannot say, nor can we tell how many of them succumbed, but he had not set any of them on shore when he turned back from Carthagena... on the 11ᵗʰ they met.* (Drake and Lane) *Drake had much to offer – his motley crew of passengers, the small boats he had seized at San Augustín...* **He did not have much food to spare**. [53] (author's emphasis) Again, what did he do with 300 South American Indians and 100 Negro slaves? If he did not have much food to spare, would he risk the lives of his men, many of them sick, to take the slaves and feed them? *...sickness had depleted their ranks... potable water was not very easy to find ...estimates of Drake's strength varied from 1200 to fewer than 500...*[54] What about the mixture of Indians and Blacks? Could that be considered an easy task? *...at Cartagena there had been disagreement among the English officers.* [55] Quinn further questions: *Were some lost in the storm? Were they all set on shore...? If not, did they die or were they killed on the way to England or were they landed at Portsmouth?* [56] Quinn's words are very interesting: *It is ironical, however, that the whole sequence of colonization was destroyed, inadvertently, by Drake.* [57]

Further English Voyages by Irene Wright, contains a wealth of information about Drake. The following are some interesting passages: *galley slaves whom the Spaniards had unchained.* [58] This is different from what has been written, crediting Drake with freeing prisoners.

CF Primrose Log. P. 16 and A. de I., 147-6-5 Santo Domingo 49- Don Diego de Osorio to the Crown, Santo Domingo, June 30, 1586. Also Acts Privy Council, New Series, XIV, p. 205 mention of Turks, galley slaves, Drake took to England upon his return. Other remained at large in the Island or made off with French Corsairs. The author continues: *...they carried with them everything they cared to take... galley slaves, negroes...from Santo Domingo to Cartagena.* [59] Did Drake leave the slaves at Cartagena? Again, Irene Wright relates that*... he obtained further amounts from their masters for the return of the slaves...* [60]A word of caution by the author: *...they should be compared with Bigg's discourse and the Primrose log.* [61] Which narration are we going to accept, the detailed one by Captain Walter Gibbs or the results of an interrogation done in Cuba by a Spanish official as translated by Irene Wright? It is hard to believe that the English narration so full of details, would miss entirely such an important occurrence as the coming aboard of hundreds of slaves as free passengers. About the deposition Ms. Wright adds *...deposition made at Havana on June 26, 1586 by an Aragonese seaman... this person must have made another probable early deposition... Although it is difficult to give much credence to a man who asserted that Drake was a Portuguese... Drake's address to his prisoners, presumably to his Moorish prisoners...(his assurance that he would return them to their own country...)*[62] Were they Turkish or Moorish from South Spain, and to which country would he take them? The vessels were not necessarily equipped to rescue and house large quantities of people for long periods. By then Portugal was being governed by a Spanish King.

Kennedy writes: *...Given the desperate circumstances of these people, it makes exceedingly good sense that they would have abandoned the island as quickly as feasible. Why would they wait for either the English or, worse still, pursuing Spanish or Portuguese ships to come recapture them?* [63]

A possible answer may be given by historian George Malcom Thompson who writes: *It had released many galley slaves, a hundred of whom, Turks, the Queen sent to Grand Seignior...*[64] This may indicate that Drake brought 100 Turk galley slaves to England. The expedition was commercial not humanitarian, and the only reason he brought the Turks was because they had a value.If so, why would he leave any on Roanoke?

There is still the question of Turk slaves returned to Turkey via England an event which some writers may be connecting with Drake's freed slaves in Santo Domingo or Cartagena. Charles Boxer invites the reader to what may be a partial explanation. *By the last quarter of the 16th century, the sugar trade of Brazil was very profitable, and between 1589 and 1591, Elizabethan privateers captured 69 ships.* [65] Would it be possible that the captured people were sent to London and were sold as slaves?

When looking into the possibility of Muslim slaves brought to America by Spaniards, a question arises. Under the terms of the contract dated March 20, 1565, the king of Spain directed Pedro Menéndez to bring *four members of the Society of Jesus, and ten or twelve religious of any other order he desired to preserve his colonists from the contamination of heresy and see that there were no Jews, Moors or Marranos among them.* [66] The King did allow Menéndez to import 500 *negro* slaves. [67] The Moors and Turks would have arrived before 1585, at Pardo's time, and 20 years before Drake. Would the Spaniards bring them to Santo Domingo? With the Inquisition firmly in place, would they allow Muslims to come to America? If they were *conversos*, why would they be sent as slaves after being converted? Now let us examine the naval activity.

From the English voyage's chart at the end of this Chapter, it can be seen that the area was quite busy with sailing ships. If Drake had put ashore his motley passengers, what happened to them? Even if they were in a hurry to leave, they would not have gone very far. Not much later, Grenville did quite a bit of exploring. He received information from the Indians that Drake and Lane had gone, but no word of anyone else in the area. According to David Quinn, Drake had perhaps 300 South American Indians and 100 Negro slaves to dispose of as a free labor for the Roanoke settlers. [68] Either these numbers were exaggerated or Drake never picked up any large number of slaves or Indians. If Drake took them, were they lost in the storm? Did they die or were they killed on the way to England? This is doubtful. Drake was already low on provisions. Most likely, the crew would have a hard time accepting them on board since they blamed them for the many who died due to sickness brought on board previously. They were so anxious to leave that they did not even wait for their three lost countrymen.

The only trace found was relative to the shipping of approximately 100 ex-galley slaves from England to the Turkish dominions. This may have nothing to do with Drake. They also could have been captured by the English somewhere else, or from the Spaniards on their return trip.

Grenville and Raleigh Voyages - 1586

Grenville departed Bideford on April 27, and on May 2 he encountered a ship from Spain belonging to Breton merchants. He took wine and oil, and on Cape Finisterre boarded two more vessels, one of them a Norman, took their goods, and sent them to England. [69] On May 8 Grenville captured a Dutch fly boat with cargo bound for Spain. He kept the cargo and the boat. Next he stopped at Porto Santo,

Madeira for water. However, the islanders fought so bravely that the English returned to their ships, according to Diaz, the Spanish narrator, and left the Islands without getting any fresh water. [70]

Grenville sailed for Virginia, arriving at Port Ferdinand during the end of the second week or into the third week of July. By then another ship sent by Raleigh with supplies had already left Roanoke. Although this date is very important, apparently it is not possible to know exactly. However, Hakluyt tells us [71] that this supply ship arrived *Immediately* after Lane's men left with Drake. It may have arrived between the 20th and 25th of June and left by the end of the month or the first week of July. (See Chart at the end of the Chapter)

Grenville would have arrived sometime in the middle of July, and departed by the end of August after having made some explorations leaving 15 or 18 men, which along with the three early ones were the first lost colonists. Obviously his priority was in piracy, and picking off prizes, not colonizing or establishing any settlement.

Another interesting fact in the Grenville voyage is that on the way to England he stopped in the Azores, headed for a trip to Newfoundland for fresh supplies, and returned to the Azores Islands, where he overtook a bark with passengers and a cargo of hides at Vila Franca do Campo, São Miguel Island, and another ship off Terceira Island. [72] That indicates how easy it was for the Portuguese to go from the Azores to the North American east coast.

1587 - John White Voyages and the Rescue Voyages of 1588 -1590

On May 8, 1587, John White sailed with Captain William and the Portuguese pilot Simão Fernandes, together with women and children. They arrived in Virginia on July 22 and on August 18, his granddaughter (Virginia Dare) was born. On August 27 he left to get supplies, never to see his family again.

In the Roanoke Colony were left 83 men, 17 women, 11 children, plus two that were born there, less one dead, George Howe, killed on arrival, for a total of 112 human beings. [73] John White and Simão Fernandes – the Portuguese pilot – returned to England with the Indians Manteo and Towaye. [74]

John White was employed as an artist on the North American voyages by Raleigh. [75] His tale is a piece of autobiography. As such, it is not necessarily history. It tells what he experienced. It does not relate fully in any sense what happened. [76]

On April 22, 1588, John White departed with Captain Facy. He was a seaman whose mind was wholly set on prize taking without being too careful whether or not he overstepped the delicate line between privateering and piracy. [77]

Because of the priority placed on prize catching, first they boarded a Scottish ship, then a Breton. They stole what they could, then chased a Flushing ship. After that, they were the ones being chased by the French, who engaged them in a fierce battle resulting in many casualties. They returned to England and arrived on May 22. That was the end of the Roanoke Colony, and of the 1588 rescue trip.

John White was sent back in 1590 to look for the English settlers left there in

1587 and found the Roanoke Island deserted. The story of this trip begins with John Watts, the greatest of privateering entrepreneurs, and his partners in the Thames in January 1590. After several problems, John White left on March 20. [79] He chased and captured a number of Spanish vessels, and finally arrived in Virginia on August 15 to find out that all the colonists had vanished, leaving only the letters *CRO* carved on a tree, and on one post the word *CROATAN*. [80]

That was the last communication from the colonists. No one was ever found.

Another aspect is the fact that due to hardships throughout the rest of Europe, and the rising of English power under Queen Elizabeth I, many continental Europeans emigrated to England. England employed Venetians, Portuguese and Genovese mariners in their early sea exploration. It is therefore possible that many of the first settlers of the Roanoke Colony may have been foreigners. Some of the names of the Roanoke colonists certainly are not typically English as shown on the list of Colonists at the end of this chapter.

Ruth Wetmore, an experienced archaeologist that has worked in the Southeast for many years, is of the opinion that at least a few of the Roanoke Colony settlers were Portuguese. [81] At least one of them, Simão Fernandes was. Some of the other names could very easily be considered of Portuguese roots. Also, Simão Fernandes, being Portuguese, probably had Portuguese servants or friends that he referred to as being part of the group while in England.

It is also interesting to note that in the Santo Domingo Island, a place practically destroyed by Drake, more than half of the population was Portuguese, according to the high court or *Audiencia*. [82]

John Smith, Pocahontas and Jamestown - 1607

All the attempts by the English to settle Virginia in the 16th century failed including the Roanoke Colony. The same almost happened to Jamestown due to several reasons. On the other hand, by the middle of the 16th century, well before Roanoke, the Portuguese were already settled in several parts of the world, and exporting sugar, spices, etc., to Europe - much of it to England.

John Smith was born in Willoughby, Lincolnshire, England in 1580 and died in London, June 1631. He was an English explorer, and principal founder of the first permanent English settlement in North America at Jamestown, Virginia.

At the age of 20, his adventuresome spirit found an outlet in the war against the Turks being fought in Hungary. In one of his narratives, he describes how he was about to be put to death, then saved when the chief's 13 year old daughter, Pocahontas, threw herself between him and his executioners. (See *The Gentleman of Elvas* book in Chapter VII for a similar story that actually happened 60 years earlier in Florida.)

John Smith's writings include *The General History of Virginia, New England, and the Summer Isles (1624); The True Travels, Adventures and Observations of Captain John Smith in Europe, Asia, Africa and America (1630).*

Blacks from Cape Verde - Turks

If Drake's release is one of the keys to help find Melungeon or other groups' ancestry, then research should be directed to the National Archives *Torre do Tombo* in Portugal for Cape Verde, *Archivo General de Indias* in Seville and *Archivo General de Simancas*, both in Spain, for Turk slaves. There are records of almost every person taken to the West Indies by Spain in the 16th and 17th centuries, including slaves, Turks and other nationalities.

According to records of the 16th century, Turkish slaves were very valuable, and families brought them in small numbers (one or two per family) to the New World as servants. One final point is the distinction between Turks and Moors.

In 1548, Jeronimo Butaca had a Turkish slave. [83] Portugal and Spain classified most Muslims as Moors. *It is not altogether clear whether our sources systematically distinguish between Turks and Moors.* [84]

List of the Colonists who arrived at Roanoke

John White *	Ananias Dare	Roger Baille
Christopher Cooper	Thomas Steuens	John Sampson *
Dyonis Harvie *	William Willes	John Brooke *
Cutbert White	John Bright *	Clement Taylor
William Sole	John Cotsmur *	Roger Pratt
George Howe	Simão Fernandes	Nicholas Johnnson *
Thomas Warner	Anthony Cage	John Jones *
John Tydway *	Ambrose Viccars	Edmond English
Thomas Topan	Henry Berrye	Richard Berrye
John Spendlove *	John Hemmington *	Thomas Butler
Edward Powell	Humfrey Newton	Thomas Colman
Thomas Gramme	Marke Bennet	John Gibles *
John Stilman *	Peter Little	John Wyles *
Brian Wyles	Geroge Martyn	Hugh Pattenson
John Farre *	John Bridger *	Griffen Jones *
Richard Shaberdge	John Burden *	James Hynde *
Thomas Ellis	William Browne	Michael Myllet
Thomas Smith	Richard Kemme	Thomas Harris
Richard Taverner *	John Earnest *	Henry Johnson *
John Starte *	Richard Darige	William Lucas
Arnold Archard	John Wright *	James Lassie *
John Cheven *	Thomas Hewet	William Berde (Verde)
William Dutton	Morris Allen	William Waters
Richard Arthur	John Chapman *	William Clement
Robert Little	Hugh Tayler	Richard Wildeye
Lewes Wotton	Michael Bishop	Henry Browne

Henry Rufoote	Richard Tomkins	Henry Dorrell
Charles Florrie	Henry Milton	Henry Payne
Thomas Harris	William Nicholes	Thomas Pheuens
	Women:	
Elyoner Dare	Margery Harvie	Agnes Wood
Wenefrid Powell	Joyce Archard	Jane Jones *
Elizabeth Glane	Jane Pierce	Audry Tappan
Alis Chapman	Emme Merrimoth	Colman
Margaret Lawrence	Joan Warren *	Jane Mannering *
Rose Payne	Elizabeth Viccars	
	Children:	
John Sampson *	Robert Ellis	Ambrose Viccars
Thomas Archard	Thomas Humfrey	Thomas Smart
George Howe	John Pratt *	William Wythers

The previous list does not include Virginia Dare, the first English child born in Virginia, and Harvie.

   * The letters *I* and *u* were used in the 16th century. For the benefit of the reader they were substituted by the letters *J* and *v* to denote modern spelling.

The 16th Century Virginia-Roanoke Voyages Chronology Chart

April 27,1584		Barlowe/Amadas/Fernandes leaves England
July 13,1584		Arrival in Roanoke to explore area
September 15,1584		Return to England with two Indians
April 19,1585		Leave England with 100 colonists
July 27,1585		Arrive at the Roanoke Island
August 25,1585		Grenville leaves for England, arrives October
Sept.14,1585		Drake leaves England
Jan. 1,1586		Drake arrives in Española
May 2,1586		Grenville leaves England
May 26,1586		Drake in Santo Domingo
May 27,1586		Drake in St. Augustine
June 9,1586	*	Drake arrives in Roanoke
June 18,1586	*	Drake and Lane departed with colonists
June 20,25, 1586	*	Raleigh's supply ship arrived
June 30, July 7,1586	*	Raleigh's supply ship departed
July 15,1586	*	Grenville ship arrives in Roanoke, leaves 15 men
July 28,1586	*	Drake arrives in England, after Lane
August 8,18, 1586	*	Eight ships sighted off Santa Elena
August 25,1586	*	Grenville departed Roanoke
April 26,1587	*	John White leaves England with 126 colonists
July 22,1587	*	John White arrives at Port Ferdinand
Aug.18,1587	*	First English child is born in Virginia

August 27,1587	*	John White returns to England
Sept.17,1587		John White in Azores
Oct.18,1587		Pilot Simão Fernandes arrives in England
Nov. 8,1587		John White arrives in Southampton
April 22,1588		White leaves England with 7 men and 4 women
May 22,1588		White returns without ever reaching Virginia
March 20,1590		White departs England on the *Hopewell*
May 26,1590		*Hopewell* attacks Spanish ships
August 15,1590		White arrives in Virginia, no one at Roanoke
October 30,1590		White returns to England, no colonists found

* Voyages related to the Lost Roanoke Colony

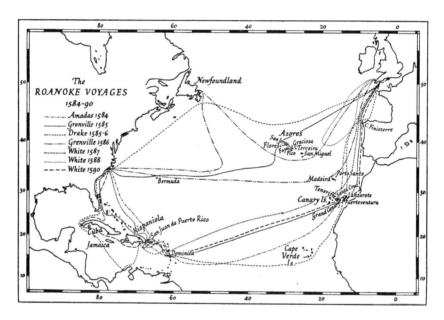

Fig. 35 - Map of the Roanoke voyages 1584-1590 [78]

Notes

[1] Encyclopedia Britannica, 1993
[2] As Berlengas e os Piratas by José de Almeida Santos, p. 1994
[3] Set Fair for Roanoke by David Quinn, p.20
[4] The Portuguese in America by Manoel da Silveira Cardozo, p. 10
[5] Sir Francis Drake by George Malcom Thompson, pp. 105-106
[6] Ibid, p. 191

[7] The Melungeons by N. Brent Kennedy, p.110

[8] Ibid, p.110

[9] North America Discovery by David Beers Quinn, p. 202

[10] The Melungeons by N. Brent Kennedy , p.111

[11] Espanhol-Português Dicionario, p. 269, Porto Editora

[12] Sir Francis Drake by George Malcom Thompson, pp. 75

[13] Espanhol-Português Dicionario, p. 269, Porto Editora

[14] The Melungeons by N. Brent Kennedy, p.120

[15] The Portuguese Seaborne Empire by Charles R. Boxer. p.45

[16] The Melungeons by N. Brent Kennedy, p.120

[17] Ibid , p.111

[18] The Roanoke Voyages by David B. Quinn, Vol. I, p. 79

[19] Ibid, p. 80

[20] Ibid, p. 81

[21] The Roanoke Canal by Peggy Jo Cobb Braswell, p. 9

[22] Photo by Outer Banks Photographer, Ray Mathews,
cover of Sprint Carolina Phone Co.

[23] The Melungeons by Bonnie Ball, p.37

[24] The Melungeons by N. Brent Kennedy, p.81

[25] The Melungeons by Bonnie Ball, p.12

[26] Ibid, p.45, Douglas L. Rights, American Indian in N.C.

[27] Ibid, p. 26

[28] The Only Land I Know by Adolph L. Dial and David K. Eliades, p. 187

[29] Ibid, p. ix

[30] The Indians of Southeastern U.S. by J. Anthony Paredes, p. 49

[31] The Roanoke Voyages by David B. Quinn, p.169,170

[32] Ibid, p. 158, Vol. 1

[33] Set Fair for Roanoke by David Quinn, p. 258

[34] Harvard Classics, Vol. 33, narrative by Captain Walter Biggs, p. 250

[34a] American History Illustrated, May 1969, pp. 22-27 by Walter Spearman

[35] Ibid, p. 237, 268

[36] Biggs' narratives were also used by David Beers Quinn

[37] The Roanoke Voyages by David B. Quinn, Vol. II, p. 786

[38] Ibid, p. 812

[39] Ibid, p. 793

[40] Ibid, p. 498

[41] Set Fair for Roanoke by David Quinn, p.132

[42] Turks, Moors, Blacks... by David B. Quinn
(Terrae Incognitae 14, 1982, p. 98)

[43] Set Fair for Roanoke by David Quinn, p.132

[44] Turks, Moors, Blacks... by David B. Quinn
(Terrae Incognitae 14, 1982, p. 97)

[45] Set Fair for Roanoke by David Quinn, p.132, p.131

[46] Ibid, pp. 343-4

[47] The Roanoke Voyages by David B. Quinn, Vol. I, p. 251
[48] Turks, Moors, Blacks... by David B. Quinn
  (Terrae Incognitae 14, 1982, p. 99)
[49] Ibid, p. 98
[50] The Roanoke Voyages by David B. Quinn, Vol. I, p. 251
[51] Turks, Moors, Blacks... by David B. Quinn
  (Terrae Incognitae 14, 1982, p. 104)
[52] The Roanoke Voyages by David B. Quinn, Vol. II, p. 588
[53] Ibid, Vol. I, pp.252,253
[54] Further English Voyages by Irene Wright, p. lvii
[55] Ibid, p. lvii
[56] The Roanoke Voyages by David B. Quinn, Vol. I, p. 254
[57] Ibid, Vol. .I, p.466
[58] Further English Voyages by Irene Wright, p. xl
[59] Ibid, p. xli
[60] Ibid, p. lvii
[61] Ibid, p. xlii
[62] Ibid, p. lvii
[63] The Melungeons by N. Brent Kennedy, p.112
[64] Sir Francis Drake by George Malcom Thompson, p. 193
[65] The Portuguese Seaborne Empire by Charles Boxer, p. 105
[66] The Catholic Historical Review, V.LI, No.3, Oct. 1965, by
  Mathew J. Connolly, p. 308
[67] Ibid, p. 307
[68] The Roanoke Voyages by David B. Quinn, Vol. I, p.254,5
[69] Ibid, Vol. .I, p.465
[70] Ibid, Vol. II, p. 789
[71] Ibid, Vol. I, p.479, note 4.
[72] The Roanoke Voyages by David B. Quinn, Vol. I, p.470
[73] Ibid, Vol.II, p.499-506
[74] Ibid, Vol.II, pp. 539-541
[75] Set Fair for Roanoke by David Quinn, p.24
[76] Ibid, p.273
[77] The Roanoke Voyages by David B. Quinn, Vol.II, pp.555,6
[78] Ibid, Vol. I, inside front cover, based on the Hakluyt Society of London.
[79] Ibid, pp. 579,580
[80] Ibid, Vol.II, pp.579,593
[81] Ruth Wetmore while on a Cherokee excavation site in
  Macon County. Oct. 1995
[82] The Portuguese in America by Manoel da Silveira Cardozo, p. 13
[83] Economia Mundial by Vitorino Magalhães Godinho, p. 547
[84] Turks, Moors, Blacks... by David B. Quinn
  (Terrae Incognitae 14, 1982, p. 104)

Chapter V

Origins of Portugal, Lusitania - The Make-up of Its People

The Melungeons and other groups have been traditionally connected with the Portuguese people because of oral information transmitted from generation to generation, and second, due to a Mediterranean, African or Oriental appearance.

This and the following chapters will describe the origins of the Portuguese people, their history and presence in North America and throughout the world. That knowledge will help the reader to better relate what has been written about the Melungeons, and provide the basis for a conclusion where the Portuguese connection is concerned.

Brief History to the 15ᵗʰ Century

Eis aqui, quasi cume da cabeça
De Europa toda, o Reino Lusitano,
Onde a terra se acaba e o mar começa
E onde o Febo repousa no oceano.

Behold her seated here, both head and key
of Europe all, the Lusitanian queen;
where endeth land and where beginneth sea;
where Phoebus goeth down in ocean green.

Lusiadas by Luis Vaz de Camões iii 20 [1]

God gave the Portuguese a small land for their birthplace,
but all the world to die in. [2]

This is a traditional saying that truly describes the fate of the many Portuguese spread out all over the world. It may also be translated as *God gave the Portuguese a small country as a cradle, but all the world as their grave yard.* [3]

It may seem that this book is overly biased towards the Portuguese ancestry, but in order to understand the Melungeon odyssey and their possible Portuguese ancestry, some basic Portuguese history would help. The Melungeons should have their place in history, in much the same way as the Portuguese, who so often are completely forgotten.

Unfortunately, there is very little published in English, and whatever is written most often represents a distorted view of the facts and ignores many others much more important. But as Kennedy said in his book, the winners write the History. This does not help when you try to research the Melungeons.

A.J.R. Russell-Wood wrote in his book *A WORLD ON THE MOVE: Portugal is a province of Spain, isn't? The capital of Brazil is Buenos Aires, They speak Spanish in Brazil, very few people speak Portuguese it is a Spanish dialect. Such statements testify to the ignorance concerning the Portuguese-speaking world...Laborers in the field of Latin American history are resigned to textbooks purporting to be histories of Spain and Portugal in the New World ,only to discover that the Portuguese part has about the same ratio to the Spanish as has the visible part of an iceberg to the bulk under water, namely one ninth...How is it that every school boy of the English speaking world can rattle off the names of Cortes, Pizarro, [Hernando] de Soto, Cabeza de Vaca, Balboa, Ponce de Leon and others of their ilk? And yet, when questioned about the pantheon of Portuguese explorers, that selfsame schoolboy would be hard pressed to name one other than the anglicized and inappropriately named Henry the Navigator.* [He also voiced the need to:] *bring the broader framework not only of a Portuguese age of discoveries, but also of the global nature of the Portuguese series of initiatives and to emphasize the sheer dynamic of the Portuguese enterprise which transcended the limitations of individuals and constraints of time and space.*

Also to better understand the resilience of the Portuguese people we should place them ...*within the broader framework not only of a Portuguese age of discoveries, but also of the global nature of the Portuguese series of initiatives; secondly, to emphasize the sheer dynamic of the Portuguese enterprise which transcended the limitations of individuals and constraints of time and space.* [4]

Celtics, Carthaginians, Phoenicians, Greeks, Jews, Romans Suevis, Allans, Vandals, Visigoths, Berbers and Moors Ancestors of the Portuguese Population

Portugal's people are made up of many races, such as the Celtics, Carthaginians, Phoenicians, Greeks, Jews, Romans, Suevis, Allans, Vandals, Visigoths, Berbers and Moors.

After the last invasion of the Moors (A.D. 711) up to the present day, no other people has had an influence on the physical makeup of the Portuguese, except for the little difference that the Crusaders may have made in the 12th and 13th centuries.

Not even the black slaves brought in during the 15th and 16th century made much difference; naturally that means that some of the Portuguese have Negroid blood as well as other races.

The Moors and the Berbers had been in Portugal for at least four centuries, and by the 1500's they were Portuguese, just as the English arriving in America in the 1600's are Americans today.

What it really means is that the Portuguese people's appearance has not changed much for many centuries.

There is a difference, however, between the North and the South of Portugal. It is easy to find fair skin, blond or red hair and blue eyes in the North, and dark skin, black hair and brown eyes in the South, where the Moors stayed the longest. The Arabs never fully conquered the northern provinces.

That was the end of invasions into what is known today as Portugal till the 1800's, when Napoleon's army invaded Portugal and Spain. But they did not stay long or had any impact except for the destruction and death caused to the population.

Now let us review the origins of Portugal and its people. In order to better understand the variety and composition of the Portuguese population, the reader should know what peoples inhabited what is today Portugal, taking into consideration that this is the oldest country in Europe that has maintained its geographic borders for more than 800 years.

The following is a summary of Portugal's origin in the Iberian Peninsula, and where the Portuguese people came from.

Starting with the Iberians, believed to be the original people or the natives of the Iberian Peninsula, Portugal was invaded, conquered and settled by a variety of races in the following order:

Celts and Celtiberians

The Celtics, also called Gauls, Galicians, Gaelic, being the ancient Irish language: The Celtics were barbarian tribes widespread in transalpine Europe and the Iberian Peninsula (Spain and Portugal).

This race formed the Celtiberians, tribes of mixed Iberian and Celtic stock, from the 3rd century B.C. onward. *This could provide a partial explanation for the Welsh as a possible origin of the Melungeons.*[5] The Celts' presence and influence extended from the North Sea to the Mediterranean, the Black Sea and to the westernmost point in Europe located in Sintra, Portugal. [6]

The Phoenicians

The Phoenicians, originally from an ancient region corresponding to modern Lebanon, with adjoining parts of modern Syria and Israel: Its inhabitants, the Phoenicians, were notable merchants, traders and colonizers of the Mediterranean in the 1st millennium BC. One of the chief cities of Phoenicia was Berot (modern Beirut).

It is not certain what the Phoenicians called themselves in their own language; it appears to have been KenaZani (Akkadian: Kinahna), *Canaanites*. In Hebrew the word *KenaZani* has the secondary meaning of merchant, a term that well characterizes the Phoenicians. [7]

Just recently in 1995, during excavations for a high-rise apartment building, a Phoenician village was discovered across from Lisbon, the Portuguese capital, on the south shore of the Tagus River. It was the largest ever found in the Iberian Peninsula. [8]

The Carthaginians

The Carthaginians' interest in the Atlantic coast of Morocco was stimulated by the more prosaic attraction of the abundant fish. Himilco's voyage also was known to the Greeks and Romans. He sailed north along the Atlantic coast of Spain, Portugal, and France and reached the territory of the Oestrymnides, a tribe living in Brittany. Carthage, a great city of antiquity, traditionally founded on the north coast of Africa by the Phoenicians of Tyre in 814 B.C., is now a residential suburb of the city of Tunis. Its Phoenician name means New Town.[9]

The Carthaginian invasion has assumed historic importance for the Iberian Peninsula as it supplied their army, the Celtiberian infantry and the superb Andalucian cavalry, which helped their General Hannibal devastate Italy. [10]

The Greeks - 600 BC

The Greek presence in the Iberian Peninsula is known to have occupied in the 7th century B.C., when a Greek navy merchant by the name Kolaios returned to Greece with a rich cargo of precious metals. These voyages were followed by others and in order to protect them, the Greeks founded numerous colonies along the Portuguese Atlantic coast. They also founded the French city of Marseille (Massalia) in 600 B.C. The Carthaginians retaliated and after battles in 530 B.C., the Greeks found the Straits of Gibraltar closed, and that was the end of their presence in the peninsula.

The Greek presence gave a powerful stimulus to start the formation of the Iberian culture during the 5th century B.C. The colonies were absorbed by the natives, but they also left magnificent temples and statues. [11] Signs of their staying have been found in the past in Portugal and just recently near Tavira-Algarve. Greek coins and utensils of this same time period were also found. [12]

There is a tradition that the name of the Portuguese capital, Lisbon stems from the name Ulysses (Odysseus) or Olisipo, which is a Greek legend of a hero during the Trojan War and the famous wooden horse of Troy. The Greek poet Homer recounts Odysseus's adventures in his epic poems *The Odyssey* and *The Iliad*. [13]

The Jews in Portugal

According to legend, the first Jews came to the Iberian Peninsula at the time of Nebuchadnezzar, king of the Chaldeans (6th century B.C.) or even before, at the time of Solomon, who reigned in Israel from 974 B.C. to 937 B.C. While these hypotheses may lie in the legendary domain, it has been ascertained that the Jewish presence in Iberia preceded and accompanied that of the Romans. From the 5th century onward the Jews reinforced their position and remained active in peninsular society during the Visigoth and Muslim occupations.

When the kingdom of Portugal was formed in the 12th century, there were already a number of important Jewish communities in several cities re-conquered by the Christians. These included the flourishing commune in Santarem which was discovered by the first king of Portugal, Afonso Henriques (1139-1185). Generally speaking, Portuguese Jews enjoyed the protection of the crown during the first dynasty. [14]

We know therefore that Jews had settled in what is known today as Portugal and Spain as early as the first century A.D. during its occupation by the Romans. They were later persecuted by Reccard, the Visigoth king, also forcing them to embrace Christianity. These Jews would later become the Portuguese Jews and part of the so-called Sephardic Jews, of Spain and Portugal.

In the 1400's there were approximately 30,000 Jews in Portugal, a number which doubled when the Spanish Catholic Kings expelled them from Spain. In turn they sought refuge in Portugal as well as others parts of Europe and North Africa. Many that could not pay for their passage were reduced to slavery. [15]

It is important that a separation be made between the Jews of Portugal and the Jews of Spain. Although they were both Sephardim, each group had its own culture and language. The same happened with Jews all over the world. Their religion is what binds them together, not necessarily the culture or language.

Isaac Abrabanel, a well known Jewish leader, worked with his father for King Afonso V, and in 1471 when the Portuguese conquered Arzila, 250 Moroccan Jews were captured and brought in as slaves. Abrabanel traveled to the countryside to redeem these North-African Jews.[16] His father was the treasurer for Prince Fernando [17] who died in Fez, Morocco, as a captive of the Moors. Prince Fernando was the brother of Henry the Navigator.

King Manuel I was one of the most sympathetic kings to his Jewish subjects, and when he succeeded João II in 1495, one of his first acts was to free those slaves. However, when this same king decided to marry Isabel, daughter of the Spanish king, he would have to agree to have them expelled, which he did, giving ten months for the Jews to leave Portugal.

King Manuel I valued their contribution and did not want to lose so many productive subjects. He took several measures to prevent their departure. When 20,000 individuals were gathered together to board the vessels, he ordered everyone not professing the Catholic faith to come and assemble in the main square in Lisbon, and from the balcony had the bishop baptize everyone with a single blessing. After that, the king told the people that they were all Catholics and could go home. Only seven or eight found the strength to resist baptism. [18] When the Spanish princess arrived to marry the King, everyone in Portugal was officially Christian. King Manuel, whom some exiles called the *Holly King* and the *Jewish King* in their chronicles, [19] did as much as he could to protect the Jews, hoping that they would eventually assimilate and become Christians. In 1497 the King also forbade all inquiries concerning religious beliefs of those who accepted Christianity in the following 20 years, and in April 1512 he extended the period of grace until 1534. In this manner assimilation of the Jews in Portugal began. [20]

Today there are still plenty of signs of their early stay. In 1985, construction in the Portuguese city of Tomar, near the Tomar Synagogue, uncovered the locale where the purification would take place was discovered. This was called the *mikev*. This synagogue is one of the oldest in Portugal, and believed to date back to the 15th century.

The Jews may have played a very important part in the period of the discoveries.

Portuguese history shows that they were often appointed to very important places within the government.

An interesting note: The Portuguese people in 1995 elected Jorge Sampaio, a Jew, for the highest elected office in the nation, president of the Portuguese Republic. What would the Inquisition say about that?

The Romans, the Lusitanos and Lusitania - 100 B.C. - A.D. 200

The Romans had a great impact in Portugal which is still being felt today. The Portuguese language, along with many others, derives from Latin. Also vestiges of the administrative and law system still remain, along with plenty of Roman ruin sites all over Portugal. Some of the most recent ones that the author became aware of, unfortunately are not open to the public except once or twice a year.

These are underground swimming pools and Roman baths located right in the center of downtown Lisbon, and accessible through a manhole located where two major streets, *Rua da Conceição* and *Rua Augusta* intersect.

Other famous ruins are located in Conimbriga as well as many other locations. The two major Portuguese cities date back from Roman times: Porto – Portus Cale, Portugal's name origin – and Lisbon (Olisipo). Porto was originally a Roman settlement.

Lusus is a mythical name connected with the first settler of the westernmost part of the Iberian Peninsula, and *Luso* or *Lusitano* today means born in the Roman province of Lusitania, of the Roman Empire, which was located more or less where Portugal is today. Today it is synonymous with Portuguese.

A Portuguese-American is called in Portuguese a Luso-Americano. The Lusitanos fought hard against the Romans under the leadership of Viriato before they gave up their independence. It took the Roman Empire many decades, with their almighty army, to subjugate the Lusitanos (Portuguese).

The word Lusitano derives from Lusitania (lux + tania) lux=light and tania=land or land of the sunshine.

Suevi, Suebi, Swabians, Vandals, Alanis - A.D. 409, Visigoths - A.D. 456

Suevi or Suebi were Germanic people. The Suevis came from a Suevi Kingdom also in Bavaria and Switzerland, ancestors of the Swabians. The Vandals, also a Germanic group came about the same time. They maintained a kingdom in North Africa from A.D. 429 to A.D. 533 and captured Rome in 455. Because of the way they damaged Rome, the name Vandal was adopted to mean destruction.

Another Germanic tribe, the Alanis, which was a nomadic pastoral people from a region northeast of the Black Sea, invaded the Iberian Peninsula, and later crossed into Africa with the Vandals.

The Visigoths were a Germanic religious people that drove out the Vandals and set up an independent kingdom in the Iberian Peninsula, until destroyed by the Muslims in A.D. 711. The Visigoths and Suebis did not have the same effect during their colonizing period as the Romans and later the Arabs.

Arabs and Berbers - A.D. 711 - A.D. 1143

The last major invasion of the Iberian Peninsula was accomplished by the Arabs, Berbers, and Moors. They stayed in Portugal for a little more than 400 years and left behind much of their advanced civilization. The conquering Arabs did not care what religion their subjects professed so long as unbelievers paid a special tax.

In 710 an Arab-Berber army set out for the Iberian Peninsula and defeated King Roderick in 711, raided into and through the Iberian Peninsula, and ruled in the name of the Umayyad caliph.

The Berbers are a Caucasoid people and indigenous of North Africa, largely scattered in tribes across Morocco, a territory comprising the western portion of Algeria, Tunisia, Libya and Egypt, which in classical times constituted the Roman province of Mauretania. Despite Roman colonization of the area and an invasion by the Arabs in the 7th century A.D., rural Berber tribes remained relatively autonomous until the 12th century, when invading Bedouin Arabs wrecked the Berbers' peasant economy and converted many of the settled tribes to nomads. Almoravids, a confederation of Saharan Berber tribes built an empire in Muslim Iberian Peninsula during the 11th and 12th centuries.

The Moors themselves never used the term. They were Arabs from Damascus and Medina, leading armies of North African Berbers converts. Most married into Spanish and Visigoth families or took fair-skinned Galician slaves as wifes; they brought no women with them. From this heady mix of race and culture sprang the Moorish civilization that would last 900 years in Spain and 500 in Portugal.[21] Muslims never became a majority throughout their 700-year Andalusian presence. Non-Muslims entered into the Muslim realm as Mozarabs, Christians who had adopted the language and manners, rather than the faith, of the Arabs. Given essentially the same administrative arrangements, the Iberian Christian population was later restored to dominance.

Reconquest of the Iberian Peninsula

Although the traditional beginning of the *Reconquista* goes back to c.a. 718, when the Christian Asturians opposed the Moors at the Battle of Covadonga, the impulse toward reconquest was not strong during the first three centuries of Muslim hegemony. It was in the 11th century, when Moorish unity broke down and the Christian kingdoms of northern Spain began to be affected by an aggressive anti-Muslim crusading spirit, that the movement began in earnest. A series of wars followed, and by the mid-13th century most of the peninsula had been subjected to Christian rule, though the continued existence of a Moorish enclave around Granada in southern Spain served to keep the spirit of the *Reconquista* alive until the end of the 15th century. Many historians believe that subsequent Spanish emphasis on religious uniformity, evidenced by the strong influence of the Inquisition and the expulsion of people of Moorish and Jewish descent, can be traced back to this crusading struggle of the Middle Ages, with the help of adventurers of Germanic origin.

County of Portugal -1096, Origin of Portugal - 1143

From the Frank aristocracy came the knights Raimundo and Henrique, to help Afonso VI of Leon and Castille. These two married his daughters, and the County of Portucale was given to Henrique of Bologne. This county eventually would become the kingdom of Portugal. Henrique married Teresa, born around 1091. The word *Portucale* appeared for the first time in A.D. 954. Right after the reconquest movement, simultaneously initiated from the north and the east, the kingdoms of Leon and Navarra were formed. This last one was divided into three other kingdoms: Navarra, Castille and Leon. Later on, the County of Portugal separated from Leon. The word Leon derives from the Latin *legione*, a Roman legion that stationed in the area. In time, Castille and Leon, through union and conquest, managed to get the remaining peninsular kingdoms, including Granada in the late 15th century. Afonso Henriques, son of Henrique, eventually made Portugal an independent kingdom and the Portuguese monarchy was constituted in 1143 with Afonso Henriques as the first king. The kingdom enlarged quickly at the cost of the Moors, through the conquest of Alentejo and Algarve, thus expelling them from Lusitania, the Roman province that became Portugal.

It is interesting to note that one of the ways used by the Moors to get accepted in the Iberian Peninsula was the same one utilized by the first Portuguese king, Afonso Henriques, and that was to secure consent for the use of their own religion and marriage between both races, a strategy which apparently has worked well in the last eight centuries. [22]

The reconquest of Portugal ended in the 1200's and most of the Moors accepted the new way of life, which after all did not change much. However, eventually and gradually, most accepted Catholicism, and the Portuguese also took advantage of their more advanced civilization. The Portuguese king was most interested in keeping the towns and villages with the people, but there were not enough Portuguese, and that was the biggest problem in centuries to come. By the 1400's and 1500's, Portugal's Moors were for the most part non-existent. After living in Portugal, they became and felt Portuguese. It has been said that the Portuguese did not have a feeling of nationality. This is not true, and as Professor Saraiva, a Portuguese historian, stated: At the time when the Portuguese had to affirm their nationality, they changed their military patron from Santiago which was Spanish to Saint George. The Portuguese did not want to have the same Patron Saint as the Spanish. [23]

First Portuguese Naval Battle and End of the Reconquest - 1180

It took place in 1180, when Knight Fuas Roupinho defeated the Moors in a naval battle off Cabo Espichel and chased them all the way to Algarve and to Ceuta. The fleet constituted of about 20 galleys and some other smaller transportation boats. They had 150 oarsmen and 40 soldiers, 6 sailors, all under the command of four or five officers.[24]

Algarve was the last area to be re-conquered, but the Arab population that lived there stayed in Faro, Loulé and Silves, as the others had done in Lisbon, following the rule since the reconquest of Toledo that put an end to the extermination of the Muslim people. [25]

Portuguese Merchant Navy and the Sargasso Sea - 1254

Such a navy existed already in 1254. There are documents indicating important coastal traffic, under the reign of King Fernando (1345-1383), which shows that the sea was an important part of the Portuguese life and economy.[26]

At the very beginning of the 13ᵗʰ century, Portuguese merchants had already found their way to England, and had judged it worth while, for the sake of trading with that country. Early commercial ties with England are apparent as well as the presence of Portuguese, Bartholomew of Portugal is one of four Portuguese citizens of that country already established in London in the year 1220, according to a royal order of the king of England, and another in 1208, *Considering the hard struggle for independence from which the Portuguese kingdom had but recently emerged.* [27] The tuna fishery in Algarve, an industry explored since Roman times, was one of the many industries that King Fernando protected. He also gave free lumber to anyone that would build a ship larger than 100 tons and would exempt other construction materials of taxes. [28] The people of Lisbon and Porto made an actual treaty with King Edward III of England in 1353.

Between the 13ᵗʰ and 14ᵗʰ centuries, possible sporadic discovery voyages were made, but without continuity or persistence. [29]

Due to insufficient documentation, some historians admit that by the 1450's, the Portuguese had reached or at least seen some of the Antilles, the American and Brazilian northeast, Newfoundland and Greenland. During those voyages they discovered the western part of the Azorean islands… having reached without a doubt the Sargasso Sea and gathered information to draw a complete map with precise winds and the Atlantic currents. [30]

The Sargasso Sea or Gulf Sea Weed (Berry Sea) is part of the North Atlantic Ocean west of the Azores and east of the West Indies and located approximately between 20° and 35° north latitude.

The Bermuda Islands are within the northwestern portion of the sea. It is the calm center of the clockwise-turning, subtropical gyre that dominates the North Atlantic. It is bounded on the west and north by the Gulf Stream and on the south by the North Equatorial Current. [31]

Early Discoveries and Naval Construction - 1336-1456

A joint effort between the Portuguese and the Genoese may have taken place around 1336, where the Genoese Admiral Emanuel Pezagno may have been contracted by King Diniz to sail the Atlantic with Portuguese ships, discovering the *Fortunate Isles* or the Canary Islands. Also, Lanzarotto Malocello was probably with the admiral. From that date on these islands began to be represented for the first time on Genoese and Mediterranean charts, such as the one of Angelino Dalorto (Dulcert).

There is a text attributed to the Italian writer Giovanni Bocaccio that speaks of a voyage to these islands in 1341 by *other Hispanics* that appears to refer to the Portuguese. Also, the Portuguese King Afonso IV wrote a letter to the Pope making territorial claims to the islands. [32]

Between 1385 and 1456, out of a total of 46 ships engaged in the maritime trade between Portugal, England and Flanders, 83% were owned by the Portuguese.[33] We can easily see that the Portuguese, by the time discoveries started in the 15th century, were well prepared for high sea navigation and could very well have been on the east coast of North America, as some historians claim.

From the 12th century on, there was much trade between Portugal and Bristol: *...ships left the Bristol channel for Portugal, where they took on salt, and then sailed for Icelandic waters to fish, returned to Portugal to sell this fish and to buy wine, oil, and salt, and finally returned with this cargo to Bristol.* [34]

Portugal - England Alliance and Elizabethan English - 1386

Portugal has the oldest alliance in the world with England, which dates back to May 9, 1386, and is known as the Treaty of Windsor. Unfortunately, the Portuguese paid a very high price in later centuries. But that is another story.

King João I of Portugal married an English princess, Philippa of Lancaster (1387), sister of Henry IV, King of England, who introduced various English habits into Portugal. Out of this marriage, four sons and a daughter were born, one of their most famous sons was Infante D. Henrique – Henry the Navigator. They all spoke English, and this language was widely used in the Portuguese court. The heavy trade with England carried well into the 16th and 17th centuries.

Catherine of Gaunt, Phillipa's sister, also married King Juan II of Castile, which helped to maintain peace between Castile and Portugal for a while. Keeping with a tradition of close ties between Portugal and England, Charles II of England married a Portuguese princess, Catherine of Braganza, who also introduced Portuguese habits into England, such as the famous tea time and furniture from India. The New York borough of Queens was named after her. Therefore it is safe to assume that during the reign of Elizabeth I, Queen of England, (1558-1603), people involved in the work of navigation would have acquired English speaking habits of the time. (See note "a")

Taking all of the above into consideration, still it is hard to believe that the

Portuguese brought with them enough Elizabethan English speaking habits that would survive for one hundred years without any contact with the English. I am inclined to rule out that they (Melungeons) were the only ones who spoke Elizabethan English when they were found by early explorers.

There is also a remote possibility that even one survivor of the Lost Roanoke Colony taught enough English to a Melungeon or Portuguese that eventually would have been used by the group. John Lawson in, a passage related to language learning wrote in the 1700's: *...being of a French-man's Opinion, how that an English Wife teaches her Husband more English in one Night, than a School Master in a week..*

Notes

[a] I recall, as a young teenager after World War II in Lisbon which was constantly visited by the U.S. Navy, when we all tried to mimic the English language to get along better with the many sailors showing up all over Lisbon. As all teenage boys of that time, we were very jealous of them, since the girls would fall head over heels every time they would see the American sailors.

[1] Camões is Portugal's poet born before England's Shakespeare
[2] Padre Antonio Vieira, 1640, Portuguese Missionary
[3] National Geographic Magazine, November 1992 by Merle Severy
[4] A World on the Move by A.J.R. Russel-Wood, pp. 4-6
[5] The Melungeons by Bonnie Ball, p.31
[6] National Geographic Magazine by Merle Severy, p. 558 (May 1977)
[7] Encyclopedia Britannica (1994)
[8] Luso-Americano Newspaper, Newark, NJ
[9] Encyclopedia Britannica, 1993
[10] Historia da Civilização Iberica, by Oliveira Martins, p.57-8
[11] Dicionario de Historia de Portugal, by Joel Serrão, V. III, p. 154
[12] The Portuguese Post, May 14, 1996
[13] Microsoft Encarta 96 Encyclopedia CD-Rom
[14] The Jews in Portugal by ICEP, p. 2
[15] Historia da Origem e... Inquisição by Alexandre Herculano, pp. 67-69
[16] The Jews of Spain by Jane Gerber, p. xxi
[17] Historia de Portugal by Damião Peres, p. 656
[18] Historia da Origem e... Inquisição by Alexandre Herculano, pp. 76-77
[19] Historia dos Judeus in Portugal by Meyer Kayserling, p. 132
[20] O Sacrificio de Isaac by Manuel da Costa Fontes, pp. 58-59
[21] National Geographic Magazine, July 1988, p. 88
[22] Historia da Civilização Iberica, by Oliveira Martins, p.163
[23] Interview with Professor Saraiva, July 1995
[24] Correio da Manhã, 26 June 1995, by Antonio Pires, p.2
[25] Fomento Rural e Emigração by Oliveira Martins, p. 24
[26] Portugal nos Mares by Oliveira Martins, p.23

[27] The Commercial Relations of England and Portugal by
Shillington & Chapman, p. 25
[28] Fomento Rural e Emigração by Oliveira Martins, p.83
[29] Historia de Portugal by Oliveira Marques, Vol. I, p. 244
[30] Ibid, Vol. I, p. 264-7
[31] Grolier Encyclopedia, 1995
[32] Portugal and the Discovery of the Atlantic by
Alfredo Pinheiro Marques, pp. 22-23
[33] The Portuguese Seaborne Empire by Charles R. Boxer, p. 7
[34] A Future to Inherit by David Biggs, p. 7

Fig. 36 - Map of Portugal, the Westernmost European Nation,
and the one closest to the United States.

Chapter VI
The Beginning of the Age of Discovery

Enough for us that the hidden half of the Globe is brought to light,
and the Portuguese daily go farther beyond the equator.
Thus shores unknown will soon become accessible; for one in emulation of
another sets forth in labours and mighty perils. [1]

The Discoveries period is the one most likely responsible for bringing the Melungeon ancestors to America. Since the Portuguese were the ones to pioneer navigation, and discoveries of new lands, it is only proper to dedicate this Chapter to that time frame, and how the Portuguese had the means to bring their people to this Continent, but also other races with a different ethnic background.

Fig. 37 - Ship of Discovery, Portuguese caravel of the 15th Century [2]
Painting of the model used by Vasco da Gama

Action on the Sea and Reaction to the Land

Genoa was, in the 13th century, the most active maritime power. It is known that in 1291 two Genoese galleys commanded by the Vivaldi brothers, with two

Franciscan friars on board, sailed into the Atlantic and disappeared forever without a slightest trace, although between 1292 and 1304 several expeditions were sent from Genoa in search of them.

The next great expedition into the Atlantic was Portuguese; it sailed from Lisbon in 1336, probably under the command of the Genoese Lanzarotto Malocello, then serving Portugal and a Portuguese subject. He succeeded, and these expeditions were followed by others from Castile. [3]

After that, Portugal became the Atlantic sea power in the early 15th century. [4] The exploits and influence, through four centuries of Europe's first great maritime empire, at their peak virtually girdled the earth. [5]

The caravel – diminutive of *caravos* – as the name implies originated with the caravos, ships used by the Arabs since ancient times. Prince Henry's shipbuilders produced the famous caravel, which combined some of the cargo capacity features of the Arab caravos with the maneuverability of the Douro River caravels. Interesting to note is the fact that Prince Henry was born in Porto by the Douro River.

When it was recognized that the Latin caravels on long trips had to use the round sails to take advantage of the winds in different directions, the round caravel was created in Portugal in the beginning of the 16th century. It was extensively used on the routes to India as part of the armed fleet.

Besides the caravels, Prince Henry also had seamen that later in 1622 were described by Richard Hawkins – a contemporary Englishman and a competent judge –...*the Spaniards and Portingals doe exceede all that I have seene, I meane for their care, which is chiefest in navigation. And I wish in this, and in all their workes of Discipline and reformation, we should follow their examples...In every Ship of moment...whilst they Navigate, the Pilot...never depart, day or night, from the sight of the Compass.* [6]

If the Melungeons and other groups were Portuguese as they said they were, first the Portuguese presence on the East Coast must be proven, which apparently is not hard to do - as we shall see.

Not everyone may know the extent of the Portuguese presence on the East Coast. It is quite substantial, and their contribution to this continent's development has been recognized throughout the years. The following are the facts recorded by many writers, although some of them do state: *There is little concrete evidence of Portuguese activity in northeastern North America between the 1520's and the 1560's.*

Historians cannot ignore that the Portuguese were the closest Europeans to North America: less than two weeks, with good weather, from the Azores. For a long time they had the capabilities, as well as the know-how of safely navigating in open oceans. ...*For from the said Azores to the said Canada is not more than 400 leagues.* [7]

Not all historians agree that the Portuguese were great and courageous navigators. Ferdinand Braudel, writer of *The Mediterranean and the Mediterranean World in the Age of Philip II,* dedicated just a few paragraphs to the Portuguese. ...*how the*

Portuguese, at the beginning of the 15th century, tackled the immense problem of navigation in the high seas, in the Atlantic, which was entirely new to them. [8]

Yes, the Atlantic was new to them, but so it was to everyone else. On the other hand, it is known that the Portuguese merchant marine were in Flanders and the British Isles since the 13th century. How did they get there? Was the Atlantic really new to the Portuguese when more than half of their nation borders on the ocean? *A position that deprived her of the cream of Mediterranean trade.* [9] How did the fishermen make their livelihood? Just fishing within sight of the coast? Why would the Portuguese venture out in the open seas?

Very simple. There is such a thing as survival, and when it comes to surviving you do whatever it takes. Portugal had nowhere to go but to the sea.

What about the other European kingdoms? First of all, they had fertile agricultural lands, which are scarce in Portugal, and when the numerous small kingdoms wanted to enlarge their empires, all they had to do was to invade nearby lands.

Dr. Braudel goes on to repeat the words of Georg Friederici, a German writer *...the Portuguese discoverers, following the endless African coast line, that in the lifetime of Henry the Navigator they were primarily timid and fearful coast-huggers, with no spirit of adventure.* [10] The world is full of injustices, and this is a typical example. Major powers of the world and their scholars not only ignored the Portuguese, but also laid on them derogatory epitaphs.

How did the Portuguese venture on the high seas being so *timid and fearful*? If timid and fearful people were able to do it, what happened to the others that we assume were courageous? My answer is to look at the results: the courageous followed the timid and fearful to the places discovered by the Portuguese.

Fortunately there are other historians that do justice to the Portuguese, such as the five professors from four major universities who wrote the book *A History of the Western World - Ancient Times to 1715*. They made reference to the *Technical Superiority of the Portuguese - The Portuguese were first. A maritime people, whose interest in European affairs was never great, their eyes were turned naturally to the sea. They were also a crusading people, hard-bitten fighters who had won back their land from the Moors.* [11]

Most Portuguese do agree that they were the worst business people in the world. At one time they had most major markets and lost them. As a matter of fact, they should go into the *Guinness Book of Records* for that.

Henry the Navigator (Infante D. Henrique) in his Lifetime

At the time of Prince Henry, and in 1300 years since the Roman geographer Claudius Ptolomeu (c.a. A.D. 73-151) of Alexandria, knowledge of the world did not advance much. Europe's northern people touched Iceland, Greenland, Labrador and possibly New York. All these voyages had no method, or were not followed, and their scientific value, if any, was lost. [12]

The love of adventure manifested in seeking new scenes beyond the wide seas, became for two or three generations an absorbing passion with multitudes. Nowhere was this spirit more prevalent or more fruitful than in Portugal. To her sons must be given the credit of having taken the lead in the maritime discovery of the period, and foremost among them must be ranked Prince Henry, the Navigator. [13]

Fig. 38 - Henry the Navigator and Prince João, later King João II, who said No! to Christopher Columbus. Contemporary portrait. Courtesy of the Biblioteca Nacional, Lisbon, Portugaal

Prince Henry the Navigator is a term coined in the 18th century. Infante D. Henrique in Portuguese, was born in the city of Porto on March 4, 1394, and died on November 13, 1460. During this period, very important events took place. The following are just some of them that may have opened the oceans for the Melungeons – or other groups, including Portuguese – presence in North America.

While the Portuguese prepared their first venture in North Africa, much secrecy was involved, and almost failed due to the fact that Portuguese Queen Filipa – Henry's mother – had a Black Jew as a servant who saw a letter revealing the expedition to Ceuta, supposedly a very well kept secret. The conquering of Ceuta on Aug. 21, 1415, was the beginning of the march from west to east. In that expedition were used 240 ships – 27 galleys triremes, 63 round transport boats and 120 others – 50,000 men of which 30,000 were oarsmen and soldiers. Also was a boat loaded with armed soldiers that moved fast, with the vigorous impulse of the oarsmen. Henry's purpose was to gather more information about the Far East and the caravans arriving there with precious and rare merchandise from India, China, etc. Apparently in that battle there was no mention of capture of Moors as slaves.

One of the best sources of information that Henry had was his brother Pedro, duke of Coimbra, who traveled extensively in Europe. From 1425 to 1428 he spent much time traveling throughout Europe. The first visit was to Castile's King Juan II, his cousin. After that to England, where he intervened with success in a conflict between John de Gaunt and his uncle the Duke of Gloucester. Then he went to Bruges, Cologne, Vienna, Hungary, Romania, Venice, Florence, Rome, Catalonia and Aragon. In the Italian Peninsula he stayed for a long while because that area of the Mediterranean had intense relations with the Arab world. Here Prince Pedro visited the naval yards and casually gathered important information on the construction of ships, which he passed along to Henry. There were plenty of myths about islands having been discovered by the Phoenicians and others may be taken seriously according to the evidence presented, such as the Antilles, Seven Cities, etc. [14]

The first Portuguese settlement attempt was on Madeira island, which almost failed in the beginning but prospered later on with vine plants that came from Chipre Island and sugar cane from Sicily.

It was not until 1435 that the Portuguese navigators first met black people, south of Cape Bojador, off Northeast Africa.

Henry's father, King João I, died and his son Duarte was crowned. During that same period, it was in Portugal that the Jews found relative security, in spite of the friction and disagreements. At the time King Duarte was crowned, the Jewish community was disseminated all over Portugal and had reached large proportions, a nation within a nation.

Antão Gonçalves captured ten Berbers in the East Sahara in 1441, with different tones of skin color, darker and light. Out of these, one seemed to be a noble Berber. His name was Adahu. He spoke Arabic and appeared to be a well traveled man with much knowledge. They were taken to Portugal, and Henry obtained valuable information. That Berber later arranged, for himself and two more, a return trip to the Sahara, with the promise that he would give in exchange ten black slaves.

In 1443 the first shipment of black slaves arrived in Portugal from Africa, south of the Sahara desert. After that, village was thrown against village, kingdom against kingdom, on a ferocious hunting for slaves by the black chiefs that lasted several centuries.

In 1445, voluntary wealthy navigators wanted to equip ships and, on their own, sail across the sea in search of fortune. The art of navigation was well known, even by the fishermen that would venture much further south – Rio de Ouro – to fill their nets. *Not only the adventurers, wanted to go on Maritimes voyages, but also many others, just for the honor of serving under Henry, the Navigator.* [15] The Berbers of the Sahara region would eagerly await the arrival of the Portuguese caravels. On one of the voyages they climbed aboard the ships in groups, where they spent all day having fun. That did not last long due to Gomes Pires, who having been cheated by one of the Berbers, threw all of them out, captured 80, and brought them to Portugal.[16] That was the only capture of Berbers known. Would their descendants emigrate later in the 16th century to America?

During that period Diogo Gomes, (1440-84) a Portuguese explorer, was sent by Prince Henry to investigate the West African coast about 1456.

The so-called *Catalan Atlas* of 1375 was made for the King of Aragon by Abraham Cresques, a Jew of Palma of Mayorca working for the king. As the persecution of the Jews resumed in Aragon late in the 14th century, Abraham's son Jehuda, who was carrying on his father's work, was forced to emigrate. *Accepting the invitation of Prince Henry, he took refuge in Portugal, where he helped the Portuguese prepare the maps for their overseas discoveries.* [17]

This Jew must be the same one mentioned by Oliveira Matins, a 19th century Portuguese historian. In his book *Portugal nos Mares* the name is spelled differently, *Jafuda*. He had such a reputation and credit as a cosmographer that he was known as the Compasses' Jew or *o Judeu das Bússolas*.

Later on he changed his name to Jaime Ribes due to persecution in Aragon against the Jews and may be the one that later taught at the primitive Sagres School of Navigation with Prince Henry the Navigator. [18]

The techniques for marking latitudes were developed by the Portuguese in the 15th century by mariners sailing down the coast of Africa.

Between 1419 and 1433, about 20 sea exploratory voyages were made by the Portuguese, and for many of them no records were found of their discoveries.

Due to the scarcity of human and material resources, the Portuguese King João II left the west explorations up to private enterprise. *Only the African Coast explorations were made at the expenses of the Crown.* [19] That may also explain the privately financed trips of which no records were made.

Portuguese Secrecy of Navigation - Portuguese Navigators

Bonnie Ball writes: *It is not beyond the realm of possibility that some Portuguese sailors could in fact be ancestors of the Melungeons, for their unrecorded explorations could have easily reached into North America.* [20]

The breach of secrecy, passing of secrets to Spain or any other nation, was punishable by death, and that was a deterrent.[21] Unfortunately, not keeping records did not help the historians but did help the Portuguese then, as it took many years for the other European nations to accomplish the same as the Portuguese did around the world. *In 1531 and during the reigning of King João III, the silence of the best pilots was paid a high price, and the indiscretion of the cartographers could result in severe punishments or even summary.* [22]

Fernand Braudel notes that King João II ordered the Portuguese pilot who told him that it was possible to get back from the coast of Mina with any ship in good condition, to remain silent on threat of imprisonment. [23] However, Morrison does not give much credit to this alleged secrecy by the Portuguese, thus discounting any early discoveries by the Portuguese navigators based on oral history. But on the other hand he fully credits Cabot's discovery of Newfoundland under the English flag, based solely on oral versions of his voyage.

It was the secrecy that enabled King João II to sign the Treaty of Tordesilles, advantageous to Portugal. During King Manuel I's reign, the death penalty was established for anyone divulging navigation secrets. [24]

Although hard proof may not be available, the oldest sources available demonstrate that astronomical navigation was invented and developed by the Portuguese in the late 15th century. *Again to some extent this has been created by the existence of policies of secrecy.* [25]

Skelton points out that Portuguese maps went to *humanist Konrad Peutinger (1465-1547) who had particular opportunities for collecting in Portugal.* [26]

Allied to secrecy and stealing is also the destruction of many documents, to the point that the Portuguese do not even know the precise date of the death of Camões, Portugal's great epic poet (sometime between 1579 and 1580) nor the location of his tomb. [26a] *Not a single manuscript with his own hand writing has survived...* [27] He was well known by his contemporaries, and famous throughout Europe with his epic poems being translated and published. It is therefore not surprising that documentation proving the Portuguese discoveries is not available.

Historian Morison does not accept the Portuguese policy of secrecy as an excuse for not having records and states that the secrecy was to protect Portugal, but apparently ended up benefiting Spain, England and France, as it would be very hard to keep secrets in the 15th century. However, secrecy existed then and still does today in practically every country. There are spies and counter spies and double agents. Back then it was no different.

Holland also benefited in no small way, as stated in the *History of the Western World - Ancient Times to 1715 ...The Portuguese tended to be close with the secrets of navigation on the sea road to the Indies, secrets which they patiently accumulated over nearly two centuries of exploration. Fortunately for the Dutch, a Netherlander, Jan Huyghen van Linschoten, who had spent six years with the Portuguese in India, published a very informative book of sailing directions. Equipped with this guide, in 1595 a Dutch expedition...* [28]

Russell Miller in his book *The East Indiamen,* adds: *Until its publication in*

1596, information about the Orient had been sparse and details of Portuguese trade there a well kept secret. [29]

There is one factor, however that historians sometimes forget: in the 15th century illiteracy was common among most fishermen, sailors, and possible some of the early navigators. Only a chosen few could read or write. How could they keep records if they could not write? That was the best secret, except sailors did a lot of gossip, and that is why the oral stories told throughout the centuries should not be completely disregarded.

In order to help solve the problem, according to one chronicle, a Captain decided to tie a bundle of garlic over one side of the ship and a handful of onions over the other. Then the pilot would shout to the helmsmen, *onion your helm* or *Garlic your elm.* [29a]

Louis André Vigneras, a professor at George Washington University makes this point quite clear: *...The armada de Sancho de Archiniea, bringing in supplies and reinforcements from Spain, finally reached St. Augustine on June 20 (1566). With this fleet came a man who would play a leading role...He was Domingo Fernández, a pilot whom the Spanish general placed implicit trust. Although an* **illiterate** *man who could not even sign his own name, Fernández must have been a first class pilot...And since Fernández was one of the few pilots who knew the coast of Florida...he acted more or less as (piloto mayor).* [30]

João Rocha Pinto, in his book about ship log books, concludes that there were no log books during the major part of the 16th century, and that only after 1530 do we start seeing an attempt to record the daily navigation. Some narrations were made, but there was far from a daily record of the voyages. Only towards the end of the 16th century evolved the daily practice of recording the magnetic needle deviation of the latitude and longitude. [31]

The passage of Neville Williams' book *Great Lives* about Drake, shows that secrecy existed and the Portuguese were not the only ones to keep secret their plans. Francis Drake did not reveal the full purpose of his voyages or his intentions of sailing into the Pacific, in advance to his crew. He gave his officer colleagues on board the bare information necessary to conduct the ship to the next port. [32] Some historians still do not believe that the Portuguese had a strong policy of secrecy during the early period of the discoveries. [33]

Charles Boxer, who wrote Portuguese *Roteiros* (logbooks, 1500-1700), mentions the ones kept by João de Castro in 1538: *because the needle of the compass varied on board ship*, when moved from one place to another, he concluded that this was due to the fact that it had been placed near a cannon, and that the iron attracted to itself the needle and made it move. *...noted 128 years before it was vaguely suggested by Denis of Dieppe.* [34]

Portuguese Navigators Working for other Countries

During the times of Portuguese discoveries, at least 68 Portuguese navigators worked for Spain - 25 for France, six for England and one for Holland. [35] Kennedy said it better: *The Portuguese did indeed play a major but unheralded role in the Spanish expeditions.*[36]

The number of the Portuguese navigators that worked for Portugal is definitely much greater. These were the registered ones, but it is believed that there were many more. However, Portugal also had foreign men working in the navy, but mostly cartographers or astrologers.

In 1457 the Venetian Alvise Ca' da Mosto (Cadamosto), envoy of the Portuguese Prince Henry the Navigator, explored the Ziguinchor harbor, a river-port town, in southwestern Senegal, lying along the Casamance River, and discovered the river Gambia in 1455, plus the Senegal in 1457. [37] He said when he saw the first caravel, *it was the best ship on the sea, and that was not a place where it could not navigate.* Another foreign navigator, Amerigo Vespucci – later he lent his name to the North and South American continents – worked for Portugal in 1501-02, and helped to explore the South American coast of Brazil before he went to work for Spain in 1503. [38] Also several Spanish sailors joined the Portuguese expeditions of Pedro Álvares Cabral to Brasil and India.[39]

During an interview with professor and Portuguese historian Dr. Saraiva, he stated that Queen Isabel of Castile, was known to have said that the best nanny she knew was the king of Portugal, because he raised the gentlemen (fidalgos) from little children and would give them to her when they were already grown up.[40] This was true, as Portuguese men were and still are fond of Spanish women; many Portuguese nobles would go to Spain, and eventually marry there.

Discovery of Madeira Island - 1424

These islands off North Africa's Atlantic coast may have been visited by Arabs and others before the Portuguese, but no attempt was ever made to claim or settle them. There is a legend about the main island, Madeira, known by Madeirans, which may have been started and perpetuated by the English. The legend has its beginnings in England, when a couple in love did not have the approval of the parents. They decided to run away in a boat with a small crew and, due to a storm landed in Madeira. Later the young maiden died, was buried and an inscription was made in the tombstone. Her lover died shortly after and the crew left the island to tell the story. As in all legends, there are no dates. The name of the Englishman was Machin and the lady was Anna de Harfet. [41] There is today a place in Madeira called Machico. There are, however, other stories, such as one about a merchant also called Machico who conducted business in Portuguese ports during the 1370s. [42]

Whoever had been there provided information for Prince Henry's later discovery. By 1417 or 1419 the Portuguese navigators João Gonçalves Zarco, Tristão Vaz Teixeira and Bartolomeu Perestrelo, may have landed there. The names of the islands derived from the Latin, such as ("legname" wood) for the main island. The others, Porto Santo and Desertas, did not need translation.

The Portuguese, after arriving in Porto Santo, planted crops. However, in the beginning this turned out a complete failure due to a rabbit. Apparently someone gave Bartolomeu Perestrelo, a pregnant rabbit as he was leaving Portugal. During the voyage little rabbits were born, and later, on arrival he put them loose on the island. Naturally the rabbits proliferated and ate all the crops. But, as tradition has it, the first female and male children born on the island were named Adam and Eve.[43] Later, the slaves from the Canary Islands provided a large part of the population. [44]

Pizzigano Map - 1424

There is cartographic evidence that the Portuguese were in Newfoundland before August 22, 1424, according to the Italian Zuanne Pizzigano's nautical chart. He may have been Italian, but the names he used were Portuguese. Dr. Manuel Luciano da Silva describes it in detail in his book *The True Antilles*. This chart would represent a Venetian adaptation of a Portuguese cartographic design which made its way to Italy, documenting real discoveries in the west made by the Portuguese at this early stage. [45]

This opinion is shared by the Portuguese historian Armando Cortesão and Lieutenant-Commander Avelino Teixeira da Mota, who wrote: *we are convinced...which in this chart lie westward of the Azores...visited by unknown Portuguese at an early date, probably just before 1424.* [46] This view is not necessarily shared by all historians. On this same map, a note appears in the middle of the Atlantic naming the area as the Sargasso Sea, knowledge obtained from the Portuguese, thus indicating they had been much farther west, possibly close to the North American continent.

Dr. Silva has discovered that the proper latitudinal position of the Antilles on a present map places them in approximately the same location as Newfoundland and Nova Scotia in Canada. There are also Portuguese names on the same map. [47] The Pizzigano map, now in the University of Minnesota library, was studied by historian Armando Cortesão in 1950. The Portuguese presence in the Antilles is confirmed by the reputed discovery, by the Soviet historian Tspernick in 1959, of a letter from King Fernando and Queen Isabel of Spain which states that Columbus knew of the existence of land in the Antilles before starting out on his voyage, because he had heard about this from a sailor, Alonzo Sanches, who had mapped the Antilles. A study of this map may be read in Vol. II of *Historia da Cartografia Portuguesa* by Armando Cortesão.

A Portuguese by the name of Dualmo, if we are to believe the British historian A. Davies, sailed from the Azores in 1487 and discovered America five years ahead of Columbus. [48] Also, with Prince Henry's encouragement at least one enterprising navigator seems to have reached the Maritime Provinces of Canada around 1424. Unfortunately we do not know his name, but the Pizzigano map gives us the cartographic evidence of his visit. [49]

The historian Samuel Eliot Morison calls the isles drawn on this map *The Fabulous Antilles Group* and dismisses the *discoveries because the names appeared only on Italian, Spanish, or other maps but never on Portuguese map.*[50] Again, secrecy would have been one reason for not recording lands discovered in maps, such as the Antilles. One should ask, what does Morison mean by Italian map in the 15th century since there was no such country as Italy? Probably he means one of the Republics in the Italic Peninsula. If so, the words most likely were in Latin.

In the 15th century there was no abundance of maps showing the exact position of continents, much less countries or islands. However with all the secrecy, the earliest map showing the East Coast of North America was made in Portugal, as we shall see in the following pages.

Professor Morison not only rejected Dr. Cortesão's conclusions but he also had some harsh words for the Portuguese University of Coimbra. [51]

Discovery of the Azores - 1427-32

These Islands were the westernmost known place in the Atlantic and historians point to 1427 as a possible early date of the discovery by Diogo de Silves. The most cited date of discovery is August 14, 1432, by Gonçalo Velho Cabral however there is no documentary proof. The actual distance between the Azores, the most westward landfall and the North American Continent was unknown at that time.

The Azores were the most important stop, first for the Portuguese when exploring the west coast of Africa, after for the Spaniards when going or returning from the West Indies and later for the English privateers awaiting the return of the Spanish galleons laden with treasure. Many battles were fought off the Azores, and in one of them which took place off Flores Island in 1591, Grenville, an English vice-admiral at the time, was killed and his vessel *Revenge* sunk in a storm on the way to Cadiz as a Spanish prize. [52] Also, *Pedro de Valdez* (or Pedro Menéndes de Aviles, the founder of St. Augustine) *was defeated in the Battle of Salga on July 25th 1581, when attempting to invade Terceira Island.* [53]

Portuguese in Labrador and Newfoundland - 1452-74

History, in order to be believed, must have solid proof of written records plus other archaeological or anthropological findings. The explorers had their names recorded for posterity. However, the true pioneers of discovery in eastern North America were very often the fishermen, from whom the navigators received information brought back from their fishing trips.Their knowledge was considered valuable news to the navigators. John Bartlet Brebner wrote about the European fishermen of Newfoundland. *These nameless men, Portuguese, Basques, Bretons and Englishmen, were the really consistent maintainers of European contact with north-eastern North America, rather than the explorers who from time to time got their names recorded in documents of state.* [54]

Right after the settlement of the Azores, the fever of discovery filled the mind of many seamen, who asked the king to grant them special advantages of lands or islands that they eventually would discover. Based on obscure and imprecise information of various documents, some historians believe the Portuguese navigators arrived in Newfoundland or at least on nearby waters, shortly after 1450, and certainly before 1480. This affirmation is extremely bold after reading the documentation. [55] The above commentary was written by Luis de Albuquerque in a book by Maria da Graça Pericão. He may be right, but after some investigation, no proof has been presented in one way or the other. This historian also said that there was no such a thing as a navigation School of Sagres. [56] Well, it all depends what was meant in the 15th century as a School. Did it have a large building and a Faculty staff, professors, etc. such as the University of Coimbra in those days? Most likely not. But what would you call a place where learned men met to discuss and learn from each other, as well as teach those around them?

The Greek philosopher Plato taught in a garden called Academus, and Aristotle his pupil started his school of logic, metaphysics, etc., in a garden called Lyceum. Should we say that those schools never existed?

Based on Chapter IX of the *Historia de Colon* (Italian translation), written by his son Fernando Colon, and Chapter XIII of the *Historia de las Indias* by Las Casas, a voyage was made to the banks of Newfoundland by the Portuguese Diogo de Teive and the Spanish Pero Vasquez de la Frontera. [57]

Columbus's son Fernando wrote that his father collected information in Portugal about an island 200 leagues from the Azores and Canaries, and that some Portuguese sailors were pushed there by a storm, but afterwards could not get back since they did not know the way. [58]

Possible voyages by Álvaro Martins Homem and João Vaz Corte Real may have been made to Canada, but nothing was ever recorded, except that in a letter by the Princess Dona Brites, a voyage was made in 1472 or 1474. [59] Another Terceiran, João Fernandes, called o *Lavrador* from his occupation as a farmer or small landowner, went on a voyage of exploration to the north in 1492 (or 1499) together with one Pedro de Barcelos. It has been surmised, chiefly from maps showing the Land of Labrador, that Fernandes discovered what is now known as Labrador; but closer investigation suggests that the land he visited is the present Greenland. [60] Secrecy is one of the reasons presented; however, historians scorn that. The distance from Azores is rather close, and fishermen were known to venture out to sea for long periods of time in search of good fishing, which the banks of Newfoundland provided.

Bartolomeu Dias and Cape of Good Hope - 1488

Four years before Columbus' first voyage, Dias, a Portuguese navigator, rounded the Cape of Good Hope in South Africa. That may have nothing to do with the presence of the Portuguese on the U.S. East Coast but, as we will discover later, it does present us with an interesting possibility, as the traffic of caravels for the following 50 years was so heavy that vessels almost bumped into each other, and many disappeared without a trace, not having reached their chartered destination. Later in 1500, Dias' Caravel was lost in the same area, when going to India as part of the Cabral fleet. [61]

Fig. 39 - This is considered as the only authentic Columbus portrait 1507-15. Courtesy of Biblioteca Nacional, Madrid.

Columbus in America - 1467-92

When the grandchildren of famous Portuguese navigators were already sailing, Christopher Columbus, of questionable Genovese birth, crossed the Atlantic and landed on the West Indies. Skelton points out that *before 1500 Portugal had a hydrographic office charged with the custody and correction of sea charts.* [62]

Certainly it must have been easy for Columbus to attain the sea navigation knowledge he needed. He derived much of his nautical knowledge and interests from the Portuguese.

Historian Samuel Eliot Morison, a much cited author, states with conviction:

...without the preliminary work of the Portuguese, the... Voyage of Columbus could not have attained its object. [63]

Rev. George Patterson, on his presentation to the Royal Society of Canada in 1890 said: *There is no reason to believe that it was in these explorations that*

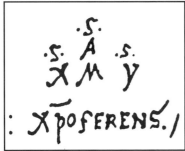

Fig. 40-Columbus's Signature

Columbus was led to those conclusions, which issued in the discovery of America, he was in Portugal from 1470 to 1484, during which time he made several voyages to the coast of Guinea in the Portuguese service. [64]

A famous Norwegian historian and seafarer, Thor Heyerdhal, claimed that Columbus arrived in America in 1467, and not in 1492. [65] He goes on to say that archive studies show that Columbus was in America long before he discovered it, on a Danish-Portuguese expedition to the Davis Strait in 1467. This Norwegian researcher, who gained fame for his daring 1947 trans-Atlantic voyage aboard a flimsy raft, said that Columbus did not accidentally stumble onto the American continent while looking for India, as most historians believe. Instead, he knew exactly where to sail because he traveled with a Danish-Portuguese expedition to Greenland as a teenage crew member.

To his credit, it can be said that at that time (1448-1481), Portuguese King Afonso V was trying to reach East India using the northern route, and negotiated with the Danish King Christian for a joint venture.

Portuguese association with Danish and English exploration is well known. Close relationships between Portugal and Denmark in the 15th century were a result of royal marriages and the visit of Prince Pedro – brother of Henry the Navigator – to Denmark in 1426, after evidently hearing reports of expeditions to Greenland.

The Portuguese king supplied ships and crews, and the Danish king supplied two Norwegians, Didrick Pining and Hans Pothorst. João Vaz Corte Real was made viceroy for whatever they would discover. The narration of this voyage is a brief one because of the reluctance of Portugal to publicize their discoveries, and so this adventure was so shrouded in secrecy that its discoveries were not made known. [66]

Armando Cortesão stated: ...*beside Pinzón in Castile, there was in Portugal many that were convinced the existence of such lands (America) and even already been there.* [67] That only proves that the Portuguese knew for a long time where America was, except no one was interested in this continent. Their aim was to reach India or the Far East. We have to draw a similar parallel: The Chinese knew where Europe was in the 15th century and how to get there, they also had the resources to make the voyage, and they did not do it because they were not interested and ...*deliberately turned their backs on maritime expansion before the end of the*

15th century. [68] The original narrative of his (Columbus) third voyage tells us that he arrived on Porto Santo on Thursday June 7th, 1498, where he stopped to take wood, water and supplies and to hear mass. Next Columbus arrived in Madeira on Sunday, June 10, was very well received in Funchal and with much rejoicing, because he was well known there, having been a *citizen thereof during some time.* [69]

Fig. 41 - Vasco da Gama, portrait painting. Courtesy of the Museu Nacional de Arte Antiga, Portugal.

Vasco da Gama
Sea Route to India - 1498

Six years after Columbus discovered America, trying to get to India or the Far East – without ever getting there – the Portuguese found the sea route to India, quickly establishing a profitable trade. Vasco da Gama's fleet was composed of four caravels and 160 men, all well chosen as the best sailors that Portugal had, many of them nobles.

Vasco da Gama departed on July 9, 1497 and arrived in May 1498 in Calicut. His ships cruised uncharted seas for 4,500 miles, a voyage of 96 days, without a glimpse of land. Columbus had sailed for 3,500 miles after he left the Canaries, when he sighted the Bahamas. [69a] *Gama's 23,800 mile to India and back stands unique in navigation history.* [69b]

A contemporary narration mentions the effects of s*curvy*, without knowing at the time that it could be cured just by eating fresh fruits. Not untill the 18th century both were connected by Captain James Cook. Dr. Luciano da Silva has also written a medical article about Camões and scurvy.

A poem from the Lusiads. *This masterpiece of Camões, one of the world's greatest epic poems, is the finest monument to Vasco da Gama's genius.* [69c]

> Nor less of pomp the Lusitanian shows
> When, with his gallant retinue, advance
> The Armada's boats, midway to welcome those
> Of the Melindan on the bay's expense
> Clad in the vogue of Spain, Da Gama goes
> All but the cloak, a gorgeous robe of France,
> The web Venetian satin, and the dye
> A glorious crimson that delights the eye. [69d]

Fig. 42 - Painting by José Velloso Salgado, Sociedade de Geografia de Lisboa, depicting Vasco da Gama at the Court of the Zamorin of Calicut in India.

The Forgotten Portuguese

Fig. 43 - Pedro Álvares Cabral as depicted in an 18th century engraving [70]

Vasco da Gama's discovery may not be related with the U.S. East Coast, but, as we will find later in one of the next chapters, it may have something to do with the subject being researched.

Also in this same year, Duarte Pacheco Pereira may have reached Florida. [71] The following year the Spanish Alonso de Ojeda, accompanied by the Florentine Amerigo Vespucci, sailed to the mouth of the Orinoco and explored the coast of Venezuela. It is interesting to note that Vasco da Gama's route to India brought his fleet quite close to Brazil; hence, he may already have known of the existence of lands to the west.

Pedro Álvares Cabral in Brazil by Accident - 1500

The Brazilian discovery by accident has been one lie perpetuated by less informed writers. Here is what Charles Ralph Boxer says in his book *The Portuguese Seaborne Empire: ...during three years the Portuguese were making secret voyages in the south Atlantic in order to familiarize themselves with the sailing conditions there.* [72]

Cabral explored well over a thousand miles of the Brazilian sea coast, a fact in itself that he had previous knowledge of the area. This fact was reported by Venetian diplomats, in conflict with the veiled letter that King Manuel I sent to the Pope. [73]

Kennedy in his book, probably due to an oversight, wrote: *Renowned Portuguese explorer Pedro Álvares Cabral discovered Brazil in 1500 by accident. Rounding the southern tip of Africa and heading northward on his return to Portugal, Cabral made a miscalculation that took him farther west than he intended. Where the South American and African continents are at their closest, Cabral unexpectedly "bumped" into Brazil.* [74] Actually he landed in Brazil when he was heading southward on the way to Africa. Most likely Kennedy will make a correction in the next edition.

As for Cabral's accidental discovery, that he *unexpectedly "bumped" into Brazil*, it is a well known fact that he was not the first Portuguese navigator to arrive in Brazil. Others preceded him. Kennedy quotes Zvi Dor-Ner rather differently due to the generally accepted belief about Cabral's discovery.

Here is how Zvi Dor-Ner describes Cabral's landing on the coast of Brazil: *In*

1500 the Portuguese explorer Pedro Álvares Cabral, who had been following Vasco da Gama's route to India via Africa's Cape of Good Hope, swung far to the west after rounding the bulge of Africa and became the first person in recorded history to land on the coast of Brazil. [75] The book *Civilization in the West* written by Christopher Brinton and Robert Lee Wolf from Harvard University and Robert Lee Wolf from the University of Rochester, notes: *It may be that this was not accidental as it seems.* [76] By 1500 the Spanish were well launched in exploration, and Columbus' voyages were well known. In 1493, after Columbus' first voyage, Pope Alexander VI had granted to Spain all lands south and west of a north-south line drawn in the Atlantic between the Azores and the Cape Verde Islands. In 1494, the Portuguese, by the Treaty of Tordesilles with Spain, succeeded in having this line moved 270 leagues farther west. Thus Brazil fell into the sphere of the Portuguese, who may have known about it all along, and who only announced their landing there after Cabral's voyage. *In any case, it was now determined that Brazil alone in Latin America would be Portuguese; everything else lay on the Spanish side of the line.* [77] There is, however, a little known fact: In the 18th century, Uruguay was located on the Portuguese side, but later was exchanged by the Portuguese for Amazons, which was on the Spanish side. Because of that, Uruguay's language is Spanish and the Amazons', Portuguese.

Duarte Pacheco Pereira, Portuguese sea captain and explorer, may have discovered Brazil in 1498, two years before Pedro Álvares Cabral explored the Brazilian coast. Because of his military exploits in India, the poet Camões called him Aquiles Lusitano (the Portuguese Achilles). The only indication that he may have been in Brazil in 1498 is his writing of the *Esmeraldo situ orbis*, where he states that the king had ordered him to discover the western part beyond the great ocean. [78]

Pacheco Pereira, reared at the Portuguese court, was an educated man, serving as a squire to King João II. He became an expert cartographer as well as a pilot and shipmaster. He explored the coast of Africa in 1488, returning with Bartolomeu Dias, who had discovered the Cape of Good Hope. Pereira sailed with Dias in 1500 on the voyage during which Cabral claimed Brazil for the king of Portugal. In 1504 Pacheco Pereira helped defend the Portuguese trading station at Cochin, India, against attacks by the ruler of Calicut. With about 200 Portuguese, Pereira successfully held off armies that numbered well over 20,000 men.

Returning to Portugal in 1505, Pereira received many honors. He collected his log books and charts and wrote a valuable account of Portuguese exploration – published in modern editions in 1892 and 1903. He was appointed governor of São Jorge da Mina but fell into disgrace when enemies reported that he had embezzled official funds. He was exonerated, but he died shortly thereafter in poverty. The narrative of the third voyage of Columbus in 1498 reads that Columbus said, *he wished to go south… and that he wishes to see what was the idea of King João II of Portugal, who said that there was mainland to the south.* [79]

This and other facts should not be ignored when establishing what the Portuguese discovered.

As a matter of interest, it also should be noted that Antonio Galvão wrote a book in 1550, translated into English in 1601 and reprinted in 1862 with notes by the admiral Bethune. Galvão states that in 1428 Prince Pedro – brother of Henry the Navigator – received in Venice a world map that supposedly showed the African and South American continents. In 1447 Andrea Biancho, a Venetian cartographer working for Fra Mauro, was in Lisbon on the way to London. While in London he made a nine-page atlas based on information obtained in Portugal. That same information may have been related to a 1447 voyage that was reported in Galvão's book. The Biancho atlas shows a large island located 1500 miles west of Cape Verde, which in itself is amazing, taking into consideration that it was in error by only 20 miles. [80]

Much has been written about the discovery of Brazil; however, the end is still not in sight, with more information being unveiled as time passes. One example of this is Chapter V of Jaime Cortesão's book *Os Descobrimentos Portugueses*.

Cortesão and his brother, Dr. Armando Cortesão are history professors and have to their credit many books. American historian Samuel Eliot Morison has also refered to their books, not necessarily always agreeing with each other. One of the chapters, *Viagens pré-calabrinas ao Brasil* or *Voyages pre-Cabral to Brazil* in English, caught my attention and presents a different story. When Martin Afonso de Sousa, working for Spain, in 1531, on the way to Argentina, anchored in Cananeia (state of São Paulo) met a man in exile (*degredado*) that history would call the Bachelor of Cananeia. Pêro Lopes mentioned this man on the exploration's log book as having been there (Brazil) for a good 30 years.

If this was the case he had lived there since 1501. This does not seem to make sense; and then, to make matters worse, Diogo Garcia, a Portuguese pilot also working for Spain wrote in Spanish about events in 1527: *...E aqui fuímos a tomar refresco en San Vicente, que está en 20 grados e alli vive un Bachieller y unos yernos suyos mucho tiempo ha que ha bien treinta años.* [81] In English: *...here we went to have refreshment in San Vicente, which is at 20 degrees and there lives a Bachelor and his sons-in-law for a long time, a good thirty years.* Diogo Garcia, in 1530, when he returned to Andalucia, Spain, refered to the arrival of the *Bachelor of Cananeia* in 1497 or 1500. The expression *bien treinta años,* a good thirty years, must mean more than thirty.

Rui Diaz de Guzmãn qualifies the Bachelor as a Portuguese gentleman or *Fidalgo* and calls him Duarte Pires in his book *La Argentina,* written in 1612. Then by chance a document dated April 24, 1499, was found, which mentions a certain exiled Bachelor and no other name. The common designation is *Bachelor* and *exiled*, which led Dr. Cortesão to believe that it was the same person. The reference is part of a long will by Álvaro de Caminha, Captain of São Tomé Island, off west Africa, which also describes the colonization of that isle, in which Jewish babies took part, sent there by King João II. [82]

By this document it can be concluded that there existed on the island a deposit of exiled persons. At least 65 names are mentioned.

The same document mentions the Bachelor and the way his belongings should be disposed of, without mentioning that he was dead, but rather that he was absent from the island. It is assumed with certainty that he was the same person being mentioned, the Bachelor in Africa and South America. But if that was the case, how did he get to Cananeia?

Admiral Gago Coutinho, another famous Portuguese – historian and pilot – admitted Bartolomeu Dias as being one of the discoverers of Brazil. This navigator was the first European to go around the tip of South Africa in 1488, opening the way to the Portuguese sea route to India.

Bartolomeu Dias was on São Tomé Island and left towards the end of 1497. Is this the same Bartolomeu Dias, or another navigator with the same name that took the Bachelor to Cananeia? Another Portuguese already mentioned had the same task, that is to go from São Tomé to explore the Brazilian coast in 1498. [83]

This fact enforces the previous assumption - and Cortesão believes - that the Bachelor of São Tomé left that island at the end of the 15th century in a caravel commanded by Bartolomeu Dias. We should not overlook the fact that, in order to reach the southern tip of Africa, any sailing ship must sail west towards South America to catch the proper winds and currents going in a southeast direction. Trade winds and currents (Brazilian current) were the cause of many shipwrecks. Bartolomeu Dias knew that in 1488, and Duarte Pacheco knew in 1498.

1498 - 1998 - 500 Years Later

Portugal is celebrating the 500 years of the Discovery of the Sea Route to India in 1998. Lisbon was chosen as the site for the World Expo in 1998. The theme, is the Oceans, thus remembring their contribuition to mankind by making it possible for the approximation of cultures from all over the world.

Vasco da Gama discovery's, raised his native Portugal to the peak of wealth and power among the nations of Europe.

16th Century astrolabe. Lisbon Maritime Museum. The Portuguese were the first sailors to use the astrolabe, a device for taking the altitudes of celestial bodies, as navigational instrument.

Notes

[1] The Discoverers by Daniel J. Borstin, p. 145 (Peter Martyr d'Anghiera)

[2] Model of a Caravel Nau São Rafael of the "Museu da Marinha de Lisboa"

[3] Portvgaliae Monvmenta Cartografica by Armando Cortesão, pp. xxv-xxix

[4] The European Discovery of America by Samuel Eliot Morison, p. 94

[5] The Portuguese Seaborne Empire by Charles R. Boxer, front cover

[6] Portuguese Roteiros by C.R. Boxer, p. 185

[7] Newfoundland from Fisheries to Colony by David Beers Quinn, p.183

[8] The Mediterranean World by Fernand Braudel, p. 108

[9] The Colonial Experience by David Hawke, p. 8

[10] The Mediterranean World by Fernand Braudel, p. 108

[11] A History of the Western World by
Clough - Garsoian - Hicks - Brandenburg - Gay, p. 367

[12] Infante D. Henrique e sua época by Mario Domingues, p.19

[13] The Portuguese in the NE Coast of America by Rev. George Patterson, p. 127

[14] Infante D. Henrique e sua época by Mario Domingues, p.154

[15] Ibid, p.276, first edition

[16] Ibid, pp.67,70,82,88,120,133,206-331

[17] The Discoverers by Daniel J. Boorstin, p. 150

[18] Historia de Portugal by Oliveira Marques, Vol. I, p. 264-7

[19] Colombo em Portugal, Marinha Portuguesa, p.15

[20] The Melungeons by Bonnie Ball, p.29, Aug.22/1937,
Nashville Banner, James Aswell

[21] Interview with Professor José Hermano Saraiva, July 1995

[22] Portugal nos Mares by Oliveira Martins, p.280,1

[23] The Structures of Everyday Life by Fernand Braudel, p. 412

[24] Historia da Expansão Portuguesa no Mundo by Antonio Baião, p.19

[25] Portugal and the Discovery of the Atlantic by
Alfredo Pinheiro Marques, p. 80

[26] Maps by R. A. Skelton, p. 41

[26a] June 10, 1580 has been established as Portugal's National Day.
The Visconde de Juromenha discovered in a document found in the
Torre do Tombo (Portuguese National Archives) that
Luis Vaz de Camões, died on that date. Some historians still dispute it.

[27] Luis de Camões by Vasco Graça Moura, p. 17

[28] A History of the Western World by
Clough-Garsoian-Hicks-Brandenburg-Gay, pp. 452-453

[29] The East Indiamen by Russel Miller, p. 26

[29a] National Geographic Magazine, November 1927, p. 511

[30] A Spanish Discovery of North Carolina by L. A. Vigneras, p. 403

[31] Houve diários de bordo durante os séculos XV e XVI? by
João Rocha Pinto, pp. 404-416

[32] Ibid, p. 270

[33] Great Lives, Sir Francis Drake by Neville Williams, p.88
[34] Portuguese Roteiros by C. R. Boxer, pp. 174-175
[35] Felisberto Roliz, Maps
[36] N. Brent Kennedy letter to Victor Marques of CNN (March 2, 1995)
[37] Encyclopedia Britannica, 1993
[38] Historia de España, Historia 16, p.507
[39] Knight of the Americas by Miguel Albornoz, p. 14
[40] Interview with Professor José Hermano Saraiva, July 1995
[41] As Saudades da Terra by Gaspar Frutuoso, p. 4
[42] Portugal and the Discovery of the Atlantic by
    Alfredo Pinheiro Marques, pp. 33-34
[43] Ibid, p. 38
[44] Os Escravos noArquipelago da Madeira bu Alberto Vieira, p. 48
[45] Portugal and the Discovery of the Atlantic by
    Alfredo Pinheiro Marques, p. 50
[46] Portvgaliae Monvmenta Cartografica by Armando Cortesão, p. xxxiii
[47] The True Antilles by Dr. Manuel Luciano da Silva, p. 6
[48] The Portuguese Americans by Leo Pap, p. 3
[49] Anomalies in Archaeology by W. David Crocket, p. 129
[50] The European Discovery of America by Samuel Eliot Morison, p. 102
[51] Historia da cartografia Portuguesa by Armando Cortesão, pp. 129-130
[52] The Sea Dogs by Neville Williams, p.203
[53] Azores Island a History by James H. Guill, Vol.5-329
[54] The Explorers of North America by John Bartlet Brebner, p. 114
[55] The Discovery of Florida by Maria da Graça Pericão, p. 122
[56] National Geographic Society by Merle Severy, p. 72 (November 1992)
[57] A Viagem de Diogo de Teive...de la Frontera ao
    Banco da Terra Nova by Jaime Cortesão, p. 5
[58] Historia da cartografia Portuguesa by Armando Cortesão, pp. 129-130
[59] Portuguese Pilgrims by Dr. Manuel Luciano da Silva, p. 28
[60] The Portuguese-Americans by Leo Pap, p. 4
[61] Historia de Portugal - Oliveira Marques, p.104,Vol. II.
[62] Maps by R. A. Skelton, p. 40
[63] Portuguese voyages to America in the 15th century by
    Samuel Eliot Morison, p.5
[64] Portuguese in Canada by Rev. George Patterson, p. 127
[65] Associated Press News Release, Summer of 1995
[66] Anomalies in Archaeology by W. David Crocket, p. 132
[67] Cartografia e Cartógrafos Portugueses dos séculos 15 e 16 by
    Armando Cortesão, p. 230
[68] The British Empire by Gerald S. Graham, p. 12
[69] The Northmen, Columbus and Cabot by Edward Bourne, p. 320
[69a] National Geographic Magazine, Nov. 1927, p. 516

[69b] Ibid, p. 507

[69c] Ibid, p. 550

[69d] Ibid, p. 531

[70] Historia de Portugal by Damião Peres, V. III, p. 595

[71] Historia de Portugal by Joaquim Verissimo Serrão, V. III, p.110

[72] The Portuguese Seaborne Empire by Charles R. Boxer. p. 36

[73] Historia de Portugal by Damião Peres, p. 598

[74] The Melungeons by Brent Kennedy, p.114

[75] Columbus and the Age of Discovery, 300., by Zvi Dor-Ner, p.300, 1991

[76] Civilization in the West by Christopher & Brinton, Wolff, p.293

[77] Ibid

[78] Historia de Portugal by Damião Peres, p. 596

[79] The Northmen, Columbus and Cabot by Olson and Bourne, p. 326

[80] Historia de Portugal by Damião Peres, pp. 591-2

[81] Os Descobrimentos Portugueses by Jaime Cortesão, p. 64

[82] Crónica d'el Rey D. João II by Rui de Pina, p. 1019

[83] Os Descobrimentos Portugueses by Jaime Cortesão, p. 67

* * *

Tratado da Esfera, used later by Portuguese kings as a symbol of discoveries around the world. Guia Nautico de Evora, c. 1516.

Sphere Armilar, used since the 16th century in the center of the Portuguese flag, including the present one.

Chapter VII

Portuguese Presence in North America - 15th and 16th Centuries

Giving due recognition to the presence of other nations on the field, however, enough has been adduced to show that the Portuguese occupied a prominent, I think I may say the foremost, place in the exploration of the north-east coast of America in the 16th century. [1]

This chapter shows the presence of Portuguese people in North America, and therefore the very likely possibility of the Melungeons and other groups having Portuguese ancestry, either directly or indirectly through intermarriage with other races, cultures and ethnic backgrounds.

Colonizing Process and Portuguese Methods

The first attempts at colonizing by the Portuguese were done by leaving domestic animals on the islands, such as pigs, cows and poultry to be used later as means of survival. Contrary to popular belief, the Portuguese were more concerned with trade than with conquest, [2] and it is reasonable to understand why.

Prince Henry adopted a method of releasing livestock in the places discovered in order to establish a claim of sovereignty as well as to re-supply the ships. He started that in Porto Santo, Madeira, Azores, and so on, which became an established practice.

According to a document dated January 1568 which spoke of a land *...where cattle were said to have been released in Prince Edward Island in Canada...* (French explorers... Breton Marquis de la Roche put down settlers who found cattle.) According to historian Marc Lescarbot, who wrote in 1608, the cattle had been released by a nobleman of the time of Francis I.

Samuel de Champlain also found cattle on the island during his voyage of 1613... *and stated that they have been left by the Portuguese.* [3]

Portuguese records show that in their colonizing process, Portugal actually encouraged their people to marry and mix with the natives, because they just did not have enough population to settle the immense world that they were discovering. Therefore they relied on later generations to keep the colonies for Portugal, which was the last colonial power to give them independence. William Freitas, Ph.D., professor from Stanford University, wrote that the *Portuguese settlement was family oriented.* [4] In 1550 the king promoted the importation of settlers from the Azores, to Brazil, however he preferred married couples. [5]

The Portuguese were and still are known as one of the peoples that better adapt to the culture of other peoples in which they have to live.

The society developed in the colonies was, in its evolution, less protected by consciousness of race, which was practically *non existent in the cosmopolitan and plastic-minded Portuguese.* [6] It may be an exaggeration to say that there was not racial discrimination at all, but it is true that the Portuguese were more liberal in this respect than the Dutch, the English or the French colonizers. [7]

The result is that presently that are many white Portuguese who proudly call themselves Angolans, Mozambiqueans, East Indians, Chinese and others. They have told the author, that they will be willing to return to Africa as soon as the war ends and the political situation is settled. They may be white, but have a strong nationalistic feeling of the African nation where they were born. A few years ago on a visit Macau, off the China mainland, the author spoke with a few people born in Macau with Oriental appearance. When asked about Portugal, they replied that they were sorry they could not speak Portuguese well or any at all, but they treasure their Portuguese Citizenship in their place of birth, although they have never been in Portugal.

Naturally, and due to miscegenation, you'll be able to find a Portuguese outside Portugal with different skin color and appearance.

Merchant Navy and Marine Traffic - 1500's

In the beginning of the 16th century there were already wealthy owners of fishing fleets, and in 1518-19 the overseas commerce represented 68% of the crown's income.[8] The New-Christians, as the people forced to convert mostly from Judaism were called, formed for the most part a middle class of merchants and capitalists. As such, they had access to the ships and commercial expeditions, which they financed on their own or by the Portuguese crown. While studying emigration patterns of the Portuguese, let us keep in mind that during the beginning of the 16th century, a strong possibility was being developed for the union of the crowns of Portugal and Spain in the same manner as Castille united with Aragon in the previous century. Such a union had been the dream of kings of both Portugal and Castille since the 13th century. In order for that to happen, quite a few marriages were arranged - first the Portuguese King Manuel I with Isabel, then with Maria also of Castille, and the third one with her niece Leonor, all of them Spanish princesses. After that we had the Spanish King Carlos I with the Portuguese Princess Isabel and out of that marriage was born Prince Felipe, who eventually would inherit the Portuguese crown and become Filipe I of Portugal and Felipe II of Spain.

All of these marriages worried the people, as they meant that eventually Portugal would be governed by a Spanish king if the Portuguese King did not provide an heir to the throne. That nationalistic fear, coupled with the risk of being persecuted by the recently installed Inquisition, could be another reason to look for refuge in another land even at a great danger. This new religious organization was given great support by King João III, and followinh his death, by his son, the King Sebastião.

The prospect of an Iberian union brought several concordance laws between Portugal and Spain with which the people of the south province of Algarve did not agree in 1568. In 1563 there were regular maritime commercial routes between the Americas, India, Portugal and Spain, and some of these shipping enterprises were using Portuguese boats without registration, both in Lisbon and   Algarve. How many ships were contracted by unscrupulous businessmen with unknown destinations? Who knows?

It is known, for example, that a Portuguese caravel was sent from Seville and, when returning from Peru with 100,000 ducats in gold and silver, was taken by the French. Merchant capitalists controlled part of the Portuguese marine traffic and performed relevant acts in the Portuguese enterprises developed by the crown.

Between 1497 and 1692 a total of 806 ships left from Portugal to India and only 425 returned, and that was only the recorded traffic. [9]

Foundation of Spain - 1500's

Any Portuguese in America is confronted with the constant confusion that Portugal is part of Spain. Fletcher states it better: *Spain as a term for the whole peninsular land mass between the Pyrenees and the Straits of Gibraltar is open to objection that it will inevitably suggest the modern state of Spain and thereby exclude the area covered by modern Portugal... Castille...was a modest County by the year 1000 of the kingdom of Leon...* [10] just like Portugal in 1096 AD.

It was not until the beginning of the 16th century that Spanish Monarchy was founded, as well as a nation much like the one we know today. The personal union of Castille and Aragon, caused by the marriage of Fernando and Isabel, was just a simple dynastic union and not a true national union. The territories had the same kings. Each one had its own institutions, currency and customs, just like any independent territory. Only in 1556 was King Felipe II able to reign over Spain, after his brief matrimony with Mary Tudor, Queen of England. [11]

Portuguese in Canada - Newfoundland and Corte Real - Maine

Fifty years ago, Admiral Samuel E. Morison (1887-1976) wrote that for the first quarter of the 16th century, *Newfoundland was in fact an outlying transatlantic province of the great and growing Portuguese empire.* [12] Another historian described the early discovery of Florida: *Alberto Cantino, the Italian agent who reported the return of the Corte Real ships to Lisbon (1501)...* [13]

There has been considerable debate on the question of the earliest Portuguese crossing to North America. One Portuguese author has argued that the honor of the first landfall in North America after the Norsemen should go to the Portuguese. [14] It has been claimed that in 1452, acting on orders of Prince Henry of Portugal, Diogo de Teive set out from Lisbon with a Spanish pilot to explore far into the Atlantic. The results of this expedition were known to Christopher Columbus and a member of the Pinzón family.

Bartolomé de las Casas, a 16th century historian, stated that the Portuguese had made voyages to the American shoreline 40 years before Columbus.

Meanwhile, Diogo de Teive in 1452, João Vaz Corte Real in 1471 and Álvaro Martins Homem in 1473 had already made voyages to the West, trying in vain to discover a sea-route to India. Due to the secrecy of the navigation imposed by the Portuguese king, very little was recorded, and also due to the fact that there was rarely anything interesting to record, as most of the time they found nothing but icebergs and frozen wasteland. The best evidence of the trip to Canada, which may have departed from Norway or Denmark and probably took place in 1472, is seen in a globe made by Martin Behaim – known in Portugal as Martinho de Boémia – a German Jewish geographer, in 1492.

In the early 1470's João Vaz Corte Real and some Danes visited Greenland and probably Labrador. Gibbs in his book *Future to Inherit,* cites Oleson: *All in all, there can be little doubt that the two Portuguese visited Greenland, Labrador and Hudson Bay.* [15] For this he received a captaincy in the Azores islands as a reward for having made a voyage to Newfoundland – *Land of the Cod Fish* – and the younger Corte Real explored the coast of Labrador.

The historian Samuel Eliot Morison dismisses Corte Real's trip because the alleged discovery was based on a statement in the *Saudades da Terra* – which Morison translates incorrectly as *Souvenirs of the Land* – by Gaspar Frutuoso born in 1522, because he was a notoriously unreliable collector of gossip. [16]

Probes into the Atlantic continued with Fernão Teles de Meneses and Fernão Dulmo from the Azores as well as Afonso do Estreito from Madeira.

In support of the argument of early exploration of the North American shoreline, one can point to the large numbers of Portuguese names that survive in anglicized form, on the Atlantic coast. [17] João's son Gaspar Corte Real also traveled deep into the Atlantic, and during one of the trips, he sailed south as far as Florida and received several benefits from King Manuel I. This Portuguese navigator makes the first authenticated European landing on the northern continent of the Western Hemisphere in 1500-1501. On a second expedition and while looking for a passage to the Pacific Ocean, they came upon a river and, very disappointed exclaimed repeatedly, *Cá-nada*, meaning in Portuguese, there was nothing. The words caught the attention of the natives, and were remembered and repeated by them when they saw other Europeans, such as Jacques Cartier in 1534. [18] This story may not be true; however it is a folk tradition with the fishermen from long ago, and the author has heard it said in Portugal many times since he was a child.

...and this seems to indicate that the Portuguese had entered the River St. Lawrence before Cartier, and frequented at least its mouth for such points had become well known and their names established. [19] *And here we may say that there is a strong reason to believe that the name Canada itself was derived from the Portuguese. ...The view commonly held is, that it is a modification of the Indian word Kanata, signifying a village or cluster of dwellings, and that the French mistook the natives pointing to their village as Kanata, and they supposed they meant the country. This we do not think likely, and besides, from his vocabulary of Indian words, we know that Cartier did not mistake the meaning of this one. But the word pronounced Canáda is pure Portuguese.* [20] The word in Portuguese meant in the 15th century the same as it means today - a double palisade in a river to indicate the passage or crossing, also a narrow path in the fields or old walled road.

The Portuguese having ascended the river St. Lawrence, either persuaded themselves that it was a channel...Cartier, on his 2nd voyage...one of the tribes up the river, told him that there began the great river...the highway to Canada...that the farther it went the narrower it became and that there...Canada...the fresh water began. [21]

Parkman in 1865 writes that the name Canada has been a point of discussion... It is appended to the journal of Cartier's second voyage as a name of a town or a village... Lescarbot affirms that Canada is simply an Indian proper name, of which it is vain to seek a meaning. Well... this is possible, but the fact remains that most Indian names had a meaning, and *Canada* did not, which means that it will remain a point of discussion. [22]

For further information see Dr. John E. Manahan's report at the University of Virginia under the title *Peter Francisco, Virginia Giant of the Revolution*, where he goes into detail relating to the origin of the name Canada and the St. Lawrence River, *Rio São Lourenço* in Portuguese. [23]

The last expedition by the Corte Real brothers was in 1500-01. Gaspar did not return. The same happened with his brother Miguel. *Kohl says that comparing this map* (Cantino) *with the present map of Newfoundland, "we must come to the conclusion that Corte Real entered and explored nearly every bay and gulf on the east coast of Newfoundland.* [24] Can we assume that being in the northeast, he also would have gone south to Maine and New England? There are however some vestiges that suggest Miguel was in New England. Inscriptions found on a rock near Dighton, MA, which has been the cause for some controversy.

Dr. Luciano da Silva has studied these inscriptions, together with other scientists, and concluded that the name Miguel Corte Real and the date 1511 was inscribed in the stone. Professor Edmund Burke Delabarre of Brown University made an exhaustive study of the so-called Dighton Rock and was able to detect recognizable European inscriptions on its surface, such as the date 1511. It remained for Joseph Damasco Fragoso, a language instructor at New York University in 1951, to recognize the existence of four crosses of the Order of Christ on the rock. Dr. Silva has also pointed out that the Newport Tower's eight arches bear a definite resemblance to the Castle of Tomar in Portugal, built by the Templar Knights who later became the Order of Christ.

David Biggs and Grace Anderson, in their book *A Future to Inherit* published in 1976, mentions that it is probably safe to discount the theory put forward by Delabarre. It is also possible that these two writers did not read Dr. Silva book, published in 1974, which goes into detail on Delabarre theories and adds new discoveries.

Scandinavian researcher Jorgen D. Simeonson said that the Newport Tower could have been built by French, Italians, Spanish, Portuguese or Dutch, and concluded that it was probably built between 1492 and 1620, which indicates Corte Real's date 1511 is the right place at the right time.

There is still another mystery about the Fort Ninigret. William B. Goodwin concluded in 1932 that it was Dutch in origin, mainly because of some blue pottery with the letter *R* inscribed on it. He believes that this was the initial of Isaac de Rasier, secretary of the Dutch Indies. However, experts told him that it was Spanish in origin.

Again Dr. Silva points out that many think of Portugal as being part of Spain and do not know that Portugal has a long tradition of blue and white pottery. The Portuguese royal flag's colors are blue and white, and Dr. Silva also notes the *R* might well have been a part of Miguel Corte Real's name. All the discoveries, as mentioned before, were protected by secrecy, which makes it harder to find any documents, and the few made were destroyed by fires, earthquakes or taken by the Spaniards during the 60 years of domination, and later during the French invasion by Napoleon's forces. All the diaries, books, letters and route maps were destroyed. As if this were not enough, the Inquisition burned many, suspecting that some of them were subversive material against the Church.

Another problem surfaced in a letter dated October 22, 1443, from King Afonso V, who complained that navigators' records had been haphazard and slovenly, not *marked accurately on sailing charts... except as it pleased the men who made them.* [25] No wonder historians have a hard time to write who did what and when. And that is why Samuel Elliot Morison concludes that there is lack of evidence of a Portuguese discovery of America. On the other hand, the same writer gives other non-Portuguese navigators credit for their achievements without clear evidence.

Were the Portuguese the first colonists? O. Louis Mazzatenta of the National Geographic Society wrote about a tower near Cape Cod commemorating the Pilgrims' first landing in 1620 and a conversation with a Portuguese-American sailor. *I was told by a Portuguese sailor. When those Pilgrims arrived, we had the harbor all buoyed out for them.* [26]

Cod Fish in Newfoundland

Leo Pap writes about Portuguese in Canada and the landmarks left by fishermen: *Reverend George Patterson pointed out in May 28th , 1891, in his address before the Royal Society of Canada, each of these rival groups (Basque, Breton, English and Galician) would strive to locate the best fishing grounds, thus in turn contributing to the overall knowledge of the coast. Nevertheless, such extensive onshore commercial activity by other nationalities never challenged Portugal's territorial claims and left little impact on the nomenclature of the east Newfoundland coast, which at every significant landmark remained Portuguese.* [27]

Nothing is known of the Portuguese settlers – as distinct from explorers – in the 16th or the first third of the 17th century within the territory now constituting the United States. However, during that period the Portuguese kept in close contact with the *northeastern corner of North America through fishing enterprises.* [28] Apart from the beginning of the cod fishery at Newfoundland in 1502, in which the English were followed by other European nations, they left much of the exploration of southeastern North America to the Spanish. [29]

The name *bacallao* as most non-Portuguese call the cod fish, is written in

Portuguese as *bacalhau* with a sound totally different from the Spanish. Most non-Portuguese people can't pronounce the sound of the letters *lh* and replace them as *ll*. Most often the Spaniards do that. Some historians point to the Basques as the possible originators of the word *bacallao*. [30] While on a trip to Scandinavia, the author asked a fisherman in an outdoor market the name for cod fish. He answered *"Bacallao* and we export a lot of it to Portugal". He did not know that the author had been born in Portugal.

For centuries cod fish was a staple food of the Portuguese diet. Salted and dried, it was highly portable and served as an important source of protein. It is also known for its nutritional value. You can ask any Portuguese how many ways there are to cook cod fish, and the answer will be 365 - one for each day of the year.

Portuguese Settlements in Canada

João Álvares Fagundes, a nobleman from Viana do Castelo, conducted extensive explorations sometime around 1520 south and west of Cape Race, Newfoundland.[31]

According to *Tratado das Ilhas Novas*, written by Francisco de Sousa in 1570, a company formed in 1521 in Viana do Castelo (home town of Fagundes) was given a grant by the Portuguese king and sent two vessels to Newfoundland waters in order to colonize the territory frequented by the fishermen. This writer's account says that *Portuguese who came from Viana do Castelo (in northern Portugal) and the Azores to people the New Codfishland, some 60 years ago... the natives were friendly...having lost their ships, the Portuguese stayed there.* [32]

The colonists first settled at what is now Ingonish, a small village on the coast of Cape Breton Island. But after spending a winter there, they moved to another unknown location and built a town of some 80 homes. [33] *...up to 400 Portuguese, English, and other European vessels swarmed around Newfoundland every year* [34] and by 1550 the town of Aveiro, Portugal, was sending 150 fishing boats to the Great Banks.

To magnify the presence and influence of the Portuguese in North America in the 16th century, there were places in Canada named Fagundes, as shown in 54 different maps dated between the early 1500's and 1600. [35]

The above may be part of another possible settlement in Nova Scotia by the Portuguese fisherman who founded the St. Peters Colony, but did not survive.

Anthony Parkhurst, an English merchant, would buy salt from the Portuguese and recorded their activities. In 1578 he reported 50 Portuguese boats and also encountered Portuguese when he explored the coast of Cape Breton. Later in 1668, Marie l'Incarnacion from Quebec wrote to her son in France of a vessel just arrived with *Portuguese*, Germans and Hollanders. There were also Moorish, *Portuguese* and French women. [36]

Cannons of the 16th century have been found nearby which have been a subject of controversy. Archaeologists are still investigating.

During 1562 and 1568 there are records showing initiatives of the Barcelos family in Sable Island and elsewhere. In the Praia da Vitoria papers in the Arquivo

Publico de Angra, Terceira Island, Azores has a petition and depositions on behalf of Manoel de Barcelos relating to expeditions sent to the Island of Barcelona of São Bardão, which has been identified with Sable Island, although there is a possibility of Barcelos' expeditions to Cape Breton as well. They were found by Manuel C. Baptista de Lima and published by him in a paper titled: *A Ilha Terceira e a colonização do Nordeste do Continente Americano no Seculo XVI.* Also in *Boletim do Instituto Histórico da Ilha Terceira, XVIII (1963), 5'37, app. I-xiii* and another valuable paper, *Uma tentativa açoriana de colonização da ilha denominada 'Barcellona' no século XVI,* at the *Congreso Internacional da Historia dos Descobrimentos, Actas (6 Vols., Lisboa, 1960-1961), V, part I, 161-167.* [37]

Again, on March 2, 1567, there was a report of a proposed Portuguese plan for an expedition to Canada. The indications of Portuguese activity with regard to northeastern North America include a suggestion that a fleet was ready to go to Canada by way of the Azores to find a land route to the Pacific. Frenchman Pierre de Monluc's recent raid into Madeira had diverted their attention and the expedition was postponed.

John and Sebastian Cabot - 1480-97 and 1539-40

Englishmen may have sighted Newfoundland as early as the 1480's, and John Cabot clearly delineated eastern Newfoundland, which he thought was Asia, in 1497. Sebastian Cabot's attempt in 1508-09 to get around it by a northwesterly route to reach Asia also failed. [38]

It has been stated by some historians that Cabot's crew was mostly Portuguese, which is not too difficult to believe taking into consideration that by then, Portugal had a surplus of seamen. Dr. Manoel da Silveira Cardozo, a professor at the Catholic University in Washington, D.C., wrote in 1958:

The Pilots in the first English expeditions to the New World were Portuguese, already during King Henry VII. [39] In the same manner, that Corte Real's first voyage to Newfoundland in 1474 is questioned by historians, so should Cabot's claim for England be questioned.

While looking at hypothetical discoveries of America, a French writer made an ambitious claim, that America was discovered by a Frenchman in 1488. Apparently Cousin, a navigator of Dieppe, being at sea off the African coast, was forced westward, it is said, by winds and currents to within sight of an unknown shore. On board was Martin Alonso Pinzón, who later went to Spain, met Columbus, told him the discovery and joined him on his voyage of 1492. [40]

Although John Cabot – born Giovanno Caboto in Genoa of Venetian Citizenship – is mentioned by the English to have been in Newfoundland before the 1500's, nothing was recorded till June 24, 1540, when he reached Labrador and Nova Scotia, returning to Lisbon, Portugal, on August 6. On this trip he notes vast cod fish banks off the coast of Newfoundland. He had previously settled in England, where King Henry VII granted him a patent to search for new lands, since England did not recognize the Tordesilles Treaty between Spain and Portugal.

Alberto Cantino Map - 1502

In his book *Sixteenth Century America*, Carl Ortwin Sauer wrote: *The Cantino map is the earliest known representation of Florida and Florida Strait.* [41] Between the short period of 1492 and 1504, there were 81 overseas expeditions, of which 17 were Portuguese, two French and nine English, all along the North American east coast, from Labrador to Florida and beyond. [42]

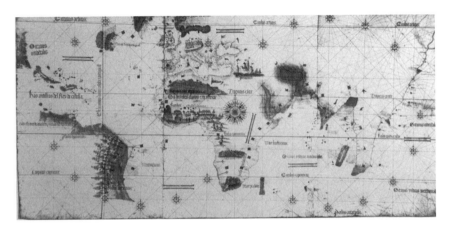

Fig. 44 - Planisferio "Cantino" (1502), Biblioteca Nacional, Portugal. The U.S. East Coast, Florida is shown on the upper left. Newfoundland is shown to the upper right, purposefully too far east to fall on the Portuguese side of the Tordesilles Treaty.

Anyone who studies cartography knows of the existence of a Portuguese map dated 1502, the so-called Cantino Map – a world chart showing the Portuguese discoveries – after Alberto Cantino, a secret agent working for Ercole d'Este in Lisbon. Ercole was the heir to Duke Borso d'Este in Ferrara of the Italian peninsula.[43] He may have had it purchased in Lisbon, Portugal and then forwarded to Ferrara, according to the following account: *...was sent by Cantino...with a note dated date November 19th, 1502, showing that it must have been constructed immediately after the return of the vessels of Gaspar's 2nd voyage. It gives a representation of the coast of the U.S. from Florida northward.* [44] This map shows the Florida peninsula and the U.S. East Coast. However, that same writer states that in the late 15th century there were no typical portolan Portuguese charts showing the graduated meridian, or any other indications of astronomical navigation, such as the equator and the two tropics. [45]

On the other hand, the historians say that Florida was discovered by the Spanish explorer Juan Ponce de Leon, who looked for the Fountain of Youth in 1513. The Portuguese knew where Florida was located before the Spaniards discovered it. Therefore there is a possibility that the Portuguese may have reached Florida according to Cantino's map, before the official discovery by Ponce de Leon in 1513. [46]

This map may be considered the most important one in the history of cartography, because it provides the first view of the world as we know it today.

Equally important was the publication in the 15th century of a Latin translation of Ptolemy's *Guide to Geography*, which had been forgotten throughout the most of the Middle Ages. Reprinted in 1475, the Geography reached its 7th edition in 1490. It reappeared in 1507, and the 11th edition, published in Strasbourg in 1513, included new maps.A planisphere was modeled after the Cantino map. [47] Based on that, this map certainly credits the Portuguese with the knowledge of the existence of lands to the west.

The Cantino and the Reinel maps give a clear indication that the Portuguese were the early explorers in that region. Pedro Reinel, in the words of Herrera, was a Portuguese pilot of much fame, [48] and the map with his name is preserved in the Royal Library of Munich. The following are names given to places by the Portuguese as shown on these maps dated 1502 and 1505:

Fig. 45 - Magellan's signature [49]

Ilha da Fortuna, Fortune – *Ilha da Tormenta*, Cape Tormentine – *Cabo do Marco*, Cape Mark – *Cabo São João*, Cape St. John – *São Pedro*, St. Peter – *Ilha das Aves*, Bird Island – *Cabo das Gamas*, Deer Island – *Cabo da Boaventura*, Bonaventure – *Ilha do Frey Luis*, Freels Island – *Baia de Santa Ciria*, Trinity Bay - *Baia da Conceição*, Conception Bay – *Cabo da Espera*, Cape Speer – *Rio São Francisco*, Cape St. Francis – *Cabo Raso*, Cape Race - *Baixos do medo*, Shoals of Terror – *Portugal cove* and Portuguese cove – *Ilha do Batel*, Battle Island – *Baia Funda*, Bay of Fundy - *Porto do Refugio*, Port Refuge – *Rio dos Jardins*, Jordan River – *Porto Formoso*, Port Joli (French).

Fernão de Magalhães (Magellan) 1519-21

After having served the Portuguese King Manuel I, first in Africa and later in India, Magellan went to the King to request some form of recognition. Otherwise, he would go to Spain and offer his services. To which the King replied that he did not care, in not so kind a manner.

While in Spain, Magellan married the daughter of an influential Portuguese who controlled the Spanish voyages to the West Indies. [50] Just as with Columbus, history would repeat itself. That is when Magellan went to Spain and did the first circunmnavigation, although he did not complete it. He was killed in the Philippines, and the Spaniard Sebastião del Cano finished it.

With the Magellan fleet were also 30 Portuguese working for Castile at the time. With him was the Portuguese navigator Estevão Gomes – who later explored the east coast of North America – and his brother-in-law Duarte Barbosa, João

BRAZÃO DE FERNÃO DE MAGALHÃES

Fig. 46 - Magellan's family crest [51]

Lopes de Carvalho pilot of the vessel *Concepción*, Estevão Dias and others. [52]

Five of the Spanish vessels had Portuguese pilots. [53] Not only did Magellan give his name to the Strait in South-America, but he also named the Pacific Ocean, due to the calm, stormless waters in which they were able to navigate for 12,000 miles. [54]

On March 6, 1521, Magellan anchored for refreshment and supplies at Guam. There they were greeted by good natured but greedy natives, who swarmed all three ships, on deck and below, promptly removing everything movable. Magellan christened these the Isles of Thieves, now known as the Marianas. [55]

Verrazano in Madeira - 1524

Giovanni di Verrazzano of Florence, working for France, departed January 17, 1524, from Madeira Island with 50 men. Some must have been Portuguese.[56] He was the first European to sight New York and Narragansett Bay.

Before the Europeans came, the Delaware (or Lenni Lenape) Indians had long occupied the region. Almost a century passed before colonization began with the arrival in 1609 of the English navigator Henry Hudson, who sent a party to explore Sandy Hook Bay. The first permanent European settlement was at Bergen (now Jersey City) in 1660.

While France was looking to the New World to establish her colonies, she was at the same time engaged in the corsair and piracy business against Portugal. It has been estimated that in 1540 about 10,000 Portuguese were victims of French piracy, with a great loss. As a comparison, Carlos V, the Spanish emperor, received just a little more than the equivalent value in gold from America for the period 1526 to 1530. [57]

New England and the Portuguese

The presence of the Portuguese on the North America continent may be noticed in many ways.

The existence of a tower constructed out of stone in Rhode Island, called the Newport Tower is a strange fact. It is believed to have been built by Portuguese navigators in the 16th century. The date was recently confirmed by Danish scientists.

Archaeological Anomalies is the name of a book published in 1994 and written by W. David Crocket. As the name implies, in the archaeological sense something is out of time and place. This book brings up some interesting points and disputes long established theories. The following paragraphs are some of the anomalies

Fig. 47 - Newport Tower with eight arches

mentioned by the author.

The Newport Tower or the *Old Stone Mill in Rhode Island was probably built about 1600 by the State's first Governor Benedict Arnold*, so the sign says. It also tells us of legends that *ascribe its erection to Norseman during their supposed visit about 1000 A.D.* Governor Arnold might well have adapted an existing structure for this purpose (windmill) ... A revolving top of some sort would have had to be built in order for the mechanism to take advantage of the wind directions. The Newport Tower is not perfectly circular. In addition to plastered columns, there is a fireplace in the structure with an interesting feature of an internally built double flue. No miller in his right mind would have allowed a fireplace in his mill.

In January of 1993, a team of Scandinavian researchers led by businessman Jorgen D. Siemonson visited Newport in order to discover, through radiocarbon dating, the age of the Newport Tower's mortar... and in September of the same year the group announced that the tower could have been built any time between 1450 and 1700, but probably before Newport was settled by the British... *and after taking careful measurements used in its construction, announced that the unit of measurement used in its construction was not the British foot but rather the ell, from Central and Southern Europe.* [58] It also may mean the that it was the work of the Vikings.

Dr. Manuel Luciano da Silva, also of Rhode Island (Bristol), stated in an interview to the reporter James A. Merolla that the dates of the samples taken by the Scandinavian scientists were between 1500 and 1650, plus or minus 50 years, which could place them anywhere between 1450 and 1700, as stated above by Mr. Crocket. These dates would coincide with Dr. Silva's long documented theory that the tower was built sometime in the early 16th century, the peak century for Portuguese exploration around the world. [59]

Proceeding south the first Europeans to set foot on New England were Portuguese. [60] However, larger settlements did not occur until the 1800's, when the whaling industry attracted many Portuguese fishermen from the Azores and the Cape Verde Islands. Actually, most of the 200,000 who emigrated to the United States in the late 1800's settled in southeastern New England, where to this day they still live and form an important part of this area of the U.S.

In 1699 Isaac da Costa, a Huguenot (Lutheran) of Portuguese ancestry, arrived in Boston from England. Benjamin Franklin da Costa, a clergyman and writer born in 1831, was one of his descendants.

Portuguese Navigator Estevão Gomes - 1525

Next we have Estevão Gomes, a pilot who navigated under Fernão de Magalhães – already mentioned – in 1519 and had been in the East Indies, was appointed by Emperor Charles V to find a northwest passage to India, but failed in his mission. He did, however, important exploring. [61]

He left La Coruña at the end of 1524 or early 1525 and steered for Newfoundland, sailed on to Nova Scotia, down North American coast, perhaps as far as Cape May or even beyond Chesapeake Bay. Later research done by Louis André Vigneras proved that Gomes sailed from Florida to Newfoundland, which makes sense since that was the way most navigation was done, to take advantage of the winds and currents. A few months earlier Verrazano, working for France, also made the voyage in a south-north direction. [62]

On his course, Gomes charted the coastline of Maine, Massachusetts, Connecticut, New York (Hudson River), New Jersey and Delaware. The Portuguese cartographers Diogo Ribeiro and Chaves drew the official sailing chart. [63]

There is a Spanish map made in 1529 showing the area as *Tiera de Estevã Gomez* (Land of Estevão Gomes), which includes a brief description of the navigator's accomplishments. To the northeast, the Map also shows *Tiera Nova de Corte Real*, and *Tierra del Labrador*, referring to voyages and Portuguese navigators and explorers. It is assumed by many historians that he went all the way to Florida–or started from Florida all the way to New England–chartering the complete East Coast. We can conclude and without a doubt that the Portuguese knew the East Coast, including the state of Virginia.

Much later, in 1542-43, another Portuguese navigator, again working for Spain, for the first time reached California, which he carefully explored all the way to the Bay of San Francisco. His name was João Rodrigues Cabrilho – a Portuguese mariner as the Spanish chronicler Antonio Herrera calls him – born in the north of Portugal in a place called Lapela, Cabril, near the city of Montalegre, province of Trás-os-Montes. This name is well known by the Portuguese living in the United States, who hold a yearly Festival in his honor in California, with a "Cabrilho state holiday" on September 28. Recently, Cabrillo – as he is known in the U.S. – was honored by the U.S. Postal Service with issuance of a commemorative stamp. According to some scholars, Cabrilho's place of birth has not been definitely established.

Cabeza de Vaca expedition into the Southeast and California - 1527-42

Portuguese were also part of this expedition. The original narrative by Alvar Nuñez Cabeza de Vaca, spells Cabeza as the Portuguese do, Cabeça with a ç instead of a z. The island of Malhado [64] – presumably the Galveston Island or Vellasco – is also spelled in Portuguese with the *lh* instead of *ll* as it would be written in Spanish. As spoken, the resemblance is less evident than in written form. [65] Malhado, when pronounced as Portuguese *Mal olhado,* has almost the same sound and means a superstitious curse by someone on a place or person, also misfortune or ill fate.

In the same narrative he mentions: *These men were excellent swimmers. One of them was Álvaro Fernandes, a Portuguese sailor and carpenter…*[66] This same name is mentioned again in the Hernando de Soto expedition as the possible author of the narrative by the Gentleman of Elvas. Would it be the same person? It is also interesting that when Cabeza de Vaca met the natives, he was told by signs that there were men like them nearby. Apparently they were the crew from an early expedition in November 1528 whose boat was shipwrecked.

As part of this expedition there was also an Arabian Black called Estevanico, a native of Azamor, a Moroccan town conquered by the Portuguese in 1513 and later abandoned by King João III in 1541. The author also quotes Fernão Alves de Castanheda as the source of some of the information published in his book. [67]

After his adventure in the Southeast, Cabeça de Vaca returned to Spain, leaving Havana with a Spanish galleon loaded with silver and gold. When near the island of Corvo, Azores, he was attacked by the French that already had seized a caravel with a cargo of slaves. A Portuguese fleet of nine ships under the command of Diogo da Silveira, returning from India laden with spices, managed to rescue him and his ship, arriving in Lisbon on 1537.

Portuguese Soldiers on Hernando de Soto Expedition of 1539-41

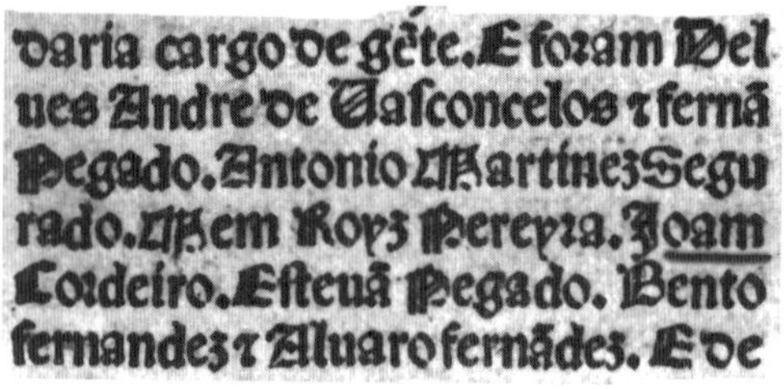
daria cargo de gēte. E foram Del
ues Andre de Uasconcelos e fernã
Pegado. Antonio Martinez Segu
rado. Mem Roys Pereyra. Joam
Cordeiro. Esteuã Pegado. Bento
fernandez e Aluaro fernãdes. E de

Fig. 48 - List of Portuguese with Hernando de Soto expedition. Notice the name Joam in Portuguese.

The latest biography of Hernando de Soto was written by David Ewing Duncan, who refers to the explorer as Hernando de Soto or Soto and not the anglicized version of *de Soto*.[1]

The author's middle name is Sousa, but is connected to the first name by ***de***; then the last name *Sousa* as in Manuel de Sousa, would be Sousa not *de Sousa*. On many of his personal documents, very often, the middle name is switched from Sousa to DeSousa, which is not correct. The author will also always refer to *Soto* or Hernando de Soto, rather than *de Soto*.

The Spanish conquistador Hernando de Soto was probably the first European to enter southern Appalachia in 1539-40. At least 100 of the 600 men that disembarked with Soto in 1539 were Portuguese The ship commanded by André de Vasconcellos, one of the larger ones among the six carrying the expeditionary force, was entirely filed with Portuguese.[2]

Writer Miguel Albornoz describes Hernando de Soto as a man who explored the area of ten states of the union: Florida, Georgia, Alabama, South Carolina, North Carolina, Tennessee, Mississippi, Arkansas, Louisiana and Texas. This area was the property of war-like, proud Indian nations, and hostile toward white men well into the 19th century. Then it took the might

of fully equipped modern armies to overcome decisively the resistance of tribes that three centuries earlier, a man had tried to subdue with only a thousand brave Spanish and Portuguese soldiers mounted on 350 horses.[70] In the temple of Cofitachequi, Hernando de Soto... also found a variety of European items including a knife or dirk, glass beads, rosaries, and Biscayan axes. [71] All members of the expedition agreed that these materials must have originated from Ayllon's 1526 expedition. [72] That also points to a European presence of Basques, and possibly Portuguese, near the North Carolina mountains.

Fig. 49 - Plaque in Hiwassee N.C., marking the area Hernando de Soto explored nearby.

Hernando de Soto's information gathered by the Roosevelt appointed Swanton Commission in 1938, is based on a book titled The narrative of a Gentleman of Elvas. Álvaro Fernandes was probably the writer of the first recorded discovery and navigation of the Mississippi river. [73] Historian Theodore H. Lewis, honorary member of the Mississippi Historical Society wrote about this book: *Nevertheless, when the narrative is considered as a whole, it is decidedly the best full account that has been handed down to us.* [74] The name of the book is *Hardships suffered by Governor Fernando de Soto and certain Portuguese gentlemen during the discovery of the Province of Florida. Now newly set forth by a Gentleman of Elvas.*[75] The

name in Portuguese is *Relação verdadeira dos trabalhos que o Governador D. Fernando de Soto e certos fidalgos Portugueses passaram no descobrimento da provincia da Florida*. James Alexander Robertson translated this book from the Portuguese original in 1933. Only two originals still exist, one in London and another one in Lisbon, Portugal. This book was used extensively by the Hernando de Soto Swanton Research Commission, and it should be subjected to a deeper study by a Portuguese scholar that could relate

Fig. 50 - A Plaque in Highlands N.C. honoring Hernando de Soto

the writings to the Melungeons or other groups.

The Swanton Commission book describes in several pages the presence of Portuguese men during the expedition. Two of them, Captain Vasconcelos of Portugal and Gonçalo Silvestre [76] ... *he being a nobleman and a hidalgo (fidalgo, gentleman) He was a very good soldier and often a commander...* [77]

Many of Hernando de Soto's former companions in arms went with him, several from Seville, and a number of Portuguese led by André de Vasconcelos. *The Gentleman from Elvas* gives a lively picture of this gathering of adventurous souls for the new enterprise. He tells us that the Portuguese, among whom he was of course numbered, left Elvas (the city) on January 15 ...*Two more Portuguese have been added...* [78] ...*In the above enumeration are included at least 19 Portuguese, probably more, and who entered mainly through the province of Badajoz...One of the Berbers also remained behind as they were passing through the Appalachian mountains and was perhaps the one who is said by Elvas to have married the Lady of Cofitachequi, though he states this man was a slave of André de Vasconcellos, ...the leading man in the Portuguese contingent* [79] ...*Álvaro Afonso, João Álvares de Valverde, Abião Lopes, Gavião Lopes, Manuel de Torres, Simão Rodrigues do Marão, Mem Roiz Pereira, Domingo Sardinha, Fernão*

Pegado, Estevão Pegado, Antonio Martins Segurado, etc. [80, 81] The above proves again that there were plenty of Portuguese and also some Berbers or Moors on the east coast of the North American continent. There is a possible calculation of at least 100 Portuguese soldiers that occupied one of the larger of the six ships. [82] Besides Elvas there is also another narrative by Rangel, Hernando de Soto's secretary. *A. Oviedo, Historia General,* first published in 1981, includes the narrative of Rodrigo Ranjel who wrote a day by day account of their activities. Ranjel's original document is not known to have survived, *and the degree to which Oviedo modified the text is unknown.* [83] It should be noted that the Gentleman of Elvas, unlike Rangel, does not put himself forward, but was so modest that only once does he refer to himself, while on a march through Florida, and that was on the occasion of the death of some relatives while

Fig. 51 - The Front Page of the Gentleman of Elvas Book

at Aminoya. Ranjel's translation follows closely the original book written by the Portuguese Gentleman of Elvas, which has survived.

Also another book about Florida was published in Lisbon, Portugal in 1605, titled *La Florida del Inca*, later translated with notes by Sylvia Hilton, and published in 1982 and 1986.[84]

Pocahontas, John Smith and the Gentleman of Elvas

While doing the research for this book, the author obtained a copy, No. 354 of the original book, translated and transcribed by James Robertson in 1933. The Gentleman of Elvas, or Álvaro Fernandes, was a Portuguese nobleman who joined the Hernando de Soto expedition along with 30 other Portuguese.

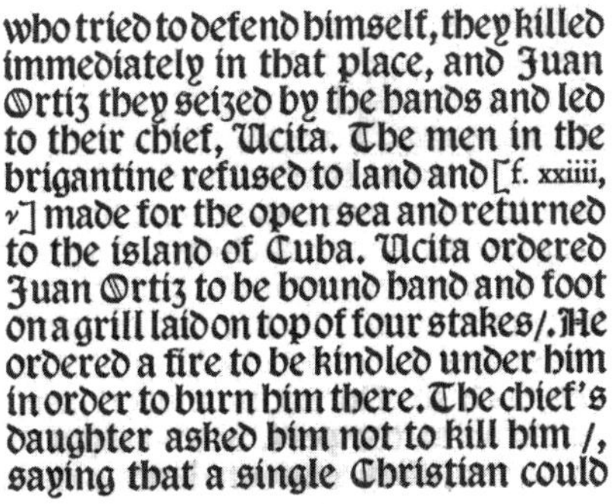

who tried to defend himself, they killed immediately in that place, and Juan Ortiz they seized by the hands and led to their chief, Ucita. The men in the brigantine refused to land and [f. xxiiii, v] made for the open sea and returned to the island of Cuba. Ucita ordered Juan Ortiz to be bound hand and foot on a grill laid on top of four stakes/.He ordered a fire to be kindled under him in order to burn him there. The chief's daughter asked him not to kill him /, saying that a single Christian could

Fig. 52 - Translation of a story similar to Pocahontas written in 1540 by The Gentleman of Elvas.

While crossing the Southeast he wrote a book describing the journey. As one of the few survivors, when he returned to Portugal, the book was printed and a copy made its way to the Spanish archives in 1544.

Later this book was published in 1557 in the Portuguese city of Évora, and another copy went to London but published under a different name.

That same book was used by the first English settlers to find their way around, and also to make them aware of the different Indian nations in the New World. Thirteen editions were made of the original, and one was given to the first English settlers when they came to America. Translations were also made in French and Dutch.

The book narrates an interesting story about an Indian girl named Ulele that saved a Spanish captain named Ortiz from being killed. The story happened more than 60 years before John Smith set foot on American soil.

The following is the original story as translated by James Alexander Robertson in 1933: *...many Indians came...seized them...The other man who tried to defend himself, they killed...and Juan Ortiz they seized by the hands and led to their chief Ucita...Ucita ordered Juan Ortiz to be bound hand and foot on a grill laid on top of four stakes. He ordered a fire to be kindled under him in order to burn him there. The chief's daughter asked him not to kill him saying that a single Christian could not do him any ill or good, and that it would be more to his honor to hold him captive. Ucita granted this and ordered him taken care of and as soon as he was well, gave him charge of guarding the temple, for at night the wolves would carry the corpses from inside it...One night the wolves carried off from him the corpse of a child, the son of one of the principal Indians. Going after it, he threw a club which struck the wolf carrying the body, which finding itself wounded*

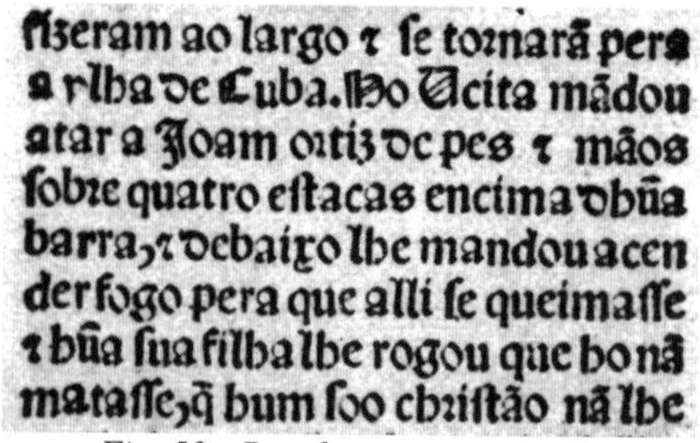

fizeram ao largo τ fe tornará pera
a rlba ɔe Cuba. Ho Ucita mãdou
atar a Joam oitiȝ ɔc pes τ mãos
fobȝe quatro eſtacas encima ɔbũa
barra,ȝ ɔebaiȝo lbe mandou acen
der fogo pera que alli fe queimaſſe
τ bũa fua filba lbe rogou que bonã
mataſſe,q̃ bum foo cbȝiſtão nã lbe

Fig. 53 - Pocahontas story in the
original Portuguese as written in 1540

abandoned it and went off to die nearby. He not knowing what he had done as it was night, returned to the Temple. At daybreak, when he found the body of the child gone, he became very sad. As soon as Ucita learned of it, he determined to have him killed. He sent along the trail where he said the wolves had gone and they found the boy's corpse and farther on the dead wolf. Whereupon Ucita was greatly pleased with the Christian and at the watch he had kept in the Temple, and thenceforward showed him great honor. ...another chief...Mocoço...came and burned the town...Juan Ortiz learned from the girl...that her father had determined to sacrifice him the next day; and she told him that she should go to Mocoço, ...At night since he did nit know the way, the Indian woman went a half a league from the town and put him on it. [85] Juan Ortiz after many years and tribulations, finally met Governor Hernando de Soto.

On July 10, 1995, Associated Press released a story that was picked by major newspapers all over the U.S., saying that John Smith read the book and made up the story. I do not think Disney's movie director of *Pocahontas* read the book. The Portuguese newspaper Luso-Americano of New Jersey published an article by the author also about this book. Unfortunately, very few people know about it, including the Portuguese, and that book, if read carefully, should give us more clues about the Portuguese in the Southeast.

Don Juan Onate Had Portuguese Soldiers

Early Spanish and Portuguese New World settlers were of a varied ethnic mix, not only in the Southeast but elsewhere. For example, (Don Juan de Onate) himself was Basque and a number of his soldiers were Portuguese. [86]

The Basque whaling industry was also well known in the late 1560's, according to an article written by James A. Tuck and published in the *National Geographic Magazine* of July 1985. The Basques' early presence in the New World had been recognized by a few scholars. It remained for historical geographer Selma Huxley Barkham to reveal the scope of their operation. [87]

The finding of a Basque galleon off the coast of Labrador provided all the proof needed. Their crew, most likely, included many Portuguese whalers. Centuries later, the Portuguese became part of the American whaling industry. Only the Basques had shown no urge to expansion, [88, 89] therefore their presence may be limited to the fishing industry and a few other separate incidents, except for their presence in Newfoundland as whalers. [90]

Fig. 54 - The Discovery of the Mississippi by Hernando de Soto, AD 1541, romanticized on a large canvas (144" x 216") by William H. Powell, 1853, hangs in the rotunda of the U.S. Capitol. Courtesy, architect of the Capitol.

Portuguese in Peru and Mexico

It is well known that the Portuguese were the first Europeans in the Pacific Ocean. Aleixo Garcia was the first Portuguese to contact the Inca Empire between 1521 and 1525. He was shipwrecked in one of the Spanish expeditions to Argentina with a few of his compatriots. Coming from Santa Catarina (Brazil), he climbed to the Andes in Bolivia, heading an army of *Chiriguanos* Indians, being the first European to step in the empire of the Incas years before Francisco Pizarro. The omission of Aleixo in the history books has been an injustice, according to the American Charles E. Nowell.

Even the Spanish discoverer Alvar Nuñez Cabeza de Vaca who explored Paraguay and the southern United States, wrote years later: ...*the old timers said that Garcia, the Portuguese made war in those lands with many Indians and having with him only five Christians.* Another *conquistador,* and one of the first, was Lope Martin Pereira accompanied by Frei Pedro Português or Frei Pedro dos Algarves, the founder of the church of San Francisco in Cuzco in 1534. In this same city appears Ximon Português in the list of the founders.

João Fernandes is another possible Portuguese admiral of Pedro Alvarado's fleet, mentioned by him as one of the two Portuguese pilots who arrived in 1532, when he wrote to Emperor Carlos V. Genes de Mafra was designated as the master pilot by Alvarado. [91] The other probable pilot was Gonçalo da Costa. Gaspar Rico is also the name of a Portuguese master pilot with the Spanish fleet under the command of Rui Lopes de Villalobos. [92]

Many Portuguese Jews went to Brazil as well as to other South American countries, and along with them also Catholic and non-Catholic Portuguese running away from the Inquisition, but most likely for economic reasons. The thousands of Portuguese arrived in Peru from Portugal or Brasil and gradually settled in Mexico, Peru and La Plata.

Portuguese merchants and capital reached relevant importance that could not be ignored, contributing 35% in 1635 annually to the Spanish treasury in silver. However, by the first quarter of the 17th century, the Spanish colonists and the Inquisition, using Judaism and other excuses, started to persecute them. Gonçalo de Reparaz, a well known historian, describes the Portuguese presence in Peru:. *...the streets of Lima were full of them...* The Portuguese not only preferred the mines, commerce and navigation, but also did not disdain the *agriculture...In 1571 we found five Lusitanos in the Andes, near Lima.* Also James Lockhard said: *...they were numerous in the farming and gardening...overwhelming predominant in this role... Portuguese sailors occupied prominent places in the Pacific navigation.* The Portuguese dominated the commerce so much that the Castilians believed that in order to succeed they had to associate themselves with the Portuguese. *The well to do people trusted them and loaned money, they were the Lords of the Land, they were honest and paid the interest punctually.* [93]

All the above can be confirmed by reading the index of 68 legal documents in the archives of Lima, Peru where one or more Portuguese are mentioned. [94]

If the Portuguese were in Peru, during the 16th and 17th centuries and in such large numbers, actively participating in the making of that nation, why is it so hard for many historians to believe that the Portuguese were also in North America, a place much closer to Portugal than Peru?

Who would think that the Portuguese had anything to do with Mexico? Well, Cortês, the founder of Mexico, had Portuguese in his expedition . Bernal Diaz del Castilho noted that the name Castillo Blanco was given by Portuguese, due to the fact that the locals reminded them of Castelo Branco in Portugal. After conquering Mexico, other Portuguese came, and one of them was an architect responsible for the only signs of the *Manuelino* style in New Spain. [95]

Portuguese in the Southwest - 1541

One group of a Spanish expedition led by Francisco Vasquez de Coronado pushed into Arizona and discovered the Grand Canyon in September 1540. In April 1541, Coronado led his army across northern Texas into Oklahoma and Arkansas, and then with a smaller group he pushed north into Kansas, reaching close to the Nebraska border in July..

From the muster roll records it appears that there were five Portuguese among Coronado's men. One of them, the soldier André do Campo, was with friar Juan de Padilla when the latter was killed by hostile Indians at Quivira; but André himself escaped, reaching New Spain from Panuco. [96]

Portuguese Navigator and Drake - 1555

On 15 Nov. 1555, the fleet sailed from Plymouth. The Portuguese pilot, Nuno da Silva, who spent 15 years aboard, noted with a practiced eye, 'Drake's ship is very stout and very strong. *More important than the capture of the Mary was the acquisition of her pilot, Nuno da Silva, whose Drake pressed into his service. He was a most experienced navigator and the English captain was fascinated by his collection of charts and nautical instruments.*

Nuno was to stay aboard the *Pelican*, where he was honorably treated, feeding at the captain's table for some 15 months. *By now Drake had divulged to his officers that he intended to sail into the Pacific, and the Portuguese pilot caught the adventurous spirit of his captor to travel into the new discovered parts of the world.* [97] Nuno's experience in the South Atlantic was considerable, and once they reached the South American coast, he displayed detailed knowledge.

Another Portuguese is mentioned as having worked for Drake. Pedro Sanhez made the following deposition in Havana after Drake ransacked San Domingo and Cartagena in 1585: *Their admiral is a Portuguese and is called Don Francisco Dragon; and all the pilots are Portuguese and Genoese, and the ships' masters also, all well acquainted with this course and the ports of Indies.* [97a]

If the English had at their service Portuguese and other foreigners, it is reasonable to assume that some or most of the early immigrants, such as the colonists of the Lost Roanoke Colony and later colonies, were Portuguese or other nationalities.

Portuguese Pilot in Virginia - 1560

Simão Fernandes – a Portuguese pilot – had guided them skillfully to their destination, where he had apparently been previously on a Spanish expedition in the 1560's. [98]

John Lawson the first Carolina historian wrote in 1700: *The Indians, which were the Inhabitants of America, when the Spaniards and other Europeans discover'd the several parts of this Country.* [99] The only other Europeans in the early 1500's that visited the US east coast were the Portuguese. The French came in the 2nd half of the century as well as the English.

Was Pardo a Portuguese Explorer? - 1565

In Chapter I, the possibility of *Juan Pardo* being a Portuguese working for Spain in the 16th century was mentioned by Kennedy, according to information given to him by historian and researcher Eloy Gallegos. The author decided to do his own investigation, and establish if he was or was not Portuguese. Since *Pardo* is not a popular Portuguese name – there are only two names listed in the 1996 Lisbon telephone directory – a visit to the Portuguese National Archives *Torre do Tombo* and with the help of Pedro Penteado, one of the archivists, produced some results.

However, there is a transcription of the original in Spanish written by Charles

Fig. 55 - The King of Portugal João II, name written as Juan in Tordesilles

Fig. 56 - The name of the Portuguese King João II as written in Portugal on the Treaty of Tordesilles (1494)

He was able to ascertain that during King João III reign (1521-1557) one Pardo was mentioned in the *Chancelarias de D. João III* (Chancellery or king's Official Documents), and recorded several times when he applied for official licenses and/or permissions. The time period is about ten years prior to the Pardo's presence in the Southeast (1565/1570).

A coincidence is worth mentioning. He was born in the city of Aveiro, a traditional place for Portuguese seaman, explorers and navigators. The Pardo's name and dates can be seen on the original documents of the 1500's. Seeing is not the same as reading, because it is very difficult to read much more than his name. Only an expert reader trained in Paleography is able to do it properly.

Fig. 57 - Juan Pardo signature, notice the symbol on the left over the third letter

The pictures show the name of the Portuguese King João II written in Spanish (Juan) on the famous Treaty of Tordesilles, and on the same document written later by Portuguese. The Pardo from Aveiro was written as *Joam Pardo* not Juan, as in Spanish.

When researching the North Carolina archives in Raleigh for the document signed by Pardo, when he explored the Southeast in 1565-09 for Spain, it could not be found.

However there is a transcription of the original in Spanish written by Charles Hudson of *The Pardo Relation* written and signed by Pardo. [100] On this document several words are written in Portuguese. In some places a word is written in Spanish, and the some word in other parts of the text is written in Portuguese. I caution the reader for the possibility of a mixture of the Galician language. But then again the Galician language was much closer to Portuguese after the 15th century. [101] The same does not happen with the documents written by Juan la Bandera (Vandera), the notary that gave the narration of most of the expedition. The original document, *Bandera Relacion* dated April 1, 1569, does state that he is a native of *quenca* "*natural de la ciudad de quenca... rreyno de España*".[102] Most likely the name *quenca* must apply to the modern name of the city of Cuenca in Spain. The name *Juan* in Portugal during the 15th and 16th centuries was written as *Yoam, Yoao, Joa'o* or *Joam*, but never *Juan*. Unfortunately the above does not help the Portuguese theory, although it may show close links to Portugal. Another document states that Pardo is a resident of Seville. [103]

After investigating in the *Archivo General de Indias* in Seville with the help of one of the archivists, I was able to obtain a copy of Pardo's signature as he signed in one of the Bandera's documents. I found it interesting that the name as signed does not look like Juan and does show what looks like the character ~ over the vowel *a* as in Portuguese *ã*. [104] See Fig. 58. Again, more research is needed, and it is up to the reader to arrive at some conclusion.

Spanish Confirms Portuguese Settled in Newfoundland

Pedro Menéndes de Aviles – the founder of St. Augustine in Florida – who in 1566 ordered an expedition to the Carolinas, had Antonio Pereira, a native of Porto, listed as one of the Portuguese member of the forces. [105] Aviles, also in 1568, considered the Portuguese to have colonized Terra Nova two to three years before. The evidence of Pedro Menéndez de Aviles was taken before the inquisitor Juan de Ovando during the course of inquiries being made at Fuenterrabia. The following are some of the excerpts of the inquiries:

The Portuguese fortified in Terra Nova and Florida. He says that on the coasts of Florida and Terra Nova, which are in his charge, and the discovery of which has been made… two years ago (1566)… the Portuguese settled after he had taken possession of that land in the name of his majesty and fought the Huguenots [luteranos]. And it is said they have fortified more than two hundred leagues inland from the conquest of that discovery.

These certain persons, inhabitants of Fuenterrabia, who were with them, speaking in the presence of Don Juan de Acuña… wrote that the French had told him there in *San Sebastian that they had seen colonies of Portuguese in Florida, each village of very big Indians, and their company have entered by way of Tierra Nova which he understands to be a branch of the sea between the land of Florida. And this he had given to the Royal Council of the Indies.*

It appears that unless they are beaten out of there… they are certain to fortify themselves there, to go later from there, especially in view of the ease with which they can be supplied from the Azores (which are King of Portugal's) and from which the sailing time in good weather is twelve to fifteen days. [106]

There is also a story of a Biscayan sailing with a French Pirate ship which was shipwrecked, and the Biscayan rescued by a Portuguese vessel. [107]

Another isolated incident also confirms early presence in Canada, when Tomás André was brought before the Aveiro (fishing town in northern Portugal) judge for having an English passport dated August 17, 1583, and related to fishing in Newfoundland. All the above indicates, in sum, that the Portuguese knew well the northeast coast of the North-American continent since the late 1400's.

Portuguese Helped the Spaniards in Florida - 1567, Corte Real - 1574

During the first half of the 16th century, French corsair activity made itself felt near the Portuguese coast. The following is a sample of correspondence in which

Portuguese presence in America was mentioned.

A Frenchman, M. de Fourquevaux, wrote a letter to Queen Catherine de Medicis. This letter was part of documents between him and the king of France, Charles IX.

I am assured, Madame, that they will not be in the aforesaid country [Portugal] so enthusiastic nor so ardent as to set out their army against the said (Algerians) pirates, as they were recently against the late Captain Monluc –Pierre de Monluc who had attacked Madeira in revenge for Portuguese help to Spain in Florida – ; and I am informed that if it had not been for the Madeira alarm a little while ago throughout all the islands subject to the King of Portugal, a fleet which is set for the Azores would have gone to Terre Neuve, to take possession of the land and people in the Grand Bay of Canada (The Strait of Belle Isle). [108]

Kennedy, in a letter to CNN (Cable News Network) also gives a good indication of the Portuguese presence: *...following examples already uncovered from the Archives by Dr. Lyon and Dr. DePratter: Portuguese seaman Juan Fernández de Cea (João Fernandes de Ceia) was given permission by the Spanish to sail to Florida and dig for treasure (January 26, 1568). 50 Portuguese farmers from the Azores accompanied Pedro Menéndez de Aviles to Florida (January 26, 1573) and 100 Portuguese farmers accompanied Menéndez from the port of Bayona to Florida. (July 13, 1573).* [109]

Domingos Fernandes, a Portuguese, piloted a Spanish ship into an opening in the Outer Banks. A native of Terceira, Azores, may be the same, or a relative of Simão Fernandes.

In 1582, when Portugal was under the Spanish crown, Richard Hakluyt was completing his book about the discovery of America. He picked up from Antonio Castillo, the Spaniard who was representing Portugal at the English court, some rather vague information about a voyage up the Labrador coast by Vasques Eanes Corte Real.

In 1574 it was said that he had reached a north latitude of some 58°. Also Vasques received from Cardinal D. Henrique confirmation of the Newfoundland charter granted to Manoel Corte Real on July 12, 1574, by King Sebastião who had died in 1578. All that took some legal shape, when a royal permission was received on May 4, 1567, to appoint a governor with legal qualifications to administer the proposed (or actual?) Portuguese settlement. [110]

Also in 1574, there was a Portuguese attempt to find a northwest passage by Eanes Corte Real from the island of Terceira in the Azores, who had been on a Labrador voyage. [111]

Defeat in Alcacer-Quibir (Ksar el Kebir) and the Union - 1578-80

On August 4, 1578, Portuguese King Sebastião is defeated by the Moors at the battle of Alcacer-Quibir. In this battle the Moors were helped for the first time by the Turks (Ottoman Empire).

In that battle the Portuguese king died, and many Portuguese nobles, along with two other Moorish kings.

This defeat marked the beginning of the fall of the short lived Portuguese Empire and supremacy throughout the world, which led to the 60 year union of the Portuguese and Spanish kingdoms by Felipe II of Spain, the Portuguese King's uncle.

In 1580, Felipe II of Spain became Filipe I of Portugal. He was the son of the Portuguese Princess Isabel of Portugal and the grandson of the Portuguese King Manuel I. Many historians erroneously write that the King of Spain conquered Portugal in 1580. According to established monarchy laws, and with agreements previously made between the monarchs of Spain and Portugal, if one of the kingdoms did not have a direct descendant, whoever survived would reign over both crowns. Due to family ties, Felipe was the natural heir to the Portuguese crown. Felipe II of Spain was also the son of the Emperor Carlos V of Austria and Germany.

For centuries it was the dream of both Portuguese and Spanish kings to unite both kingdoms. Many times the king of Portugal had the opportunity of also becoming the king of Spain. Had that happened, Portugal and Spain would ironically have become one country. But Castille waited too long, and the spirit of nationhood settled in Portugal after the 13th century.

During the period of Portuguese and Spanish union, many Portuguese navigators under the Spanish flag were in North America. One of them was Vincente Gonçalves, a pilot sent by Pedro Menéndez de Aviles to reconnoiter Chesapeake Bay in May 1588. [113]

Later in 1593, a large contingent of Portuguese soldiers arrived in San Juan, Puerto Rico. Filipe I gave them orders to sail from Lisbon. Many of the men brought their wives, and others married on the Island. From these men descend many Puerto Rican families.

Portuguese in New Mexico - 1596

Portuguese soldiers were among Don Juan de Oñate's group of colonists going to settle New Mexico. Unfortunately, life was not very kind to two of them. Two Spanish Brothers, Juan and Matias Rodriguéz, convinced João Gonçalves and Manuel Português – two Portuguese, unhappy with Oñate – to leave New Mexico, which they did by taking their horses and some food with them. They got caught later and were executed, after being seized through trickery as their captors had previously promised their lives would be spared.

However, they realized later that they were going to be executed and begged to be allowed to confess to a priest. That last request was denied. They were beheaded and had their hands chopped off.

The Spanish brothers were permitted to escape as they were friends of one of their captors. [114] After the war with Mexico, one of the first chronicles of the area in the 17th century was written by Benevides Memorial, a Portuguese friar from the Azorean St. Michael island. [115]

One of the distinguished family names in New Mexico is Chaves. Manuel Antonio

Chaves, son of Julian Chaves and Maria Luz Garcia, was born on October 18, 1818. He became famous in the battles with hostile Navajo, Ute and Apache Indians, earning the name of *El Leoncito* or The Little Lion. There is indication that he was of Portuguese ancestry. [116]

The name can be traced back to the Portuguese city Chaves in Portugal. The spelling of the name in Portuguese ends with an *s* and Spanish with a *z.*

Manuel Brazil is another Portuguese, found in New Mexico as a cattle rancher during the years 1870 to 1880. He was also a commissioner in Roberts County, but is better remembered as the man responsible for the capture of Billy the Kid, a well known outlaw of the western frontier. [117] Brazil was born in Rosais, São Jorge, Azores in 1850 as Manuel Silvestre Brazil and possibly arrived in the U.S. when he was a teenager. [118]

Portuguese Navigators, Soldiers and Explorers in the North American East Coast Before Sir Walter Raleigh - 1587

The following chart shows just a few of the names that explored the coast of North America before the first attempt to establish an English colony. There are many more to be added as research continues.

1470-02	João Vaz Corte Real, Newfoundland
1492-05	João Fernandes Labrador and Pedro Barcelos in Newfoundland and Labrador
1500-01	Gaspar Corte Real , Greenland and Canadian coast
1519-21	João Álvaro Fagundes, Greenland and Canadian coast
1525	Estevão Gomes, East Coast, from Newfoundland to Chesapeake Bay and possibly Florida.
1540	André de Vasconcelos and at least 30 Portuguese soldiers took part in Hernando de Soto's expedition to the Southeast.
1555	Nuno da Silva, captured by Drake and later worked as a pilot in his South American expedition
1568	João Fernandes de Ceia to Florida
1578	Manuel and Vasques Corte Real to Labrador and Newfoundland
1585	Don Francisco Dragon, an admiral with Drake

Portuguese Navigators in 15th and 16th century North America.

Portuguese Log Book Value

Raleigh paid £60 – a colossal price in those days – for an original *Roteiro* or logbook written by the Portuguese navigator João de Castro about the Red Sea, showing that he appreciated and valued Castro's talents. [119]

Rulers of Portugal to 1580

Dynasty of Burgundy

Afonso Henriques	1128-1185	Sancho I	1185-1211
Afonso II	1211-1223	Sancho II	1223-1248
Afonso III (a)	1248-1279	Dinis	1279-1325
Afonso IV	1325-1357	Pedro I	1357-1367
Fernando	1367-1383	Leonor Teles (c)	1383-1385

Dynasty of Avis

João I	1385-1343	Duarte	1433-1438
Afonso V (b)	1438-1481	João II	1481-1495
Manuel I	1495-1521	João III	1521-1557
Sebastião	1557-1578	Henrique	1578-1580

Portuguese Dynasty Chart

(a) Regent until 1248   (b) Prince Pedro, Regent until 1448   (c) Regent

Notes

[1] Hernando de Soto by David Ewing Duncan, p. xx

[2] The Portuguese-Americans by Leo Pap, p. 241, Jaime Cortesão, p. 43-44

[1] Portuguese in North America by Rev. George Patterson, p. 162

[2] Christians and Spices by John Correia Afonso, p. 33

[3] A Future to Inherit by David Biggs, p. 9

[4] Portuguese Heritage, December 1993, p. 22

[5] Historia da Lingua Portuguesa by Serafim da Silva Neto, p. 421

[6] The Masters and the Slaves by Gilberto Freyre, p.3

[7] Christians and Spices by John Correia Afonso, p. 34

[8] Infante D.Henrique, Mario Domingues, p.8

[9] Portugal nos Mares, Oliveira Martins, p.37

[10] Moorish Spain by Richard Fletcher, p. 9

[11] Historia de España by Joseph Perez, p. 479,480, 1986

[12] João Alvares Fagundes by Richard Goertz, p. 116.
Canadian Ethnic Studies, 33. No.2 1991

[13] Sixteenth Century America by Carl Ortwin Sauer, p. 25

[14] A Future to Inherit by David Gibbs, p. 4
(Jaime Cortesão, Viagem de Diogo Teive, 1933)

[15] Early voyages and Northern Approaches by Trggvi Oleson, p. 119
(Toronto 1963)

[16] The European Discovery of America by Samuel Eliot Morison, p. 93

[17] A Future to Inherit by David Gibbs, p. 5

[18] The Portuguese in America by Manoel da Silveira Cardozo, p. 4
[19] Portuguese in America by Rev. George Patterson, p. 137
[20] Ibid, p. 138
[21] Ibid, p. 139 (Discoveru of Maine)
[22] Pioneers of France in the New World by Francis Parkman, p. 205
[23] Peter Francisco by William Arthur Moon, p. 52
[24] Portuguese in America by Rev. George Patterson, p. 138
[25] The Discoveries by Daniel J. Borstin, p. 162
[26] Little Portugal by O.Louis Mazzatenta, p. 90-107
    (Nat. Geographic Magazine, Jan. 1975)
[27] João Alvares Fagundes by Richard Goertz, p. 118.
    Canadian Ethnic Studies, 33. No.2 1991
[28] The Portuguese Americans by Leo Pap, p. 8
[29] Set Fair for Roanoke by David Quinn, p.13
[30] Pioneers of France in the New World by Francis Parkman, p. 192
[31] The Portuguese-Americans by Leo Pap, p. 5
[32] A Future to Inherit by David Gibbs, p. 8
    (Trato das Novas Ilhas by Francisco de Sousa)
[33] The Portuguese-Americans by Leo Pap, p. 9
[34] Ibid, p. 8
[35] João Alvares Fagundes by Richard Goertz, p.127-128
[36] A Future to Inherit by David Gibbs, p. 8
[37] Newfoundland, from Fisheries to Colony by David Beers Quinn, p.183
[38] Set Fair for Roanoke by David Quinn, p.12
[39] Boletim do Instituto Historica, Presença de Portugal… E. U. by
    Manoel da Silveira Cardozo, p. 9
[40] Pioneers of France in the New World by Francis Parkman, pp. 189-190
[41] Sixteenth Century America by Carl Ortwin Sauer, p. 25
[42] O nome de América e a Cartografia, by João Vidago, p. 9
    (Harrise pp. 662-700)
[43] Maps by R. A. Skelton, pp. 39-40
[44] The Portuguese in America by Rev. George Patterson, p. 136
[45] Portugal and the Discovery of the Atlantic by
    Alfredo Pinheiro Marques, p. 77
[46] Historia de Portugal by Joaquim Verissimo Serrão, V. III, p.110
[47] Pioneers of Ocean Exploration by Luis de Albuquerque, p. 13
[48] Portuguese in America by Rev. George Patterson, p. 140
[49] Historia de España by Joseph Perez, p. 479,480, 1986
[50] The Discoverers by Daniel J. Boorstin, p. 260
[51] Historia de Portugal by Damião Peres, V. III, p. 601
[52] Historia de Portugal, Vol. III, by Joaquim Verissimo Serrão, p. 30
[53] Os Pioneiros Portugueses by Dr. Luciano da Silva, p. 55
[54] Historia de Portugal by Damião Peres, V. III, p. 600
[55] The Discoverers by daniel J. Boorstin, p. 265

[56] North American Discoveries by David Quinn, p.59
[57] O Essencial sobre o corso e pirataria by Ana Maria Pereira Ferreira, p. 35
[58] Anomalies in Archaeology by W. David Crocket, p. 10
[59] The East Bay Window by James A. Merolla, Section B, December 22,1993
[60] The Portuguese-Americans by Leo Pap, p. 5
[61] Ibid, p. 5
[62] The Voyage of Esteban Gómez...by L.A. Vigneras, pp. 25-28.
(Terrae Incognitae, 1976 Vol.II)
[63] Sixteenth Century America by Carl Ortwin Sauer, p. 64
[64] Spanish Explorers in the Southern States by Frederick W. Hodge, pp. 12, 57
[65] The Spanish, Portuguese Languages by William J. Entwistle, p. 282
[66] Spanish Explorers in the Southern States by Frederick W. Hodge, p. 49
[67] Ibid, p. 126
[68] Hernando de Soto by David Ewing Duncan, p. xx
[69] The Portuguese-Americans by Leo Pap, p. 241, Jaime Cortesão, p. 43-44
[70] Knight of the Americas by Miguel Albornoz, p. 351,
also Swanton's Final Report
[71] The Gentleman of Elvas, p.65-65
[72] The Forgotten Centuries by Charles Hudson, p.100
[73] The Portuguese-Americans by Leo Pap, p. 6
[74] Spanish Explorers in the Southern States by Theodore H. Lewis, p. 130
[75] Ibid, p. I-4
[76] Ibid, p.287
[77] Ibid
[78] Ibid, p.VI-79
[79] Ibid, p. VI-82,83,85
[80] Spanish Explorers of the Southwest States by J. F. Jameson, p. 138
[81] Final Report of the United States de Soto Commission by
John R. Swanton, p. 350
[82] Os Portugueses no Descobrimento dos Estados Unidos by
Jaime Cortesão, p. 48
[83] The Forgotten Centuries by Charles Hudson, p.100
[84] Ibid
[85] The True Relation of the Fidalgo of Elvas, pp. 39-46 Chapter IX
[86] The Melungeons by N. Brent Kennedy, p.107,
The Last Conquistador by Marc Simmons
[87] National Geographic Magazine, July 1985, p. 41
[88] Ibid, pp. 41-71
[89] The Spanish, Portuguese Languages by William J. Entwistle, p. 5
[90] National Geographic Society, July 1985, pp. 41-71
[91] Os Portugueses no Vice-Reinado do Peru, by Conçalo de Reparaz, pp. 9-11

[92] Os Portugueses no Descobrimento dos Estados Unidos by
Jaime Cortesão, p. 64

[93] Historia de Portugal by A.H. de Oliveira Marques, Vol.II, pp. 171-172

[94] Os Portugueses no Vice-Reinado do Peru, by Conçalo de Reparaz, p. 41

[95] Boletim do Instituto Historica, Presença de Portugal...E. U. by
Manoel da Silveira Cardozo, p.10

[96] Spanish Explorers in the Southern States by J. F. Jameson, p. 385

[97] Great Lives, Sir Francis Drake by Neville Williams, p.88

[97a] Further English Voyages to Spanish America. 1583-1594 by Irene A. Wright
p. 212. Cf. Document No. 35. Encl. No. 2

[98] North American Discovery by David Quinn., p. 200

[99] A New Voyage to Carolina by John Lawson (Hugh Lefler), p. 172

[100] The Juan Pardo Explorations by Charles Hudson, pp. 305-310

[101] Gran Enciclopedia Gallega by Silverio Canada, Vol. 18, pp. 104-105

[102] Archivo General de Indias in Seville, signature Santo Domingo, 224

[103] Catholic Historical Review, Vol. LI,3, Oct. 1965 by
Michael V. Gannon, p. 340

[104] Archivo General de Indias, Patronato 19, ramo 22, year 1566

[105] A Spanish Discovery of North Carolina by L. A. Vigneras, p. 410

[106] Newfoundland, from Fishery to Colony by David Beers Quinn, p. 186

[107] The Spanish Jesuit Mission in Virginia by Lewis and Albert Loomie, p. 20

[108] Newfoundland, from Fishery to Colony by David Beers Quinn, p. 185

[109] N. Brent Kennedy letter to Victor Marques of CNN (March 2, 1995)

[110] Newfoundland, from Fisheries to Colony by David Beers Quinn, p.185

[111] Ibid, p. 187

[113] North American Discovery by David Beers Quinn, p. 178

[114] The Last Conquistador by Marc Simmons (1991), p.119-21

[115] Boletim do Instituto Historica, Presença de Portugal... by
Manoel da Silveira Cardozo, p.10

[116] The Little Lion of the Southwest by Marc Simmons, pp. 1-11

[117] Luso-Americano, Jan.13,1993 - Manuel Brazil by Geoffrey Gomes, p. 2

[118] Ibid, Apr. 6,1994 - Manuel Brazil by Geoffrey Gomes

[119] Portuguese Roteiros by C. R. Boxer, pp. 175

Chapter VIII

Portuguese Presence after the 16th Century in North America

*If we are on a river shore and looking at the other, we must think, that a raft
or a bridge existed there, in order that the conquerors' army could cross.
The historian's logic and imagination,
allows him to put the bridge or the raft in his chronicles.* [1]

To Emigrate, the Destiny for the Portuguese
A Poem to the Emigrant, Portuguese or any Other [2]

Portuguese	English
Ao deixar a minha terra	When I left my country
Eu pensei que navegar	I thought that navigate
Era só partir para longe	Was only to leave for far away
E um dia regressar	And one day to return
Ao chegar à nova terra	Arriving at the new world
Quiz fazer dali meu lar	I wanted to make my home there
Estrangeiro eu fui para sempre	But foreign forever I was
Nunca tive o meu lugar	Never had I my place
Quem somos nós	Who are we
Em frente ao mar	Facing the sea
Com sonhos loucos	With crazy dreams
De navegar	To navigate
Quem somos nós	Who are we
Em frente ao cais	Facing the sea
Com sonhos loucos	With crazy dreams
Voltar atraz	To go back
Um Natal que eu não esqueço	A Christmas I'll never forget
Regressei ao meu país	As I returned to my country
Cada amigo que eu conheço	Each friend that I meet
Me abraça e me diz	Embraced me and told me
Que eu deixei de ser quem era	I, no longer was the same
E que estranho o meu falar	So strange is my talking
Emigrante eu fui p'ra sempre	Emigrant I was forever
Já não tenho mais um lar	No longer had a home [3]

This Chapter portrays the known Portuguese immigration to the North American continent in a broad manner. It does not, by any means replace other books that study this aspect in detail. However it may show a possible migration of Melungeons or other groups, from or to areas where larger groups of Portuguese were known to be established.

Immigrants from Portugal

Judge Shepherd in his eloquent oratory about the celebrated Melungeon case, stated that the immediate source of Melungeon origin stemmed from a group of immigrants from Portugal. [4] Adalino Cabral wrote, a paragraph as to the global impact of the Portuguese: *No European people has been longer in the New World or more continuously than the Portuguese. Perhaps this is the way it was meant to be. After all, they have proportionally furnished more emigrants to the Western World than any nation of Europe (with the possible exception of England). Having established the first of the modern empires, and on virtually all continents of the world, this errant race, not content with the enormity of its own geographical space, also emigrated to lands under the control of other sovereignties.*

They emigrated to English-speaking nations (United States, Canada, England, Australia, South Africa...) and, in each of them, the Portuguese have been affected by the dominant language, having not alternative but to employ a mixture of linguistic phenomena – borrowing or Portinglês. [5]

Geofrey Gomes, from the California State University at Hayward, wrote about one Portuguese immigrant that no one knew about and goes on to say: *...that Portuguese immigrants have been more integrated into the American experience than previously thought. Clearly, a Portuguese presence is to be found beyond the traditional geographical focal points...It makes one wonder, however, how many more like him remain to be rediscovered and salvaged from the obscurity to which they have been relegated.* [6]

Portuguese Emigration from the Azores and North of Portugal

A study made in the 19th century pointed to Minho, Beira Alta and the Azores as the areas from which most of the Portuguese were coming. Between the period of 1860 and 1888 a total of 113,280 came from Minho (north), 70,890 from Beira Alta (north central), 60,088 from the Azores, and 23,202 from the Madeira Islands, while from the rest of Portugal only 23,134 emigrated.

Portuguese Women Immigrated in the 1600's

The Dutch, by establishing New Amsterdam (New York), put a colonial wedge between the English colonies and New England. The first settlers came in 1623, and in 1643 Father Isaac Jogues, a French Jesuit missionary, arrived. In 1646 Father Jogues wrote a letter describing the colony:*...for there are in the Colony besides the Calvinists, Catholics, English Puritans...it is near this river that a gold* *mine is reported to have been found...* [7]

Leo Pap wrote: *...and...it turned out that his hostess... was a Portuguese Catholic woman...*That there were one or several Portuguese residents in New York at that time is also indicated, for instance, by the old marriage records of the Dutch Church.[8]

Much earlier, Portuguese women *endured heat, disease, snakes, jaguars, fierce Corsair and Indian attacks, and French and Dutch invasions.* [9]

Portuguese Jews in America - 1621

Due to the fact that the Jews were one of the people most displaced in the 15th and 16th centuries, there are indications that they travelled by whatever means available to different parts of the world. It is known that many, disguised as Christians and through bribery, obtained passage in caravels bound to India and Brazil to escape the Inquisition. Their presence is noted in South America in the early 16th century and then in North America in the early 17th century. It is therefore possible that some Portuguese Jews arrived on the U.S. East Coast during the early 16th century and later moved north.

Most likely, they were joined by other *cristãos novos* (new christians) who formed their own group, either based on family ties or race, which did not follow the Jews. It is important to know the pattern of Jewish migration to establish a possible Melungeon connection.

The earliest date recorded for the presence of Jews in America is 1621, with an Elias Legardo as a probable Portuguese Jew, being noted in Virginia. Before that, it is also known that in May of 1549 a ship loaded with fugitives from Portugal had arrived in Ragusa (Dubrovnik, Croatia) and Syria as well as European Turkey. These cities daily received Portuguese families looking for some religious freedom *(given to them by half Islamic tolerance.)* [10] In one of the group of Jewish refugees, were João Migueis and his brother, her aunt Beatriz Mendes, a Portuguese Jewess lady later known as Doña Gracia Nasi who became one of the most influential women in the Ottoman world.

Those vessels were loaded with *fugitives.* Did they all go to Europe or did some of them go to the New World, like the Pilgrims?

The Portuguese Jews played an important part in the development of the countries discovered by Portugal. Gilberto Freyre, a well known Brazilian writer and a social anthropologist, tells us in his classic book *The Master and the Slaves*, which was translated into English by Samuel Putnam from the original *Casa Grande & Senzala* and published by the University of California Press, *As for the Jew, there is evidence to the effect that he was one of the most active agents in the winning of a market for the sugars producers of Brazil.* [11] In 1636 Jews were arriving not only from Portugal and Spain but also from Italy, Turkey, North Africa and the Netherlands. [12]

In 1507, Portugal decreed that all Jews of whatever religions beliefs be allowed to leave Portugal, trade and buy property anywhere in the world. So they went to the Ottoman Empire, Brazil, Holland and the Dutch colonies. The descendants of these Jews came to settle in the American Colonies.[13] The date of the first arrival is not known, but there had been Portuguese Jews in the Colonies as early as 1621, already mentioned. The next date on record is 1634, of Mathias de Sousa in Maryland.

The new and modern view is that American Judaism began in May 1654 with the arrival of the first Portuguese Jews from Recife, Brazil. Just as it can be held that American history began at Jamestown and that this experience set the framework for future American history, so it can be demonstrated that the Portuguese Jews and their successor immigrants in the Colonial period set the framework for a new Jewish history. [14] The age of the Sephardim Jews in America – from the Hebrew word for Spain, *Sepharad* – is considered to be from 1621 to 1776. [15]

Francis Salvador was a prominent patriot of the Revolutionary in South Carolina and appears in history as early as 1732. He was related to a wealthy family of Portuguese Jews in England and cousin to Mrs. Mendes da Costa. While in South Carolina he was held in such esteem that he was elected to the General Assembly of S.C. He died August 1, 1776, while on an expedition against the English and Indians. Other names such as David Nunes Cardozo and Isaac N. Cardoso also fought in a militia company of Charleston, South Carolina. [16]

Collectively, the American Jews are one of the most remarkable groups in the world. A society of 6 million Jews has attained the highest economic, educational and social levels in Jewish history, and enjoyed a degree of freedom never attained by Jews in any country, in any civilization, in any age, *including the kingdoms of Judah and Israel in ancient days, and the state of Israel today.* [17]

All Sephardim Jews are from Portugal and Spain, or of Portuguese and Spanish ancestry. They were viewed by the British as *Portugals*, and a puzzle to them, after New Amsterdam was taken over by England and renamed New York in 1664. The Portuguese Jews always kept their Portuguese names after arriving in America. They were persecuted during the Inquisition but did not change their names, while others that were not persecuted, quickly changed. [18]

They kept not only their Portuguese names, but also the language. In Surinam, where many Portuguese Jews settled before coming to America, their slaves adopted the Portuguese language, and went on speaking broken Portuguese. [19] In Newport, Rhode Island, the Jews contributed to the city's commercial prosperity early in the 18th century, when trade sprang up between Portugal, West Indies and Newport. Among them were many Portuguese. The great earthquake of Portugal in 1755 brought additional Jewish settlers. [20]

Founding of Virginia Colony and the Portuguese - 1621-49

This colony was founded by respected members of the Anglican church. Many of the early settlers in Virginia were rich English merchants, and their wish in England was to become country gentlemen. This was rather difficult to achieve in England, so Virginia became their *Little England*, and although Jews were not allowed to settle in this colony, Portuguese Jews did trickle in as early as 1621, according to some sources. Those of Sephardic origin married into some of the finest of Virginia's transplanted gentry. [21] In 1649, Virginia already had an English population of 15,000 plus Black slaves. [22]

New York - Maryland - Rhode Island - 1654-58

There are records of a colony of Spanish and Portuguese Jews arriving from Recife, Brazil. The Portuguese Jews were called the Portuguese Nation.[23]

Among the varied mix of settlers in that Colony was Dr. Jacob Lumbrozo, who arrived from Portugal in 1656. There were Portuguese Jewish settlers in Newport as early as 1658. Tombstones in the first Jewish cemetery in Newport are still intact, the earliest dating from 1677.

The first synagogue, Touro Synagogue, was built in 1673, and still stands. One of the families of the Newport Jewish community was the Aaron Lopes family, who arrived from Portugal in 1750. [24] In 1655 the Portuguese Jews were excluded from serving in the military when Peter Stuyvesant was preparing for a military expedition against New Sweden. Not only were they not allowed to serve but they had to pay a special tax. [25]

New York and Emma Lazarus, 1649-1730

The first official Jewish synagogue, Shearith Israel, was built on Wall Street, and David Mendes Machado, a native of Lisbon, became the rabbi. Still in existence, this congregation is the oldest in the United States, now located on Central Park West. The original language and writings of the minutes in the synagogues of the early Jews were in Portuguese. Actually, the earliest minutes and accounts of the Congregation Shearith Israel – now the Spanish-Portuguese Synagogue on Central Park West, New York – were written in the Portuguese language. [26] In 1655 this same congregation is recorded to have petitioned the local authorities for the right to establish a Jewish cemetery in the city. A small part of that cemetery, located near New York's Chatham Square, still exists. Portuguese names can be found in the wills filed between 1665 and 1796 in the surrogate's Office of the County of New York – names like Marques, Pinheiro, Nunes, Fernandes, Machado, Pacheco da Silva and others. [27]

Isaac Mendes Seixas, a Portuguese Jew, arrived in New York from Portugal in 1730. His son Benjamin Mendes Seixas, of New York and Newport, was one of the founders of the New York Stock Exchange. Carlos Seixas, the Portuguese harpsichord baroque musician, may have been related.

Reader's Digest published an article about *The Statue of Liberty*. In it the ancestors of poet Emma Lazarus' – author of the poem *The New Colossus* – were mentioned as having emigrated from Portugal in 1649 among the first Portuguese Jews to settle in what is today New York. [28] Benjamin Nathan Cardozo, born 1870 in New York City of Portuguese ancestry, was named to the Supreme Court of the United States.

First Mailman Was Portuguese - 1693

Portuguese names appear in French-Canadian legal records in 1698 and in 1693 Montreal judicial archives show that Pedro da Silva, from Lisbon, was paid 20 sols for the transport of a bundle of letters from Montreal and Quebec City. This was the first known mail service between the two cities.

When he was 33 years old, Pedro da Silva married a 17 year old French-Canadian and had at least two daughters and seven sons. His sons had large families, one of them Jean 17, Dominique 15, Nicolas 13. The name Silva, Sylva or Dasilva is to be found in North America in the 19th and 20th centuries. [29] The town Sylva, North Carolina is located in an area where the Melungeons were known to have settled.

Savannah, Georgia - 1733

Fig. 58 - Synagogue in Savannah, GA.

There is a synagogue in Savannah where the Portuguese Jews took an active participation before the Revolutionary War in 1733. It is the third oldest in the U.S., is built using a Gothic architectural style, very unusual for a synagogue. The original Portuguese Jews did profess Catholicism to escape death by burning, but reverted to the Jewish faith as soon as they arrived in the U.S. History of this synagogue shows that the original Jews were Portuguese Sephardim.

Abraham de Lyon, who was a vintner in Portugal before coming to the United States, began the growing of grapes in Georgia in 1737.

New England – 1740's

New England has been the traditional place of choice for the Portuguese immigrant since the early times of settlement. Unfortunately, there are very few non-English records available to document the presence of the Portuguese in this area of North America. However, if a serious search is done much more can be found, and the areas to be investigated are in Holland, Belgium and France. There are a wealth of documents out there waiting to be found. Naturally you must be fluent in either one of three languages – Flemish, Dutch or French – and have paleographic reading knowledge of the 16th century. It is not impossible, and it can be done.

Aaron Lopes, baptized as a Catholic, fled Portugal in the early 1740's. He settled in Newport, Rhode Island, where he openly professed Judaism. He became one of the wealthiest merchants and shippers of his day, building the whaling industry, and owning at one time about 30 ships. Lopes was one of the founders of the Touro Synagogue in Newport.

José Dias, a Portuguese who settled on Martha's Vineyard, served in the American Revolutionary War. He was captured by the British and died in their custody in 1781. Moses Seixas, who died in 1809, was the grand master of the Masonic Order of Rhode Island and was the cashier of the Bank of R.I. Also in Rhode Island, James Lucena about 1769 began the manufacture of Castile soap.

Antone S. Sylvia, a native of the Azores, arrived in 1855 in New Bedford, Massachusetts, at the age of 15. He began as a clerk in the Joseph Frazer Whaling Outfitting Co., New Bedford, and in 1862 became the sole proprietor of the business and a millionaire.

The presence of the Portuguese mariners made itself well known from the beginning of the 19th century for the following century. Names like George A. M. Brier (Silva), George M. Chase, Henry Clay, Francis J. Sylvia, Manuel King Sylvia and many more. A book titled *They Ploughed the Seas* by Pat Amaral provides a wealth of information about the Portuguese presence in New England in the early 19th century. It should be known that most of the Portuguese were born in the Azores Islands, and many of them became ship owners, master mariners and whaling masters such as John E. Simmons, born in Faial. [30]

The US Revolution and the First Census – 1779-90

After the Declaration of Independence, the crew of one of the earliest American warships, *Bonhomme Richard*, under the command of John Paul Jones, one of the founders of the American Navy, was mostly constituted by Portuguese. By the 18th century American ships traveled regularly between New England, Portugal and the Caribbean. These ships brought in the Madeira wine so much appreciated by George Washington. [31]

There are records dating back to the colonial period that point to an already fairly large Portuguese population in the United States. The study made in 1920 was based on Portuguese family names existing in 1790, when the first census was taken. At that time it was shown that the population of Portuguese origin was estimated at 24,000. [32]

Pennsylvania, Portuguese from Lisbon, 1769–1805

While searching for the possible Portuguese Melungeon roots, other Portuguese groups, who may or may not be connected with the Melungeons, were discovered. The following pages describe a particular and interesting group that also suffered discrimination until very recently.

Fig. 59 - Association Booklet
Courtesy Antonio Matinho

Leo Pap mentions the possibility that they may have come from Pennsylvania. This is doubtful, however. There are records of a group coming into Pennsylvania from Lisbon, Portugal, but it is not connected with the group or groups discussed in this book.

By the 18th century there were communications and easier means of transportation as compared with the 16th and 17th centuries. From 1794 to 1799, Portugal already had a diplomatic mission headed by Cipriano Ferreira. [33] Later, the Abade José Correia da Serra was the Portuguese diplomat (1816-1820) in the U.S. representing Portugal during the Thomas Jefferson administration (1801-1820). That was before the Portuguese government recognized the American independence. Portugal, being an old ally of England, was under pressure not to recognize it. Portugal, however, was one of the first three nations, along with France and Holland, to do so in February 15, 1783.

When the American Revolution started, Portugal was governed by one its fiercest dictators, Prime Minister Marquis of Pombal, whose iron fisted government in time of crisis benefited the people and the nation. He, however, sided with Great Britain in some of the measures taken.

On Sept. 10, 1813, a major U.S. naval victory took place in the War of 1812, ensuring U.S. control over Lake Erie. Commandant Oliver Perry's fleet of nine ships engaged six British warships. Portuguese names were found in the muster roll, and since Perry was living in Newport, Rhode Island, at the time, it is only natural that he would pick up Portuguese settlers and seamen living there.

Later in the 19th century we encounter signs of a very well organized Portuguese community in Erie, Pennsylvania. An organization called the Holly Trinity Portuguese Association was founded in 1874. The name indicates that it was a religious association; however, the Portuguese usually form an organization that serves as a social as well as a religious gathering. Jacob Mendez da Costa, a Medical doctor of Portuguese and Spanish ancestry, studied at the Jefferson Medical College in 1849, where in 1872 he was elected professor. He was active in the foundation of the Pathological Society in 1857, serving as its first secretary. Costa also has to his credit medical writings. [34]

Peter Francisco, the Portuguese Patriot

Peter Francisco, born Pedro Francisco in Azores, was kidnapped presumably by Moorish pirates from his home in Terceira Island and left on a dock in Virginia in 1765 when he was approximately 5 years old.

Fig. 60- Peter Francisco in 1828 painting. Courtesy of Virginia State Library

He grew up to be a giant of a man who served the American Revolution with fierce pride and performed outstanding feats of strength and heroism. [36] To appreciate better his tremendous contribution to the American Revolution, note the words of General George Washington: *Without him we would have lost two battles, perhaps the War, and with it our freedom. He was truly a One-Man-Army.* [37] Dr. John Manahan reported to the University of Virginia the following under the title *Peter Francisco, Virginia Giant of the Revolution* a lengthy document from which is the following quote: *He (Peter Francisco) was of a dark complexion, with black eyes...* [38] Again this color description is similar to the one given to the Melungeons.

Francisco was known to have fought in various northern battles and is reputed to have slain 11 British in one battle and captured a 1,100 pound cannon and turned it on the enemy.

Abade Correia da Serra and Thomas Jefferson's Monticello

The third President of the U.S., Thomas Jefferson, took 25 years to build his dream house, Monticello. The room used by *abade* José Francisco Correia da Serra (1750-1823) was recently refurbished. It was inaugurated on June 18, 1995, after a restoration project financed by the Foundation for the Luso-American Development (FLAD).

Correia da Serra was known to the American President's family as *abade – abbot* in English – because of his original Portuguese title. President Jefferson is known to have invited Correia da Serra to give his opinion of the Philadelphia University articles and by-laws. [39] He was also a scientist, botanist, polyglot and founder of the Portuguese Sciences Academy.

Fig. 61 - The "Abade" José Correia da Serra room

To be admired is the meticulous work done to restore the room. The highlight of the room is an 18th century Portuguese Arraiolos rug that was donated by FLAD, previously restored in the *Arte Antiga* museum in Lisbon. Correia da Serra was a university professor in the U. S. and, after being introduced into the circle of enlightened individuals with whom President Jefferson enjoyed spending time, Correia da Serra won the President's respect and friendship.

He lived in the U.S. until 1820, the year in which he returned to Portugal to spend the last three years of his life. By that time he had been Jefferson's guest in Monticello on numerous occasions, accepting the President's repeated invitation to *come and make yourself at home.* [40]

Fig. 62 - Abade José C. da Serra [35]

Dr. Manuel Luciano da Silva, an historian and researcher of the Portuguese in America, was awarded on November 4, 1995, the Peter Francisco Medal, and during this event it was mentioned that Humberto Carreiro discovered that Monticello, the famous home of President Thomas Jefferson, in Virginia was the property of a Portuguese Jewish family, Machado Philips Levy, who saved Monticello from destruction.

Portuguese in Virginia and Washington, D.C.

One of the most famous Americans was born in Washington, D.C., on November 6, 1854, and his name was John Philip Sousa, son of the Portuguese John António Sousa and German Maria Elizabeth Trinkaus. [41] He grew up to become the famous march composer of *Stars and Stripes Forever*. President Ronald Reagan, in 1987 approved a law that made the *Stars and Stripes Forever* the official march of the United States.

In Virginia, it is interesting to find the existence of a large thoroughfare "Portugee Rd." which is not far from the Richmond Airport in Virginia.

During an interview with Isabel Paul of the Enrico County Library, she stated that the name Portugee dates to the early 1800's, however, in 1887 was called White Oak Swampy Road, and before that was called New Road, a name given to any road where the naming presented a problem. Isabel could not tell the author, the exact date when the road was finally named Portugee. The issue of the 1978 Enrico County Historical, page 44, had additional

Fig. 63 - Sign near Richmond, VA. by Linda Aguiar

information on naming of roads. After some more research, the author came across Dr. Lewis Manarin – a member of the Enrico Historical Society – whom he interviewed. The author was told of a legend dating back to the late 1700's and early 1800's, that in the neighborhood there was a Portuguese settlement, and the road now called Portugee Rd. led to it.

Later the settlement was abandoned and the name disappeared, to show up 50 years later. Dr. Lewis Manarin also informed of a Jim Walthal which later the author had the opportunity of talking to, and the result is an amazing story that just started to unfold and promises to be very interesting. Mr. James B. Walthal was kind enough to provide the author with the information related to his relatives. His great grandfather José Vieira Ramos came to this country in the 1830's under amazing circumstances. Before proceeding with his story, let us review Portugal's situation in the early 1800's.

France's Napoleon had just made a pact with Russia in 1807, which left him free to turn against Britain, Sweden and Portugal. Spain had been Napoleon's ally since 1796. He then summoned Portugal to close all ports to the British and declared war on Britain. A French army of 30,000 crossed Spain and invaded Portugal, while the Portuguese royal family fled to Brazil, which later proved to be the starting of the independence process for the largest South American country, then a Portuguese colony.

While in Portugal, the Napoleonic forces occupied Porto (Oporto), a northern city, and also other places in Portugal. The war with France lasted until 1814, and during that time, Jim's grandfather, as a very young man, apparently fought against Napoleon's army during the occupation and later the retreat under pressure of the Portuguese and British allied army. The part of the Napoleonic wars fought in Portugal and Spain contributed considerably to Napoleon's eventual downfall.

After that, José Vieira Ramos returned to his native Azores, where he got himself involved in some kind of rebellion against the government. The details are rather sketchy. He, together with other participants in the rebellion, were put aboard a ship and deported to another island, presumably Tarrafal in Cabo Verde, the favorite place for the Portuguese government's political prisoners.

He knew what was in store for him and his companions, and they together mutinied and took over the ship's command, forcing it to go west towards the American East coast, landing in southeast Virginia.

The American government considered them refugees and gave them some land as a place of settlement near what is today Portugee Road in the suburbs of Richmond, Virginia. Some of them stayed for a while and others moved to the city, including Jim's great-grandfather, who met a Virginian lady, married, and had children whom he encouraged to learn music. One of the children was Manly Burrows Ramos, a name borrowed from one of the Baptist ministers, which he held in high regard. Manly was Jim's grandfather and father of Alice Ramos, the mother of Jim.

One of the offspring became a pharmacist, another a school teacher, and so on. José Ramos Vieira was naturalized as an American citizen in 1836, one of the earliest, and joined the Baptist Church, where he was held in the highest respect. When he died in 1895, he was the oldest member of the Baptist Church.

Portuguese in Illinois and President Lincoln - 1846

The state of Illinois received the first group of Portuguese in 1846 under unique circumstances. A Protestant English missionary on the way to the Orient stopped in Madeira, and due to his wife's illness he had to stay. While there he was able to convert a number of Madeirans.

After a while the Catholic clergy became hostile. A few years later, this group left the Madeira Island, went to the British West Indies and Trinidad to work on a plantation. Due to climate and work conditions they did not adapt well, and the first group of 130 eventually wound up in Springfield after overcoming quite a number of problems.

Although they found work conditions unbearable in Trinidad, [43] they were good workers, which is reflected in a favorable report on them by the governor that sparked the beginning of the emigration to Bermuda of many Portuguese.

Other groups also went to Jacksonville, and for the next few years many more of the original group joined them. Many of the traditions no longer exist except for a place still called the Portuguese Hill and a few typically Portuguese family names. In Springfield also lived Abraham Lincoln, who later became President, and a member of his household staff was Frances Affonsa, one of a Portuguese refugee group from Madeira. Manuel de Fraita (Freitas), another Portuguese that Frances liked, would come to visit Frances at Lincoln's place and they had supper together. It is believed they got married.

President Abraham Lincoln, a Melungeon Descendant?

Fig. 64 - Portrait of President Lincoln by Chicago photographer Alexander Hesler, taken in Springfield June 3, 1860. One of the few photographs showing Lincoln without a beard. [42]

Anyone reading President Abraham Lincoln's biography, would see good indications that his mother, Nancy Hanks may have descended from Melungeons.

The sixteenth President of the United States was born on February 12, 1809, in a log cabin in a backwoods farm of Kentucky, near a place called Hodgenville in what is now Lauren County. Samuel Lincoln, the President's ancestor, emigrated to Massachusetts in 1638.

Later his grandson Abraham Lincoln, crossed the mountains from Virginia and settled in Kentucky. His son Thomas Lincoln worked under Joseph Hanks learning carpentry and later married his niece Nancy, who gave birth to Abraham Lincoln, and 50 years later would be nominated for President.

Not much is known of his mother, except that she was the illegitimate daughter of a Virginia planter and a woman called Lucy Hanks. [44] Abraham Lincoln said of his mother, "I owe everything that I am to her," explaining further, that he inherited from her, *the mental qualities which distinguished him from the house of Lincoln.* [45]

From the above, and also from Nancy's physical features, it is possible to assume she is of Melungeon descent. It is also written that her name was Nancy Sparrows Hank, and her mother was Lucy. Studying Lincoln's genealogy on his mother's side is a monumental task, as many doubts are presented along the way. No clear decision has been reached by the historians, or at least their opinion is not unanimous. [46] Also, the description of Nancy Hanks adds another common factor: *Her dark skin, dark brown hair, keen little gray eyes, outstanding forehead...* [47] As to the description of his father Tom Lincoln, it is somewhat similar to his son

Abraham, according to Carl Sandburg: *As Tom Lincoln came to his full growth he was about 5 feet, nine inches tall...His dark hazel eyes...coarse black hair.* [48]

Portuguese and Moor, According to Abraham Lincoln

Further research into President Lincoln's life reveals a connection with dark complexioned people and the Portuguese. While working as a lawyer in Springfield, he accepted a case from a Portuguese called Dungey. The name written in Portuguese, *Dungue*, is not very common, and may indicate that in the 1850's, Dungey's past generations had already been established.

As to the Portuguese Dungey's case, this was the result of him being called a *negro* by his brother-in-law, named Spencer. It was a crime under Illinois laws then for a white to marry a *negro;* therefore, the words were slanderous and Dungey had Lincoln bring a slander suit in which Spencer stated that Dungey, a *Black Bill is a negro and it will be easily proved if called for.*

Lincoln, when addressing the jury, accused Spencer of having called Dungey a *nigger* and argued: *Gentlemen of the jury, my client is not a negro, though it is not a crime to be a negro - no crime to be borne with a black skin. But my client is not a negro. His skin may not be as white as ours, but I say he is not a negro, though he may be a Moor. Not only had Spencer called Dungey a nigger but he had followed it up with adding a nigger married to a white woman.* The jury gave a verdict of $600.00 to the Portuguese. [49]

When reading *Alex Stewart, Portrait of a Pioneer* by John Rice Irwin, the founder and director of the Museum of Appalachia in Norris, Tennessee, it is interesting to note what he wrote: *...when I enrolled in Lincoln Memorial University in Harrogate, Tennessee, a small college in full view of Cumberland Gap. Abraham Lincoln had suggested the college be built to educate the mountain people, the majority of whom had remained loyal to the Union throughout the Civil War.* [50] There are indications that well known figures may be Melungeon descendants. Since Kennedy's book was published, a number of personalities have come forward and shown interest in Melungeon genealogy.

Portuguese in Hawaii

Of more than one million people living in Hawaii, 20 percent have Portuguese blood. [51] It is not hard to believe that a Portuguese may have been its discoverer. English historians record Captain James Cook as the discoverer of the islands in 1778, however, other historians refer Juan Gaetano (João Caetano), who was a Portuguese navigator working for Spain, as the discoverer in 1555. Hawaiian traditions tell of the arrival of mysterious foreigners who remained and intermarried.[52] *In 1527, Fernando Cortez, the conqueror of Mexico, dispatched a fleet of three vessels to the Spice Islands (the Moluccas) by way of Guam and the Philippines... and two ships disappeared* [53] which reinforces the Hawaiian oral traditions of a shipwreck about the same time. In 1542 the Spanish sent another

Fig. 65 - Lusitana Street in Honolulu, Hawaii

fleet with João Caetano as chief navigator. *Jean de La Perouse, the famous navigator who followed.*

Captain Cook to Hawaii in the 1780's was convinced that Caetano had discovered Hawaii, and wrote the voyage as follows: "It appears certain that these islands were discovered for the first time by Caetano in 1542". [54]

After Caetano's voyage, the Spanish produced a number of charts indicating a group of several large islands known to them as *Isla de Mesa.* After some debate, it was assumed to be the same group seen by Caetano. Honolulu Professor A. Mouritz also concluded that a relationship existed with Caetano's discovery.

Captain Cook, the official discoverer, asked if the Spanish knew the location of Hawaii, why did they not make use of the islands to provision their ships? The answer again is secrecy, also given by the Portuguese to justify the lack of detailed information about their discoveries. We know that in late 16th century the Spanish were at war with the English who were also already navigating in the Pacific. It is natural to assume that the Spanish did not want the enemy to know the location of any islands in the Pacific, and strict orders were issued to avoid any mention of the *Isla de Mesa* group.

Eventually the charts fell into the British hands, possibly in the 1740's, 30 years before Captain Cook arrived in Hawaii in January 1778. [55]

It is hard to believe that, with so many Portuguese and Spaniards sailing the Pacific Ocean since the beginning of the 16th century, the islands would await discovery by Europeans for more than 200 years. Magellan and many others sailed the Pacific in the early 1500's. Portuguese were living in the islands as early as 1794, however the earliest Portuguese visitor was John Elliot de Castro, of whom details are available. He first arrived there in 1814 [56] and later became Secretary of Foreign Affairs to King Kamehamea (1790-1918). Portuguese emigration did not occur in great numbers until late 19th century. Between 1878 and 1899 approximately 11,937 Portuguese immigrants landed in Hawaii, most of them after a lengthy voyage of more than three months. [57]

After the overthrow of the monarchy, three of 18 delegates to the Constitutional Convention were Portuguese, and two out of six from the Oahu District were also Portuguese. Between 1909 and 1929 no less than 31 members of the territorial legislature were ethnically Portuguese.

Jacinto Pereira, known as Jason Perry, was born in Faial, Azores, in 1826. One of the most distinguished among the early Portuguese in Hawaii, he served as a consular agent and was instrumental in getting the Hawaiian authorities to recruit laborers from Madeira. By 1913, it is estimated that just from the Azores Islands, around 10,000 had settled in Hawaii, officially known as the *sister islands to the Azores*.[58]

Fernando dos Santos, editor of the Portuguese-American newspaper *Luso-Americano,* wrote a book titled *The Portuguese in Hawaii* based on many interviews with Portuguese descendants in Hawaii and provides an actual picture of the Portuguese making of the youngest American state.

The four-string ukelele most people believe to be native to Hawaii, is of Portuguese origin. It was brought over by the Portuguese emigrants when a large percentage of Madeirans emigrated to Hawaii in the early 19th century. Today it is a symbol of Hawaiian music. In continental Portugal is called the *cavaquinho* or *braguinha,* with possible origins in the Portuguese city of Braga. This musical instrument is very popular in the north of Portugal and in the Madeira Islands.

The name ukelele means *jumping flea* in Hawaiian. King Kalakaua became fond of the original *braguinha* and started the trend. Three Madeira immigrants, Augusto Dias, José do Espirito Santo and Manuel Nunes, set up a business manufacturing the instrument in Honolulu. It was produced in Hawaii by a Portuguese between 1877 and 1878, and Arthur Godfrey made it very popular through television. [59] I was told by Mariano Rego, an Azorean musician, that the braguinha, was brought into Hawaii by an immigrant from Madeira by the name Barbosa. Also from Hawaii, the steel guitar evolved from the Portuguese *viola* or guitar when a native Hawaiian boy got the idea of using his pocket knife to get a special sound effect.

Portuguese in Louisiana

In a New Orleans cemetery, a Delaney tombstone has several Portuguese names. The earliest one is D.N. Manuel Pereira, dated 1837, Teodoso Pereira, 1841, Maria Joaquina Pereira in 1849 and others with more recent dates.

Fig. 66 - New Orleans Mausoleum of a Portuguese family.
Photo courtesy Ilidio Pereira

Fig. 67 - Mausoleum - Proud members of the New Lusitanos Benevolent Association inspect their new society tomb in the Girod Street Cemetery on the day of its dedication in October 1859. The tomb was decorated with black velvet panels trimmed with silver. Tomb designed by N.J. de Pouilly. Courtesy Leonard V. Huber Collection

In August 1853, the Portuguese Beneficence Society celebrated its fifth year with 430 members. The Portuguese had one of the best halls in New Orleans, and in 1891, 1892 and 1893 the Knights of Joy Parade, as well as New Year's Eve events were held there. [60]

Several associations were formed, such as the Portuguese Benevolent Society in 1857, the Portuguese Society in 1855, the Portuguese Benevolent Association in 1870, the Lusitano Benevolent Society in 1848, and the New Lusitanos Benevolent Association after that.

On Delacroix Island, Louisiana, lived a group of people called *The Islenos* who in the 1970's were still speaking 18th century Spanish brought to Louisiana by their ancestors. *Linguistic studies have found the presence of Portuguese, French and English...*[61]

That may also indicate the presence of the Portuguese at an early period.

Portuguese in Nevada

It is known that during the latter half of the 18th century a group of emigrants from Madeira, as part of an exodus that began in the 1840's from Funchal, eventually wound up on the Midwestern frontier.

First to California at the time of the gold rush, beginning in 1849, came thousands of Azoreans, Madeirans and Cape Verdeans, who also made their way to Hawaii. This restless population of the 1850's and 1860's, now in California's Sierra Nevada, came down to Nevada, Oregon, Washington, Idaho and the South Dakota Black Hills.

It is in Nevada that in 1853 some Portuguese surnames are recognized. Solomon Nunes de Carvalho, a Sephardim Jew, David Nunes and Sara d'Azevedo, a Jewess. The greatest part of Virginia City population was foreign born, and among them were some Portuguese. The Surrey County of 1875 census lists 109 males born in Portugal. Seventy five percent were miners, including one woman, which was extremely rare. The same data indicates that many Portuguese appear to have preferred to operate small businesses, such as grocery stores, restaurants and others. [62]

Donald Warrin has made extensive studies in this area.

Portuguese in California

The presence of Portuguese in California goes back to the 16th century, with explorers and navigators already mentioned. Later, in the 18th century, José Manuel Machado was placed in command of the Presidio at the San Diego Mission in 1769, in the 19th century Antonio José Rocha, also known as Don Antonio Rocha settled in Los Angeles, in 1815.

Rocha was born in Minho, Portugal, on January 18, 1790, and died in 1837. His peasant background, as well as the tragic consequences of the Napoleonic Wars, combined to obscure all but scattered bits of information. However, it is assumed that he may have embarked in Madeira aboard the Canadian schooner *Columbia*, bound for Monterey, California, where he arrived in November of 1814. Later he married to Maria Josefa and had several children. [63] His son, Antonio José Rocha, served as the district judge of Balboa, 1868-1873.

Also, there was a Portuguese in the Spanish army stationed at the Presidio in Santa Barbara (1798-99). His name was José Antonio de Azevedo, he was a native of Lisbon, Portugal. [64]

It is interesting to note that just about the same time we have other Portuguese arriving in Virginia, also consequences of the Napoleonic Wars mentioned earlier. Rocha built his house, which later was sold to the municipality and became the first City-County Municipal building of Los Angeles. There is still another: Carlos Pedro Diogo Andrade also arrived in California shortly after 1825 and moved to Sacramento in 1846.

These are not the only ones. Francisco José da Silva and João Soito Freitas, both from the Azores, are but a few of the many Portuguese who went to California in the early 1800's. Some of them drifted north to Oregon and into the Rocky Mountain territories. [65]

Captain Antonio Mendes, said to have been the first person to navigate the Sacramento River, arrived in San Francisco in 1853. He was borne in Terceira, Azores, and joined the crew of a whaling expedition bound for the China sea. He tried his hand at mining, then bought some ships and, later in life, farmed in Sutter

County. Pporfessor Eduardo Mayone Dias has made extensive studies about the Portuguese presence in California.

Portuguese in Wyoming

John *Portugee* Phillips was born in 1832 as Manuel Filipe Cardoso in the Azores. Leo Pap, in his well researched book *The Portuguese-Americans,* describes an interesting part of his life where he became a sort of Paul Revere of the West. While working at Fort Kearney, along the Bozeman Trail in Wyoming, he volunteered to break through the siege lines to seek help at the next fort. This meant riding 240 miles through hostile territory, in freezing snow, which earned him special praise in Congress. That almost impossible task was called a much greater feat than the famous ride of Paul Revere. [66]

Antonio Monteiro was another Portuguese in the Rocky Mountains in the 1830's. He worked for John Jacob Astor's American Fur Company in the fur trade business, with Spaniards and French. Born in the city of Porto, Portugal, son of José Soares Monteiro and Ana Maria Manuel Monteiro.

Monteiro commanded a 50 man expedition into Crow Indian country, and it was in this expedition that he made his most significant contribution to the history of the Western frontier by establishing a trade post, which consisted of a cluster of cabins and came to be known as Portuguese houses. [67]

Portuguese in Idaho

Gold attracted also the Portuguese to this state, and in 1862 there are records of Portuguese being in the gold mines of Idaho and the rush to Boise. ...*Late in the summer of 1862, the opinion of old miners that a rich deposit would be found ... finding to be rich for fifteen miles... While encamped... they were fired upon by some Shoshones who had hung upon their trail for several days. Grimes, Wilson, Splawn and the Portuguese pursue the attacking party... Grimes was shot...the eleven returned to Walla Walla...bringing with them... between $4,000 and $5,000 in gold-dust...*[68] The name of the four Portuguese miners are unknown as well as another Englishman also with the group.

Portuguese in Missouri

The Portuguese may have arrived there in 1803 when a Portuguese Jew by the name Salomão Barbosa accompanied the famous Louis and Clark explorations to the West as a cartographer. Also, a priest named Father Himalaya was contracted as a scientist by the U.S. armed forces, and some inventions have been attributed to him. Later in 1904, when the Worlds Fair was held in St. Louis, Portugal had a pavilion there. The grandson of the director for the Portuguese exhibit still lives in St. Louis, owning a gallery called Gomes Gallery. Manuel Luis da Ponte, who had a weekly radio talk show in St. Louis when the author visited that city while doing the research for this book, provided the above information. [69]

Antonio Monteiro, a fur trader, also came to Missouri and returned in 1839-40 to Wyoming but later moved to northern New Mexico where he married and had two children. His presence in this state was noticed until 1845.

Portuguese in the Bermudas

It is rather difficult to talk about Portuguese and Spanish navigators without mentioning the Bermuda Islands. After all, situated in the Atlantic Ocean, they are about 570 miles (900 km) east of Cape Hatteras (North Carolina), an area where navigation activity has occurred since the early 1500's .

The Spanish navigator Fernández de Oviedo sailed close to the islands in 1515 and attributed their discovery to his countryman Juan de Bermúdez. probably between 1503 and 1511. In 1612 Bermuda was included in the third charter of the Virginia Company, and 60 English settlers were sent to colonize the islands. Indian and African slaves were transported to Bermuda beginning in 1616, and soon the slave population outnumbered the white settlers.

There is an inscription on a rock that marks one of the intrusions by Portuguese navigators in the overseas dominions of Castile.

The story relates to a Portuguese merchant ship that left Santo Domingo with their men and shipwrecked off Bermuda in 1543, but all the men were able to save themselves. [70] They stayed there for 60 days and left a mark with a Portuguese Cross of Christ, the letters *JR* and the date 1543.

About three-fifths of the population are descended from African slaves brought to Bermuda before Britain outlawed the slave trade in 1807. Whites include the British and descendants of Portuguese laborers from Madeira and the Azores who went to Bermuda in the mid-19th century. English is the major and official language, but some Portuguese is also spoken. It is believed that between 15 and 20 percent of the population have Portuguese ancestry. The Portuguese population is estimated between 3,000 and 5,000 thousand.

The Portuguese do participate actively in the social and political life of the islands. Trevor Monis is a member of the Bermuda parliament (1996) and is one of four already in the House of Assembly. The others are Ernest DeCouto, Harry Soares, Clarence Terceira. [71]

North Carolina - Searching for Roots in 20th Century
Gaston, Northampton County, N.C. by the Virginia Border - 1958

The next illustration is the title – not so long ago – of an article occupying the full center page of the Virginia newspaper *The Virginian Pilot* on January 26, 1958. The article was written by Luther J. Carter and was accompanied by three large photographs depicting the school and a group of Portuguese children playing. The following is a transcription of the article in its entirety, so that the reader can make a proper judgment of the circumstances of these *Portuguese* people as they were classified.

The Virginian-Pilot **FEATU**
and
The Portsmouth Star   SEC

Century-Old Stigma Remains

'Portuguese' Youngsters Segregated in Carolina

Fig. 68 - Article title about the Portuguese in 1958

JACKSON, N.C.—A tiny group of "Portuguese" children occupies a narrow, forsaken middle zone in Northampton County's Segregated school system.

Eighteen pupils, aged 6 to 16, attend the Bethany School, a one classroom cinder-block building tucked away in a pine grove in the County's northwest corner just below Emporia, VA.

The shabbily clad children come from widely scattered homes in Gaston township, some of them walking six miles to reach the school.

These innocents bear a stigma imprinted at least 100 years ago. The approximately 16 "Portuguese" families now living in the County are further isolated from their white and Negro neighbors by a 35 year old legislative act creating for them the separate school.

Why? For one thing, there is a widely held belief among the county's white residents that these people are descendants of Northerners who mingled with five Negroes in pre-Civil War days, with some intermarriage taking place.

The origin of these people, and how they came to be known as Portuguese is obscure. Apparently illiterate, just as some still are today, they left little or no records relating to their history. Hearsay speculation, unsubstantiated theories are all that is left.

The hard lot of the present day "Portuguese" is easy enough to document, however. Unwilling to associate with the Negroes, and generally unwanted by the whites, their tradition of ill luck and ignorance is being perpetuated. Only those who leave the County appear to have a chance to escape this curious web of circumstance.

***Strange Blend** - The Bethany School is a strange blend of the modern and antiquated. Built several years ago to replace an older building that burned, its front consists largely of glass and steel framing, and, inside, modern circular light fixtures hang above the rows of desks.*

Against the rear wall there is a pot-bellied coal stove. Behind the building one sees a hand operated water pump and privy.

The teacher, Miss Osceola T. Crew, a slim, white-haired spinster who 17 years

Fig. 69 - These "Portuguese" children are delighted with themselves, like children anywhere. But what of the future, as fugitive students and citizens apart?

ago went to the school after the superintendent asked her if she wanted to do some *"mission work,"* occupies a role that has all but vanished in American education.

The grades are from the first through the eighth and she teaches them all. In nearly every grade the children vary one to three years in age, and most are over age for their grade. One third-grader, a 15-year-old child has recently had a brain tumor removed, Miss Crew described as *"almost a mental case."*

Slow Progress - *The other children, she says, are of average ability, with a few above average. Their progress is slow because of poor attendance.*

State Law fixes the public school year 180 days. Miss Crew estimates that, on the average, her pupils are in class somewhere around 100 days.

Various reasons are given for this. She says most of the children come from farm homes whose *"economic condition is terrible."* In the spring and fall the parents want the children to help with the crops. Normally attendance is best in mid-winter, but when a reporter visited the school recently one third of the class was absent. *"Hog killing time,"* Miss Crew explained...

Hog killing time. Something typical of Portugal; a very special time in rural

Fig. 70 - The building where the Portuguese School classes were held in 1958 for the segregated Portuguese children is still standing. Shown in the photo is Mr. Tom Willey.

communities of the mainland and with islanders of yesteryear, when complete families, neighbors and friends gather together in sometimes, a few days feast. This is still an important event today with the Portuguese people.

The fact that the County operates no school bus for these children contributes to the bad attendance, particularly in inclement weather. Miss Crew picks up some of the pupils each morning, but others must walk.

Another explanation, which appears especially important where the older children are concerned, is indifference. Some of the pupils regard the Bethany School as an academic dead end. The County provides no high school education for the Portuguese. They are not allowed to attend the white schools and do not wish to attend the Negro schools.

How it Happened - How did this came about? Judge W.H.S. Burgwyn of Woodland, who has served in both the state House of Representatives and Senate, caused to be passed by the 1923 session of the General Assembly a Law stating "that the people known as 'Portuguese' shall have a separate school from the white and colored schools...."

Two years later, the Assembly enacted a Law permitting the same people to register themselves as "Portuguese" on the voter registration books.

Burgwyn hazily recalled the 1923 school Law, but when first asked about the registration Law he drew a blank. His best recollection was that he introduced the school bill at the request of the Portuguese. The County school officials were in accord with the proposal but did not originate it.

"I don't know why they call themselves Portuguese," Burgwyn says, then indicates he introduced the bills chiefly out of sympathy.

A Forlorn Group - "I had a distinct belief that they were not Negroes," he explains. "I just thought they were a forlorn group of people. They were not accepted by white people and they didn't want to associate with Negroes."

Many were "blue-eyed and sandy-haired," he remembers and bore names that were not of English origin. (However pupils now attending the Bethany School have such names as Bass, Scott, Peters, Turner, and Hobbs.)

Before the enactment of special school Law the Portuguese apparently did not

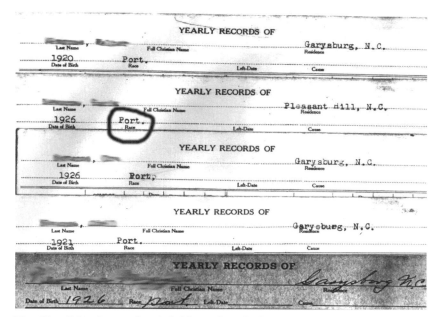

Fig. 71 - *School records of children classified as Portuguese race born in the 1920's. See word "Port." circled. Names have been covered for privacy.*

send their children to school at all or sent them to a private school. Miss Crew has heard that Bethany Mission Church (now the Bethany Methodist Church where the Portuguese still go) and a private school were organized during the decades immediately after the turn of the century.

Fig. 72 - *The sign today means what it says.*

Has no Illusions *- N. L. Turner, a pleasant easy going man, has been superintendent of County schools for 19 years. He has no illusions about the quality of education provided the Portuguese but seems to see no way of giving them something better. He thinks that consolidating the Bethany School with white schools wouldn't work "The white folks just never accepted them here," he remarks. A step towards consolidation might be to admit pupils finishing Bethany to the white school at Gaston. But not long ago a girl who wanted to enter this school was rejected. For such a pupil the County will offer to pay only $25 a month towards his room and board if he wants to attend high school in another community.*

Fig. 73 Northampton County Courthouse in 1995

Some pupils have done this and been readily accepted by white schools. Rarely one is rebuffed. Asked about the lack of school bus service for the Bethany pupils, 'Turner replies, "They never asked for any. The fact is that they're so scattered you couldn't get them."

The poor attendance of the pupils, coupled with the fact that there is no high school for them, raises the question of the enforcement of the compulsory attendance Law. "The Law is not enforced," Turner says without hesitation. "It is not enforced anywhere, not in this County or anywhere else." He believes the regular attendance of pupils is virtually impossible without the cooperation of parents and suggests that cooperation of Bethany families s often lacking.

What about the future? What's to become of the Portuguese?

With the air of one who prefers to let history run a free course, Turner replies, "It'll take care of itself. There aren't half as many of them now as when I first came here. They'll eventually go away. Some will marry colored, others will marry white." Meanwhile, Miss Crew works patiently with her pupils. She teaches them about DaGama, Magellan, the other great Portuguese explorers. "I try to give them a sense of pride, she says."

Meanwhile in Portugal
Human Dignity and Respect for Someone else's Name

That was the title – translated to English – in the largest Portuguese newspaper *Diario de Noticias* out of Lisbon, Portugal, on March 11, 1958. Apparently it was referring to the article published by *The Virginian Pilot* previously. This newspaper was considered to be the official voice of the Portuguese government, a dictatorship under Salazar at the time, and in this article it was demanding that the American government – North Carolina – would cease to call this people Portuguese. It goes on to repeat much of the *Virginian Pilot* article, translated to Portuguese.

An official from the Embassy of Portugal in Washington, by the name Bernardo Teixeira, press and cultural affairs attaché, visited the area in March 1958 and reported that the families in question *"were all completely white, related to each other, with Anglo surnames; they claimed to have been in Northampton County since the construction of the Roanoke Rapids Canal, c.1820, when their (allegedly*

DIGNIDADE HUMANA

e respeito pelo nome alheio

Fig. 74 - Copy of the article published in the Portuguese newspaper Diario de Noticias

Portuguese ancestors came from Pennsylvania or from Portugal to work on the canal; and they have been locally described as 'Portygee,' never as Croatan or Melungeon, as far back as at least 100 years".

It is reported, according to the records of Pennsylvania Colony, from 1727 to the Revolution, that there were some Portuguese. Scattered lists of immigrants landing at Philadelphia from Lisbon or Amsterdam between 1769 and 1805 include a number of Portuguese names, some undoubtedly belonging to persons of Jewish descent. [72]

The Portuguese newspaper ends the article with a veiled threat, stating that only a few miles away in Norfolk, is the (NATO) North Atlantic Treaty Organization headquarters, of which Portugal was and still is a member, and if nothing is done about, the Portuguese voice would be heard in protest.

Roanoke Rapids - March 3, 1958

The Portuguese from Gaston were again in the news. This time the *Sunday Herald* of Roanoke Rapids featured a front page story with the title *Northampton's Portuguese Go Elsewhere For Higher Education*. Dick Kern wrote the story that describes the education problem with the *Portuguese Community* in the County of Northampton. His remarks are interesting: *Many veteran public officials admit it*

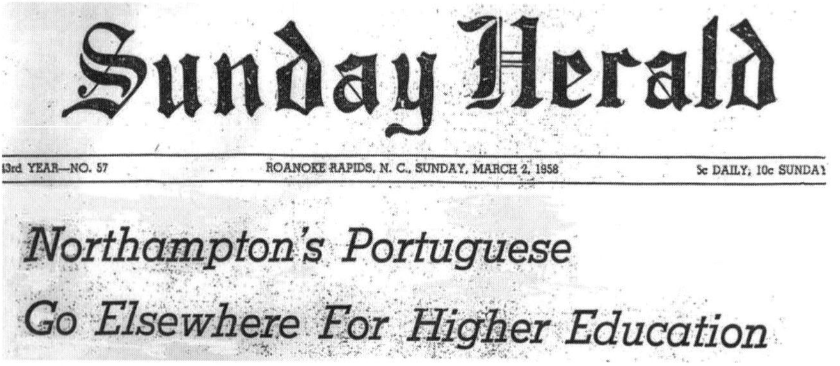
Sunday Herald

43rd YEAR—NO. 57 ROANOKE RAPIDS, N. C., SUNDAY, MARCH 2, 1958 5c DAILY, 10c SUNDAY

Northampton's Portuguese

Go Elsewhere For Higher Education

Fig. 75 - Roanoke newspaper March 3, 1958

Fig. 76 - Glenn Scott beside the plaque describing the historical Roanoke canal and honoring the Portuguese immigrants who build it.

is one of the most unique situations in the state, if not the nation. The people are registered on election books as Portuguese, but still are not accepted for what they are by many people who often call them resentful names. [73]

Gaston, NC

The author did visit the Gaston area in North Carolina and, while searching for anyone that could help, he met Reverend Simpson from the United Methodist Church, who pointed him to Mr. Willey. At the time he found that there are still a number of families living in the area, known to be descendants of Portuguese left over from a much larger group. These people do not want to talk about it due to discrimination suffered that ended just recently. The local people feel guilty about it, and they are quick to point out that *we are all united now.* Even during the second world war they were refused service in the armed forces and had to move to a different county.

They, just like the Melungeons, do not speak Portuguese or keep any Portuguese culture, and use English names such as Turner, Bass, Scott and Hobbs. They were there in the early 1800's and worked on the Roanoake River waterways canal, having moved from the mountains.

On researching the local library and the few historical records available, the author found that the Roanoke waterway was constructed by several groups of people who provided labor. However, the description terminated with ... *and others*, probably referring to persons that the historians did not wanted to name by group.

The Gaston Portuguese children of 1958 as adults

Later the author returned to Gaston and talked with Glenn Scott, one of the descendants of the Portuguese families living in the area for almost two hundred years. After the first few words of introduction, the author told him that he was Portuguese. That seemed to have had an impact, as from that moment on, he was much more friendly and communicative.

Someone told him that their ancestors may have came from Brazil, Pennsylvania or the mountains looking for work, and established themselves in the area after the

Fig. 77 - Present Generation of the Portuguese from Gaston

building of the Roanoke canal was completed.

Scott offered the author a tour of the area. The place where the canal was built is a beautiful trail to visit and enjoy.

It is not likely that this group originated from Brazil or Pennsylvania, unless they belonged to one of the groups in the Pennsylvania mountains.

If the Gaston's Portuguese came from Pennsylvania, it is hard to believe that they would have lost all signs of Portuguese culture, including all surnames, since the 1800's, a time when communications and regular travel between Portugal and the U.S. were frequent. An official Portuguese diplomat was already in place. Also, and while doing research for this book, the author spoke with descendants of Portuguese immigrants who arrived in 1830, and who still remembered their ancestry and family names.

One of many persons that have been assisting in this research obtained a copy of a letter – now an historic document – addressed to the Portuguese Consulate in Philadelphia from the Portuguese Embassy in Washington, testifying to the truth of this incident with the following message to (In Portuguese): *Exmo. Sr. Vice-Consul de Portugal em Philadelphia.*

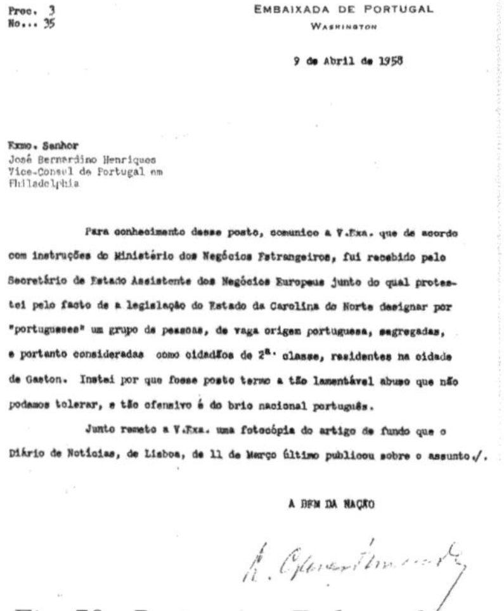

Para conhecimento desse posto, comunico a V. Exa. que de acordo com instruções do Ministério dos Negocios Estrangeiros, fui recebido pelo Secretário de Estado Assistente dos Negócios Europeus junto do qual protestei pelo facto de a legislação do estado da Carolina do Norte designar por "portugueses" um grupo de pessoas, de vaga origem portuguesa, segregadas, e portanto consideradas como cidadãos de 2ª classe, residentes

Fig. 78 - Portuguese Embassy letter

na cidade de Gaston. Instei por que fosse posto termo a tão lamentável abuso que não podemos tolerar, e tão ofensivo é do brio nacional português.

CHAPTER 602

AN ACT TO PROVIDE SEPARATE SCHOOLS FOR THAT RACE OF PEOPLE IN GASTON TOWNSHIP, NORTHAMPTON COUNTY, KNOWN AS THE "PORTUGUESE."

The General Assembly of North Carolina do enact:

Separate school.
Proviso: school building.
Teachers supplied.

SECTION 1. That the race of people known as "Portuguese" in Gaston Township, Northampton County, shall have a separate school from the white or colored schools in said county : *Provided,* said Portuguese shall furnish a suitable building situate in Gaston Township for said school, said building to be approved by the county board of education for said county of Northampton.

SEC. 2. That after said building shall have been provided as aforesaid, the board of education for Northampton County is hereby 687 empowered and directed to provide teachers for said school for said race, and said teacher or teachers shall be paid as other teachers in said county are paid without extra tax on said race of people, except as they may vote same upon themselves. The teachers of said school shall be either of the said race known as Portuguese or white persons, as in the discretion of the board of education for Northampton County it may deem proper.

Payment of teachers.
Teachers of Portuguese or white race.

SEC. 3. This act shall be in force from and after June fifteenth, one thousand nine hundred and twenty-three.

When act effective.

Ratified this the 6th day of March, A.D. 1923.

Fig. 79 - Record as ratified on 3/6/1923

AFTERNOON SESSION

SENATE CHAMBER,
MONDAY, March 5, 1923.

The Senate meets pursuant to recess, and is called to order by Honorable W. B. Cooper, Lieutenant-Governor.

The President names Senator Woodson as a member of the commission to investigate as to the advisability of renovating the Canova statue of Washington.

Upon motion of Senator Woodson, S. B. 1182, A bill to repeal subsection 7 of section 5151 of the Consolidated Statutes, relating to Confederate pensions, and providing for an appropriation of $500,000 for additional pensions, is taken from the Committee on Pensions and referred to the Committee on Appropriations.

Passes its second and third readings and is ordered enrolled.

S. B. 1463, H. B. 1661, A bill to provide separate schools for that race of people in Gaston Township, Northampton County, known as "Portuguese."

Passes its second and third readings and is ordered enrolled. *(CHAPTER 602)*

Fig. 80 - Record as passed on March 5/1923.

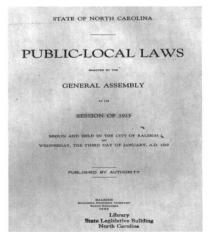

Fig. 81 - Record Book of the N.C. General Assembly of 1923.

Junto remeto a V. Exa. uma fotocópia do artigo de fundo que o Diario de Noticias, de Lisboa, de 11 de Março último publicou sobre o assunto.

A Bem da Nação, [74] (signature not legible).

Follows the translation in English: *Mr. Vice-Consul of Portugal in Philadelphia: for your information and according to instructions received from the Ministry of Foreign Affairs, I was received by the Assistant Secretary of European Affairs, and protested the fact that legislation of the State of North Carolina has designated as "Portuguese" a group of persons, of vague portuguese origin, segregated, thus considered as second class citizens, residents in the city of Gaston.*

I insisted that this intoreable abuse be terminated, and so offensive it is to the Portuguese national pride.

Enclosed find a copy of the article as published by the "Diario de Noticias" of Lisbon, dated March 11th last.

To the Good of the Nation....

The Embassy letter and other documents are now part of the history of the Portuguese making of America.

Roanoke Canal Built by Portuguese Immigrants

The Roanoke Canal contains some of the most impressive and best preserved early 19th century canal construction in the nation. Begun before 1819 and completed in 1823, the Roanoke Canal was built as

One of the aqueducts built by Portuguese in the early 1800's

Fig 82 - Glenn Scott and the aqueduct built by his Portuguese ancestors

the North Carolina segment of the ambitious Roanoke navigation system designed to connect the Blue Ridge mountains of Virginia with Norfolk, over a distance of 400 miles.

The canal was constructed by hand and has an aqueduct built of local granite that spans 30 feet in a single arch. It is one of the area's most impressive engineering accomplishments.

According to local tradition, it was built by Portuguese immigrants, many of whom remained in the area. It is interesting to note that this construction was built to connect the Blue Ridge Mountains to the seacoast by water. The Blue Ridge Mountains, is the home of many Melungeons. Presently, part of the remaining aqueduct is located near Gaston, where many families known as the Portuguese still live. They, like the Melungeons do not speak Portuguese or keep any Portuguese culture, and use English names such as Turner, Bass, Scott, Hobbs. The plaque, in a simple way, does honor the Portuguese. Research at the Raleigh archives of North Carolina, produced a copy of the General Assembly laws passed in 1923, as shown on Fig. 79 and 80. They were there in the early 1800's and worked on the Roanoake river waterways canal, having moved from the mountains.

Luther J. Carter was the journalist who wrote the story about the Portuguese from Gaston, and now, almost 38 years later, he still remembers the article vividly. He could not add any more than what was published. However, he said that the Portuguese government did send a protest note to the State Department.

The governor of North Carolina, in order to appease the Portuguese government, called the Portuguese ambassador in Washington and sent him a gift with the emblem of North Carolina (Tar Heel).

Robert Mason, at the time the editor of the *Virginian Pilot* also followed the story. The author contacted Mason. He remembers the article, the meeting with Bernardo Teixeira and the fact that he began to rage and criticize the Americans and North Carolina – while having a coffee at a restaurant – for the conditions that they forced the *Portuguese* people to endure. At that time, Mason warned him, *if you don't shut up, I will call the waiter and tell him that you're Portuguese, and I am sure that they he'll throw you out of this restaurant.* Mason also recalls that he was for the most part interested in the young Portuguese girls. *"Well, they were good-looking too, I can add",* said Mason. The Portuguese diplomat also mentioned that these people reminded him of people from the Azores Islands. Later, Teixeira got quite upset for getting a traffic ticket from the local Police. In a later interview, Mason added that he believes that these Portuguese people are connected with the Melungeons and also the possible shipwrecks off the coast of North Carolina.

Notes

[1] La España del siglo X, Fray Justo Perez del Urbel, p.12

[2] Roberto Leal and Márcia Lúcia, CD

[3] Translation by Melissa Mira Knippel

[4] Memoirs of Judge Lewis Shepherd, 1915, p.87-88

[5] Portinglês, Vol.4, p. 1348, by Adalino Cabral

[6] U.P.E.C., Summer 1988 issue, Antonio Monteiro by Geofrey L. Gomes, p. 7

[7] Makers of America by Wayne Moquin, p. 85

[8] The Portuguese-Americans by Leo Pap, p. 11

[9] Portuguese Settlement, by William Freitas, Ph.D., Portuguese Heritage, 12/1993, p. 22

[10] Historia da Inquisição em Portugal by Alexandre Herculano, pp. 98-99

[11] The Master and the Slaves by Gilberto Freyre, p xii

[12] Farewell España by Howard M. Sachar, p. 352

[13] The Jews in America by Max I. Dimont, p.28

[14] Ibid, p.11-12

[15] The Jews in America in Colonial and Revolutionary times by Leon Huhner, pp. 16-31

[16] The Jews of South Carolina by Leon Huhner, p. 50-51

[17] The Jews in America by Max I. Dimont, p.240

[18] Boletim do Inst. Historica, Presença de Portugal, by Manoel da Silveira Cardozo,p. 11

[19] Historia da Lingua Portuguesa by Serafim da Silva Neto, p. 528

[20] The Jews of Newport by Hugh Huhner, pp. 4-6

[21] Ibid, p.49

[22] Makers of America by Wayne Moquin, p. 85

[23] Ibid, p.91

[24] The Portuguese-Americans by Leo Pap, p.44

[25] The Makers of America by Wayne Moquin, p. 127

[26] The Portuguese-Americans by Leo Pap, pp. 10-11

[27] Ibid

[28] Our Fair Lady:the Statue of Liberty, Reader's Digest, July 1986, pp. 191-197

[29] A Future to Inherit by David Gibbs, p. 9

[30] They Ploughed the Seas by Pat Amaral, pp. 132-133

Notes (Cont.)

[31] Boletim do Instituto Historica, Presença de Portugal... by Manoel da Silveira Cardozo, p. 13

[32] Ibid, p.15

[33] Photo from article by Henrique Mano, *Luso-Americano*, Nov.22nd 1996, p. 14

[34] Dictionary of American Biography by Allen Johnson, Vol. V, p. 24

[35] Luso-Americano by Henrique Mano

[36] Peter Francisco by William Arthur Moon, cover painting

[37] America's Great Soldier (Esquire Magazine, March 1942) by Robert Buckner

[38] Peter Francisco by William Arthur Moon, p. 52

[39] Dicionario de História de Portugal, Vol. V, p. 540

[40] FLAD Newsletter, August 1993, p. 8

[41] Encyclopedia Britannica, Vol.20, p. 953 (1967 edition)

[42] Abraham Lincoln by Carl Sandburg, p. 159

[43] The Portuguese Immigrants by Leo Pap, pp. 23-24

[44] In the Footsteps of the Lincolns by Ida M. Tarbell, p. 82

[45] Abraham Lincoln by Lord Charnwood, p. 6

[46] In the Footsteps of the Lincolns by Ida M. Tarbel, p. 84

[47] The Prairie Years by Carl Sandburg, Vol.II, p. 52

[48] Ibid, Vol.I, p. 13

[49] Ibid, Vol.I, p. 6-7

[50] Alex Stewart Portraid of a Pioneer by John Rice Irwin, p. 12

[51] The Portuguese in Hawaii by Fernando dos Santos, p. 5

[52] The Portuguese Immigrants by Carlos Almeida, UPEC, p.14

[53] The Portuguese in Hawaii by John Henry Felix and Peter F. Senecal, p. 150

[54] Ibid, p. 151

[55] Ibid, pp. 153-154

[56] The Portuguese-Americans by Leo Pap, p 31

[57] Ibid, pp. 14,15

[58] Azores Islands a History by James H. Guill, Vol. 5-651

[59] Ibid, p.18

[60] New Orleans Public Library Documents

[61] New Orleans Times Picayune of July 5, by John R. Kemp,

[62] Portuguese Immigrants in Nevada by Donald Warrin, UPEC Life 1989

[63] California History, Sept. 1987, El Portuguese by Eduardo M. Dias and David E. Bertão, p. 188

[64] Geoffrey Gomes, California State University at Hayward

[65] The Portuguese Americans by Leo Pap, p. 30

[66] Ibid

[67] U.P.E.C., Summer 1988 issue, Antonio Monteiro... by Geofrey L. Gomes, p. 6-8

[68] The Works of Hubert Howe Bancroft, Vol. XXXI, p. 259

[69] Interview with Manuel da Ponte in April 1996

[70] Eprigrafia Portuguesa by João Vidago, p. 174 (Oviedo Y Valdés p. 577)

[71] Luso-Americano, 4/10/96, p. 6-7

[72] Portuguese-Americans by Leo Pap, p. 242-3

[73] Northampton's Portuguese... by Dick Kern (Sunday Herald, March 2nd 1958, f. page)

[74] Embassy of Portugal letter dated 1958

Chapter IX

Portugal Leads the Way

Animals leave nothing, people leave history

Portugal, the first modern national state to reach its present size by the 13th century, led the way in the attempt to reach the Far East by water. Her good location and her seamen, trained in the school established by Infante D. Henrique (Henry the Navigator 1394-1460), provided ideal conditions. The poverty of her people, unable to buy high-priced luxuries and her desire to expand territorially, as well as a holdover of the crusading spirit, were major reasons for her enterprising spirit. The route sought was around the tip of southern Africa and success was finally achieved when Vasco da Gama reached India in 1498. [1] That single event was to affect the world in an unforeseen way.

Portugal began its overseas expansion in 1415, establishing colonies in the 1500's (Goa, Damão e Diu), and in other parts of the world. [2]

There has been some controversy by historians or scholars about the existence of the Sagres school for navigation in the 15th century . They doubt that possibility. Well, they maybe right if they refer to the Sagres school in the same manner as the modern naval learning institutions we know today. Most likely it did not have elaborate buildings or a proper faculty, but the first school known to men was just a few bench seats in a park.

The Portuguese Sea Route to East India

The discovery of America, and of a passage to the East Indies by way of the Cape of Good Hope, are the two greatest and most important events recorded in the history of mankind. [3] The reader probably will be thinking, what has East India to do with the Melungeons or the Portuguese in North America? As it will be shown, it may have the most logical explanation for the origin and arrival time of the people – who later would form the Melungeons and other groups – on the North American continent.

As we read in the previous chapter, Bartolomeu Dias rounded the southern tip of Africa in 1488, which he called the Cape of Good Hope, *Cabo da Boa Esperança*, also Cape of Storms or *Cabo das Tormentas*.

He accomplished that, nearly five years before Columbus made his first landfall in the Caribbean, in what he thought were the East Indies.

Ten years later, Vasco da Gama, following the Bartolomeu Dias route, found the seaway to India. He was to die in that same area when he was part of Cabral's fleet to India. The Portuguese discovered what Columbus was seeking: the fabled East Indies. They also chartered new sealanes halfway round the globe to Japan. [4] The Portuguese, by their discoveries, not only extended the limits of the world known to Europe, but contributed greatly to its more accurate representation.

At the end of the 15th century, the introduction of a scale of latitudes was made, and in 1502 the Cantino map was already showing the Portuguese discovery of India. [5] Also shown on that same map is the Caribbean and Florida.

The Search for India by Land - 1487

Pero da Covilhã and Afonso Paiva, of Portuguese Jewish origin, traveled to India by land. On the way they separated, Covilhã did get to India, and on the way back to Portugal he met emissaries from the Portuguese King, ordering him to go back and get more information. It is not known if Covilhã's letter ever got to Portugal, but if it did, the king would know then that the shortest way to India by sea would be to follow the African coast to the south, turn north and east.

This information was kept secret and may have been the basis for Portuguese King João II's rejection of the Columbus proposal.

The Portuguese in East India - 1498

Trade, not conquest, attracted the Portuguese to India, and the 16th century brought two factors into Indian history, the *Mughuls* who came by land and the Portuguese by sea. *These two carried India into a new age.* [6]

Vasco da Gama, a Portuguese navigator, found a searoute to India in 1498, and from that date, Portugal changed drastically during a golden age that lasted only fifty years. During that time, trade, traveling and emigration were very heavy to the Far East.

Later in 1540 Vasco da Gama's son, with an armed force, kept the Turks on alert over a period of 15 years. [7]

Right from the beginning, the Portuguese government was involved in fostering mixed marriages of Portuguese and East Indians. According to royal plans, actual official intermarriages began in Goa by 1509. Each couple was granted an important subsidy or dowry in money, which rapidly increased the number of weddings.

In three or four years more than 500 marriages took place, mostly in Goa, but a few in Cannanore and Cochin also.[8] Duarte Pacheco Pereira became famous by his defense of the Cambalaan Pass against the Calicut's rajá during the beginning of Portuguese settlements in Canará (modern Karnatka). [9]

The intermarriages of Portuguese with the natives were common all over the Far East, as well as in Africa and Brazil.

In India, these intermarriages meant improved status to Muslim women, and the descendants of these marriages are still today all over the East, with Portuguese names and Portuguese words embedded in their speech. [10]

Out of one of these mixed marriages came Manuel Godinho de Heredia, who was no longer a pure-blooded Portuguese. His father, João de Heredia, married Helena Vassiva, daughter of the King of Supa, João Tubinanga.

Manuel was then a mixture of Malay–Portuguese and became famous for having claimed the discovery of the Isle of Gold in 1601, later called Australia.

Only in 1606 did the Dutch ship *Het Duifken* reach this continent, claiming its discovery. [11]

Malacca and Malaysia - 1509

The Portuguese arrived in Malaysia in 1509, occupied it for two years and controlled it for 130. The Dutch defeated the Portuguese in 1641, however, they were not able to erase all vestiges of the Portuguese presence. Today there's still a dialect derived from Portuguese and the Catholic religion. The *Portugis,* as they are called in Malacca, still have folkloric dances which are predominantly Portuguese, such as the *Vira* and *corridinho.* [12]

The Moluccas Sea and Moluccas (Maluku) Islands, today part of Indonesia, were originally named by the Portuguese as *Ilhas Malucas* in 1511, and also known as the Spice Islands. A film documentary presented by PBS-TV with the title *Ring of Fire*, demonstrates vividly the Portuguese presence on these remote islands during a festival on the Aru and Garuda islands. The Portuguese were the first Westerners to be seen by the natives. Echoes of the past are seen in a Portuguese soldier's helmet of the 16th century, used as a symbol, having Portuguese music in the background (fado) sung by Amalia Rodrigues. [13]

North Carolina, Graveyard of the Atlantic

David Stick wrote a book about shipwrecks in the Outer Banks of North Carolina. Although he was not able to find any records of early shipwrecks, he presents us with an impressive story of many ships lost in that area, starting with the Spanish brigantine of the fleet under the command of Lucas Vasquez de Ayllon in 1526 en route to Cape Fear in the Spanish colony of Chicora. [14] In order for the reader to better understand that part of the North Carolina coast, let us read what David Stick wrote: *You can stand on Cape Point at Hatteras on a stormy day and watch two oceans come together in an awesome display of savage fury...the northbound Gulf Stream and the cold currents coming down from the Arctic run head-on into each other...Seafaring men call it the Graveyard of the Atlantic.* [15]

It is important to note that not only ships bound to the West Indies or the American coast met their final destination at the graveyard...*Ships of many nationalities, of almost every shape and size, bound to and from the ports of Europe, Africa, and even Asia.* [16] The reason for so many vessels lost is due to the fact that this section of the North Carolina coast extends out into the sea from the South Carolina coast to Cape Hatteras. Mr. Stick goes on to say, *...the past history and the present day life of the entire coast of N.C. are closely integrated with shipwrecks.* [17] *...there are entire villages today populated with descendants of shipwrecked mariners.* [18]

Verrazano reported to the King of France that he explored the Outer Banks (North Carolina) and landed on the coast in 1524 at latitude of 34° – approximately the same as the Portuguese Madeira Islands – just above Cape Fear. [19] In this same area there are at least two known shipwrecks, in 1559 and 1564. [20]

Shipwrecked Portuguese Caravels

The East India trade book records written by Luis de Figueiredo Falcão show that between 1497 and 1692 a total of 806 ships left Portugal on their way to India and only 425 returned. Out of these, 381 ships that did not return, 285 stayed in India, 20 ran aground, 6 burned, 4 were captured by enemy forces or pirates and 66 were lost or shipwrecked.

The maritime connection from Lisbon to the Far East between 1497 and 1580 was by 620 ships with an average of six to seven ships per year. However, in 1505 the fleet was comprised of 28 caravels, and during the early 16th century, each fleet had 14 to 15 ships. [21]

From 1495 to 1578, 100 ships were lost by accident, shipwreck or piracy. The larger losses occurred in the early 1500's on the returning trips, as these were the most dangerous. The size of each ship was about 500 to 600 tons with a crew of 123 persons, or an average of 175 including passengers. [22]

On the same note, in 1591, of the 22 ships that left for India, only two arrived in Portugal. [23] Pedro Álvares Cabral, the official discoverer of Brazil, departed Lisbon, Portugal on March 15, 1500, with a Calicut, India destination. Cabral commanded a fleet of 13 ships in 1500, fewer than half arrived in India. The first one to disappear, without anybody ever knowing how, was the one commanded by Vasco de Atayde when he was off the Cape Verde Islands, south of the Canary Islands and in the same latitude as the Caribbean Sea, thus subjected to the equatorial currents, which could erroneously bring ships to the East Coast instead of South America, the original destination. See map on page 350.

After passing the Canary Islands and Cape verde, going in a westerly direction, it separated from the fleet and was never found. [24] Where did this shop go?

Carlos de Passos wrote that there were 27 shipwrecks lost due to storms and 12 to other causes in the period of 122 years. But many more occurred without anyone ever having any knowledge. Only after 1527 did narratives start to appear, and before that all is ignored, though the shipwrecks did happen. [25]

Bernardo Gomes de Brito, author of the book *The Tragic History of the Sea,* published in the 18th century, describes the losses of Portuguese ships on the voyage to or from India, while the west coast of India was under the rule of Portugal. [26] These are very interesting facts. Where did these vessels go or where were they shipwrecked? On the way to India, or on the way to Portugal? In either direction it is very easy to be pushed in a westerly direction, by currents or by winds, towards the North American continent. Could some of the ships have made their way to the east seacoast of America, on purpose or forced by forces of nature, before or after rounding the Cape of Good Hope in South Africa? The fleets to India always left Lisbon in March for the 18-month return trip. If they left later they would not take advantage of the southeast winds in order to arrive in India by September.

On the return trip from India the fleet would leave in January, but not later than February 15.

If during the many regular voyages any one of the southbound ships would be

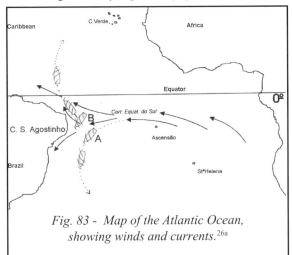

Fig. 83 - Map of the Atlantic Ocean, showing winds and currents.[26a]

forced westward by winds and currents after passing the Canary Islands, or on the return trip from India while approaching the equator, they would arrive on the U.S. East Coast during late spring, shipwrecked, mutinied, pirated or looking for lands to the west, known to exist. That time of arrival would give the settlers plenty of time to prepare for the winter, thus guaranteeing their survival, which the English were not able to do almost a hundred years later.

Illustration Fig. 83 above, shows how the winds and currents afected the caravels. It also tell us that as soon as a sailing vessel rounds the Cape of Good Hope, it will be pushed by these same winds and currents. The wind is an important factor, and in this case is the southeast trade wind that would prevail, pushing the vessels towards the west and the north of Brazil and the equator. As they get near the equator, the south equatorial ocean currents also give them a push again to the northwest.

Once they go past the equator, again, the north equatorial currents will do the rest of the job of getting the ships into the Gulf Stream, towards the U.S. East Coast and Cape Hatteras, the easternmost point before the Gulf Stream, again pushes them towards the east in a clockwise motion. The same situation occurs on the way south past the Canary Islands, when the ships are naturally pushed west toward the Caribbean. If their destination is India or Brazil, then the vessels must negotiate the most difficult part of the voyage before they reach the equator, according to Commander Malhão Pereira of the *Sagres*, a Portuguese navy school windjammer. See page 350 for map and details about a 1996 Conference.

We can conclude without a doubt it is very easy for a caravel to wind up on the shores of the U.S. East Coast, either going to India or Brazil or on the return trip.

These trade winds and currents brought Columbus to America, and all future navigators. The author's question: would it be possible for the Portuguese ships to wind up on the U.S. East Coast? Let us also keep in mind that most of the losses and shipwrecks occurred on the return trip. Or could the passengers have demanded that they be taken to America, which they knew about? Also life in India may not have been the land of milk and honey the Portuguese expected. Naturally, if that was the case, then they and everyone else on board, immediately became outlaws and avoided contact with anyone, taking refuge anywhere.

Shipwreck with Women and Children

One of the most tragic stories of the sea is the shipwreck of the galleon *S. João* in 1552 off the East African coast. Manuel de Sousa Sepulveda, the Captain, his wife and children all perished, along with many slaves and servants, in very tragic circumstances. [27]

Another tragic story is the shipwreck of the *Garça* in one of the Hakluyt Society works. *Francisco Barreto, the captain of the ship, and all the other officers, seeing the state she was in and that there was nothing else to do but abandone her, they agreed to trans-ship to the Aguia the women and children and other useless mouths in the first place.... decided to make a muster of all in his ship, so as to organize and accommodate them in the best way; and he found that they amounted to 1,037 souls, between gentlemen, soldiers, seamen, slaves, women and children.* [28]

In 1537, captain and ship owner Duarte Tristão, with his vessel *São Miguel* departed from Mozambique on the return trip to Portugal loaded with riches, disappearing without a trace. [29] These events point to the fact that complete families traveled in those days. The Portuguese nobles took their families with them as well as an enormous number of people in one ship alone.

See Appendix E for a chart of Portuguese shipwrecks known, page 329.

English and French Corsairs

Not only shipwrecks prevented many vessels from arriving safely in Portugal, but also the corsairs and pirates awaiting the Spanish and Portuguese galleons loaded with riches returning home. During the first half of the 16th century, the French corsairs were very active in attacking Portuguese ships off Portugal's coast and the islands. The third quarter of the 1500's saw plenty of action by English corsairs, Drake being the most famous.

Out of five ships that left Goa, India on January 10, 1592, only one arrived safely in Lisbon on July 17, 1592. The second, *Bom Jesus,* having as captain Manuel de Sousa Coutinho, his wife, many nobles, soldiers, sailors and slaves shipwrecked off the east Africa coast with no survivors. The third, *São Bernardo,* disappeared without a trace. The fourth was beached and burned on the Flores Island by its crew to avoid being captured by the English. The English were still able to salvage part of the cargo. The fifth, *Madre de Deus*, commanded by Fernão Mendonça Furtado, was attacked by a large English fleet of corsairs and captured after a fierce battle. It had aboard almost 600 persons, including women, children and slaves. [30] John Burrough, who was in command of the squadron, gave orders for the *Madre de Deus* to proceed to Dartmouth, where it caused great admiration. Russell Miller described it: *Pandemonium broke loose in England's Dartmouth harbor...when the Madre de Deus...dropped anchor...She was the biggest ship anyone in Elizabethan England ever seen...She stretched 165 feet in length, and had a beam of 47 feet and a burden of nearly 1600 tons – about three times the capacity of the largest English ships. Her seven decks...were studded with 32 brass guns...Chests were crammed with gold and silver coins, flawless pearls, amber, jewelry set with large diamonds and vials of precious musk...425 tons of pepper, 45 tons of cloves, 35 tons of cinnamon...*[31] and much more including cochineal, mace, nutmeg, benjamim (an aromatic substance) and ebony.

This is an example of the many battles fought on the high seas by the Portuguese, causing eventual loss of many lives and the capture by the enemy of Portuguese and Indian nobles for ransom. Did the English capture and take any of them to England? Did they later come to America as part of Jamestown Colony, to be established in 1607?

Fig. 84 - Map of Western India showing a native boy from Goa [48]

Portuguese Emigration to and from India

Emigrant families from Portugal going to India, or others returning home with their relatives – some of them of mixed marriages, as encouraged by the Portuguese government – were good candidates for arrival in North America instead of their chartered destination. Afonso de Albuquerque thought that it was necessary to create, in a place so far from Portugal, a strong and solid nucleus of roots, and to achieve that he promoted the marriage of good women and clean men. To those in mixed marriages he conceded favors, giving a home, land, cattle and a horse to start life. Later, in 1529, there were already more than a thousand children, sons and daughters of Portuguese in Goa.

The list of 54 weddings shows that 25 women were Moors from India –possibly Turkish – five were from Canará, and the rest from Malabar, Java, Burma and nearby lands. [32] In India, after the marriages, there were two classes among the European population, the *casados* (married) and soldiers.

That did not happen only in India, but also in Abyssinia (modern Ethiopia) when in 1646, Pedro Barreto de Resende wrote that he found a thousand men, children and grandchildren of 400 Portuguese, from when Cristóvão da Gama passed by the area with their women, children as well as their elders more than 100 years before. [33]

According to historians of the 16th century, India was absorbing the best of 8,000 men per year, and it is possible that the Portuguese population would have been reduced to less than half from the 16[34] century to the next.[34]

Fidelino de Figueiredo wrote that each India-bound ship transported an average of 250 persons. Between 1497 and 1527, the first 30 years of the Portuguese Empire in the Far East, 320 vessels departed to India and transported 80,000 persons, including soldiers and passengers. [35]

By 1570 there were 16,000 Portuguese in India. [36] In 1589, Paulo de Lima – a Portuguese captain – departed from Goa in India with a caravel loaded with spices and slaves. He had with him his wife and servants. Also aboard were many passengers, soldiers returning... and women. [37] It is also a fact that more than 10,000 men disappeared or died at sea. And to confirm that, Boxer also writes: *...during the 16th century approximately 2,400 people left Portugal yearly overseas, the great majority of them being able bodied and unmarried young men, bound for golden Goa, and... few of them returned.* [38]

João de Lucena, a 16th century priest and chronicler, wrote the life of St. Francis Xavier. St. Francis was born in Pamplona, Navarra (a name very familiar with the Melungeons), Spain in 1497 as Francisco Jasso Xavier and died in China on Dec. 2, 1552. He served as an evangelist for the Portuguese King João III from 1541 until he died. For his work the Catholic Church later made him a saint. Lucena describes what life was like aboard the ships going to India: *...what thing is an India nau* (ship) *put to sea on sails with 600, 800 and sometimes more than 1000 inside herself, men, women, little boys, free, slaves, nobles, common people, merchants, soldiers and sea people. Someone that compared it to a large village, was not exaggerating.* [39]

There is another fact that should not be ignored: the Portuguese Jews also signed up in many ships going to India, secretly, to avoid the Inquisition.

During the 17th century the Portuguese Jewish Diaspora stretched rapidly from the Ottoman Empire to Goa on the Indian subcontinent, from Denmark and Northern Germany all the way to Brazil and the islands of the Caribbean. Though so widely scattered, its members retained their identity as Portuguese Jews, seeing themselves as citizens of a nation uniquely heroic and tragic past.[40] Would they have any advantage by identifing themselves as Portuguese if they were not? Why not Spanish or other nationality?

The major emigration movements from the Azores were registered around the 16th century, towards Africa and India. [41] From the above information, we know that complete families traveled between Portugal and India,

Fig. 85 - Map of Western India, showing Karnataka, formerly Canará

which means they could settle and survive wherever they would go. Also, a large Portuguese population was traveling. Many vessels were not arriving at their destination, and no one ever heard of them. The trend established long ago continued in the 18th century, when it was recorded that many orphan girls went to India. [42] In any event, the Portuguese were the first Europeans to establish themselves in India, and the last ones to leave. *Four and half centuries were to pass between the conquest of Goa and the lowering of the Portuguese flag in that territory in 1961.* [43]

Rejected in India

Kennedy brings to our attention a possible fact that may help make the connection when he wrote: *Streams of escaping or exiled Moors made their way abroad, and historical records even depict a shipload of these hapless people seeking asylum in India, vainly claiming to be "sunburned Portuguese" in an effort to explain their ruddy complexions. However, the Catholic friar at Bombay, upon hearing their plea, knew better and denied them entry.* [44]

A further study of his source tells us that in 1589, the religious order of the Franciscans was still admitting *mestiços* as novices in Goa (India), though they had been ordered not to by their superiors in Portugal. Only 50 years later, a determined attempt was made by the European born Franciscans friars at Goa to prevent any Creole from holding office. The Creoles later defeated this order, and Friar Miguel da Purificação, who had been born near Bombay, argued that the many dark-complexioned Portuguese who came out to India were in reality Mulattos... contaminated with Negro blood, *"although they allege that they got sunburn during the voyage".* [45] From this we have to assume two things, one that they indeed were accepted in India, and two, that the problem was only in the fact that these dark Portuguese were not being allowed to hold office within the Catholic Church, and he was referring exclusively to the friars. Furthermore, we are now in the early 17th century, many years after Drake's famous Roanoke rescue and the massive expulsion of Moors from Spain, which occurred in the late 15th and early 16th centuries.

If we add to the fact that a trip from the Mediterranean to India would be quite costly just for food and water alone, it is difficult to believe that their ship would have made it all the way to India, without Portuguese knowledge or authorization. This fact may not be important, but it may point to the many missionaries in East Africa that were looking for a position in India, and these missionaries were definitely a mixture of African, Portuguese and Indian, thus explaining the dark complexion, which you find today in many Portuguese living in Portugal and elsewhere, who descend from East Indian families.

Portuguese East India Men and Women

From the above, we may also have overlooked another aspect, and that is the possibility of East Indians, living in some of the Portuguese colonies in India, and having already intermarried with local people, produced a new generation of Indian-

Fig. 86 - Photo of a Melungeon child and Melungeon young man taken by Doris Ulmann in the 1920's. Used with special permission from the Berea College and the Doris Ulmann Foundation [51]

Portuguese. Fernão Vaz Dourado was a famous cartographer born during the early 1500's in India of an Indian mother, and produced many atlases often known as the Vaz Dourado type. [46] The classification of Moors (to all the Muslims) by the Portuguese may have brought the same name to the North American East Coast, to anyone originating from any of the areas controlled by the Ottoman Empire. [47]

Let us look further into this possibility and read what William H. Gilbert, Jr., a well known anthropologist, wrote in his book *Peoples of India* about racial types of this nation: *The physical types of the people of India show a wide range in all the characteristic features of skin color, nose and head form, hair, and stature...The color of the skin ranges from dead black... to the ivory skin of the Kashmiri beauty and the wheat color of the higher casts of upper India. ...A third element in the racial typology of India is a strain similar to the Mediterranean peoples of southern Europe.*

This may provide us with a connection, but it also may add confusion to the already confused puzzle as Gilbert adds the next paragraph:

A fourth racial type is a generally reminiscent of the Nordic type of Europe, except that the complexion is more brunet. Its traits include long-headedness; a tall stature; a long face; prominent, narrow nose; usually straight hair, with body and head hair well developed; and occasional light eyes or hair. Among the Kaffirs and the Pathans, the skin color of this type is mainly a rosy white tint, and an appreciable number possess gray-blue eyes and chestnut hair.

This description adds strength to a possible connection to the Melungeons, if we recall the first encounters of the English with Indians in 1584 and John Lawson with the Hatteras in 1700.

James Adair in his thesis: *Doubtless the idea that the Carolina natives were backward cousins of the people of Bombay and Calcutta influenced, to a certain extent, many of the old descriptions of their dress and ornaments.* [49] It is quite interesting the parallel established by the writer with the East Indians.

See Appendix D for a chart showing the wedding of Portuguese men and East Indian women, page 327.

Canará Melungeon Name

The name Canará may help to put the puzzle together. As mentioned in Chapter II, Kennedy revealed to us in his book that his great uncle's name was Canara Nash, and this name was common among the earliest Melungeon families.

Battles took place in 1509 involving many nationalities, between Muslims and Portuguese, and among them was a very confused population with their *junks* (type of boats used in the far east) from Diu on the Gujerât, and from Calicut (Kalikodu) on the Canará. [50]

Kennedy, a Melungeon descendant, also has darker skin and blue eyes, as well as some Mediterranean and East Indian resemblance. He himself said that often he was mistaken as a Turk, when he visited Turkey for the first time. Let us keep in mind that the Turks (Ottoman Empire) were very active in India during the 16th century. Also the name Canara is mentioned again in similar circumstances by Charles R. Boxer. [52]

Another coincidence shows up when you look up an older map of India and verify that there is a large area in northwest India named Canará by the Portuguese, later named Karnataka. This area is located near Goa, which the Portuguese held till 1956, and very active since 1498, when Vasco da Gama found the sea route to India. Karnataka, or Canará (Kannara in English), is rather large and divided into

*Fig. 87 - Photo of a Melungeon young man taken
by Doris Ulmann in the Appalachians ca. 1930.
Used with special permission from the Berea
College and the Doris Ulmann Foundation.*

north and south regions, which had their own language, called *Canarês* or *Canarim,* except Goa with its own language, Konkani. It is known as a land of seafarers even today. The name *Canarim* was erroneously applied by the Portuguese to the people of Goa. [53] Fig. 84 shows the area of Karnataka, and to the north, the cities where the Portuguese built their empire of the Indias. (Goa Damão and Diu.) Bombay was also part of the Portuguese Empire, but it was given to King Charles II as a dowry of the portuguese Princess *Catarina de Bragança.* Also notice the artist's conception of a typical Christian boy native of Goa. His face denotes a Mediterranean resemblance and would be quite at home in any Portuguese village. All of the above describes the Portuguese connection of the name Canará (Karnatka), the English and the people from India.

Let us keep in mind that Portuguese families, some of mixed marriages and others not, were traveling back and forth on a regular basis between Portugal and India. If they wound up on the East coast, that would explain the variety among the Melungeon groups or others that may have separated and formed other communities mixed with the local Indians, such as the Lumbees.

Also, the cover page of the *National Geographic Magazine* of June 1985 gives another example of a Far East face with red-brown color and striking greenish-blue eyes, of a girl refugee from Afghanistan, not far from the west coast of India. Since we are looking at strange coincidences, the name *Kannada* (a corruption of the name Karnatka) is the name for a large area of India and sounds just like *Canada.* The Portuguese were the early explorers and settlers in both places.

Portuguese in Australia

The Dutch in 1606, and English in 1770, have long been known to have reached Australia. However, for more than two centuries a debate has been going on about

Fig. 88 - Cas Goins, daughter Gladys Goins, wife Ritter Jane Sergen and son Homer Goins, a Melungeon family in the early 1900's.
Photos Courtesy of Pat Rice,Sheppersdville Kentucky.

other Europeans who may have preceded them. [54]

The Dauphin or Harleian map shows inscriptions on the apparent continent (Java-la-Grande) Australia south of Indonesia that derived from Portuguese sources. The presumption was that some Portuguese mariners were really the first Europeans to reach Australia. Numerous writers have upheld and elaborated upon this theory. Apparently the case for an early Portuguese discovery of Australia rests entirely on imagined resemblance between the continent of Java-la-Grande on the Dieppe map and Australia.

Counter argument is the justification of the way the names were written, which was according to the way they sounded. The author presented an example that I have to disagree with. He says that *Queensborough* sounds just like *Coimbra*. [55] Well, does it? You the English-speaking reader, what do you think?

Kenneth McIntire and Ian McKiggan are the two strongest advocates of the Portuguese discovery. The only argument left is to use common sense. The Portuguese were in Indonesia, close to Australia, and used native pilots whenever possible. Sumatra was known in the 16th century as *Taprobana*, a name made famous by the Portuguese national poet Camões.

The Portuguese conquered Malacca and were in the Moluccas in the 16th century. The distance from these islands to the north or west coast of Australia is only a few hundred miles. Timor, which is very close to Australia, was visited by the Portuguese in 1514 and became active in the third quarter of the 16th century with the presence of missionaries.

Timor was part of Portugal until 1975, when Indonesia annexed it. Their people did not accept the annexation and have been rebelling for the last 20 years. Their leaders, Dr. José Ramos Horta and Bishop Carlos Filipe Ximenes Belo, have recently been awarded the Nobel Peace Prize for their activities.

Is it possible that the Portuguese and the area's native pilots did not know about Australia? Most likely they did, but since there was no immediate trading value, it was ignored. Manuel Godinho de Heredia – half Malay – in 1601 claimed the discovery of the Isle of Gold, later called Australia.

Let us remember that Portugal and Spain had signed the Tordesilles Treaty, which would enable Spain to claim ownership of Australia. So why tell the world about new lands that Portugal could not claim under the treaty?

Just recently (1996) a Portuguese silver coin from the 16th century was found in a beach near Melbourne, Australia. The Australian State Museum in Victoria has confirmed the coin's country of origin and the date; however, coin experts disagree. One other 15th century coin has also been found and is now awaiting confirmation from experts in Portugal.

Some Portuguese historians, including Admiral Gago Coutinho, believe that Gomes de Sequeira discovered York Peninsula in Australia and spent some months there living in peace with the natives. This conclusion is based on the Gastaldi map published in 1554. [56]

Gomes de Sequeira stayed away from his base for eight months, and the question is, where did he spend the winter of 1525? He visited New Guinea which is approximately 100 miles from Cape York in Australia.

He also recorded a discovery of a large island inhabited by Pacific natives. We should keep in mind that discussions were under way as to whom the Spice Islands belonged, Portugal or Spain. The argument was settled when Portugal bought them. Later it was discovered that they were on the Portuguese side of the Tordesilles Treaty. So Portugal had paid for what was already hers.

Asiatic and Oriental Appearance

Dr. Edward T. Price, in his doctoral dissertation on mixed-blood groups, published in 1951, wrote:... *An Oriental appearance is occasionally attributed to them, but they are commonly thought to be of at least partly Portuguese descent.* [57] Louise Davis of the Nashville *Tennessean* describes Mrs. Bell, a Melungeon lady, after an interview: ...*her skin had the red-brown color of an Asiatic.* [58] Is this a coincidence? In the mountains of Tennessee? Again she writes that the *Encyclopedia Americana* states: *Chinese sailors were known to have made their way to Portugal and intermarried with the Portuguese, and the slightly Oriental strain is one of the clues to the occasional slant eyes and silky skin of some of the Melungeons.* [59] Arthur Estabrook writes in 1926: ...*in Ad County, Virginia there is a group of "red skinned people" who have considered themselves white.* [60] The Asiatic appearance, with its varied colors, is possible and easy to explain, if we interject the Portuguese element: they were on the Arabian coast and throughout Asia during the early 16th

Fig. 89 - Cas Goins, a Melungeon c. 1945
Photos Courtesy of Pat Rice,
Sheppersdville Kentucky.

century, with the consequent miscegenation well documented and recorded. In 1952 North Callahan wrote: *...Colony of strange people with dark complexions of a reddish-brown hue was found in the upper Smokies.* [61]

Bonnie Ball, a teacher who taught the Melungeon offspring, wrote of her own personal experience and knowledge: *Their skin was dark and oily, showing more of a coppery color than of, say, Ethiopians or darker members of the white race.* [62] *...They* (Melungeons) *had a noticeable red color that was constant throughout their family...* [63] Again, *...She* (Melungeon student) *was very dark, with dark eyes and drooping eyelids; however, her nose and mouth were more oriental than Caucasian or Ethiopian.* [64] Jean Patterson Bible, on their possible ancestry, also writes: *The most likely tradition of the Asiatic or European strain in the Melungeon heritage, according to a majority of Melungeons, and one shared by a number of early and later Tennessee historians...* [65] An Oriental appearance is not common with the Portuguese, but you can still find looks that maybe resemble Oriental. This explains the discrimination the Melungeons had to suffer because of the color of their skin, but also points to an origin.

Henry Price, an attorney in Rogersville, Tennessee, wrote about the Melungeons in 1971 as someone that lived with the Melungeons and studied them for 25 years: *As a rule the young men are quite handsome and the young girls are strikingly beautiful. The later...might suggest Eurasian and Polynesian ancestry.* [66]

Speaking of Asiatic appearance, the ethnologist Mooney cited a reference made by Barton in 1797 relating to white people and also to moon-eyed people. This is rather interesting and should not be ignored: *There is a dim but persistence of a strange white race preceding the Cherokee...The Cheerake tell us, they found it possessed by certain 'moon-eyed people' who could not see in the day time...He seems to consider them an albino race. Haywood, twenty six years later, says that the invading Cherokee found "white people" near the head of the Little Tennessee.* [67]

It can be concluded that there is a long road ahead before the early history of America can be completed.

Portuguese in Japan and China - Portuguese Language in the Far East

The Portuguese arrived on the southeast coast of China in 1513 and were considered no threat. After a period of hostilities and clandestine trade, the Canton provincial governor signed a treaty in 1550. Eventually the Portuguese were allowed to set up shop in Macau, where they still are today. It will be handed over to the Chinese in 1999, making Portugal the longest standing colonial power in the Far East. In 1543, the Portuguese Antonio Peixoto, Antonio da Mota and Francisco Zeimoto were the first Europeans to arrive in Japan, and Europe's first major port in Japan, the city of Nagasaki, was founded in 1570 by the Portuguese seeking a harbor for their ships. [68] In the following century (1660), Portuguese navigators went from Japan to Lisbon by way of the Arctic.

In 1544, on the way to Japan, Portuguese explorer Fernão Mendes Pinto discovered and named Formosa [69] – meaning *beautiful* – the Island of Taiwan off the China mainland, as well as the Formosa straits. The origin of the Chinese name Taiwan is not known. Some of the small islands (Penghu Islands) are also known as the islands of the *Pescadores*, a Portuguese name. In Indonesia the *Flores* Island name was also given by the Portuguese.

The Portuguese language is the fifth most spoken language in the world after Mandarin Chinese, English, Hindi and Spanish. It is also the third European language ahead of German and Italian, as well as one of the oldest in Europe, with a rich literary tradition. It is the official language in seven independent countries and spoken by 200 million people. English is, however, the most widely spoken language in the world, and considered to be the current *lingua franca*.

The spreading of the Portuguese language began in 1430 in the Azores and Madeira islands, 100 years before the first attempt to populate Brazil. In 1551 the English Winham visited Guinea and the King of Benim spoke Portuguese to the English, a language that he had learn in infancy. It is not surprising the importance given to the Portuguese language, if we take into consideration that Portugal was the only country in Europe that spoke only one language, *a linguistic unity absent elsewhere in Europe.* [70]

This is just to show the expansion of the Portuguese language in the world, and it is a *fact that Portuguese today has more words of Asian, African and Amerindian origin than any other European Language...* [71] It is one result of the far- reaching dialogue between civilizations, in which the Portuguese were the pioneers. [72] Between the 16th and 18th centuries, the Portuguese language in creole versions was used as the international language of the Orient and along the African coast. In 1658 the Dutch governor, Van Goens, decreed that it would be forbidden for the slaves to speak Portuguese among themselves, with the Dutch or foreigners. [73] He tried to stop its use in Ceylon (modern Sri Lanka) and Java, in vain. Even the Danish and English missionaries preached in Portuguese right up to the dawn of the 19th century. In order for the French priests to be understood, they had a Portuguese interpreter repeating the sermon aloud in Portuguese. In South Africa it was the second language during the 17th and 18th centuries, and it is not surprising to find words of Portuguese origin in the Dutch, French and English languages.

See Appendix F for a glossary of words with Portuguese roots used in Japan.

Notes

[1] Colonial America by Oscar Theodore Barck, Jr. , p. 3

[2] The Melungeons by Bonnie Ball, P. 29

[3] The Conquest of Paradise by Kirkpatrick Sale, p. 3 (Adam Smith)

[4] National Geographic Magazine by Merle Severy, p.57, November 1992

[5] Christian and Spices by John Correia Afonso, p. 33

[6] History of India by Romila Thapar, p.336, 1974

[7] The Ottoman Centuries, by Lord Kinross, 1977,
New York Morrow Quill, p.246

[8] History of Portugal by Oliveira Marques, p. 249-250

[9] Portugal nos Mares by Oliveira Martins, p. 270

[10] National Geographic Magazine by Merle Severy, p. 79 (November 1992)

[11] Portugal nos Mares by Oliveira Martins, p. 151-3

[12] Lusa News Agency by Brian Oneil, Luso-Americano, April 25/1995

[13] Ring of Fire by Lorne and Lawrence Blair (PBS TV), VHS tape

[14] Graveyard of the Atlantic by David Stick, p. 5

[15] Ibid, p. 1, Ibid, p. 2, Ibid, p. 3, Ibid, p. 4

[19] The Outer Banks of North Carolina by David Stick, p. 13

[20] Ibid, pp. 13,14

[21] Historia de Portugal by Joaquim Verissimo Serrão, V. III, pp. 159-162

[22] Historia de Portugal by Oliveira Martins, p. 299

[23] Os Navios de Vasco da Gama byJoão Brás de Oliveira, p. 14

[24] Historia de Portugal by Joaquim Verissimo Serrão, V. III, pp. 102

[25] Navegação Portuguesa dos Séculos XV e XVII by Carlos de Passos, pp. 10-11

[26] Portuguese Voyages by Charles David Ley, p. xviii

[26a] Map by Navy Commander Malhão Pereira, presented at the Marine Academy

[27] Historia Tragico-Maritima by Bernardino Gomes de Brito
(Damião Peres), p. 23-39

[28] The Tragic History of the Sea by Father Manoel Barradas
(C. R. Boxer), p. 40-43

[29] Peregrinação by Fernão Mendes Pinto, p. 22

[30] Batalhas e Combates da Marinha Portuguesa by
Saturnino Monteiro, pp. 269-272

[31] The East Indiamen by Russel Miller, p. 8

[32] Historia da Lingua Portuguesa by Serafim da Silva Neto, p. 533

[33] Ibid, pp. 518-536

[34] Fomento Rural e Emigração by Oliveira Martins, p.32

[35] Estudos de Historia Americana by Fidelino de Figueiredo, p. 21
[36] History of Portugal by Oliveira Martins, p.299
[37] Ibid, p.291
[38] The Portuguese Seaborne Empire by Charles R. Boxer, p.52
[39] Historia da Vida do Padre Francisco Xavier by João de Lucena, Vol. 1, p. 44
[40] The Jews of Spain by Jane S. Gerber, P. 188-189
[41] Portuguese Immigrants by Carlos Almeida, UPEC, p.4
[42] Historia da Lingua Portuguesa by Serafim da Silva Neto, p. 533
[43] Christians and Spices by John Correia Afonso, p. 34
[44] The Melungeons by Brent Kennedy, p. 103
[45] The Portuguese Seaborne Empire by Charles R. Boxer, p.252-3
[46] Japan in Early Portuguese Maps by Alfredo Pinheiro Marques, p. 15
[47] Ibid, p.44
[48] National Geographic Society, December 1984, Peoples of Southeast Asia Map
[49] The Red Carolinians by Chapman J. Milling, pp. 7-8
[50] Historia de Portugal by Oliveira Martins, p.231, 286, 288
[51] National Geographic Society Dec. 1984, Peoples of Southeast Asia Map
[52] The Portuguese Seaborne Empire by Charles R. Boxer, p.41
[53] Glossário Luso-Asiático by Sebastião Rudolfo Delgado, pp. 196-197
[54] The Portuguese Discovery of Australia by W. A. Richardson, p. 5
[55] Ibid, p. 12
[56] Onde Teria Invernado Gomes de Sequeira em 1525 by
      Gago Coutinho, p. 1525
[57] The Melungeons by Bonnie Ball, p.8, Edward Price, Geographical Review,V.41
[58] The Mystery of the Melungeons by Louise Davis, p. 11
      (Nashville Tennesseean 9/29/1963)
[59] Ibid
[60] Mongrel Virginias by Arthur H. Estabrook, 182
[61] Smoky Mountain Country by North Callahan, p. 162
[62] The Melungeons by Bonnie Ball, p. v
[63] Ibid, p. 56
[64] Ibid, p. 89
[65] The Melungeons by Jean Patterson Bible, p. 93
[66] Melungeons: The Vanishing Colonoy of Newman's Ridge
      by Henry R.Price, p. 1
[67] History, Myths, and Sacred Formulas of the Cherokees by
      James Mooney, p. 22
[68] National Geographic Magazine by Merle Severy, p. 90 (November 1992)
[69] Portugal nos Mares by Oliveira Marques, p. 316
[70] The Colonial Experience by David Hawke, p. 8
[71] The Dawn of a New Age by Luis Filipe Barreto, p. 7
      (The Courier–Unesco–1989/4)
[72] The Dawn of an era by Luis Filipe Barreto, Unesco, p. 7
[73] Historia da Lingua Portuguesa by Serafim da Silva Neto, pp. 421-514-518

Chapter X

The Turkish-Ottoman Melungeon and other Group Connections

The Ottoman Empire played an important role in the world, mostly on the East, but since it controlled vast portions of the Mediterranean and their constant wars with Spain and other eastern Mediterranean countries, it is possible that their people may have played an important role in the Melungeon make-up. There are many Melungeon descendants who believe their ancestors were Turks. It is therefore important for the reader to know a little about the Ottoman Empire.

Also, it is important to underline the fact that this book is not concerned with who was the victor, but only if any Turks were made captives, including women or children. Also if they were transported to the U.S. willing or not.

The Ottoman Empire was created by Turkish tribes in Anatolia and lasted from the decline of the Byzantine Empire in the 14th century until the establishment of Turkey as a republic in 1922.

The first period of Ottoman history, from 1300 to 1481, was one of almost continuous expansion through war, alliance and outright purchase of territory. In 1453 Constantinople was taken, and in subsequent years Morea, Trebizond, Bosnia, Albania, the Crimea and other areas were conquered or annexed. Under Selim I (1512-20), Ottoman expansion resumed. His defeat of the Mamelukes in 1516-17 doubled the size of the empire at a stroke by adding to it Syria, Palestine, Egypt and Algeria. The reign of his son Süleyman I (1520-66), known in Europe as *the Magnificent*, was a golden age of Ottoman power and grandeur. He conquered Hungary from the Habsburgs, annexed Tripoli, extended the empire southeastward through Mesopotamia to the Persian Gulf, and made the Ottoman navy dominant in the eastern Mediterranean.

Although they were often at war with the West, it was common to see Ottoman Empire trading ships flying Christian, Islamic or Judaic symbols when they were carrying mixed nationalities. Many of the merchants were also Jews.[1]

Süleyman himself overran Iraq, and even challenged Portuguese dominion of the Indian Ocean from his bases in Suez and Basra. The Ottomans began to spread their empire from a corner of Anatolia, and during the 17th century, when Turkish expansion was at its peak, the Ottoman Empire reached into central Europe to include what is now Hungary and Romania and most of the other present-day Balkan states. It also included what is now Syria, Iraq, Israel, Egypt and north Africa as far west as Algeria.

Morocco is the only north African country where the Portuguese conquered some of the towns. Because of its lack of natural harbors, its rugged mountainous interior and its distance, throughout its history from imperial centers in the east, Morocco remained relatively isolated until the early 20th century. The Ottoman Empire did not reach that far west – Algeria being the westernmost country – and no battles of consequence were fought against the Portuguese. They did have an

Fig. 90 - Map of Europe and North Africa, 16th Century.(Hammond Historical Atlas)

encounter with a Portuguese fleet of 30 Caravels and other ships, possibly a total of 70, on June 15, 1501, to fight against the Turks in aid of Venice. The Portuguese were supposed to conquer Mazalquibir, the Oran defense castle, which they were unable to do. They finally returned to Lisbon on December 25.[2] Later, another fleet of 1500 men, led by the Portuguese Prince Luis as part of an alliance with Spain against the Turks, went to Tunis in 1535. The Portuguese officially maintained neutrality not to anger the Turks in India. By doing this, they were hoping that helping Spain against Barbarossa would alleviate the military pressure of the Moors in north Africa.

However, the Red Sea and the Indian Ocean saw quite a bit of action between the Turks and the Portuguese. Most Red Sea actions were primarily to investigate or spoil Turkish naval preparations. By the time the Turks arrived in India, the Portuguese were already firmly settled. [3]

Let us take a look at the map showing northwest Africa and the south of Portugal. The area controlled by the Ottoman Empire was called the Barbary States. We can see that the Turks did not come that far west. Also, we must make a distinction between Turks and Moors or Berbers, although any non-Christian in the Mediterranean was given the generic Moor name.

The Hadrami chroniclers on Portuguese activities reveal several battles, one in the Islamic year 908, or Christian year 1502-03. When a battle took place, the Portuguese captured seven vessels and took some prisoners. [4]

Whenever prisoners were taken, very often they were exchanged or ransomed. In 1517, *...some of the Franks went to the port of Aden...the Emir Mardjãn gave them water...and ransomed some prisoners from them.* [5]

The author R. B. Sergeant mentions Batticalá (modern Bhatkal) as *one of most important ports of Kanara* [Portuguese Canará] *and must have been well known at least to all the Gulf Arabs as it was a great center of horse trade.* In 1529-30, arrived on this port a Portuguese vessel with Muslim prisoners, [6] and in the following year a ship with families is mentioned. *...with their children and women, and Salm²n's² children and servants, on board.* [7]

A Turkish gun (1530-31) is preserved to this day in the Tower of London, with Arab inscriptions. One of them reads, *Entering into the land of India, Portugal* (Burtukãl) *the accursed, in Cairo the preserved, year 937 H. (A.D. 1530-1).* [8]

Turkish Influence in the West

For the first time…*Turkish influence and the Ottoman Empire was to be extended, in 1578 to Morocco. Here the Sheriff of Fez* [town where Henry's – the Navigator – brother Fernando died in prison under the most horrible conditions many years before] *called for the aid of the Turks against the Portuguese, who landed a large force in support of the pretender. This was granted with alacrity, for fear of Spanish cooperation with Portugal and a great battle was won against the Portuguese at Alcazarquivir in which their King, Sebastian was killed,, together with the pretender and a quarter of their army. Thus started the decline of Portugal, of which Philip speedily took advantage by its armed occupation.* [9] Let us keep that in mind when we look into the possibility of the Turks being the major component of the Melungeon people. Kennedy maintains: *Moorish and Turkish naval heroes soon evolved, most notably two dark-skinned, red-haired Moorish brothers…* [one of them]…*was known to Europeans as Barbarossa, literally "Redbeard." From the very early 1500's until almost 1546… Barbarossa fought the Spanish at every opportunity along the North African coast. The Spanish and Portuguese continued to wage naval warfare against the unrelenting Moors and Ottoman (Turkish) Empire well into the 1600's, with both sides filling their galleys with oarsmen captured from each other.* [10] Barbarossa's activities were mostly in the Mediterranean, although there was limited Moor or Turkish piracy and French corsair action along the Portuguese coast. The Moors avoided the area because the Portuguese king had implemented a coast guard fleet between the Azores and the continent to protect the Indian fleet returning from India loaded with spices. The French did it mostly to challenge the Portuguese and Spanish closed-seas policy.

The pirate Berbers used Argel and Tunis as their nest, and from this point they attacked southern Europe, which they did also in 1530 from Tripoli. Dragut, a Turkish pirate, had previously conquered that city.

Dragut captured men and women and later demanded high ransoms. However most of the young women wound up in harems.

Pirate ships, French, English, Turks, and others from Argelia, managed to assault 220 Portuguese ships returning from India and Brazil between 1549 and 1550. [11]

Moors and Turks Freed by the Portuguese

Kennedy reveals yet another possibility: …*And, of course, if Drake could have deposited Moors and Turks off our shores, might there not have been other, more obscure incidences of this nature? Emancipados freed by the Portuguese themselves, for example? Undoubtedly there were.* [12] First, we have to accept the possibility of Drake having dropped them off on our shores. Second, we have to question how the *emancipados* – if there were any – got here. On the other hand, if the Turks were galley slaves, they were an expensive commodity to let go that easily. Also, most *emancipados,* or new Christians – Cristãos novos – were Jews.

The Moors in Portugal had already been absorbed by the Portuguese community at large by the 15th and 16th centuries. Finally, Portugal did not have any quantity of Turkish captives to speak of in the 16th century. Let us keep in mind that Portugal's major problem was the small size of its population.

The only way the Portuguese could have Turkish slaves would be the result of battles fought in the Indian Ocean. If the Portuguese had Turkish prisoners, they would not have sent them all the way from the Indian Ocean to Brazil. Instead, they would have traded them for Portuguese prisoners, and the Muslims had many.

What happened to the supposedly captured Turks? David Beers Quinn offers a possible answer: *The only trace we find of the passengers is of negotiations to send home some 100 ex-galley slaves to the Turkish dominions.* [13]

We should not rule out the possibility of these Moors, Muslims or Turks having been captured galley slaves at the Battle of LePanto, where the Ottoman Empire had a tremendous loss. Portugal was also involved as an ally in this battle. Again, a separation between the Spanish and Portuguese must be made. The Portuguese did not wage naval warfare against the Turks in the Mediterranean. A possible connection with the Turks is viable, but only if we take into consideration that the Ottoman Empire ruled most Mediterranean countries, except for the northwest coast of Africa, where Portugal was most active. It is questionable whether everyone under the Ottoman Empire should be considered a Turk.

Turkish slaves were men only, and if they intermarried with Indian women, the Melungeons would have a different look, and they probably have, and may be the origin of the Lumbees or other Indian tribes of North Carolina such as the Powatans, Croatans or others.

Portugal was involved only with the Moors or Berbers of Northwest Africa, and records show that, when attacked by the Portuguese, they were never helped by the Turks or asked for their help, with one exception in 1578. No record of large numbers of Turks made prisoners by Portugal in the 16th century was found in Portuguese history books. The slaves used in Madeira came from Morocco in the 15th century.

Most likely Kennedy is referring to Spanish, not Portuguese, battles. As for oarsmen captured by the Portuguese, most battles with the Moors were inland. However, the Portuguese did battle the Turks in the Indian Ocean, quite far from the Mediterranean. That may be the best connection between the Portuguese and the Turks.

The Turk Name and Portuguese-Captured Algerians

Kennedy makes a possible connection with the Berbers: *Even without Drake it is an established fact that the sixteenth-century Spanish and Portuguese regularly used captured Algerians (probably North African Berbers) as galley slaves for both their Mediterranean and New World seafaring endeavors.* [14]

Again, we have to assume that Kennedy is talking about the Spanish and not the Portuguese, as they did not normally get that far east, with the exceptions mentioned above. However, the Portuguese did bring to Portugal Berber slaves captured along the West African coast, mostly in the 15th century.

As for the name *Turk*, it was discovered through consultation with more than one history professor and older people that the English used to call anyone who spoke a foreign language, or whose culture could not be recognized or understood, a Turk. Similarly the Brazilians and Mexicans call the Americans or anyone who does not speak like a native, a *gringo*.

Francisco Coronado, on his famous expedition to Mexico in 1542, had an encounter with an Indian slave called Turk: ... *He had been led there by an Indian Turk ...and saw that they have been deceived by the Turk...and with Ysopete. The Turk was taken along in chains.* [15]

This was not a connection with the Turks. Apparently, what happened was that when the Spaniards saw that particular Indian, due to his unusual appearance or because he looked like one, they called him *Turk*. [16] He is believed to be an Indian from the Pawnee tribe. [17] However, some Melungeon families stated that their ancestors have said that they were Turks.

The Ottoman Empire in the 15th and 16th centuries controlled most of the Mediterranean, also Persia and parts of India, before the Portuguese arrived. They could have played a part also, but I doubt that the Turks could have been the main element according to the studies made so far.

See Chapter X for the Turkish activities during that period and their possible interaction with the Portuguese. Within these parameters, it was established that the Melungeons' ancestors could be any one of the following nationalities: Spanish, Portuguese, Turkish or from any of the countries in the Far East, such as India. Turkish may mean any native of the countries controlled by the Ottoman Empire, including all on the East Mediterranean and north Africa, except the westernmost part.

Galley Slaves and the Battle of LePanto - 1571

A galley was a large seagoing vessel propelled primarily by oars. The Egyptians, Cretans and other ancient peoples used sail-equipped galleys for both war and commerce. Though the advent of the lateen (fore-and-aft) sail and the stern rudder rendered the galley obsolete for commerce, it retained its military importance into the 16th century. It played the leading role at the Battle of Lepanto [18] in 1571 in the eastern Mediterranean.

Rowing in the galleys, particularly those belonging to the Ottoman Empire that sailed the Mediterranean, was another form of brutal slave labor. Tens of thousands of Slavs, victims of Crimean Tartar slave raids, first suffered a hellish existence in the Crimea itself, and then ended their days rowing on Ottoman triremes. [19]

Portugal did not have many galley-type vessels in terms of the 16th century except in the Indian Ocean. Also, galleys were used in the Battle of LePanto which took place in 1571, and was fought between allied Christian forces and the Ottoman Turks . The Venetians formed an alliance with Pope Pius V and Felipe II of Spain (May 25, 1571). Felipe sent his half brother, Don Juan of Austria, to command the allied forces. On October 7, 1571, the Battle of LePanto in the Gulf of LePanto near Corinth, off the coast of Greece, ended in defeat for an Ottoman fleet of 240 galleys. The maritime league of 212 Spanish, Venetian, Genoese and Maltese ships lost about 5,000 oarsmen and soldiers, but it captured 130 vessels with their stores and provisions.They also took 4,000 prisoners, freed 12,000 Christian galley slaves and killed 25,000 Turks. This story may give credit to Drake's capture in 1586, but not from the Portuguese – perhaps from the Spaniards. They were the ones that had the Turkish captives, not the Portuguese.

It is possible that Spain may have taken some of these Turkish galley slaves to the Caribbean Islands. Therefore, the same slaves that Drake captured 15 years later from the Spaniards were taken back to England and left with others on the shores of Virginia or the Carolinas. Subsequently they could have met with the Portuguese, who were already there, as well as other settlers and the Indians, thereby becoming part of the Melungeons.

Would the Spaniards hold them for 15 years? If so, they would be older. Would they take unconvert Muslims to the New World? On the other hand Manuel da Costa Fontes, while working on his doctor dissertation at the University of California, on Portuguese folk ballads in north America and other Portuguese folk traditions, found an extremely rare ballad remembered by the Portuguese in north America about the Battle of LePanto.

He discovered a fairly complete version in California (1970), and on January 22, 1978, Maria Soares de Sousa, a native of the island of Santa Maria, Azores, recited the following fragment in Stoughton, Massachusetts in Portuguese: [20]

A peça de D. João era de bronze e rendia;
foi deitada à meia noite p'ra defender sua Turquia
Era tanta a sangueira que pelos embornais corria;
eram tantos os corpos n'agua qu'as anauas entorpeciam.

The translation in English:
Dom João's piece of artillery was of bronze
and it worked plenty;
It was fired at midnight in order to defend* his Turkey.

There was so much blood that it flowed through the supper holes;
there were so many corpses in the water that they hindered the ships.
* should read attack

One should ask, why should such a ballad survive to these times? Did the Turks actually bring it over and pass it along to the Portuguese? Perhaps some of the Portuguese soldiers involved in that battle brought it over to North America. It certainly must have been quite popular to survive four centuries. It also points to a possible Azorean connection.

Portuguese Defeat in Morocco and the Decline - 1578

On June 24, 1578, a fleet with 940 sails and 24,000 men departed Lisbon, arriving in Morocco on July 7. [21] The biggest defeat in Portuguese history happened on August 4, when the young, stubborn and inexperienced king of Portugal, Sebastião, was killed and his army annihilated at Ksar el Kebir (*Alcacer Quibir*) in northwest Africa. Here, he and many young Portuguese noblemen – who were as foolish as their king – died or were made prisoners. With him also died a Moorish king and two Moorish princes. He went to battle not heeding the advice of Spanish King Felipe II and the pope. Just before the battle began, he stubbornly refused to listen to reason as to the best way to wage the war, using proper military positions. That was called the *Battle of the Kings*. The Portuguese noblemen who did not die were made prisoners. This defeat marked the beginning of the fall of the short-lived Portuguese Empire and supremacy throughout the world.

From that date on, the Portuguese were hard-pressed to exchange whatever Arab, Moorish or Turkish prisoners they may have had for the many young Portuguese noblemen dying in Moorish prisons. It is hard to understand how the Turks or Moors got to Brazil, and for them to be captured or freed by Drake.

Turkish Name *Rëis* and the Map

In 1929, at an Istanbul palace in Turkey, a map dated 1513 appeared showing north and South America as well as the Caribbean. [22] This map was drawn on a gazelle hide by Piri Rëis, a Gallipoli born Turkish Admiral. [23]

Admiral Rëis was appointed by the Ottomans; he assisted them in suppressing Turkish revolts in central and southern Anatolia (1526), and enjoyed the favor of Sultan Süleyman I the Magnificent. In 1551 a fleet of 30 units under the command of Rëis left the Straits of Mecca, and was sent to overtake Mascate, but failed and took refuge in Bassorah. [24] Later he was beheaded in Cairo, because he fled the Portuguese *and abandoned his fleet to the enemy.* [25]

The area drawn on the map was well known by the Portuguese of that time. See Chapter VII, on 1502 Cantino map. [26, 27]

The Portuguese Women and the Turks in India

The Portuguese fought many battles in the Indian Ocean against the Turks, such as the Battle of Hormuz (Ormuz) in 1507, of Goa in 1510, and Malacca in 1516. The towns of Ormuz and Malacca were held till 1650 when the Turks, Persians and Malayans took it back with the help of the British, Dutch and French.

The Indian Ocean and the Arabian, or Red, Sea was the stage for many battles between Moors – non-Catholics in India – as well as Turks and the Portuguese: *...here he landed troops on the Island of Diu and, armed with a number of huge cannons which had been dragged across the isthmus of Suez, laid siege to its*

Portuguese fortress. The soldiers of the garrison with the aid of their women folk, resisted with courage... defeating the Turks. [28]

The Portuguese -Turk Melungeon Connection

The Turkish connection with the Melungeons and the Portuguese would be more acceptable if they had originated from Portugal or the Azores after having lived there for many years as Muslims. The Portuguese kings, before 1531, did allow the practice of the Muslim religion much in the same way as the Moors allowed the Christian religion when they invaded the Iberian Peninsula. The Mediterranean trade with the Portuguese ports would also justify the presence of Turks, either fleeing the Ottoman Empire or just doing business in Portugal.

Many persons wrongly assume that the Portuguese fought most battles in the Mediterranean and North Africa, which is not the case. The capture of Turks or Moors in the Mediterranean by the Portuguese has been mentioned; however it is more likely that this would have been in the Red Sea or the Indian Ocean. In this area of the world, the Portuguese and the Turks often faced each other in war-like manner, and called each other by specific names.

The Portuguese in India were called *Franks* and the Turks *Rümï* or *Rumes.* All others were called Moors. The word *Frank* in Portuguese is *Firango* or *Franguês*, which derives from *Fring,* meaning Europe, in the Persian language. [29]

The presence of Turks in North America in the 16th century, direct from the Middle East to America, it is highly unlikely. However, if one takes into consideration the encounters between the Portuguese and the Turkish (Ottoman Empire) in the Far East, the Arabian Sea and the Indian Ocean, then it is quite possible that Turks or their direct descendants were in Portuguese caravels going to or coming from India. Through shipwrecks or other cause, these ships could very well wind up on the U.S. east coast seashores.

The government of Turkey, town officials and scholars, along with Turkish National TV and newspapers have been giving the Melungeons very much attention. Brent Kennedy, with many others has visited Turkey several times. Gowen Research Foundation published a report of the tour written by Col. Carroll Heard Goyne, Jr. in the April 1997 issue of their news letter.

In a forest dedicated to the Melungeons a plaque reads essentially as follows:

This forest dedicated to the memory of the men of Cesme [Turkish town] *who were taken to America in the 16th century by the Portuguese and became Melungeons.*[30]

The following is a chart showing the battles fought since Portugal achieved her nationhood in 1143. The chart shows that most battles were fought in the Far East. The Turks were involved there, and very often they were taken captive along with their women and children. Also, the Turks took Portuguese and their families as prisoners.

See the map where battles were fought at the end of this Chapter.

Chart of Battles Between the Portuguese Navy and Turks, Moors

M	D	Y	Captain	Location	Nations Involved
7	15	1180	Fuas Roupinho	Cape Espichel	Moors, N. Africa
10	17	1182	Fuas Roupinho	Ceuta	Moors, N. Africa
7		1341	Pessanha	Ceuta	Moors, N. Africa
9		1469	King Afonso V	Portuguese Coast [1a]	French Corsair Colombo
8	31	1476	Pêro de Ataide	St. Maria -Lagos	Genoa [1b]
10/12		1502	Vasco da Gama	Mt. Deli	Mecca, Calicut, Cairo
12	31	1502	João da Nova (2-1-1503)	Cannanore	Mecca, Calicut
10/12		1504	Lopo Soares de Albergaria	Pandarane	Turks, Mecca
7	24	1504	Garcia de Melo	Larache	Moors, Pirates,N.Africa
10	18	1505	Francisco de Almeida	Onor	Mecca, Onor
11		1505	João Homem	Coulão	Mecca, Coulão
9	27	1507	Afonso de Albuquerque	Ormuz	Turks Ormuz, Oman
3	24	1508	Pêro Barreto	Chaul	Turks, Mecca
5		1508	Rui Soares	Sea of Arabia	Turks, Mecca
2	3	1509	Francisco de Almeida	Diu	Turks
3		1510	Antão de Nogueira	Sea of Arabia	Mecca, Cambaia
6		1510	Antonio de Noronha	Mandovi - Goa	Turks - Narsinga
1		1511	Jorge Botelho	Calicut	Mecca
6	24	1511	Afonso de Albuquerque	Isle of Polvoreira	Mecca
4		1517	Lopo Soares de Albergaria	Jeddah, Red Sea	Turks - Mecca
		1520	Vasco Fernandes César	Alcacer Ceguer, Africa	Moors, Pirates
3	8	1520	Miguel da Silva	Ceuta, NW Africa	Moors, Pirates
7/9		1520	João & Aires Coelho	Tangier, NW Africa	Moors, Pirates
10		1521	Vasco Fernandes César	Strait of Gibraltar	Moors and English
3		1521	Diogo Fernandes de Beja	Diu-Arabian Sea	Turks
3		1521	Simão Martins	Dabul-NW India	Turks
7	27	1521	Antonio Correia	Barem-Persian Gulf	Turks - Persia
9		1521	Nuno Fernandes Macedo	Diu-NW India	Turks
11		1522	Manuel de Sousa Tavares	Ormuz	Turks - Persia
7	14	1535	Antonio de Saldanha	Tunis	Turks [1c]
		1550	Gonçalo Vaz	Aden Gulf - Red Sea	Turks
		1551	Luis Figueira	Assab Bay - Red Sea	Turkish Pirate Cafar [1d]
		1552	Inacio Nunes Gato	Alcalá - N. Africa	Turks - Argel [1d]
		1552	Antão de Noronha	Ormuz- Red Sea	Turks - Mecca [1d]
		1553	Pêro de Ataide	Ormuz- Red Sea	Turks - Piri Reis [1e]
		1554	Fernando de Meneses	Oman Gulf	Turks - Mecca [1f]
		1555	Pedro da Cunha	Carvoeira, Algarve	Turks - Argel

Chart of Portuguese naval battles to the 16th century

See notes on the next page.

The chart shown on the previous page is part of a much larger chart compiled by the author from information available in documents and books, such as the four-volume collection of the *Batalhas e Combates da Marinha Portuguese* by Saturnino Monteiro and published by the Portuguese Navy Library in Lisbon.

This chart shows only the battles involving the Moors and, more specifically, the Turks or the Ottoman Empire up to the first half of the 16th century. It should be noted that prisoners were made on both sides and the Portuguese won and lost many battles. Also, sometimes Muslim women and children traveling to and from Mecca were made captive. The same happened when Portuguese ships were captured with families aboard. The name *Moor* was originally connected with the people of northwest Africa, Morocco area. That same name was later extended to all Muslims anywhere in the world, in the Ottoman Empire, India, Indochina, Indonesia and most of the lands in the eastern Indian Ocean.

Notes

[1a] Culam or Colombo was made prisoner, worked later for Portugal.

[1b] In this battle, all ships were destroyed by fire, 800 Genoese died, 500 French and 500 Portuguese. According to tradition, it was here that Columbus saved his life by holding onto the wreckage. *Colombo o Velho* (The Old), who was the Captain on one of the Portuguese vessels and presumably Columbus' relative.

[1c] A fleet of Spanish, Portuguese and others attacked Tunis to free that city from Barbarossa, also known as Red or Blue Beard who had an army mostly of Berber soldiers. The allied navy freed the city and 20,000 Christian prisoners.

No record of Turkish or Muslim prisoners made. Later Barbarossa recovered from the defeat and attacked Mallorca, captured a loaded Portuguese ship and made more than 6,000 prisoners. Portuguese women and children captured.

[1d] Prisoners, later exchanged.

[1e] As a result of this campaign, Süleyman had Piri Rëis executed.

[1f] End of the Ottoman Empire expansion in the Far East.

[1] 16th and 17th centuries

[2] Portugal nos Mares by Oliveira Martins, p. 72

[3] The Portuguese off the South Arabian Coast by R. B. Serjeant, p. 18

[4] Ibid, p. 43

[5] Ibid, p. 51

[6] Ibid, p. 55

[7] Ibid, p. 56

[8] Ibid, Apendix I

[9] The Ottoman Centuries, by Lord Kinross, 1977,
New York Morrow Quill, p.273

[10] The Melungeons by Brent Kennedy, pp.102-103

[11] As Berlengas e os Piratas by José de Almeida Santos, p. 14

[12] The Melungeons by Brent Kennedy, p.112

[13] The Roanoke Voyages by David Beers Quinn, vol. 1, p. 254

[14] The Melungeons by Brent Kennedy, p.112

[15] Makers of America by Wayne Moquin, p. 5 (Encyclopedia Britannica)

[16] Spanish Explorers of the Southern United States by
Theodore H. Lewis, p. 313

[17] Os Portugueses no Descobrimentos dos Estados Unidos by
Jaime Cortesão, p. 28

[18] Historia de España, Historia 16, p.507

[19] 1994 By Encyclopedia Britannica

[20] Study of the Portuguese Ballad by Manuel da Costa Fontes, pp.126, 136

[21] Historia de Portugal by Joaquim Verissimo Serrão, V.III, p. 76

[22] The Ottoman Centuries, by Lord Kinross, 1977,
New York: Morrow Quill, p.245

[23] National Geographic Magazine, Geographica page, March 1994

[24] Dicionario de Historia de Portugal, Vol. III, by Joel Serrão, p. 499

[25] The Ottoman Centuries, by Lord Kinross, 1977,
New York: Morrow Quill, pp.245

[26] It is also a coincidence that Reis is a very common name in
Portugal, Lisbon the capital, alone has more 150 "Reis" names in its
telephone book.
In Portuguese the name does not have a symbol over the letter "e".

[27] Brent Kennedy, report to the Gowen Foundation, 1995

[28] The Ottoman Centuries, by Lord Kinross, 1977,
New York Morrow Quill, p.244

[29] Os Portugueses na India by Agostinho de Carvalho, p. 99

[30] Gowen Research Foundation Newsletter by Col Carrol Heard Goyne, Jr.
April 1997

Damião de Gois, Lisbon
1546 Biblioteca Nacional.
A contemporary engraving of a
Royal historian, humanist and
afmous writer.

Damianvs A Goes.
This name may be in the origin
of many Melungeon names.
Gois travelled extensively in the
Far East during the 16th century.

Next Page: *Fig. 91 - Map of the Indian Ocean*

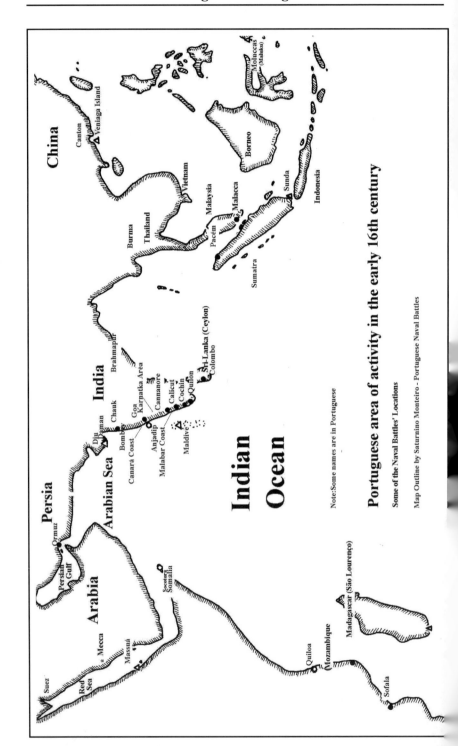

Portuguese area of activity in the early 16th century

Some of the Naval Battles' Locations

Note:Some names are in Portuguese

Map Outline by Saturnino Monteiro - Portuguese Naval Battles

Chapter XI

Conclusion

Portuguese, Melungeon and/or other Groups' Connections and Root

From hypothesis to hypothesis, the truth eventually will be found [1]

The following are guidelines established to set the hypothesis and arrive at a logical conclusion:

First, a time frame between 1500 and 1600 was established for the arrival of a group of people that would be known later on as the Melungeons, Portuguese or anyother name. Earlier or later arrivals were ruled out. If they arrived before Columbus, a totally different set of circumstances would have to be considered, and would be so speculative, almost as complex as trying to find the origin of the native Indian. If they came later, they would have had contacts with the many settlers that arrived after Jamestown. The English or other explorers did not seem to have encountered any recent arrivals. The groups said to be found were already established.

For the time frame being considered, the earliest Spanish voyages to the American Southeast occurred in the period of 1521-1526. French and Spanish colonial activities materialized only in the 1560's. The French man Jean Ribault learned of the tales about the Southeast that Lucas Vásquez de Ayllón had spread in 1523.[2] During that time period, there was not a large movement of Europeans, other than the Portuguese or the Spanish. The English, French and Dutch became active in voyages to the North American continent during the latter part of the 16th century and after. The Spanish failed in their early attempt of settling in South Carolina and the English failed in Roanoke Colony, North Carolina as well as later on in Jamestown. Only the pilgrims that arrived from England in 1620 aboard the Mayflower– after staying in Holland for some time – were able to succeed. By then the Portuguese had been exporting sugar and other products to Europe from the colonies for 100 years.

One strong factor for the possible survival of a Portuguese group in the early 1500's is the fact that they crossed with so many different races right in their own country, due to invasions as described in Chapter V. Studies have shown that the Portuguese acclimatize themselves in various parts of the world better *than almost all the other European races,* [3] and the Portuguese race appears to be endowed with a temperament that permits it to adapt itself more easily than other races to climates that are *different from that of the mother country.* [4]

Second, their nationality or place of origin ought to be established, as well as their means of arrival, and not necessarily their race. Therefore, if they were Moors, Berbers, Jews or others that came from Spain, and have been there for several generations, they would be considered Spaniards. The same would apply to

Portuguese nationals. If these parameters were not established, it would be very difficult to come up with sensible answers. How could anyone be considered Carthaginian, Phoenician, Greek, Roman, Gothic, Moorish or Berber if they all came from the European continent, except the African black slaves, who arrived at a later date. It has been established that they were not black or American Indian when they were first met by the English, or possibly the French.

The Iberian Peninsula was invaded by different races of people, and the makeup of the Portuguese people naturally reflects a bit of everyone that lived in Portugal for a long period.

As stated, the Melungeons or any other group claiming Portuguese ancestry were made up of more than one component, but they started out with a major component that may have been responsible for their presence in America. There is no such thing as pure Melungeon, European, African or other race, nowadays, all Americans are made up of many races, not necessarily a melting pot but a mosaic of cultures. We have to rule out the English, French or other Northern European countries, as well as the small Italian republics of the time. As for being Spanish, it has been shown in Chapter III that this is unlikely.

Third, it was assumed that in order for a group to survive over such a long period of time, and still hold onto its own identity and physical appearance, men and women would have to be part of the equation in the same manner as black slaves from Africa. If just black male slaves would have been brought in, then we would not have today the beautiful black skin of the slave descendants. Therefore, male slaves or soldiers were ruled out, although, if they were in the U.S., most likely they intermarried with female native Indians, Blacks or any other. Naturally, in this case their offspring would carry their genes to the present.

Preliminary calculations assumed that the Melungeons may have started out with only 200 persons. If that was the case, a group was able to survive over 14 generations, many thousands still living today.

How Important Was It To Be White?

In Elizabethan times, the need to be white was so great that even Queen Elizabeth covered her face generously with a white powder made of lead. Since everyone wanted to have a white face, they often risked their very lives, due to the corrosive action of the lead that penetrated the skin. [5]

The color of one's skin, it was important then and still plays an important part in some segments of society. Colleen McCullough, author of the well known and famous book, *The Thorn Birds,* wrote: [6]

Safely hidden in the last row of desks, Meggie dared to glance sideways at the little girl sitting next to her. A gap-toothed grin met her frightened gaze, huge black eyes staring roundly out of a dark slightly shiny face. She fascinated Meggie, used to fairness and freckles, for even Frank with his dark eyes and hair had a fair white skin. So Meggie ended in thinking her deskmate the most beautiful creature she had ever seen...

Later Meggie's parents commented: *I don't think it is such a good idea to be too thick with the Dagos', they muttered sharing the British community's instinctive mistrust of any dark or Mediterranean people. Dagos are dirty, Meggie girl, they don't wash too often, he explained lamely, wilting under the look of hurt reproach Meggie gave them.*
This is a fictitious story of the early 20th century, but in real life was also true.

Why Would the Portuguese Emigrate in the 16th Century ?

Would the Portuguese emigrate as settlers to North America willingly? Possibly, because conditions since the 1540's aggravated at a steady pace and many families went in search of better living conditions, or to survive. In the 16th century they did emigrate to Africa, Brazil and India. Why not to the North American continent? After all, it was much closer. The basic reason for emigration was probably always economical first, then religious or political as the second most important consideration.

After the first golden years of the 1500's, the economic situation was terrible. The establishing of the Inquisition did not help matters. Lisbon was visited with plagues and earthquakes during that time, but they proved easier to face than the cost of 50 years of glory. Literally half the nation's population had vanished in pursuit of wealth in the new colonies.

King Sebastião came to power in 1566 and, in the same year, the copper coin was reduced to 1/3 its value, a cruel but needed measure because the English had taken all the silver and gold. The business people, who had increased in large number after the discoveries, knew in advance and paid all debts. The poor people got caught with 2/3 less of their money. Many hanged themselves, and if that was not enough, the bubonic plague came with full force.

During the time when the plague was at its height (July and August of 1569), 700 persons died daily in Lisbon alone. There were no places for burying the dead. Huge ditches were dug and the bodies thrown in fifty at a time. It was a fast and fatal disease. More than one third of the Lisbon population succumbed to the plague, approximately 40,000 people.

Then there was the great disaster of Alcacer-Quibir (1578) in North Africa, plus the consequential Iberian union of both crowns in 1580. Life got much worse, when Felipe II of Spain became Filipe I of Portugal. He was the son of Princess Isabel of Portugal and the grandson of the Portuguese King Manuel I, as well as the son of the Emperor Carlos V. England, as a previous ally, was then an enemy of great proportions.

The high level of emigration registered in the 16th century coincided with a period of catastrophes suffered by the Portuguese, [7] as well as the prospect of an Iberian union which brought several concordance laws between Portugal and Spain. These laws faced heavy opposition from the people of Algarve in 1568. Prior to that, in 1563, there were already regular maritime commercial routes between the Americas, India, Portugal and Spain. To add more confusion for the historian and researcher, some of these shipping enterprises were using Portuguese boats without registration, both in Lisbon and Algarve, with no records ever made of their activities.

This union was accepted by most Portuguese business people and large land owners. They now could import and export to Spain duty free. To make things more palatable, the Spanish king promised complete autonomy, with separate language and control, as part of a kingdom united to Spain. As time went by, subsequent Spanish kings did not keep Felipe's promises and eventually caused the Portuguese to revolt in 1640, when their total independence was restored.

Ever since Portugal expelled the Moors in the 1200's from what is now her present territory, it had nowhere to expand, and therefore always looked to the seas as the new frontier. First it conquered some cities in Morocco. That did not prove very advantageous. The cost of keeping these towns was far greater than the economic benefit. The existence of the North American continent had been well known since the early 1500's, and the people dreamed of rich lands on the other side of the Atlantic. The large quantities of silver, gold and diamonds arriving in Portugal actually impoverished the people. [8] The merchant marine, which was a crown monopoly, was now in the hands of businessmen without scruples. Many times, anarchy was the dominant power. It is not certain if the Portuguese left Portugal proper or the islands with America as a known destination. They certainly left by the thousands for Africa, Brazil and India, however.

The Return of the Navigators

The first thing Columbus did when he returned from his voyage to America was to visit the Portuguese King João II. Both Columbus and his crew spoke of many wonders. The same happened earlier when other navigators returned from Africa, thereby starting a wave of settlers to new places recently discovered.

After Columbus, Portuguese navigators returned from India, Brazil and other locales. Later, Portuguese navigators and explorers found themselves employed by other nations. It was the case with Spain, such as Fernão de Magalhães (Magellan), Estevão Gomes, João Rodrigues Cabrilho and many others.

During the first half of the 16th century, economic conditions deteriorated to the point that emigration was the only way out even for what remained of the middle class. Portugal verified a typical contradiction of the Portuguese history: A country with lack of skilled labor was supplying other countries with their best resource, their people. Those were the prevalent conditions at the time, causing many to emigrate.

The news was tempting not only from Africa, Brazil, South and Central Americas, but also later from the North American East Coast, Newfoundland to Florida. Pardo had possibly recruited Portuguese soldiers and their families to settle the Spanish colony of Santa Elena. He already had Portuguese soldiers at his service. Would it be possible for entire Portuguese families to emigrate without leaving any record of their departure? It may be possible, because many of the records, books and notes were destroyed by fires, earthquakes, burned by the Inquisition, removed by the Spaniards during their occupation or later destroyed by Napoleon's invading army.

There is also another possibility, which is still evident presently, emigrate illegally and fill caravels with families that gave all their savings to dishonest businessmen looking for a quick profit. The emigrants arriving on American soil did not have to pay taxes to the crown or abide by any Portuguese laws if they had left illegally.

Meanwhile, Felipe II of Spain took advantage of the strong Portuguese navy, a remainder from the discovery period, and decided to invade England with the *Invincible Armada.* It turned out to be a great loss for Spain, and for Portugal in a much larger proportion. The Portuguese had paid dearly for their king's foolishness ten years before in Alcacer-Quibir.

Before the 17th Century, Caravels with Non-Anglo Settlers to the East Coast

We can assume that the Portuguese people – formerly Moors, Berbers, etc. – had plenty of information about the New World, and with all the economic woes, religious persecution, and epidemics, why not emigrate to America. After all, everyone in search of a better life was emigrating to Africa and Brazil, where they had news of an inhospitable climate with fevers and death. Knowing about the malarial, and fever stricken tropical coast of Africa and Asia, it is possible that they would attempt North America.

The information reaching Portugal was that the area of Virginia and North Carolina was one of a temperate climate with fertile soil, why not try it? Well… a possible theory, but not proven. (One of the problems for many before leaving was how to return. That did not seem to be a problem.) The prospective settlers were aware of the regular shipping routes between Africa, Brazil, Central and South Americas, as they spoke to many who returned from that part of the world. They knew of the Spanish attempts in settling the east coast during the early 1500's, and later Santa Elena colony. If these Portuguese settlers were in Santa Elena at the time it was being destroyed and abandoned, would they move to St. Augustine? Maybe not, they were also aware that a Spanish king and his army had invaded Portugal and, not being Spanish, they could have chosen to search for safer and more productive areas. Then, add the fact that there was talk of gold and jewels in the mountains.

The English and Indian attacks may also have been a contributing factor for moving towards the higher grounds away from the coast. There is still a question that some Melungeons or other groups of early settlers did not necessarily look mediterranean or Portuguese. If so, how and when did they arrive in America? A possible explanation may be the description by A.J.R. Russell-Wood of the life aboard one of the ships in the *Carreira da India* (Indian Route): *As the voyage progressed the crew became a floating United Nations with disregard for race or religion: slave and free blacks from Brazil and so-called Kaffirs (Port. Cafres) from east Africa, whose presence was sometimes essential to the continuation of a voyage: Chinese, Javanese, and Indians forcibly recruited in the ports of the Indian Ocean.* [9]

The Jesuit João de Lucena wrote a book about the life of the priest Francisco de Xavier (later St. Francis Xavier) that describes the trip to India in 1531: *...an Indian ship sailing with six hundred, eight hundred and sometimes more than a thousand persons inside, men, women, little boys, free and slaves, nobles, people, merchants, soldiers, sea people. Without a doubt, was not exaggerating the one that compared the ship to a large village.* [10] It may very well be possible for one of these ships to have arrived in America at an early date.

The story of the Jesuits aboard the vessels on the Indian route between 1541 and 1598 tells us of the main points in the voyages: *...religious life, distractions, fights, heat, diseases, accidents and presence of women.* [11]

Anthropology, Archaeology and the Archaeologists

The National Geographic Magazine story published in March 1988 and written by Joseph Judge describes the daily life of the settlers in the 16th century. His report, along with photographs by Bill Ballenberg and paintings by John Berkey, brings to life the work of archaeologists such as David Hurst Thomas. According to Kennedy, Dr. Chester DePratter of the University of South Carolina's Institute of Archaeology and Anthropology, and Dr. Stanley South, are key members of the research team excavating Santa Elena.

During excavations at a Cherokee prehistoric village and burial ground site located in an industrial park of Macon County, North Carolina, the archaeologist Ruth Y. Wetmore spoke about the Melungeons and the possible Turkish connection, she mentioned that the word Turk in those days meant anyone that did not speak English properly. Also, one reason to come to the mountains was the possibility that the sailors, hearing about gold and precious stones in the mountains, would jump ship. One would now ask what good the gold would do if they could not get back to their country.

America has a very short history in terms of Europe. However, if we look into the many Indian nations' history before the Europeans arrived, then we have a much longer history. As findings by archaeologists surfaced, they caused the following newspaper headline recently: *Cherokee remains, relics found at Macon Industrial Park.*[12] Due to economic reasons, no further study or even a preservation of the site was done, and American history was lost forever. Dave Moore, who was the archaeologist heading the excavation in Macon County, stated in an interview that another excavation is planned for a possible site where Pardo may have had a fort built, also in North Carolina, near Morgantown, by the foothills. *Pardo entered the interior with 125 soldiers on December 1st 1566. ... established a fort at Joara...same town as* Hernando *de Soto's Xuala...forts with garrisons of fifteen to thirty men were built at Chiaha, Cauchi, and Joara.*[13] This town was part of the chiefdom of Cofitachequi. Xuala, or Joara, is located near the foothills of Appalachia, close to Marion or McDowell Bottom in North Carolina.

The Azores Connection

The Azores' population originally was partially made up of some of the people from Flanders. Not only do they have common English and Flemish names, there is also an area called the *Bretanha* located in *São Miguel,* the largest of the nine island archipelago. In the north of France there is a province with the same name, Brittany. Foreign names are common in the Azores, such as Morrisons, LaBescat, Bettencourt, etc. Also, on the Faial Island, there is an area called Flamengos which originated with the Flemish from Flanders. Holland, Belgium and France share what used to be called Flanders in Europe.

Relations with Flanders date from the beginning of the Portuguese monarchy. The daughter of the first Portuguese King Afonso Henriques, Teresa, who later adopted the name Matilde in her new country, married the Flanders Count Filipe I. [14] These relations were reinforced into an alliance with Flanders in the 14th and 15th centuries due to the marriage of the Portuguese princess, Isabel of Portugal, to the King of Flanders, Philip the Good. Isabel was the sister of Henry the Navigator. Because Flanders was going through hard times such as war, death, destruction, hunger and disease, ran rampant. She requested that her brother settle the displaced Flemish in his island ventures, such as on his new found Azores. This was about the middle 15th century, however… *A voyage from Portugal to Flanders to obtain settlers was no easy matter. …combined Portuguese and Flemish fleet that carried Isabel to Flanders in 1429, left Cascais on October 17, and arrived at Sluis on Christmas day, December 25.* [15]

The Azores were rediscovered on Aug. 14-15, 1432 when the Portuguese arrived at an island later called *Santa Maria*, because it was Saint Maria's day. At that time Prince Henry ordered sheep and goats released to provide food for later expeditions. Later, Moorish prisoners captured in the Moorean wars were used there for work as well as in the Madeira Islands. Also, settlers from Flanders, Artois and Picardy, sent by Philip the Good, as well as Flemish people were entering the service of Henry the Navigator. It should be noted that it is not uncommon to find blue eyes and blonde hair among the Azoreans. *União Portuguesa do Estado da California*, Portuguese Union of the State of California, published a book, *Portuguese Immigrants,* which it states: *The popular feast of St. Mark, "Festa dos Cornos", celebrated on the 25ᵗʰ of April of each year in Faial and other islands, is another of the few testimonies of the Flemish presence, not to mention the blue eyes and blond hair adorning the Azoreans.* [16]

Dr. James H. Guill, author of the book *A History of the Azores Islands*, knows about the Melungos, and has for the last 45 years researched every possible aspect of the Azorean people. He maintains that there is a record of a certain captain leaving the Azores to go to the continent to pick up settlers, but one or two voyages never ended. He's of the opinion that some of the Melungos are descendantss of people that came from the Azores.

One such voyage to the Azores from Flanders may not have turned north to the islands at the correct time to reach the islands. One voyage may have neared the coast of North America, turned north, and encountered what is now the North Carolina coast. When colonization of this region was begun nearly two centuries later, the colonists encountered a European group calling themselves Melungeons and identifying with the Portuguese. [17]

The Azores' Portuguese Islands are only 1,100 miles from Newfoundland and 2,200 miles from New York. Portugal has the closest European point to the U.S. Azorean islands of Corvo and Flores are situated at 36° 55' N latitude (same as New York) and 24° 46' W longitude (New York 73°) while the closest point in the United Kingdom or Ireland is at 52° latitude and 10° longitude. Newfoundland is located at 48° N. latitude and 53° W. longitude. It is not very hard to imagine determined Azoreans reaching North America without much difficulty, planned voluntarily and/or by forces of nature.

As a matter of record it is known that 50 Portuguese farmers from the Azores were contracted by Pedro Menéndez de Aviles to Florida on January 26, 1573. And on July 13, 1573, 100 more Portuguese farmers followed. [18]

Azores to America in a Small Boat

Not long ago, in 1951, a married man in São Miguel Island by the name Victor Caetano was talking to his friend, a single man engaged to be married. He asked him, *Do you want go to America?* The other answered, *When? Tonight? How? No !* He replied, *in a boat that we are going to build.*

Fig. 92 - Map of the North Atlantic showing Portugal on the east and the USA on the west. Notice the distance from the Azores Islands.

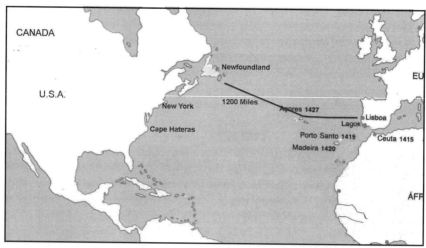

So they did, by evading the authorities and families, saying that they were building the boat for someone and being paid for it.

The boat was made of cheap lumber and measured approximately 15 feet. When the "vessel" was completed, the two men gathered some provisions and a fishing rod, and set out to sea at 1:00 AM. The following morning, the wife and family went to the police, who in turn went out on a wide search towards the west, the American coast direction. After many hours of searching, they found some signs of a boat wreckage and assumed that the two men had drowned. Meanwhile, the adventurers, instead of going west, went north, thus avoiding the police. Later they turned west, and after a couple of weeks of rowing and sailing, they were spoted by a Greek cargo boat that offered to rescue them. They refused, saying, *We're going to America*. The Greek Captain informed Portugal, and left them out in the ocean. A few days later a storm hit, damaging the small sail and mast. By then they were starving and suffering from exposure. Not giving up, they went on, eating raw fish. Already near the U.S. east coast of New England, they were spoted by the Coast Guard, which rescued them. The single one met a cousin and married her, and obtained legal status.

The married man went to Washington, D.C., and made a petition to remain in the U.S. He was refused and was told that he was going to be deported. He said, *You may deport me, but when I get back to the Azores, I will build a bigger boat and return.* [19] After much public interest, he was finally allowed legal status. A mini-series movie was made out of the story and is available in video cassettes by Henda Records. The following are the title and description in Portuguese: *O Barco e o Sonho, a partir do conto homónimo de Manuel Ferreira e do depoimento de Victor Caetano. O relato ficcionado das aventuras vividas por dois açorianos que na decada de 50 rumaram num barco à vela em direcção dos Estados Unidos.* The translation in Portuguese: *The Boat and the Dream*, from the story written by Manuel Ferreira, as told by Victor Caetano. He writes about two Azoreans that in the 50's sailed in a boat to the U.S.

Those facts are presented as evidence just to show that it was not hard for any Portuguese person to come to America from the Azores as early as the 15th century.

The favorable winds and currents would bring them in with very little effort on their part, contrary to Admiral Morison's conclusion that it would be unlikely, in early periods of navigation, for boats to reach Newfoundland from the Azores. [20]

Cherokee Indians

When the Cherokee in Virginia were encountered by white settlers in the 17th century, they occupied the Appalachian Mountains, mostly the territory of the Southeast. However, archaeological studies have been made and revealed their existence around A.D. 1000. Other studies also revealed the Lee-Pisgah ceramics dated around the same time, concluding that the Pisgah people were the Cherokee ancestors. [21]

It is known that when the Trail of Tears occurred in 1838, the Melungeons were living in the same area occupied by the Cherokees. It is also known that the Melungeons intermarried with them. Many Melungeons were known to have suffered the same fate as the Cherokees when they were moved west to the reservations, and many died along the way. Although the Melungeon-Cherokee

Fig. 93 - Lawanda Myers a member of the Cherokee Tribe.   *Fig. 94 - Jim Myers a possible Melungeon descendant.*

is not officially recognized, research points to a definite association.

There is a similarity between early Christians and the Cherokees in the interpretation of Creation and Paradise: *Although the early Cherokees did not worship personages...They viewed earth as a great island floating in a sea of water... On this island the Cherokees were the principal people. The similarities between early Christian beliefs and those of the aboriginal Cherokees are interesting. It was only in the early 1500's that the Christian concept of heaven and earth met with serious opposition. ... Prior to the "Enlightenment" and the period of exploration, the Catholic Church assumed that the earth was flat and surrounded by water.* [22]

The Cherokee had been established in the Southern mountains at least two or three centuries before their first contact with Western civilization during the incursions of Hernando de Soto in 1540 and Juan Pardo in 1566. [23] It is also possible that they may have been there much before. John Lawson was intrigued by the Indians he encountered: *...that these People might come from some Eastern Country; for when you ask them whence their fathers came, that first inhabited the Country, they will point Westward and say, where the Sun sleeps...* [24] Mooney is inclined to think that the early Spanish contacts made a considerably permanent impression on the Cherokee. [25]

Their housing is described by Timberlake in 1760 when he *noted that the Overhill Cherokee built rectangular houses...about 16 feet abroad, were sometimes 2 stories, and were often as long as 60 or 70 feet.* [26]

At least one linguistic remnant of the Spanish incursion is evident today. The Cherokee word for cow, *waca,* is unmistakably derived from the Spanish *vaca.*[27]

The Creeks, another nearby tribe also uses a similar word, *waga*. Another coincidence is that the Spaniards – in 1540's Soto expedition – were shown European articles which they were told had been obtained from white men who had entered the river's mouth many years before. [28] Other tribes were evidently encountered by Pardo and Soto expeditions. [29]

The word *vaca* is the same for Spanish and Portuguese. It is also possible that Portuguese as well as Spanish may have been in the area prior to 1540 and traded with the Indians. In practically all Spanish expeditions, Portuguese were among the troops, and the above indicates a possible Portuguese connection.

During research, Jim Myers, who owns the Log Cabin Gift Shop in Saunokee Village, Cherokee, was interviewed. Presently he is searching his genealogic family tree. Based on what he has found so far, he believes that he may be a Melungeon descendant. His wife Lawanda is a Cherokee Indian, but her maiden name is French. Jim's father's name was Harmon Myers. He told the author that about 20 years ago when he tried to search his roots, got tremendous opposition on the part of his cousins. They did not want the past to be known, possibly due to possible illegitimacy and having been registered in the U.S. Census as Mulattos. Jim is of a medium-heavy stature, with brown eyes and light complexion. His grandmother was an English lady, a possible descendant of Sam Houston. She was a teacher and, when he started to ask her questions about the past, she started to cry and asked him not to do it.

Apparently, what Jim has been able to find out is that some of his ancestors were registered as Mulattos and, based on the area where they lived, they could not be black, because the blacks registered lived in a totally different area. His great-grandparents worked in iron foundries, which is where a lot of Melungeons worked. Jim and his wife certainly have fine European features, as can be seen on the pictures. Jimmy's name was given to me by the office of Charles Taylor, federal Congressman for the Franklin area, who also is interested in this research.

Attempts were made to contact someone from the Cherokee tribe or get more information. Nothing else was available than what has been written by books sold at the Heritage museum, which did not help this research. However, the connection between the Cherokees and the Portuguese pops up once in a while.[30] Dromgoole also mentions... *The Malungeons believe themselves to be of Cherokee and Portuguese extraction.* [31] ...*the master of the house, who claims to be an Indian, and who, without a doubt, possesses Indian blood...boast largely of his Cherokee grandfather...*[32]

Coincidences? Hypothesis?

In the beginning, some questions related to the Melungeons were presented. Not all the answers were found. However, some coincidences shown are hard to ignore. It is up to you, the reader, to draw his/her own conclusions after evaluating the evidence presented. Here are some possible facts which may give the answer to Portuguese ancestry:

1. The origin of the name Melungeon is Portuguese.
2. The Portuguese knew that America existed and where it was.
3. The Melungeons always affirmed that they were Portuguese.
4. The Melungeons had physical characteristics similar to those of the Portuguese.
5. The English considered them Portuguese.
6. The census registered the Melungeons as Portuguese.
7. Declarations of their ancestors pointed to a Portuguese origin.
8. They were considered Portuguese by the courts and the laws.
9. Some of the original names pointed to a Portuguese origin.
10. Since the Portuguese were emigrating to Africa, Brazil and India they would also have come to North America.
11. There were regular means of transportation between Portugal, Spain and the New World.
12. The Melungeons, as well as the Portuguese, were precious metal craftsmen.
13. The Portuguese name survived to our days among the Melungeons.
14. Portuguese farmers were brought in by Pedro Menéndez in 1573.
15. What other modern language has names still in use that are very similar to Melungeon, such as Melungo, Mulango, Malange? Only the Portuguese language has these names still in the dictionary.

Portuguese Ancestry Claims

1. *The older Melungeons always claimed positively that they were Portuguese.* [33]
2. *And yet, no matter how distant their settlements lay from one another, they invariably claimed to be Portuguese.* [34] *I assumed the Melungeons were telling the truth, that is, that they were indeed Portuguese.* [35]
3. *They called themselves Portuguese and were found in the regions mentioned by our first pioneers of civilization there. They must come of some Colony emanating from Portugal.* [36]
4. *The present day Melungeons claim to be of Portuguese descent.* [37]
5. *The most plausible theory seems to be the theory which holds that the Melungeons are of Portuguese extraction. This theory is verified by the Melungeons who from early dates have claimed to be Portuguese.* [38]
6. *Burnett (1889)...who considered themselves of Portuguese extraction.* [39]
7. *Possibly they...descended from Portuguese or Spanish...* [40]
8. *[B]ut when all the racial ethnic theories failed, the people* (Melungeons) *themselves still maintained they were Portuguese.* [41]

The above are just a few, and an example of the many Portuguese ancestry claims. There are many more. At the time this book is being written, excavations are being conducted by archaeologists who may came up with new discoveries, on a site believed to be the place where Pardo built one of his forts.

Archaeologists and anthropologists may indeed provide many answers. They are in the ground. Time will tell, as long as the "digging" does not stop. For now, this book may not give a solid proof that the major component of the Melungeon people was Portuguese. However, all indications are that they were early European settlers, if not the first ones. Although some of the Melungeons may have originated outside Portugal proper, they were Portuguese by nationality. The Melungeons may have come from Portugal continental, the Azores, Madeira, or other Atlantic islands, Africa, Brazil or the Far East. All of these places, or part of them, were Portuguese territory and under the Portuguese flag. This is the only logical explanation why the Melungeons are so diverse in physical appearance. There is yet so very much to be done.

Notes

Portuguese Historians - Professor and author José Hermano Saraiva, Ph.D. is a well known historian and has many books to his credit. Also he has a weekly program about the History of Portugal on the RTP, Portuguese TV network. During an interview with the author, and after he read portions of Kennedy's book, Professor Saraiva requested a copy, which Kennedy sent. His final comment was, *it is very important that the subject should be studied.* He leans heavily on the Azores theory, and stated that a number of ships left the islands or the continent and were never heard of. He also mentioned that in the Azores, Santa Maria Island, Bay of Cré, 150 meters from the Chapel of the Angels, are buried some 16th century canons that marked the locale where Columbus landed in 1493 when returning from his first voyage. It is also interesting to know that *Historia Concisa de Portugal,* a book written by Professor Saraiva, has been translated into the Chinese language. He also told the author, that no writer ever attempted to write Columbus' life story before he arrived or even while he was in Portugal. That should be done in order to shed more light on his accomplishments, as well as possible earlier navigation.

Professor and author Artur Teodoro de Matos, Ph.D. president of Damião de Gois Institute at the Torre do Tombo in Lisbon, stated in an interview that he also was interested in the subject, and he recommended that it should be studied further. Professor Matos lived in the Far East for a number of years.

[1] Historia da Civilização Iberica, Oliveira Martins, p.41
[2] New Andalucia by Paul E. Hoffman, p. ix
[3] The Masters and the Slaves by Gilberto Freyre, p. 9
[4] Ibid, Studies by Emile Béringer of the Climate...Pernambuco
[5] Correio da Manhã, 2 Jul. 1995, p. 27
[6] Thorn Birds by Colleen McCullough, pp. 27,32 (also a movie)
[7] Fomento Rural e Emigração by Oliveira Martins, p.172
[8] Historia da Civilização Iberica, Oliveira Martins, p. .270
[9] Men Under Stress:The Social Environment...the Carreira da India by
A.J.R. Russell-Wood, p. 23

Notes (Cont.)

[10] História da vida do Padre Francisco de Xavier by Padre João de Lucena, p. 44
[11] As Relações de Viagens dos Jesuitas na Carreira das Naus da India
by José Wicki, p. 8
[12] Asheville Citizen, p. 3B, Dec. 29, 95
[13] The Forgotten Centuries by Charles Hudson, p.202, 203
[14] Historia de Portugal by Damião Peres, p. 641
[15] Azores Island A History by James H. Guill, Vol. 5-141
[16] Portuguese Immigrants by Carlos Almeida, UPEC, p.1
[17] Azores Islands, A History by James H. Guill, Vol. 5-141
[18] N. Brent Kennedy letter to Victor Marques of CNN
[19] Interview with Mariano Rego from Toronto
[20] A Future to inherit by Anderson and Higgs, p. 7
[21] The Buffalo Ridge Cherokee by Horace R. Rice, p. 14
[22] The Cherokee Perspective by Lawrence French and Jim Hornbuckle, p. 4
[23] Acculturation of the Eastern Cherokees by Leonard Bloom, N.H.R.,
Vol. 19, 1942, p. 331
[24] A New Voyage to Carolina by John Lawson (Hugh Lefler), p. 173
[25] Ibid, p. 332
[26] Red Carolinians by Chapman J. Milling, p. 12
[27] A New Voyage to Carolina by John Lawson (Hugh Lefler), p. 332
[28] Myths of the Cherokee by James Mooney, p. 193
[29] Catawba Nation and its neighbors by Frank G. Speck,
N.H.R. V.16-1939 pp. 405-6
[30] Cherokee is located in the mountains of Western North Carolina
[31] The Malungeons by Will Allen Dromgoole, p. 479
[32] Ibid, p. 477
[33] The Melungeons by Bonnie Ball, p. vi
[34] The Melungeons by N. Brent Kennedy, pp.11-12
[35] Ibid, p. 93
[36] History of Tennessee by Hale and Merrit, pp. 180, 181
[37] Smoky Mountain Country by North Callahan, p. 162
[38] The treatment of the Melungeon by Jacqueline Daniel Burks, p. 23
[39] Genetics in the Melungeons… by Pollitzer and Brown, p. 388
(Human Biology, Sept.1969)
[40] The Melungeons by Jean P. Bible, p. 2
(Martha Collins, Sneedville Bank President)
[41] Atlantis Dwelling place of the Gods by Henriette Mertz, p.58

Appendix A
Common Surnames, Places and Portinglês [1] Words
(names that may indicate Melungeon and other group connections)
Place Names used in North America

The following is a list of names used by people of Portuguese ancestry, including the Melungeons, and other groups of people that may be connected with the Portuguese. All of these may be coincidence but are worth considering. Some of them belong to the Santa Elena settlers. [2] Others are the result of the author's literary research and personal interviews.

English/Melungeon	Portuguese	English/Melungeon	Portuguese
A		Bowman	
Adams	Adão	Bradby	
Adkins		Bragans	Bragança
Allmond		Brandon	Brandão
Amadas	Amada, Almada	Branham	
Amador	Amador	Braveboy	
Andrews	Andrade	Brier	Silva
Ashworth		Brigman	
B		Brogan	
Bacalieu (Canada)	Bacalhau	Brown	Browne, Abrão
Barber	Barbosa	Bruym, Brum	Brum
Barker	Barqueiro	Bulcan	Bulcão
Barnes		Bullion	Bulhão
Barrett	Barreto	Bunch	
Bass		Burgess	Borges
Battle Island (Canada)	Batel	Burrows	Barros
Bean		Burton	
Beckler		Bush	Bucho
Bedgood		Butters	
Bell	Bela	Buxton	
Bennett		Byrd	
Berry		**C**	
Bettencourt	Bethencourt	Calloe	Calhau
Beverly		Canara	Canará
Bolin, Bolton		Canara	Caneiro/a
Bolling, Boulden		Canara	Canhardo
Boone		Canário	
Borling, Bowlin		Carrico	Carriço
Boteilho	Botelho	Carter	
Bowling		Casar	Casar

English/Melungeon	Portuguese	English/Melungeon	Portuguese
Casteel / Steel	Castilho	Dial, Dial, Dick	
Caton	Caetano	Doodes	
Caudill	Caudilho	Doyle	
Chavis, Chavers	Chaves	Driggers	Drummond
Chula (Georgia)	Chula	Dungey	Dungue
Clark		**E**	
Cole	Calero	Elvis	Elvas
Coleman		Ely	Elias
Coles		Emery	Amaral
Colings		Epps	
Colley		Eulalia	Eulalia
Collier		Evans	
Collins	Colina	**F**	
Colyer		Farilham, Canada	Farelhão
Conception (Canada)	Conceição	Fellow	Fialho
Cook		Fermeuse, Canada	Formoso
Coone	Cunha	Ferry	Ferreira
Cory, Corey	Correia	Fields	Campos
Costello	Castelo	Fisher	Ficher
Costmore		Fletcher	
Counts	Condes	Fratus	Freitas
Cox		Freates	Freitas
Coxe		Freels (Canada)	Frey Luis
Cravalho	Carvalho	Freeman	
Crémaillière (Canada)	Caramelo	Fretard	Freitas
Criel		Fundy (Canada)	Funda
Cross	Cruz	**G**	
Cubans	Cubano	Gallagher	Galego
Cumba	Macumba	Garland	
Cumbo		Garrett	Garret
Cumbow		Gawen, Gawne	
Curry	Correia	Gawin	
Custalow	Castelo	Gibbens	
D		Gibbs	
Dare		Gibson, Gipson	
Davis	David	Goain, Goane	Goeses
Day	Dias	Goains, Goen, Goene	Gois
Delp		Goan	
Deluz	da Luz	Goens, Goine, Going	Goes
Denham, Denhan	Dinho, Godinho	Goings, Goune	Goios
Dennis	Dinis	Goins, Goin, Goines	Góis/Goiás

English/Melungeon	Portuguese	English/Melungeon	Portuguese
Gormes, Games	Gomes	Jason	Jacinto
Gorven, Gorvens		Joe King	Joaquim
Gouen		Judy	Juvenalia
Gowain, Gowans		**K**	
Gowan, Gowane		Keith, Keyes, Keys	Chaves
Gowen, Gowene		Kennedy	Canadei
Gowin, Gowine		**L**	
Gowing, Gown		Labrador (Canada)	Lavrador
Gowne, Gowyn		Langston	
Gowyne, Goyen		Lasie	
Goyne, Goyenne		Lawson	
Graham		Leviner	
Grants		Locklear	LaBescat
Greaves	Graves	Lopes	Lopes
Groom		Lowry	
Gwinn		Lucas, Lucus	Lucas
H		Lula	Lula
Haires	Aires	Lumbees	
Hale		**M**	
Hall		Maddox	
Hambricks		Maggard	
Hammond		Major	Major
Hanks		Male	
Harmon		Marks	Marques
Harris		Martin	Martins
Harvey, Harvie		Mathias, Mathews	Matias
Hatcher		Mattes	Matos,
Hawkes		Mattos	
Head		Mayle	
Helen	Helena	Mellow	Melo
Hendricks		Mendes	Mendes
Hillman		Milee	
Hogge		Miller	Melo
Holmes		Miner	Mineiro
Howe		Minor	Menor
Hunt		Mizer	
Hyatt		Moluccas (Indon.)	Maluco
I		Molungo	
Ingles	Inglês	Molyns	Molino/a
J		Moore	Moreno
Jackson, Jones		Morrison	Morrison

English/Melungeon	Portuguese	English/Melungeon	Portuguese
Moseley		Roach	Rocha
Mull	Moules	Robinson	
Mullins	Molino / a	Rogers	Rosa
Mursh			
Myer	Maia-Mayer	**S**	
N		Salvadore	Salvador
Nash (Nasi for Jews)	Nasce	Salvo (NC)	Salvo
Navarrah	Navarro/e	Sammons	
Nelson	Nelson	Sampson	
Newman		Sampson	
Niccans		Sawyer	
Nicholas, Nichols	Nicola	Schmidt	Ferreiro (a)
Noel	Noel	Scott	
Norris		Sears	Soares
O		Sedalia (NC)	Cidalia
Oliver	Oliveira	Sexton	
Ormonde	Ormonde	Shavis	
Orr		Shephard, Short	
Osborn	Osverno	Silver	Silva
Oxendine		Silvia, Sylvia	Silveira
P		Simmons	Simões
Paine		Smith	Semedo
Pattereon	Patrão	Smith	Ferreiro
Perkins		Spair , Spear , Can.	Espera
Perlrins	Pery	St. John Harbor	São João
Perry	Pereira	Stanley	
Perry	Peres, Pires	Steel	Aço, Ferro
Peters	Pita	Stevens	
Phelps		Stewart	
Philips	Filipe	Stitt	
Phipps		Swartz, Sowa	Soares
Pinder		Sweat, Sweats	
Polly		Swett	
Powell		Swindall	
R		Sylva	Silva, Sylva
Race (Canada)	Raso	Sylvester	Silvestre
Ramey		Sylvia	
Rasnick		**T**	
Reaves, Reece, Reese	Rios	Tally	
Revels, Reeves		Tarves, Tarvis	Tavares
Ries, Rivers	Reis, Rivas	Taylor	

English/Melungeon	Portuguese	English/Melungeon	Portuguese
Thompson		William (s)	Guilherme
Tobias	Tobias	Williamson	
Tolliver		Wood	Madeira
Tormentine (Canada)		Wood (s)	Matos
Tormentinha(s)	Matos,	Wyatt, Wise	
Madeira			
Wyatt	Madeira	**If not on list, add:**	
Wyatt			
Travers	Tavares	....	
Travis	Tavares		
Turley		....	
V			
Valentine	Valentim	....	
Vardy, Verry	Vieira		
Vera, Viera, Vierra	Vieira	....	
Vicars	Vigario		
Vidalia	Vidalia, Vitalia	....	
Viola (TN)	Viola		
W		....	
Wager (Wedge)	Cunha		
Walter	Valtério	....	
Ware			
Washburn		....	
Watts			
White	Branco	....	
Whited			
Wilkins			

Translation Table of Names used in this Book

Portuguese	English	Spanish	Others
Abade	Abbot		
Afonso		Alfonso	Affonso
Alcacer-Quibir	Alcazarquibir		Ksar el Kibir
Álvares		Alvarez	
Bragança		Braganza	
Cabrilho		Cabrillo	
Canara	Karnatka		Kannara
Castanheda		Castañeda	
Colombo	Columbus	Colon	

Portuguese	English	Spanish	Others
Coração	Curaçao		
Diogo		Diego	
Estevão		Esteban	
Fernandes		Fernandez	
Fernando	Fernando	Hernando	Fernão/Ferdinand
Filipe	Phillip	Felipe	
Góis	Goins	Goys	Goes
Gomes		Gomez	
Gonçalves		Gonzalves	
Henrique	Henry	Enrique	Anrique
João, Joa'o	John	Juan	Joam, Yoao
Lisboa	Lisbon	Lisboa	Olissipo
Lopes		Lopez	
Macau	Macao		
Magalhães	Magellan		
Mendes		Menendez	Mendez
Mendonça		Mendonza	
Nunes		Nunez	
Pedro	Peter	Pedro	
Porto	Oporto		
Rodrigues		Rodriguez	
Salsaparrilha	Sarsaparilla	Zarzaparrilla	
Sebastião	Sebastian	Sebastian	
Simão	Simon		
Tejo	Tagus		
Viriato	Viriatus		

Foreign name chart

Gois, Goios, Goes, Gowens, Goins, Gomes, Goans, Goa

The Góis family was a family of nobles in the Portuguese royal court. Gonçalo Gois was a knight in the 12th century who fought for the first Portuguese king, Afonso Henriques. Brites de Gois was grandmother of Filipa Perestrelo, the wife of Christopher Colon (Columbus). There were family ties with Columbus that lasted for many generations.

Jorge de Portugal, grandson of Rodrigo Afonso de Melo and Isabel de Meneses, married Isabel Colon de Toledo, Columbus granddaughter. [39]

Another famous Gois was Damião de Gois, written as *Damianvs A Goes* in the 16th century. He was born in Alenquer in 1502 and died in 1574. He was a royal historian, humanist and famous writer who married in 1538 a Dutch noble, Joana

Fig. 95 - Gois
Family Crest

van Hargen; in his time he was one of the very few that had a friendship with Saint Ignatius of Loyola and with Martin Luther a very unusual combination. Gois was also persecuted by the Inquisition due to his book, published in 1541 and banned by the Inquisition. Later he was appointed *guarda-mor* (director) of the Torre do Tombo (Portuguese National Archives). [40] Bento de Gois was a famous missionary also in the 16th century.

Goiás or Goyaz is an area in Brazil that was explored in 1592, mainly because of the existence of gold. Today, the capital of Brazil, Brasilia and the *Distrito Federal* are located in that region. The Brazilian State of Goiás capital is called Goiânia. Some of the variations of the name Goins were submitted by the Gowens Foundation, for which I am grateful. According to Edward Price, the name Goins *seems to be a peculiar marker of...mixed bloods...Further, Goins is an unusual name; though many whites are named Goins, it occurred with much greater frequency among free colored persons in 1830... (2.8 per thousand) than among the population at large in 1790...The Goins name arrived in Virginia Gowen, one "Tho: Gowen" having been listed as a passenger on the Globe in 1635.* [40a]

Price, further states that *a phenomenon as the Goins family must have a definite story behind it, but has it made its way into the records?* For anyone interested in finding the origin of certain names with possible Azorean connection, I recommend the book by James H. Guill, *Azores Islands A History.* It has over 2,000 names with their derivation and family origins.

Portinglês

Portinglês is the language of Portuguese-Speaking people in selected English-speaking communities. For perhaps the most extensive glossary of Portinglês, or English words as spoken by the Portuguese in America, see Adalino Cabral, four volumes, published in 1985 by University Microfilms International, 300 N. Zebb Road, Ann Arbor, MI 48106. This work represents a dissertation for the partial fulfillment of the requirements for the degree of doctor of philosophy.

Also see Leo Pap's *Portuguese American Speech* published in 1949 by Columbia University, New York.

Portuguese Sounds and a Very Important Name

As stated at the beginning of this appendix, the coincidences are so overwhelming to the point that they should not be ignored. For some they may be far-fetched, but for many that lived and still live in the Southeast, these coincidences make sense.

From an academic point of view they may not be accepted, but for the many interviewed, they would like to see it in print. It has been said that some names may have a Celtic, Irish or English origin.

That may be possible if one takes into consideration that the Celtic people, at one time controlled most of Europe. However, the names or coincidences are very much alive today in Portugal, and have been for hundreds of years. Also in many parts of the U.S.

Mãe longe, Portuguese phrase made up of two words. 1. *Mãe* in Portuguese means mother in English. 2. *Longe* in Portuguese means far away in English. *Mãe longe* = **Mother far away.** In Portuguese is pronounced almost like **Melunge,** with a nasal prolonged sound in the first syllable.

If someone asks a Portuguese immigrant who's left his mother in the old country, *where is your mother?*, the answer is *mother is far away* or *Mãe longe.* The spelling of mother in Portuguese is *Mãe* or *Mae* without the tilde.

An interesting coincidence is related to this name. Many families in the Southeast use the middle name Mae as in Billy Mae, Lillie Mae, Effie Mae, Ollie Mae, Dollie Mae, Lucy Mae, Mae West, Pearl Bailey Mae, Rita Mae, etc. It is also interesting that these names belong to families that claimed Portuguese ancestry and live in North Carolina. According to them, they are not connected to the Melungeons. Mae Jamison is also the name of the first American of African ancestry to travel in space, and she was born in the Southeast.

There are many Portuguese sounds that, when words are combined, can produce the same sound as an English word or name. An old Portuguese lady in her late nineties, and still enjoying full mental faculties, has a special way of doing that, since she does not speak English. Only one problem, she sometimes finds a humorous way in the translation, for example, *Kentucky.* She finds it easy to remember if she says in Portuguese *quente aqui* or *hot here*, Cherokee, *cheira aqui*, Cincinnati, *se ensina a ti*, and so on.

Another coincidence in Portuguese sounds, was found in Dromgoole's article. This writer, who lived with the Melungeons for a short period to study them, refers to their behavior and a refusal by some people to employ them as servants: *...their ignorance of defiance of the difference between **meum** and **tuum** ...they expect remuneration for the slightest service...*[41]

These are Latin words and mean *mine* and *yours*. In Portuguese they are written very similary – *meu* and *teu* – and in order to add a nasal sound at the end of the word, the letter m is added. This would be the way an English-speaking person would pronounce *mine* and *yours* in Portuguese. These same words in Spanish are written as *mio* and *tuyo* which are different.

Why did Dromgoole used Latin words? My understanding is that the writer is referring to a possibly selfish attitude, not knowing the difference between what belongs to them and what belongs to others, which in certain conditions may not be justifiable but may be explainable. These words and sounds may be irrelevant but other less probable similarities have been used when establishing connections with other groups.

English Surnames and the Name Change Game

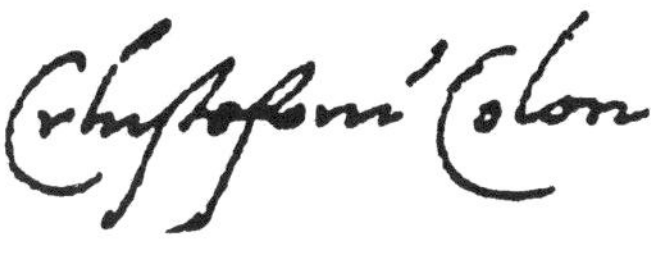

Fig.96 -Christopher Columbus' name as written by the Pope, 11

One of the first things many immigrants face when arriving in America is the most likely change of their name. Columbus is the most famous name change in history. In the books written about the Melungeons, a fact is mentioned that most had English surnames, which is not surprising when Columbus' real name was, and still is, in the Spanish-speaking world *Colón*. But very few people know him by that name in North America.

The name Colombo in Italian and Portuguese means pigeon, and it is hard to believe that he would be called that. Name change happens and is perpetuated, just like in Columbus' case. Did the name originate in Genoa ?

If Genoa was indeed the place of Columbus' birth, it hardly registers on his soul: nowhere does he refer to the home in which he was born or the way he spent a single moment of his early years. *Nowhere, also, does he use a word or phrase of substance in any Italian dialect including Genoese.* [42] Indeed, it is hard to see how, even assuming Genoese birth, one could really construe Colón as an Italian, if one can even talk about such a thing as Italy in the 15th century. The language he used in writing his letters and papers was Spanish, [43] not Genoese, Italian or Latin. No document was ever found written in Italian, not even the ones he wrote to *Italians* or his personal papers such as expenses, etc. [44] Some less informed writers blame this on the fact that Genoa did not have a written language, and it was for the most part a dialect, or that Columbus could neither read or write his native language when he left Genoa at

Fig. 97 - Christopher Columbus' name as written by the Pope, 31

24. One could hardly believe that, Genoa being one of the most important republics of the Mediterranean. And how could Columbus become the well educated man portrayed in history? But that is another story. When he arrived in Spain he was considered a Portuguese citizen, and the Spaniards later made him a Spanish citizen – not formally – and his name was forever bound to Portugal and Spain.

Dr. Luciano da Silva, a medical doctor and Portuguese history researcher has found some very interesting information in Rome: a document written by Pope Alexander VI on the 3rd and 4th days of May, 1493, clearly names Columbus as Colon, and not as Colombo, as shown and provided by Dr. Silva, to whom we owe a great deal for this discovery. The name Columbus is Latin for Colombo. Why would the pope write *Colon* when the language of the Catholic church was mostly in Latin? And why would the Spaniards call him *Colon* if latin in the 16th century was still a very common language taught in spanish colleges ?

Rui de Pina, a Portuguese writer and contemporary of Columbus, does call him *Christovam Colombo* [45] once in his chronicles, and that is where most Portuguese historians explain or justify his name. However Pina was also known to write what the king liked to read, and Pina did not like Columbus. Did he change his name on purpose? The name Colombo, or pigeon, could be considered derogatory, which would not fit well. The only reason the name Columbus is mentioned is to point out how easy it is to change a name, and not to prove that Columbus was Portuguese. According to scholars, there is not enough documentary proof available of his birth place.

Is it possible that the names of the Melungeons were quickly changed by the first English clerks in charge, due to the language, speech, inability to spell, illiteracy? Or the desire to conceal their non-Anglo origin, as it still happens in this century with Portuguese and other immigrants? A nickname was and still is very common. Very often the illiterate families were registered by their family nicknames. [46] Another very common way, still in practice, is the naming of a person by his place of birth, origin or length of stay. The name Portugal or Brazil is used as a surname in many Portuguese areas as well as in Brazil. The surname *Mira,* if one wants to give it a glorious origin, came from *Mira Ceti* the first variable star, acquiring the Latin name *Miraculous* in the 17th century. However, that may not be the origin. Most persons with the surname Mira trace their origins to a village called Mira, from where most fled after the French Napoleonic invasion of Portugal. The name in Spanish means *look* and it is not regularly used as a surname in Spain.

There is also a common misconception among some scholars that all Latin families, name their offspring by a saint's name, which is not always the case.

Anglicizing the names was done not only to be safe, but to survive in a culturally different society, in which one must do whatever is necessary. As the proverb goes, when in Rome, do as Romans do.

Fig. 98 - Caneiro village in Portugal.

Portuguese Names That May Indicate Melungeon Connections-Caneiro, Canhardo, Caneira

Many people in the old days took the name of the town as their second name. When the Ourem town historian was interviewed, he did confirm that the little village of Caneiro had a history of people emigrating to the U.S., back as far as the 17th century, and many people carried that name as their surname, and some with that name were interviewed.

This small village is located near the Castle of Ourem, originally built by the Moors and conquered by the Christians in 1136. Also nearby there is another village called Canhardo. That name can easily sound like Canara in English.

The names Caneiro and Caneira are common in Portugal. There are at least 20 other villages in Portugal with that name, as well as others in Spain, but not as many. It may not have anything to do with the Melungeons, but since they have a tradition of Moorish ancestry, and Portugal is full of stories and legends about the Moors, it is appropriate to mention one of them..

Fig. 99 - 11th Century Ourem Castle near Caneiro

In a town not far from Ourem, called Figueiró dos Vinhos, it is known that as early as the end of the 8th century A.D., Guesto Ansures rescued six noble maidens who were being taken by the Moors to Abderrhamen, King of Córdova. Every year 100 girls were sent to swell his harem, in accordance with tribute agreed on with Maregato, eighth king of Leon. This feat succeeded in breaking forever that infamous pact. Also one of the most popular stories in Portugal still being told is about the *Princesa Moura Encantada* or enchanted Moorish princess, who would take man with her to paradise.

Southeast Towns and Portuguese Names

Vidalia, famous for its sweet onions; Vitalia, Lula, Alto, Mendes, near Glenville south of Claxton; Portal near Statesboro, all in Georgia are well known Portuguese names. Dona is another one previously given to today's Blackwater village in Lee County, Virginia.

In this area lived a settlement of Melungeons, and it is believed to mean that a

Fig. 100 - Sylva in North Carolina

large tract of land was given to an heir (female). [47] The name *dona* is a Portuguese noun, and means *owner* or, as a title *dona* when addressing an older woman, usually married or widowed. The word is also used in Spain as a title, but not as commonly, and is written as *doña*. The word *owner* in Spanish is written as *dueña*.

Another strange coincidence is the name of a town in the mountains of Western North Carolina in Jackson County, where Portuguese explorers passed as part of the expeditions of Hernando de Soto in 1540 and Juan Pardo in 1567. It is an area where Melungeons used to live, and traditionally an Indian Cherokee area. A further inquiry into the town's name history shows as having originated from a Danish itinerant who passed by in the 1800's. Well that may be so, but the fact is that the name Sylva is not a Danish name, a fact confirmed by the Danish Embassy in Washington through Arcindo dos Santos, a Portuguese married to a Danish lady. He also informed us that there is not a single Sylva in the Danish capital of Copenhagen telephone book. There are, however a few Silvas, but they are Portuguese families living in Denmark. *Silva* or *silvado* is the Portuguese name for a thorny bramble fruit-bearing bush that gives wild berries, also called multiflorous rose, found in abundance in the same area. It is found in north temperate regions of the Old and New World. The farmers took advantage of their rapid spreading and used them as fences to keep animals in and people out. According to *Hernando de Soto Commission* report on the most likely route followed by the Spanish explorer in 1540, a major town named Cale was visited by the expedition,

which happens to be in the same area of the present-day city of Ocala in Florida. The original name of Portugal was *Portus Cale*. [48] In all fairness, place names or surnames can be misleading, and one has to be careful when establishing a definite connection.

Fig. 101 - Typical sign advertising Country Ham for sale at a roadside in North Carolina.

Foods in the Southeast That May Indicate Portuguese Origin

For many years I noticed the similarity of the foods used in North Carolina to that of my own in Portugal, such as turnip greens, collard greens, black-eyed peas, country ham, etc. My wife was the one that brought it to my attention, which prompted me to inquire with the local folk and asked if they knew where this type of food came from. The answer was: *the slaves brought it in.* According to sources describing the origin of foods, such as the Encyclopedia Britannica and others, these foods are classified as of Mediterranean origin, and do not grow in hot or tropical climates, as we know all slaves came from.

It is possible that the Spaniards brought some, but their impact in the Southeast was mostly in Florida; and there, this type of food is not common. The way country ham is prepared is in much the same way as the Portuguese or the Spaniards prepare it today. While I mention pork meat, lets keep in mind that the Muslims do not eat it and it is very hard to find it in Turkey, according to a Portuguese friend of mine who does business on a regular basis with Turkey. Also, his Turkish customers, when visiting Portugal do not eat it either.

It is also very interesting that only in the Southeast you are able to find a chain of restaurants serving turnip greens with ham and black eye pea salad. The name of the restaurants are *Cracker Barrel* and *Black-Eyed Pea* as well as others less known. Some of the foods very popular in the Southeast, are also part of the typical

Fig. 102 - Cracker Barrel Restaurant sign, serves turnip greens

Portuguese eating habits, more in the countryside than in the city. They are mostly vegetables, easy to grow and to take care. The way turnips and other vegetables are cultivated, and the time of the year – usually planted at the end of the summer – makes them able to survive the first fall frost, providing food for the winter. Another coincidence mentioned by Lawson, the first historian of North Carolina: *I am not a judge of the different sorts of Quinces, which they call ...Portugal...The Chestnut-Tree of Carolina...The Nut is smaller than those from Portugal, but sweeter.* [49] If the Portuguese arrived here at an early date, they would find fruits such as the quince and chestnut very similar to the ones found in Portugal. They are not exclusively Portuguese – probably they are also used by other folks – but it is interesting to note.

Typically Portuguese Foods

English	Portuguese
Mustard greens, sprout, broccoli rabe	Grêlos
Turnip greens	Nabiças
Galician cabbage, collard greens, kale	Couve Galega or Portuguesa
Cured, salted country ham	Presunto
Black-eyed pea or cowpea	Feijão Frade
Green peas to use in England in 1514	Ervilhas
Chick peas	Grão de bico
Corn meal, grits	Papas de milho
Rabbit	Coelho
Sarsaparilla	Salsaparrilha

Collard Greens - Kale is a non-heading leaf vegetable, which is eaten as a cooked green and also is an excellent source of minerals and vitamins A and C. One of the oldest cultivated vegetables, kale closely resembles wild cabbage and may be the ancestor of all the common cabbage crops. It is hardy in cold weather – in fact, its flavor is improved after it has been touched by frost. Kale is grown in the South in every season except summer, and in the North as a spring and fall crop. The reason collard and kale are being mentioned is due to the fact that the Portuguese use them in large quantities. Collard is, however, the one used in what is considered the national soup, called *caldo verde* or green soup. This soup is made using potatoes, shredded collard, onions, olive oil and one slice of Portuguese sausage or *chouriço*. According to Dr. Luciano da Silva, a medical doctor, this soup prevents cancer in the colon due to its fiber content.

A story related to kale and collard is interesting enough to repeat, and I will leave it up to the reader to draw any conclusions. During a multi-cultural festival in Florida, a Portuguese group – Portuguese-American Cultural Society – was serving their own style of food. However, the ladies selling the food were not able to sell the Portuguese soup, which was being called collard soup. Then one of the Portuguese ladies changed the sign to say kale soup and, amazingly enough, the soup started to sell and it was a success. Why?

Sarsaparilla [50] is one of the roots that the Melungeons used as a tonic. They also gathered it and sold it. It was used as an aromatic flavoring agent to mask the taste of medicines, in root beer or other carbonated beverages. This is well known in Portugal and Spain, often used as tea. The spelling in Portuguese is *Salsaparrilha* and in Spanish, *Zarzaparrilla*.

Turnip Greens - Turnips, originated in middle and eastern Asia, and by cultivation spread throughout the temperate zone. The foliage turnip does not produce an enlarged root but only a profusion of leaves which are used as a pot-herb. A variety called

Fig.103-Black-eye-Pea Restaurant near Atlanta, serves black-eyed pea salad, similar to Portuguese style.

Seven Top is widely grown in the southern United States. Cultivation started in England in 1724 mostly for stock feeding. Turnips afforded large quantities for winter feeding. [51] Henry R. Price is quoted to have written: *During the summer the Melungeons grow several root crops: turnips and potatoes are favorites.* [52] Bartram wrote that in 1775, Dr. B. S. Barton, vice-president of the American Philosophical Society, told him about the Creek and Cherokee diet: *Turnips, parsnips, salads...they have no knowledge of.* [53]

Of the cultivated greens, collards are probably the most nutritious, though turnip greens are the most popular throughout the region. Kale and mustard greens have their own advocates; preference varies by region, turnips being a hardy biennial plant cultivated for its fleshy roots and tender growing tops.

Young turnip roots are used raw in salads or as appetizers, and the young leaves may be cooked and served. The fully grown roots are also cooked and served as whole or mashed vegetables used in stews. Also used by the Portuguese is a vegetable called *broccoli raab* or *broccoli rabe*, in Portuguese *Grêlos*. It is a vegetable plant related to the turnip and grown for its pungent leafy shoots. Calcium is plentiful in nature such as leafy green vegetables, turnips, and collard greens. There are about 50 Old World species, including Portuguese cabbage. [54]

Turnips in England - After the two Whig factions were reconciled in 1720, Townshend became president of the Privy Council and (in 1721) secretary of state. Townshend earned his nickname *Turnip Townshend* for his contribution to the development of the use of turnips in crop rotation. Greek and Roman farming techniques are known from contemporary textbooks that have survived, and methods were dictated to some degree by the Mediterranean climate and by the contours of the area. The majority of the crops cultivated today on the Mediterranean coast were known at that time in England, but some were not very popular.

The olive, the vine and fruit trees were grown, as were turnips and radishes. The Arabs had introduced sugar cane and rice to some parts of southern Europe. The voyagers to North America returned with corn (maize), tobacco and the turkey. South America supplied the potato, cocoa, quinine, and some vegetable drugs, while coffee, tea and indigo came from the Orient.

The history of vegetables is imprecise, though familiar types, including the radish, turnip and onion, are known to have been in cultivation from early times. [55]

Corn or Maize, Corn Meal, Stirring Mush, Grits

Corn, a cultigen that was demonstrated in Mexico as early as 5000 B.C., first showed up in the southeastern U.S. at about A.D. 200, *but for hundreds of years it was only a minor part of the diet.* [56] The Portuguese may have been the first Europeans to recognize its value and were planting it in Portugal as well as other parts of the globe in the early 16th century. They were the first to bring corn to Europe, and it is on record that it was being planted in 1500 in Portugal and taken to China in the early 1500's. It is therefore possible that the corn meal would have been brought over by the first European settlers, where *grits* originated.

Black-eyed pea, or cowpea, is one annual plant within the pea family. In other countries they are commonly known as China bean, or black-eyed bean. The plants are believed to be native to India and the Middle East but in early times were cultivated in China. In the southern United States the cowpea or black-eyed pea is extensively grown. [57] In Portuguese they are called friar's beans, because the Jesuit friars brought them from the Far East, according to tradition.

Portuguese Quilting - Quilt, *manta de retalhos* in Portuguese used as a bedcover. I remember it more as a necessity than an art or choice as it is now known in the Southeast.

My aunt, as a dressmaker, was constantly asked by the local folk for the small pieces of cloth left over. My grandmother used to spend the evenings making a quilt out of these small pieces of cloth, at the light of a kerosene lamp, to be used as a bedcover and keep us warm during the cold winter nights.

Quilting is an ancient tradition, and uses as a bedspread is an extremely old custom, referred to in the earliest written sources, for example, the Bible. It is believed to have originated in the Middle East. Kennedy has mentioned in his book of a possible connection with the Melungeons and the Turkish tradition of quilt-making with very elaborate designs.

It may not mean anything, but I thought of mentioning it while looking for old pieces and bits of customs or culture that have survived over the years.

Music and Folklore Dance in the Southeast
Square Dance - *Baile Mandado*

There is one type of folk dance that is still being performed in the south of Portugal and, only there, it is called *Baile Mandado*. In North America it is a variation of a square dance called out by a singer. This dance, and variations of it, is very popular mostly in the Blue Ridge and Appalachian mountains. The similarity is due to the fact that the steps of both dances are called out by a man, usually the director of the group. The singing calls made by the *caller* give instructions for couples to perform a variety of movements, and are all based on a smooth, shuffling walk. So far I did not find any other dances in the world performed the same way.

Here's how the square dance came to be. In colonial days European dances were taught in the cities with figures or movement called spontaneously as the dance progressed. Although the dancers would have to learn the figures just prior to the dance – taught by the caller – they could be put together by the caller in any sequence on the spot. This method of dancing provides an interesting and spontaneous competition or challenge between the caller and the dancers, with the caller trying to fool the dancers – who were daydreaming or flirting – yet keep the dance flowing, and the dancers to execute the calls without a break in rhythmic step or motion.[58, 59]

The square dance is also said to have derived from the European quadrille – a four-couple square dance – and seems to have been more noticeable during the early 1700's [60] in the Appalachian Mountains. In Portugal it had its origins in the south of Portugal, Algarve. According to the Faro group director, it is also called the mountain quadrille or *Quadrilha Montanheira* in Portuguese, and it is one of the oldest traditional dances. The caller in Portuguese is called the *mandador* and the dancers are subject to his orders.

The quadrille was very fashionable in the late 18th and 19th centuries and was performed by English aristocrats in 1815, also in elite Parisian ballrooms. [61]

The city of Waynesville, located in the mountains of western North Carolina, is the American capital of folklore dance. It holds every year in July a Folklore Festival – *Folkmoot* – with participation of about 12 countries worldwide. In 1994, a group of folklore dancers from Faro in the south of Portugal participated with great success and again in 1996 another group from the north of Portugal – *Grupo Folclorico da Santa Marta do Portuzelo* – did attend.

By the way, neither my wife nor I was brought up in the U.S. However we always liked most types of country music. Portugal has a national song or music called *Fado*, meaning fate. The lyrics tell a story – a sad one most of the times – and it is thought to have derived from the Moors, another reminder of one of the many things that Portugal inherited while occupied by the Arabs for four centuries. Country music songs tell a folk story and also, most of the times, a sad one too. Also, it has been said that Ireland is the origin of country music. If so, that reinforces the fact that the Portuguese and Irish people may have common roots, since both had the Celts as common ancestors.

Fig.104 - Grupo Folclorico de Faro, Algarve.

A Good-bye with Flowers

During this research and while interviewing many Melungeon descendants, they stated that the Melungeon had an old custom with flowers which Jess Stuart mentions: *...It was an old custom to give flowers to a departing guest.* [62] This is also a tradition with the Portuguese which is slowly disappearing. Naturally, one may say that it is also common with other nationalities, but other nationalities may not have other coincidences shared.

Notes

[1] Portinglês Dictionary of Words spoken by Portuguese by Adalino Cabral

[2] The Melungeons by N. Brent Kennedy, p.122

[3] Names found in the early enumeration of Melungeon families.

[4] Captain Philip Amadas, voyage of 1584, The Roanoke Voyages by David B. Quinn, Vol. 1, p. 91

[5] Found in the Azores

[6] Common in the Azores Islands, and found on the telephone list of Sneedville, where many Melungeons live or lived.

[7] Ibid [8] Ibid [9] Ibid [10] Ibid [11] Ibid

[12] Names found in the early enumeration of Melungeon families. [13] Ibid

[14] Found in the Azores [15] Ibid

[16] Elvis Presley's family had roots in North Carolina, in the early 1800's.

[17] Elvas Hall was the name of a Melungeon. Elvas is the name of a large City in the south of Portugal, as well as the place where the writer of the first book about the Southeast was born, *The Gentleman of Elvas.*

[18] Names found in the early enumeration of Melungeon families.

[19] Caneiro is the name of a village near Ourem, as well as the name of 20 other villages in Portugal, and a common surname. Brent Kennedy's great-uncle name was Canara, which when pronounced in English has the same sound as in Portuguese.

[20] Found in the Azores [21] Ibid

[22] Names found in the early enumeration of Melungeon families.

[23] Found in the Azores

[24] Names found in the early enumeration of Melungeon families.

[25] See section under Gois

[26] Found in the Azores

[27] Name of a town in Georgia

[28] Names found in the early enumeration of Melungeon families.

[29] Found in the Azores

[30] Ibid [31] Ibid [32] Ibid [33] Ibid [34] Ibid [35] Ibid

[36] Silva or Sylva is a very common name in Portugal, and among the Portuguese in all Portuguese-American communities. It has been in the North-American continent at least since the 1600's.

[37] Gonçalo Silvestre, was the name of a soldier and commander – also a noble – of the Hernando de Soto expedition, in the southeast, including N. Carolina.

[38] Vidalia is a famous town in Georgia for its sweet onions

[39] Azores Islands A History by James H. Guill, Vol. 5-163

[40] Um Humanista Português, Damião de Gois by Aubrey F. G. Bell, pp. 15-27

[40a] Racial Mixtures in Eastern United States by Edward T. Price, p. 150, Los Angeles S. College

[41] The Malungeons by Will Allen Dromgoole, p. 474 (Arena, 1891)

[42] The Conquest of Paradise by Kirkpatrick Sale, p. 53

[43] Historia da Civilização Ibérica by Oliveira Martins, p.247

[44] Cartografia e Cartógrafos Portugueses dos séculos 15 e 16 by Armando Cortesão, p. 199

[45] Crónicas d'el Rey D. João II by Rui de Pina, p. 1016

[46] The Portuguese-Americans by Leo Pap, pp. 206,7

[47] N. Brent Kennedy, letter to Victor Marques of CNN

[48] Atlantis Dwelling place of the Gods by Henriette Mertz, pp. 35-56

[49] A New Voyage to Carolina by John Lawson (Hugh Lefler), p. 107

[50] The Melungeons by Edward T. Price, p. 4 (Geographical Review, April 1951)

[51] Encyclopedia Britannica, book 22, page 414.

[52] Melungeon Treatment… by Jacqueline Daniel Burks, p. 39

[53] The Indians of the Southeastern U.S. by John R. Swanton. 1946, p.286

[54] Southern Cooking by Bill Neal's, p.79.

[55] Encyclopedia Britannica, 1994 edition

[56] The Forgotten Centuries by Charles Hudson, p.7

[57] Encyclopedia Britannica, 1994 edition

[58] Southern Appalachian Square Dance by Frank X. Bonner, p.29 .

[59] The Discovery of the Dance by A. S. Barnes, P.117.

[60] Random House Dictionary, 1983

[61] Encyclopedia Britannica, 1993

[62] Daughter of the Legend by Jesse Stuart, p. 226

Part I

In Chapter VI, there is a summary of the beginnings of Portugal and the make-up of the Portuguese from the early invaders to the 12th century. Appendix A, Part I, shows a more detailed description and presents the more important events that affected Portugal and the Portuguese. Part II gives the chronology of events and information available related to the Melungeons after the 15th century as well as to Portuguese or other groups that may or may not be connected.

The Ancient and Modern World Calendars

Before reading the following chronology, it is appropriate to mention a few words about the dates and the calendar used.

The dates listed which may not necessarily be correct, are based on the western calendar. Apparently Pope João I asked monk Dionisio Pequeno or Dinosio Exiguo, who was a specialist in mathematics and astronomy, to calculate the Easter date, in order to end the irregularities of the celebration. During the study he arrived at the conclusion that Jesus Christ would have been born in the year 753 of the Roman calendar, which was used later to establish the Christian era. Based on the Bible, Christ was born when Herod was the king of Judea, and Herod's death is calculated in the year 750 of the Roman calendar.

Let us keep in mind that the Christian calendar is also called the Gregorian calendar due to a reform made in the 16th century by Pope Gregory XIII also famous for the St. Bartholomew's Massacre of Protestants. This calendar was adopted by all Catholic countries in Europe and later by others under western influence. The Eastern Orthodox Church did not accept the change and still keeps the Julian calendar for its own calculation of Easter. As for the United States, it was not until 1752 that England and America made the change; therefore all dates of events in the U.S. prior to that, would be based on the Julian calendar, which meant that George Washington's birthday, which fell on February 11, 1732, old style, became February 22, 1732, new style. [1]

The China revolution of 1911 brought a reform which introduced the calendar of the West, alongside the traditional Chinese calendar. In 1929 the Soviet Union, aiming to dissolve the Christian year, replaced the Gregorian calendar with a revolutionary calendar. The week was to have 5 days, 4 for work, the fifth free, and each month would consist of six weeks. The extra days needed to make up each year's complement of 365 or 366 days would be holidays. By 1940 the Soviet Union had returned to the familiar Gregorian calendar.

The years will get rather complicated when you take into account other civilizations. For example, the Jewish calendar corresponding to the Christian year of 1996 is 5756, which will change to 5757 on September 13. With all the scientific advance, the Jewish people know that this is arbitrary, as it was instituted between A.D. 200 and 600 , and it was thought to correspond to the creation of the world as described in the Bible.

The Islamic year in 1996 is 1416 of the Muslim era, starting a new year on May 18. The new year is based on new phases of the moon and starts when Mohammed, ran away from Mecca to Medina in the actual Saudi Arabia, which was in the year 622 of the Christian era.

While in most of the world it is 1996, the Chinese are living in the year 4693, changing again between January 21 and February 19 to the year 4694 under the sign of the mouse. The Chinese new year is celebrated during the second new moon, and the counting is not associated with any special cultural event. It is only an indication of the years since they decided to officially keep track of the count. The lunar Chinese year is divided into 12 months of 29 or 30 days and adjusted to the solar year, with the introduction of another six months cyclically. [2]

The seven day week dates back to Roman times and remains a proving witness to the early powers of astrology. The days are named after the planets as they were known in Rome 2,000 years ago. English and Italian: Sunday (Sun, Domenica); Monday (Moon, Lunedi); Tuesday (Mars, Martedi); Wednesday (Mercury, Mercolodi); Thursday (Jupiter, Giovedi); Friday (Venus, Venerdi) and Saturday (Saturn, Sabato). When people tried to extinguish ancient idolatry, they have replaced the planetary names with simple numbers. So the Quakers call their days First Day, Second Day and so on up to the Seventh Day. In modern Israel, too, the days of the week are given ordinal numbers, and the only other country in Europe and the world to use a similar method is Portugal, with the exception of Sunday and Saturday which they kept as the ancient Domenica and Sabbath.

Summary of Facts in Chronological Order
Related to the Portuguese History Before the Christian Era [3]

40,000	The *Hommo Sapiens* emerges from the Neanderthal man and later the Chancelade man appeared, who did not look much different from the average Mediterranean man of today, still living in Europe. [4] A Chancelade skeleton, human fossil remains, were discovered in a rock shelter at Chancelade in southwestern France in 1888. The skeleton was found in a curled posture — an indication of a deliberate burial below the lower Magdalenian occupation floors of the shelter; it is assumed to be of Magdalenian age (about 17,000 years old).

18,000	Paintings and engravings made in rocks, rupestrian style. These were found in the north of Portugal, Foz do Coa in 1995 when in the process of building a dam. A movement headed by João Crisóstomo started in the U.S. to save the engravings. In 1996 the newly elected government agreed to stop the construction of the dam.

15,000	Paleolithic cultures in western Portugal

4000   Iberians, name of a people that inhabited the Iberian Peninsula, a name of Greek origin, which along with Algarve (Arabic), Sephardic (Judaic) means *land of the West*

2750   Tyre is founded by mariners on the east coast of the Mediterranean and begins its rise as a great Phoenician sea power. The Greek historian Heredotus will say in 450 B.C. that Tyre was founded 2,300 years ago.

1424   Egyptian king Thutmose IV forms alliances with Babylon and leads military expeditions into Phoenicia.

1000   Phoenicians, Greeks, Carthaginians

814   Carthage is founded in North Africa by refugee Phoenician colonists.

776   Greek's first recorded Olympic Games.

700   Phoenician colonists plant olive trees in the Iberian Peninsula, and the beginning of celtic Migrations.

698   Greek colonization of the Mediterranean. In the next two centuries they will be motivated primarily by a need to find new sources of food as Greece's population expands.

600   Celtic people settle on the Iberian Peninsula and form the Celtiberians. Not long ago, similar signs of Celtic culture could be found in both Portuguese and Irish fishing villages.

562   The Phoenician city of Tyre falls to Nebuchadnezzar II after a 16 month siege.

520   Phoenician city island of Tyre has a population of 25,000; Old Tyre in the mainland is even larger.

418   Athenian forces crush Carthage.

408   *Orestes* by Euripides, who continues the theme of his 413 B.C. tragedy *Electra by Sophocles;* Euripides dies two years later in Macedonia at the age of 77.

300   Carthage in North Africa gains economic ascendancy in the Mediterranean by trading in slaves and silver from the Iberian Peninsula. Celtiberians inhabit an area around Tagus River. The Portuguese capital Lisbon is also located where this river meets the Atlantic Ocean.

280   The king of Syria loses Phoenician control to Macedonian's Ptolemy II.

195   Celtiberians submit to Romans, total submission in 133 B.C. However, Viriato and his successor Sertorio, the first Portuguese heroes, fought lengthy battles against several Roman generals.

161   Lusitania, a Roman province –what is approximately today Portugal–the Roman Galba, vexed by the bravery of the Lusitanians–natives of Portugal–ordered the massacre of 30,000. One of the survivors, Viriato, led a revolt against Rome and defeated five Roman generals in succession, forcing the last one to sign a peace treaty.
          Some historians stated that the war between the Lusitanos and the Romans lasted from 153 B.C. and 80 B.C., with Viriato followed by Sertorio, who at one time took refuge in Mauritania.

146   Carthage falls to Roman legions led by Scipio Aemilianus in six days and nights of house-to-house fighting after a long blockade. Some 900 Roman deserters torch the Temple of Aesculapius and choose death by fire rather than execution.
          Hasdrubal surrenders his garrison , and his wife contemptuously throws herself and her children into the flames of the temple. The city's ashes are plowed under, its environs become the Roman province of Africa and the Third Punic War is ended.

Christian Era

Based on the Bible, Jesus Christ was born when Herod was the king of Judea in the year 750 of the Roman calendar. The Jewish calendar year was instituted between the year 200 and 400. At that time it was thought to correspond to the time since the creation of the world, as described in the Bible approximately 4,000 years before.

409   Suevis-Suebis settle in the north of Portugal and form a kingdom with the Portuguese city Braga as their capital. The Allans invade the Iberian Peninsula and settle in the center of Portugal. The Vandals also invade and settle in the north of Portugal, and in the south of Spain. Later the Suevis occupy the center of Portugal, forming with the Visigoths the two independent kingdoms of the Iberian Peninsula, till A.D. 585 when the Visigoths dominate the whole peninsula.

416   Visigoths invade the Iberian Peninsula. They settle in the north of Portugal and gradually move to the center and south. Another group settles in the center of Spain.

439   Carthage falls October 29 to the Vandals, who have been led by Genseric. He makes Carthage his capital.

448   Suevi King Rechiar comes to the throne as a Catholic.

456   Suevis attack the Romans in Tarraconensis but are defeated by the Visigoths under Theodoric II. Described by the Bishop Hydatius of Chaves, a Portuguese city. This was the end of the Suevic kingdom.

The Islamic Era
Portugal in the 6th Century to the 16th Century

622   Mahomed, the founder of the Islamic religion, goes from Mecca to Medina in the actual Saudi Arabia, thus starting the Islamic era. To the north, the Suevi Kingdom. To the south and east, the West Gothic kingdom. From A.D. 622 to A.D. 700, this same kingdom governed the area where Portugal is today located and also part of Spain.

697   Carthage is destroyed by the Arabs, ending Byzantine rule in North Africa forever.

711   North African Arabs, Moors and Berbers invade the Iberian Peninsula.

739   Begins the reconquest of the Iberian Peninsula due to the expansion of the kingdom of Asturias due to the union of the Cantabric kingdom.

755   Political constitution of the County of Leon, independence of the Arabs and also independence of Navarre.

757   Kingdom of Asturias under Alphonso I started the reconquest of the Iberian Peninsula from the Arabs.

863   Separation and independence of the County of Galicia.

885   Galicia submits again to Leon.

967   Independent County of Castile is formed.

1073   Alphonso VI of Leon conquers Castile.

1099   Death of El Cid. Rodrigo Diaz de Bivar, or Rui Dias de Bivar, married Jimena Dias de Las Asturias from a family that later took the name Meneses, an Azorean family.[5]

1109   The County of Portugal is formed and given to Henry of Bologne. In this same year the kingdom of Aragon absorbs the kingdoms of Leon and Castile.

1140   Constitution of the Portuguese monarchy and foundation of the Kingdom of Portugal..

1147   Santarem and Lisbon are re-conquered from the Moors by the Portuguese.

1180   First naval battle won by the Portuguese against the Berbers.

1250   Portugal expels the last Arab settlement from Portugal.

1254   Seeding of the Leiria forest by King Dinis. It was already being planned to build boats, looking out to sea. Later, this forest provided the lumber to build the Caravels of discovery. Later, that same king authorized merchants to create an insurance exchange due to maritime development in Portugal.

1276   Portuguese friar Pedro Julião is elected pope and is named João XXI.

1291   The Genoese Vivaldi brothers attempt to reach the wealth of India by crossing the Atlantic. The attempt fails and the Vivaldis are lost at sea.

1308   Commercial treaty between Portugal and England.

1311   Extinction of the Order of the Templars and creation of the Order of Christ. This would have an effect on Portuguese discovery as Prince Henry would later be given this order and its wealth.

1314   King Diniz nominates Nuno Fernandes Cogominho as admiral-in-chief. On his death King Diniz called the Genoese Emanuel Pezagno to organize and command the royal fleet. He stayed in Portugal and his family – the Peçanhas – held the title of Admiral of Portugal for generations.

1325   King Diniz dies and King Afonso IV becomes king of Portugal.

1336   Canaries expedition ordered by the Portuguese king. They show up on the chart by Angelino Dalorto, Dulcorot or Dulcert. These islands proved to be of extreme importance for later navigation, including Columbus' first voyage to America. King Afonso IV, in a letter claims Portugal's right to the Canaries.

1346   The Catalan Jaume Ferrer attempts a voyage along the African coast and fails to return, another example of the difficulties encountered by Mediterranean sailors to navigate the Atlantic.

1357   King Afonso IV dies and Pedro I is crowned king Portugal.

1367   King Pedro I dies and is succeeded by Fernando.

1372   Treaty between the king of Portugal and the duke of Lancaster, and the following year is confirmed by the kings of Portugal and England as the Treaty of Westminster.

1383   Portuguese win a decisive victory against Castille in the famous battle of Aljubarrota, where 5,000 Portuguese defeated the Castilian army of 30,000, and affirm their nationality.

1386   Alliance between England and Portugal. Portugal has the oldest alliance in the world with England, that dates back to May 9, 1386, and is known as the Treaty of Windsor. The following year King João I marries Filipa, daughter of the duke of Lancaster.

1394   Henry the Navigator is born on March 4 in the city of Porto.

Portugal and the World in the 15ᵗʰ and 16ᵗʰ Centuries – Conquests and Discoveries – Early Explorations of North America

1415   August 21 - Portuguese conquer Ceuta in Morocco, and a new vessel called *the barinel* was used for the first time.

1417   Madeira Islands, off North Africa's Atlantic coast, may have been visited by Arabs and others. By 1419 Portuguese navigators João Gonçalves Zarco, Tristão Vaz Teixeira and Bartolomeu Teixeira landed there.

1419   Prince Pedro embarks on what appears to be a voyage of tourism; however it was a secret mission to obtain information for his brother Henry the Navigator, which he later uses on his voyages of discovery.

1422   Caesar's era ends and Christian era begins.

1424   Chart of Zuanne Pizzigano. There is cartographic evidence that the Portuguese were in Newfoundland before August 22, 1424, according to the Venetian cartographer and his nautical chart.[6] This map is part of a collection of 60,000 old and rare manuscripts belonging to Sir Thomas Phillips of London.

1425 Portugal wrests the Canary Islands from Castile. Madeira Islands settlement begins. Sugar cane from Sicily and vines from Cyprus are planted.

1427 Azores' possible early date of the discovery by Diogo de Silves.

1432 The Azores Islands are re-discovered in August 14,1432 by Gonçalo Velho Cabral.

1433 King João I dies and his son Duarte succeeds him. Africa's Cape Bojador, south of the Canary Islands, is rounded by the Portuguese navigator Gil Eanes.

1437 Portuguese are defeated by the Moors when trying to conquer Tangiers in Morocco. Prince Fernando is kept prisoner and dies there while awaiting the ransom demanded by Sala-ben-Sala.

1438 King Duarte dies and Prince Afonso, his heir, is still a child. Prince Pedro assumes the regency of the kingdom till 1446, when King Afonso V takes over the government of Portugal. He marries Prince Pedro's daughter in 1447.

1443 African slaves are introduced in Portugal, sold to Portuguese explorers in exchange for goods, by other blacks. The black brokers became the major traders.

1444 Portuguese explorer Nuno Tristão reaches Senegal.

1445 Portuguese explorer Diniz Dias rounds Cape Verde and 25 caravels per year trade between Africa and Portugal.

1448 Birth of Cristóbal Colón (Christopher Columbus).

1449 Prince Pedro, brother of Henry the Navigator, falls victim to the intrigue and the ambitions of the ducal house of Braganza. He may have been responsible for valuable information gathered while traveling throughout Europe and given to Henry.

1448/81 Portuguese-Danish expeditions. Portuguese King D. Afonso V and the Danish King Christian I of Denmark and Norway agree on making joint expeditions to the West between 1448 and 1481.

1450 Flemish nobleman Josue Van den Berg, who served under Prince Henry, begins to colonize Terceira Island, Azores.[7]

1452   Diogo de Teive may have visited Newfoundland, as written by Fernando Colombo, Christopher Columbus' son, in Venice, year 1571.

1453   The Turks (Ottoman Empire) conquer Constantinople (Istanbul today). This event marks the end of the Byzantine Empire and of the European crusades against Islam. Coffee is also introduced by the Turks.

1456   Diogo Gomes arrives at Guinea-Bissau, on the East African coast, and sugar from Madeira reaches Bristol, giving many Englishmen their first taste of the sweetener.

1458   Portuguese conquer Alcacer Seguer in Morocco.

1460   Henry the Navigator dies in Sagres on November 13.

1462   Portuguese begin settlement of Santiago Island, Cape Verde, with blacks from Guinea and Moors from Morocco.

1467   Columbus sees America at 16. Famous Norwegian historian and seafarer Thor Heyerdhal claimed that Columbus arrived in America in 1467 and not in 1492, while traveling with a Danish-Portuguese expedition to Greenland as a teenage crew member.[8] See 1448.

1470-2   João Vaz Corte Real, possible presence in Newfoundland. [9]

1471   Tangiers and Arzile in northwest Africa falls to the Portuguese, who have earlier taken Casablanca. Tangiers is given to England in the 17th century as a dowry of Portuguese Princess, Catherine of Braganza when she marries English King Charles II.

1472   Portuguese navigator Fernão Pó discovers the Islands of São Tomé, Prince, Cameroon off West African coast.

1473   Álvaro Martins Homem, possible presence in Newfoundland.

1474   João Vaz Corte Real makes a voyage to the "Land of the Cod Fish" and the younger Corte Real explores the coast of Labrador.

1475-6   Columbus arrives in Portugal [10] when he is approximately 24 or 25 years old, fifty years after the Portuguese initiated the conquest of the Atlantic. To understand his isolated adventure, it is important to be aware of the geographic discoveries made by the Portuguese between 1419 and 1542, from the Atlantic isles to Japan.

Sugar from Madeira is exported to Europe in large quantities as news arrives from France in this and in following years.

1479   Columbus marries the Portuguese lady Filipa Moniz de Perestrelo, daughter of the navigator Bartolomeu Perestrelo. [11] He lived ten years in Portugal. His mother-in-law gives him charts and other documents that belonged to her late husband. He also travels the Portuguese routes to the Guinea and western Atlantic, gathering information about Portuguese discoveries. Birth of Diogo Colón in Madeira, Columbus's son.

1481   King Afonso V dies and proclamation of João II as king.

1480   Convention between Castile and Portugal on how to treat the Berbers and the Moors.

1482/83   Portuguese in Malange, Africa. The expedition of Diogo Cão, ordered by King João II, discoveres the major part of Angola including the area of Malange. [12]

1483   Martin Luther is born on November 10, later inspires the reform of the church of the 16th century against the Catholic Church.

1484   Portuguese explorer Diogo Cão discovers the Congo River in West Africa, and possible voyage of Columbus to the Antilles for Portugal. Death of Columbus' wife Filipa Moniz Perestrelo. Inquisition is established in Castile.

1484/6   Columbus leaves Portugal to go to Spain and offers his services to the Spanish monarchs, after the Portuguese King João II turned him down. When he arrives in Castile, he is considered Portuguese. It is recorded that he was more fluent in Portuguese than he was in Castilian. In 1486 the Portuguese occupy Azamour in Morocco.

1487   Portuguese navigator Bartolomeu Dias round African southern tip, later called the Cape of Good Hope.

1488   Fernando Colón, son of Columbus and a Spanish woman is born in Córdova. King João II sends an enigmatic letter to Columbus in Spain, promising him that he would be welcome and his services recognized.

1489   The Portuguese king renews the alliance with the British, reconfirming the Treaty of Windsor.

1490   Portuguese explorers converts the Congo Empire to Christianity.

1492   The Catholic monarchs complete the unification of Spain by conquering Granada, the last Islamic kingdom on the Iberian Peninsula. The Jews are expelled from Spain and in October Columbus arrives in the Antilles, island of Watling - Saint Salvador – thus discovering America. Pedro de Barcelos e João Fernandes Labrador, sailing from the Azores, discovered a peninsula on the northeast coast of North America which he gave his name, Labrador. They also explored the east coast of Canada in the same area. German Behaim, a resident of Portugal, builds his famous globe in which he registers the progress of the Portuguese discoveries.

1493   Feb. 13 – Columbus stops in the Azores Islands on his return to Spain from America, and went after to Lisbon on March 4th. The Portuguese were the first to know of his discovery.
          May 4 - Pope Alexander VI establishes a line of demarcation between Portugal and Spain for dominion over the lands discovered. To the West belongs to Spain and to the East belongs to Portugal.

1494   The Treaty of Tordesilles, signed in June, divides the globe between Spain and Portugal as established in the previous year by Pope Alexander VI, giving Portugal almost 1,000 more miles to the west.

1494   To 1500, Gaspar Corte Real goes to Newfoundland to look for his father who disappeared on a previous trip. On one of these trips, Gaspar contoured the coast of Florida.

1495   King João II dies and the duke of Beja, Manuel, is crowned king of Portugal.

1496   Expulsion from Spain of Moors and Jews who refuse Baptism. Columbus returns to Spain without managing to find India. He has exhausted his human and material resources. Doubts are beginning to set in about him and his plans.

1497   After 10 years of inactivity, the Portuguese start their exploratory trips again. This period was used to carefully study all the knowledge obtained till then as to winds and currents. The years following the voyages were carefully planned and had a pre-assigned destination. Vasco da Gama sails from Lisbon on the way to India in July. Between the years 1497 and 1692, a total of 806 ships left Portugal, and, of these, only 425 returned. This was the activity registered.[13] June 24 – John Cabot, born Giovanno Caboto in Genoa, of Venetian citizenship, reaches Labrador and Nova Scotia, of which there are no records, returning to Lisbon, Portugal, on August 6.

1498 Portuguese explorer-scientist Duarte Pacheco Pereira is sent on a secret expedition and touches the South American coast. This information is later used by the Portuguese to send Pedro Álvares Cabral and officially discover Brazil in 1500. Portuguese navigator Vasco da Gama discovers the sea route to India, establishing a trade route between Europe and India, bypassing the Venetian middleman.
John Cabot and his son Sebastian coast Newfoundland and Nova Scotia; no records were kept. Possible voyages to Greenland and the North Atlantic by João Fernandes Lavrador.

1499 Spanish navigators Alonso de Ojeda, Diego de Lepe and Vicente Yanes Pinzón, with Amerigo Vespucci, sail the northern coast of South America while working for Spain. Already in Brazilian territory, they found a cross, presumably left there by Duarte Pacheco Pereira.

1500 Rediscovery of Brazil by Portuguese navigator Pedro Álvares Gouveia, later known as Cabral. The date of the first discovery was kept secret due to the negotiated treaties with Spain.
Columbus is arrested and sent back to Spain. He still is able to make another voyage at his own expense in 1502-1504.

1500 Gaspar Corte Real, a Portuguese navigator, makes the first authenticated European landing on the northern continent of the Western Hemisphere.

1501 Portugal sends a fleet to help Venice against the Turks. [14]

1502 Miguel Corte Real goes to look for his brother Gaspar to the northeast coast of North America. Does not return but left an inscription in the Dighton Rock.[15] See 1511. Also, Cape Race, Newfoundland, is shown on a Portuguese chart as *Cabo Raso*. Alberto Cantino map clearly shows Greenland and North America as well as the Florida peninsula. Corn is planted in Portugal for the first time.

1503 Fernando de Noronha discovers the islands that later receives his name.

1505 Sri Lanka (Ceylon) is discovered by the Portuguese Lourenço d'Almeida, off the coast of India.

1506 Tristão da Cunha, Portuguese navigator, finds islands in the south Atlantic that will later bear his name.

1507 The Portuguese colonize Mozambique in East Africa, where the word *Melungo* appears to have originated. The Portuguese capture Zafi in

Morocco and begin commerce in captive Moors, Berbers and Jews. Many were women, all are called white slaves. Christopher Columbus dies. Almeida da Cunha discovers Madagascar.

1509   Portuguese explorer Diogo Álvares Correia establishes the first European settlement in Brazil near Porto Seguro.

1510   European explorers probe the east coast of North America to a point north of Savannah.

1511   First Portuguese expedition to the Pacific and Malacca. Miguel Corte Real may have left a message on the Dighton Rock, with this date and the Portuguese coat of arms, according to declarations by Professor Delabarre of Brown University in 1926.

1512   The Newfoundland cod banks provide fish for Portuguese, English, French and Dutch vessels, which do the drying of the catch there for shipment back to Europe. A Portuguese caravel reaches Guangzhou (Canton). The first European ship lands in China. Diogo Garcia discovers *Rio da Prata*.

1513   Ponce de Leon rediscovers Florida while looking for the Fountain of Youth.

1514   Green peas come into use in England.

1516   Duarte Coelho discovers Cochin China (modern Vietnam) and Fernão Peres de Andrade arrives in China.

1517   Fernão Andrade and Tomé Pires land in China, and the Portuguese plant maize there.

1518   Portuguese King Manuel I requests the pope to elevate the Congo Prince D. Henrique to bishop of Utica. He becomes the first black Christian Bishop.

1519   The dollar has its origin in the "thaler" minted in Bohemia.
Fernão de Magalhães (Magellan), who has accomplished many expeditions, both in Africa and the Orient for the Portuguese King Manuel I, leaves Portugal to offer his services to Spain.

1520   Magellan, a Portuguese navigator working for Spain, rounds the straits of the southern tip of South America and stops in Guam, Marianas Isles. Álvaro Fernandes, also a Portuguese, is on Parfilo de Narvaez's expedition to the coast of Mexico.

1521 King Manuel I dies, and João III succeeds him. Aleixo Garcia crosses the South American continent from the Atlantic to Paraguay before many famed explorers. He is killed by the Indians in 1525 and Princess Isabel of Portugal marries Carlos V of Spain. Foundation of the colony of St. Peters in Nova Scotia, Canada, by Portuguese fishermen and João Fagundes de Viana.
There are eight Portuguese in the Spanish forces when Hernan Cortez conquers the Aztec capital, future Mexico City.

1522 Magellan's ships and crews return to Seville after accomplishing the first circumnavigation of the world.

1524 Probable birth of the Portuguese poet, Luis Vaz de Camões, writer of the epic poem, *The Lusiads*. Vasco da Gama dies and is buried in Cochin, India. The first book published in India is published in Cochin in 1577, while under Portuguese rule.

1526 The first English ships explore the African Guinea coast.

1527 English ship sails along the coast from Labrador to Florida and the West Indies, but nothing follows.[16] French ships in Mozambican waters, East Africa, where the name Melungeon or Melungo is used by the black people when calling whites.

1529 Chinese orange is introduced by Portuguese in Europe.

1530 Plan to colonize Brazil by the Portuguese.

1531 Earthquake in Lisbon and a papal request to establish the Inquisition in Portugal.

1533 French pirates in Brazil. Portuguese pilot Martim da Costa, working for the Spanish fleet of Fernando de Grialva, discovers lower California.[17]

1536 Pedro Nunes – 1502-1578 – a Portuguese mathematician, invents the nonius for graduating instruments, used by Pierre Vernier in 1631 and by William Oughtred in 1630 for the slide rule, a primitive analog computer. Oceans navigation treaty is signed between France and Portugal. Inquisition in Portugal is put into operation, more than three centuries after it was definitely established in France, Aragon and the north of Italy.[18] The first *auto de fé* takes place in 1540.

1539/40 Fernando Colon, Columbus' son, dies. The narratives he wrote about his father will be referred later by many historians.

1542/3 Lourenço Marques discovers bay and river in East Africa that later get his name, which changes to Maputo, after the independence of Mozambique.

1543 Portuguese Antonio Peixoto, Antonia da Mota and Francisco Zeimoto are the first Europeans to arrive in Japan. Portuguese Princess Maria of Portugal marries Prince Felipe, future King Felipe I of Spain.

1544 Fernão Mendes Pinto discovers and names Formosa (Taiwan).

1547 A law is passed in Portugal to register every ship going to Brazil.

1549 Settlement of São Salvador, Baía, Brazil.

1550's Mass emigration from the island of São Tomé to Brazil.

1553 Turks siege Ormuz, a Portuguese territory in India.

1555 Possible discovery of the Hawaiian Islands by João Caetano, a Portuguese working for Spain. History names Captain John Cook as the discoverer in 1778.

1556 Founding of Portuguese settlements in Japan. [19]

1557 King João III dies and his grandson Sebastião succeeds him. The peninsula of Macau, off the China coast near Hong-Kong, is ceded by China and later settled by Portuguese.

1558 A Portuguese caravel is sent from Seville and in 1558 is captured by the French when returning from Peru with 100,000 gold and silver (golden ducats).

1559 The first executions in an *auto de fé* took place in Seville.

1564 William Shakespeare is born. Later he is associated with the term "Elizabethan language."

1566 Great plague in many Portuguese cities causes thousands of deaths. [20]

1567 Portugal approves a law that forbids new Christians to leave for the overseas territories or colonies.

1568   The Portuguese ambassador in London, England, presents a complaint against clandestine English navigation on overseas territories.

1570   City of Nagasaki is founded in Japan by Portuguese seeking a harbor for their ships.

1571   Oct. 7 - The Battle of Lepanto, in the Gulf of LePanto near Corinth, ends in defeat for an Ottoman fleet of 240 galleys.

1572   Publishing of the epic poem *The Lusiads* by Luis de Camões.
Massacre of Protestants in Paris on St. Bartholomew's Day.

1576   French pirates attack Santa Maria Island, Azores.
Brazilian population reaches 57,000.

1577   Renewed law to forbid new Christians – recent converts to Catholicism – to leave for the colonies.

1578/79 August 4 - Portugal's King Sebastião is killed and his army annihilated at Alcacer Quibir in northwest Africa.
Luis Vaz de Camões, the greatest Portuguese poet, dies on June 10.

1580   Union of the Portuguese and Spanish crown. Felipe II of Spain becomes Filipe I of Portugal. He is the son of the Portuguese Princess Isabel of Portugal and the grandson of the Portuguese King Manuel I. Felipe II of Spain is also the son of the Emperor Carlos V of Austria and Germany.

1581   Spain's King Felipe II sends black slaves to his Florida colony of St. Augustine. They are the first blacks to be landed in North America.

1582   Catholic Europe adopts Gregorian calendar, which was ten days behind the Julian calendar.

1583   Francis Drake attacks Brazil.

1587   Francis Drake attacks the Portuguese province of Algarve in the south, sacks and burns Sagres.
February 8 - Catholic Mary Queen of Scots is executed.

1588   May 27 - Felipe II, king of Castile, invades England to terminate Elizabeth I's reign. [21] The fleet of 200 ships and 20,000 soldiers, leaves Lisbon, Portugal. Many Portuguese soldiers and ships are forced to participate, since Portugal is governed at this time by the king of Spain. The Portuguese people pay a very high price for this defeat, since their soldiers and ships took a larger and disproportionate part in this Armada. On July 30,the Spanish Invincible Armada is defeated, a turning point in Elizabethan England. English privateers attack Brazilian ports.

1589   Drake attacks Lisbon and fails. England tries to free Portugal from Spain. João da Gama sails from Macau, China, across the Pacific, making the first recorded voyage by a Portuguese ship.

1594-5   Englishman, Francis Drake attacks and sacks the Brazilian city of Recife.

1598   King Felipe II of Spain dies and is succeeded by Felipe III

1601   Manuel Godinho de Heredia born in Portuguese East India of Portuguese father and Indian mother, claims to have discovered Australia.

1617   Moors attack Porto Santo, one of the Madeira Islands, and captures almost all of the population.

1622   Turks (Persians) unite with the English against the Portuguese and capture the city of Ormuz. Moors and Turks raid the Algarve coast.

1626   Manhattan is purchased from the Indians for 60 guilders. (24 US$).

1640   Dec. 1- Portugal regains total independence from Spain.

1646   William Shakespeare dies on April 23.

1654   Portugal recovers the Brazilian territory held by the Dutch.

1660   Portuguese navigators go from Japan to Lisbon by way of the Arctic.

1662   May 31- Catherine of Braganza, daughter of Portuguese King João IV marries Charles II of England.

1664   New Amsterdam is taken by 300 English soldiers from the Dutch and becomes New York.

1671   Black population in Virginia is less than 5%. By 1715 it will be 24%.

1697   July 18 - Portuguese missionary Antonio Vieira dies, age 88 years old.

1700   Boston ships 50,000 quintals of dried cod fish to market, most to Bilbao, Porto and Lisboa.

1701   Louisiana becomes a province of Spain.

1717   Portuguese fleet, at the request of pope Clement XI, defends Venice and Corfu against a Turkish armada, defeating it, thus preventing it from becoming part of the Ottoman Empire.

1751   Benjamin Franklin discovers the electrical nature of lightning.

1755   Earthquake in Lisbon destroys city and kills thousands.

1763   Spain cedes Florida to England.

1773   December Boston Tea Party. Colonists demand independence.

1776   Declaration of Independence is signed on July 4, followed by the American Revolution.

1782   Spanish forces complete their conquest of Florida from the British.

1783   Florida is given back to Spain by England under the Versailles Treaty. Portugal recognizes U.S. Independence and signs friendship treaty.

1789   George Washington is elected the first U.S. President, to govern till 1797.

1794   Founding of the City of Toronto in Ontario, Canada. Portuguese would have been part of it.

1803   The United States purchased the Louisiana Territory from Napoleon.

1807   November - Napoleon invades Portugal. The Portuguese royal family flees to Brazil.

1814   French Napoleon's armed forces are expelled from Portugal. João Elliot d'Castro becomes secretary to the king of Hawaii.

1819   Spain sells Florida to the U.S. under the Transcontinental Treaty.

1822   Sept. 7 - Brazil declares independence from Portugal by Portuguese Prince Pedro, later called Emperor Pedro I. Independence is achieved almost peacefully, as the result of his father Prince João, later Portuguese King João VI, having moved to Brazil after Portugal was invaded by the Napoleonic army. When Prince João arrived he forms the united kingdom of Portugal and Brazil.

Part II
European Settlers, Melungeons and other Groups
Chronology in North-America

1500/25 Portuguese vessels on voyages to or from India and Brazil are shipwrecked or lost at unknown sites. At least 11 of them are recorded. Some of the caravels have complete families.

1524/5 Estevão Gomes a Portuguese navigator, who took part in the Magellan expedition, is chartered by the Emperor Carlos V to find a northwest passage to India but fails. He does however explore, the east coast of North America from Florida to Newfoundland, including Chesapeake Bay. There are maps in the archives of Seville showing the entire U.S. East Coast with that date and his name.

1526 In July, the Ayllon fleet departs from Spain with six ships carrying some 500 souls: men, women, children, soldiers, priests and the first black slaves to reach American shores. Many ships are lost and only 150 return.[22] Lucas Vásquez de Ayllón leads the first settlement attempt on the South Carolina coast.

1528 Pánfilo de Narvaéz lands at Tampa Bay with 400 men.[23]

1539/40 Hernando de Soto, the Spanish *conquistador,* lands at Tampa Bay with 600 men – many of them Portuguese – in ten ships. He was probably the first European to enter southern Appalachia.

1540 The Gentleman of Elvas writes a book about the Southeast. The well known and cited book, *Gentleman of Elvas,* is written by Álvaro Fernandes, a Portuguese nobleman who joined the Hernando de Soto expedition along with 30 other Portuguese.

1541 May 21 - Hernando de Soto dies and is buried in the Mississippi. The survivors make it to Mexico, including a few Portuguese .

1542/3 September 28 - California is discovered by the Portuguese navigator João Rodrigues Cabrilho, working for Spain. Antonio Correa, another Portuguese is Cabrilho's shipmaster. [24] João Caetano, a Portuguese navigator working for Spain, may have discovered some of the Hawaiian Islands.

1544 A copy of the book written by the Portuguese Gentleman of Elvas arrives in Spain, the first one about the American Southeast.

1545   Brazil's first confirmed export of sugar, and Luis de Góis is the first to take tobacco leaves to Europe. Jean Nicot the French ambassador in Lisbon takes a few leaves to France. The word *nicotine* derives from the ambassador's family name.

1550's It was told to the Englishman in 1584 that a Spanish ship had, in fact, been wrecked on the Outer Banks and some of her men rescued by the Secotian Indians.
The survivors had patched two boats together from the wreck and set southward, but shortly afterward the boats were found cast away along the shore and it was presumed that all drowned. [25]

1557   Publishing of the Gentleman of Elvas' book in the Portuguese city of Évora. That year or before, a copy found its way to London, England, and Spain.[26]

1558   Henrique Garcês, a Portuguese from Porto, discovers mercury in Peru, increasing production of silver greatly.

1559   Spanish colonists arrive in South Carolina and try to settle. Two years later they are forced to leave.

1560   Simão Fernandes, a Portuguese pilot, navigates the East Coast, Virginia and the Carolinas as part of a Spanish expedition.

1563   Regular maritime routes between America and the Indies, with many Portuguese ships without registration from Lisbon and Algarve.

1565   Menéndez is given the right to bring 500 Negro slaves to Florida.

1566   Early in the year, Menéndez builds a fort on Parris Island, the first of four that would stand there, and the first structure of Santa Elena. In July a troop of 250 men under Captain Juan Pardo arrives from Spain.[27]

1567   Juan Pardo reaches the Tennessee Valley. Sergeant Hernando Moyano de Morales writes a letter to Santa Elena.

1568   March 2 - Pardo returns to Santa Elena, bringing sacks filled with sorely needed corn and a description of the interior as good for bread and wine and all kinds of live stock. That hope brings settlers to Santa Elena.

January 26 - Portuguese Seaman Juan Fernández de Cea (João Fernandes de Ceia) is given permission by the Spanish to sail to Florida and dig for treasure.

1569   Two caravels unload 193 emigrants, farmers and their families. By October, the little capital – Santa Elena – numbers 327 souls.

1570   A Spanish mission to Chesapeake Bay ends when an Indian convert leads an attack.

1578-9   Simão Fernandes serves as a master under Raleigh in the *Falcon*, as an experienced pilot. [28]

1584   July - Simão Fernandes a Portuguese navigator, leads an expedition to North America under the command of Philip Amadas and Arthur Barlowe. The first colonists arrive in Roanoke, Virginia.[29] This colony is named after England's virgin queen.

1585   Raleigh sends a new expedition to Virginia under the command of his cousin, Sir Richard Grenville. Colonel Ralph Lane leads the expedition with John White and Thomas Harriot having special responsibilities. Simão Fernandes is the chief pilot and master of the ship that leaves 107 men at the colony. [30] Drake's armada sails from Plymouth, September 12, with 25 ships and 2,300 soldiers and mariners. He attacks Vigo in Spain, the island of Santiago in Portuguese Cape Verde.

1586   May 28 - Drake sacks and burns St. Augustine.
Drake arrives in Roanoke and may have deposited slaves previously released from Cartagena and Santo Domingo, Turks, blacks, etc. A few days later he departs with the colonists.

1587   John White lands 150 settlers, including 17 women, in the Virginia colony – what later is to be called the lost Roanoke Colony. *All contact with the Lost Colonists…is lacking from 1587 to at least 1603* (15 years). [31]

1607   May 14 - Jamestown, Virginia is founded by colonists from England under Captain John Smith. Within three years, only 150 of the 900 survived. American history, refers to it as the first colony of European settlers. It is assumed that the settlers planted tobacco and had the first slaves in North America, which actually only happened after 1619.[32] A fire almost destroyed it and later it had to be abandoned. The last population census of 1624 showed 183 persons.

1609   Translation of the Elvas book, written by the Portuguese Álvaro Fernandes, the Gentleman of Elvas. This book is published in London under a different title, as an incentive to English discovery and an aid to *our enterprise on foot* namely the settlement of Virginia. Two years later it is reissued.

1611   Authorized (King James I) version of the Bible is published. The original English used (Elizabethan) is still being used today in the mountain area.

1619   The first 20 black slaves arrive in the Virginia colony, brought over by a Dutch privateer for sale, *who are now wonderfully encreased.* [33]

1620   November 11/21- after a voyage of 65 days, the *Mayflower* arrives in Cap Cod and anchors in Provincetown with more than 100 passengers. These are English Puritans, Pilgrims from Holland, where they had gone to in 1607. They established the first permanent New England colony on Plymouth Bay, 37 miles (60 km) southeast of Boston.

1625   Second translation, in English, of the book written about the Southeast travels of Hernando de Soto, by the Portuguese Gentleman of Elvas

1642   Jews sail from Holland to Brazil.

1643   Isaac Jogues, a French Jesuit missionary visiting in New Amsterdam, says he heard 18 languages spoken in the seaport town, which probably included Hebrew, Mediterranean and North African dialects and a small settlement of Sephardic Jews.

1649   Black laborers in Virginia colony still number about 300.

1654   First encounters with Melungeons. French and English explorers in the Southern Appalachians reported encounters with dark-skinned, brown and blue eyed, and European featured people.

1663   Founding of what would be called later the State of North Carolina. English King Charles II issues a charter that establishes Carolina as a proprietary colony. [34] The northern part of the Carolina colony is known as Albemarle until 1691, when it is renamed North Carolina. Parts of this state would later form the State of Tennessee, which after the American Revolution caused serious problems for the State of South Carolina.

1669   John Lederer leads an expedition across the Piedmont plateau to ascend the Blue Ridge Mountains, followed by more in 1670. In one of those expeditions he reports a town of bearded men.

1671   Small English party penetrates the Ohio River watershed beyond the Blue Ridge Mountains. Thomas Wood has a man named Portugal working for him.

1673 April 1673 to August 22, 1674 - White, hairy people wearing clothes and performing a Catholic religious ritual found by James Needham and Gabriel Arthur. [35]

1683 An English shipwreck off the Africa east coast will contribute to exploration of the region. A Portuguese survivor of a wreck 42 years earlier is met. He was married to an Amapondo woman.

1685 Translation and printing of the book by the Gentleman of Elvas in French, and then translated back into English in 1686 and reissued in 1687, 1699. [36]

1705 Virginia act declares *who shall not bear office in this country*, no Negro, Mulatto or Indian. [37]

1709/45 John Lawson encounters a people that he calls the Hatteras Indians - later called the Lumbees that are different from the other Indians and is told legends about their ancestors from the coast of North Carolina. Among the families he encounters, many of them are of *Portuguese* origin, according to their legends.

1712 North Carolina and South Carolina by a division of the Carolina Colony founded in 1663.

1716 A company of Virginia colonists crosses the Blue Ridge Mountains under the leadership of Alexander Spotswood.

1718 Great Scotch-Irish immigration to America begins.

1733 Savannah, Georgia – Sephardim Portuguese Jews and others build a synagogue, the third oldest in the U.S., using a Gothic architectural style.

1745 April 26 - a land grant of 100,000 acres, is made to *John Robinson...* [38] *...They were rich, dark, and said to be Portuguese.* [39]

1750 March 5 or 6 - Dr. Thomas Walker… sets out on his tour of the land to be surveyed with companions and finds possible route used by the Melungeons to the East Tennessee Mountains, the Cumberland Gap. [40]

1767 Daniel Boone on his way to Kentucky through the Cumberland Gap.

1769 Virginia's colonists defy King George III's degree of 1763 and establish the first pioneer settlement at Watauga, in upper east Tennessee[41]

1784 John Sevier organizes State of Franklin and finds a dark-skinned, reddish-brown complexioned people supposed to be of Moorish descent, who are neither Indian or Negro, but have fine European features, and claim to be Portuguese. [42]

1789 North Carolina cedes the territories to a state later called Tennessee.

1790 Census takers' guide says, *Identify all free whites over the age of 16 and slaves.* This may have been the beginning of the term FPC – Free Persons of Color. They try to identify people like the Melungeons. [43]

1795 National census shows that there are 973 free persons who were neither white, Indian or black.

1796 The State of Tennessee is founded from the failed State of Franklin. Melungeon people have already been established there.
Translation to Dutch of the Portuguese book by the Gentleman of Elvas.

1797 Tradition of strange white race preceding the Cherokee in Tennessee. [44]

1807 Melungeons with names like Lucas, Osborne and Moore may have come into southwest Virginia.

1809/12 New printing of the book by the Gentleman of Elvas

1810 Jacob Mooney arrives in Baxter County, Arkansas, with four dark-skinned men assisting him, who could not be categorized as Negro, Indian, or white. They are simply *Lungeons.* [45]

1820 Building of the aqueduct Roanoke Canal by a group called Portuguese.

1834 Citizenship Rights – The Tennessee Constitution states that only free white men 21 and over can vote and bear arms. This could easily exclude the Melungeons and other groups not considered white at a given time and place. [46] John A. McKinney, of Hawkins County, is chairman of the Committee of the Constitutional Convention, declares that a *free person of color,* if it meant anything, meant Melungeon. [47]

1835 Citizenship Rights – The North Carolina Constitution amendment to the previous one of 1776, states that *no free negro, free mulatto, or free person of mixed blood descending from Negro ancestors to the 4th generation shall vote for the Senate or the House of Commons.*

1840 Oct. 7 - *The Whig,* Tennessee newspaper, mentions *Melungeons.*

1846/50 New printing of the book by the Gentleman of Elvas.

1848   September 6 - *Knoxville Register* mentions the *Melungeons.*

1859   Col. John Netherland's efforts restore the citizenship of the Melungeon people and runs for Governor.

1861   Abraham Lincoln is elected President and the Civil War begins in April.

1872   The Celebrated Melungeon Case – Phoenicians, Carthaginians and Portuguese. Judge Lewis Shepherd writes in his memoirs that the Melungeons descended from the Phoenicians, Carthaginians and Portuguese, or descendants of them from the southern coast of Portugal.

1877   St. Anthony Portuguese Benevolent Society is formed in Hawaii.

1884   New printing of the book by the Gentleman of Elvas, again in 1890.[48]

1886   New printing of the book by the Gentleman of Elvas in New York by Buckingham Smith. [49]

1885   Discriminatory Law – If a white man wants to marry a dark girl he can get a license, but a dark man cannot get a license to marry a white girl. That is much more difficulty.

1887   *History of East Tennessee* – This book writes about Newman's Ridge and the people that occupied it. [50]

1888   Ethnologist James Mooney writes about a strange white race preceding the Cherokee in the Tennessee area. Mooney corresponds with McDonald Furman in South Carolina about the Redbones and his interest in their heritage. [51]

1889   Swan M. Burnett writes *Notes on the Melungeons.*[52] April 13 or June 13 - *Boston Traveler* article about the Melungeons.

1891   Will Allen Dromgoole writes about *The Malungeons*. This derogatory report leaves a legacy that the Melungeons have to endure for many years to come. [53]

1899   *American Anthropologist*, vol. 2, publishes *A note on the Melungeons.*

1904-5 New printing of the book by the Gentleman of Elvas in New York and in London.

1912   December - *The Melungeons* by Paul Converse, *Southern Collegian*. Col. W. A. Henderson, president of the Tennessee Historical Society and member of the Tennessee bar, gives a description of the Melungeons.
January 12 - *Arkansas Gazette*, article by Mrs. Eliza N. Heiskell, of Memphis about the Melungeons.
October 12 - *Nashville Banner* article about the Melungeons.

1913   *History of Tennessee and Tennesseans* by W. T. Hale and Dixon L. Merritt is published, describing the Melungeons.

1915   Judge Lewis publishes his memoirs. [54] The Celebrated Melungeon Case that took place in 1872 and absorbed wide public interest, even after Judge Shepherd published his autobiography, which contained his involvement in a judicial process related to a romantic case of a Melungeon family and their descendants.
North Carolina Supreme Court holds hearings on the case: Croaton Indian School of Pembroke, N.C. vs. Three Goins Families regarding Indian qualifications for school admission. Melungeon, Redbone and Croaton Indian names appeared for these citizens of North and South Carolina in the late 1800's that might want entrance to this school. [55]

1922   New printing of the book by the Gentleman of Elvas in New York.

1923   North Carolina State House of Representatives and Senate, General Assembly pass a law stating "...*that the people known as Portuguese shall have a separate school from the white and colored schools...*"
July 29 - *The Knoxville Journal and Tribune* publishes a Melungeon article *Melungeons, Mystery Race... after South Carolina Hegira.*

1924   August 3 - *Nashville Banner*, Melungeon article by Douglas Anderson
Virginia enacts the racial integrity law or the one blood drop law.

1925   The General Assembly of the State of North Carolina enacts a law permitting *the people known as Portuguese to register themselves as Portuguese* on the voter registration books.

1929   Portuguese Indian - Mary Killen Hollyfield, descendant of Betsy Reeves, remembers that in 1929, the Reeves were known as having come from Portugal.

1933   New English translation by James Robertson of the book written by the Portuguese Gentleman of Elvas

1936   June 21 - *Chattanooga Sunday Times-Magazine*, Melungeon article.

1936   Congress creates a seven-member Hernando de Soto Expedition Commission. *Final report of the Swanton Commission* by John R. Swanton of the Smithsonian Anthropology was largely based on the book titled *The narrative of a Gentleman of Elvas.*

1937   August 22 - *Nashville Banner*, publishes "Lost Tribes of Tennessee Mountain" by James Aswell

1939   N.L. Turner is nominated superintendent of Northhampton County Schools, North Carolina, including the Bethany School in Gaston, a separate school for Portuguese .
         Tennessee Guide, NY - *The Melungeons in Oakdale*, p. 362 .

1940   Legacy from Dr. W. A. Plecker. There were only two classes of people, white (northern European) and "Colored" (those with 1/16 or more black, Indian, Asian, or southern European heritage).
         Dec. 1 - *Louisville Courier*, Melungeons article by Woodson Knight.

1941   Miss Osceola T. Crew, a teacher, is appointed by the Northampton School superintendent to teach the grades one through eight at the Portuguese School in Gaston as "mission work."
         James Aswell publishes book God Bless the Devil, Melungeon stories.

1942   Mrs. John Trotwod Moore, Virginia state librarian and archivist writes a letter to Dr. W. A. Plecker that refers to early settlers in South Carolina who migrated from Portugal about the time of the Revolutionary War and later moved to Tennessee. [56]

1944   May - *America's Mysterious Race* by Bonnie Ball (Read).

1945   July 29 - *Baltimore Sun*, publishes article by L.F. Addington, "Mountain Melungeons."* April - *Southern Literary Messenger* publishes *Who are the Melungeons* and the *American Journal of Sociology*, the article "Goins and Melungeons", Vol. 51

1947   October 18 - *Saturday Evening Post*, "Sons of the Legend."

1949   March - *Association of American Geographer Annals* of East Tennessee Melungeons, publishes "Mixed Blood Strain."

1951   April - Edward Price's doctoral dissertation on mixed-blood groups, notes that they (Melungeons) were attributed an Oriental appearance, but in reality, he thinks that the Melungeons were of Portuguese ancestry, or at least partially.[57] Geographical Review XLI-2

1958   Sunday, January 26 - "Century-Old Stigma Remains - Portuguese Youngsters Segregated in Carolina. Title of a full page article published by *The Virginian Pilot - The Portsmouth Star*, and written by Luther J. Carter. Sunday, March 2nd - *Sunday Herald* of Roanoke Rapids features a story about the Portuguese of Northampton County (Gaston). October 10 - *Knoxville Sentinel* article: "East Tennessee Melungeons have a past clouded in myth."

1957   *Eugenics Quarterly*, "American Tri-Racial Isolates."

1959   August - *Tennessee Conservationist* - "Mystery People of Tennessee."

1960   Bonnie Ball writes for the Ross County Historical Society paper read at Chillicothe, Ohio. Also writes several articles in the 60's.

1963   September 22/29 - *Nashville Tennessean*, "The Mystery of the Melungeons" by Louise Davis. [58]
June 21- *Chattanooga Sunday Times*, "Romance of the Melungeons."

1964   November 26 - *Knoxville News-Sentinel*, publishes Melungeon article.

1965   August - Graduate thesis about the Melungeons, by Phillis Barr, East Tennessee State University, Department of English Faculty.

1965-6   Dr. William S. Politzer and Dr. William Brown University of North Carolina: Health survey of Melungeons in Hancock County.

1966   October 30 - *Baltimore Sun*, article by Mary Conelly.
March 10 - *Knoxville News-Sentinel*, "Strolling" and Melungeons.
June 12 - *Knoxville News*, article "Olive Skinned Hancock Countians."

1967   August - *Tennessee Conservationist*, article about the Melungeons.

1968   Mildred Haun writes "Melungeon Colored". Dec. 1 - *Knoxville News* writes "New outdoor drama on Melungeons" by Willard Yarbrough.

1969   First performance of the Melungeon outdoor drama "Walk towards the Sunset" by Kermit Hunter. Staged at Sneedville, Tennessee, and run till 1976. Bonnie Ball's first edition of *The Melungeons*.
June 26 - *Life Magazine*, John Futterman writes "The Mystery of the Newman's Ridge." [59] March 30 - *Louisville Courier, Journal and Times Magazine* editorial about "The Melungeons."
The Melungeons, their Origin and Kin by Bonnie Ball.
Human Biology by Pollitzer & Brown, Genetics and Melungeons.

1970 November 11- *Chicago Tribune*: "Melungeons, Tennessee Mystery."
October 19 - *Knoxville Journal*: article about the Melungeons.
July - *Tennessee Conservationist*: article about the Melungeons.
November 30 - *Chattanooga Times*: article by Mouzon Peters.

1971 January - Argosy Magazine, Melungeons came from Jewish origin.
June 27 - Drama of the Melungeons, Grit, family Section.
September 5 - The Last of the Melungeons, Kingsport Times-News.
August 10, New York Times, Mysterious Hill Folk Vanishing.

1971 Nov.7- *Johnson City Chronicle*, "Melungeons" by Johnnie Neal Smith.

1972 Spring issue of the *Tennessee Valley Historical Review*: Reprints article by Louise Davis. April 19 - *Knoxville News*, "Melungeon Drama."

1973 November - *American History Illustrated*: Stinson, Byron writes about the Melungeons. [60]

1975 Jean Patterson Bible publishes a book *The Melungeons Yesterday and Today*. April - Saundra Keyes Ivey's dissertation "Oral, Printed, and Popular Traditions" related to the Melungeons of Hancock County, Tennessee for a Ph.D. degree in Philosophy at the Indiana University.
September 25 - *Knoxville Journal*, "Melungeons" by Juanita Glenn.

1981 Leo Pap of New York State University publishes his book *The Portuguese Americans*, mentions Melungeons on pages 13-14 and 241-2.

1983 From Newman's Ridge, TN, to Southeast Kentucky highlands, trail of Portuguese-English mixed clans. [61]

1988 March - *National Geographic Magazine*: Publishes an article about Santa Elena Island by Joseph Judge. Possible origin of the Melungeons.

1989 Shepperd's Satellite TV transmits program about the Melungeons.

1990 The spring issue, Vol. XV-1, of *Tennessee Anthropologist* by Dr. James Guthrie. Article about Melungeons: "Comparison of Gene Frequency."

1991 July/August - *Blue Ridge Magazine* article about the Melungeons, "Who Are These Mysterious People."

1992 July/August - *Blue Ridge Magazine*: "The Melungeon Mystery Solved. "
December 6 - *Kingsport Times*: Melungeons subject of Study by Barbara Watson.

1993   Dr. James H. Guill publishes *History of the Azores* and mentions the Melungeons on page 141. July 7- *Atlanta Constitution*: Article by Chris Wohlwend, "Mystery of the Melungeons." July 12 - *The News & Observer* of Raleigh, N.C. "The Mystery of Virginia's Melungeons" by Chris Wohlwend, Cox News Service. August 15 - *The Charlotte Observer* "Melungeons in the New World" by Bruce Anderson. First presentation of the Book-Document, *Melungeons and other Mestee Groups* by Mike McGlothlen. November 1- *Tuscaloosa News Alabama*: Story about "Melungeon Ancestry."

1994   June - *The State Magazine*: Article by Billy Arthur, "The Melungeons." February - Kennedy publishes his book *The Resurrection of a Proud People*. *Portuguese RTP TV* transmits a program about the Melungeon people. Virginia TV channel transmits a program about the Melungeons with Greg Wallace of WCYB-TV, Bristol Virginia. *New England Cable TV* transmits Melungeon program with Dr. Manuel Luciano da Silva, from the series "Portuguese Around Us".

1995   *Luso-Americano* of Newark, NJ, the largest Portuguese-language newspaper outside Portugal, publishes a series of seven articles about the Melungeons, written by the author.
         Portuguese RTP TV transmits a second program about the Melungeon people, with more extensive interviews.

1995   May and December - Trip to Turkey by Kennedy as a guest of the Turkish Government for further research of the Melungeon people.
         Dec. 7 - Article about the Melungeons by Bryon Crawford on the *Transylvania Times* of Brevard, NC.

1996   Production of the *Peter Pan* play, featuring an inter racial cast, where the pirates are played as Melungeons. May 28 - *Kingsport Times-News* "Melungeon Museum." and on October 26, "Melungeons and Turks, A Key to Mystery" by Brad Lifford.
         September - Gowen Research Foundation, Lubbock, Texas, publishes Melungeon origin research articles, and family histories of Gowen, Goin, Goyne and other spellings showing clearly Portuguese origin.

1997   April 14 - *The Wall Street Journal*: "Appalachian Clan and Web Sites."

Brief History of Slavery

This book would not be complete unless the subject of slavery would be mentioned. Most likely some of the early settlers, Melungeons and others, did intermarry and live with slaves, many times helping them to obtain their freedom. It is natural that we should look, very briefly, into their history.

From the beginning, the truth or what is known of the truth it is being stated no matter if it is politically correct or not. Therefore, the subject of slavery must be brought up, although many tried to avoid it.

Professor John T. Strunk of Harriman, Tennessee, informed the author that one of his students, Bret Wright, believed to be a Melungeon descendant, came from Hancock County. He told Mr. Strunk that he recalled stories that his grandfather had told him, that there was a dispute over a slave or the question of slavery and that his branch of the family left Hancock County because of the feud. According to Mr. Strunk, most of the Melungeons and their descendants who came to Bazeltown near Harriman intermarried with blacks, and the ones who settled in Rhea County near Dayton intermarried with whites. He also stated that most of the Melungeons that came to Harriman were named Goins. Although they intermarried with blacks, many retain a Mediterranean appearance, with gray eyes, olive complexion, light brown or dark blond hair and freckles.

The above illustrates the fact that Melungeons did live and interact with slaves. It also helps the long established traditions stated in this book.

What about the Portuguese and the slaves ? Famous Brazilian historian and sociologist Gilberto Freyre, writer of the critically acclaimed book *The Masters and the Slaves*, went into gruesome detail about slavery in Brazil, but he also said, *Although the Portuguese has been portrayed as the evil or the inventor of black slavery from Africa to the Americas, they were the only ones to treat the slaves on equal footing as other whites.* In Brazil, the use of the black slave was due to the Brazilian Indian's inability to work as a slave. Also, in the early 16th century the Spanish tried unsuccessfully to subjugate and enslave the native populations of the West Indies, without result.

Yes, the Portuguese were one of the European countries to start the slave trade and, even seen in the context of the times, it was not justifiable, at least the type of treatment dispensed to slaves. But the Portuguese were not alone, and not necessarily the worst offenders. Charles R. Boxer, famous historian, wrote: *The Portuguese empire might be moribund, decaying, corrupt, but, at least, it was far from racial prejudice.* [62] In another study made about the Jews in Cape Verde, Richard Lobban wrote: *It is essential to realize that the Portuguese were only brokers within a system…Moreover for those engaged in finger pointing…we must not forget African participation…The celebrated ancient African empires of Ghana, Mali…were all built upon the slave export business as much as the plantations* [in the] *south in the USA.* [There were also Muslims and Jews involved as brokers] *For those who single out Jews in this sorry traffic in humans, it must also be recalled that African Muslims were earlier into the trade across Sahara, down the*

Nile and in the Indian Ocean; it is in those regions of Muslim Africa that this cruel trade still continues to the very present. [63]
We should also note that African slaves contributed to the building of Brazil and... *small farmers and artisans could move up more easily in Brazilian society than they could in the southern (and northern) United States.* *...Mulattos found more chances for education in Brazil than did their counterparts elsewhere.* [64]
Most of the black population of North America is in the U.S., where 29,986,060 blacks were counted by the 1990 census; Canadian blacks numbered less than 1 percent of the population (170,340). Almost all these people are descendants of Africans brought to the New World as slaves between 1501, when Spain first permitted African slavery in its colonies, and 1808, when the U.S. banned the importation of new slaves. [65]
In chronological order, the following paragraphs point out some of the more important events in slavery that culminated with its abolition.

Slavery in the British Isles at an early date: *Slavery existed in Britain when history commenced the records of that island. It was there found in a state and condition predicated upon the same causes by which its existence is now continued and perpetuated in Africa.* [66] Although abundantly practiced there and widespread in the ancient Mediterranean world, it had nearly died out in medieval Europe. It was revived by the Portuguese in Prince Henry's time, beginning with the enslavement of Berbers in 1442.

1433 - To the surprise of the people waiting for the caravels to arrive in 1433, Gil Eanes, a Portuguese navigator, brought the first captured slaves from the Canary Islands. [67] In 1441 Antão Gonçalves captured ten Berbers in the East Sahara, and out of these, one seemed to be a noble Berber. His name was Adahu. He spoke Arabic and seems to have been a well traveled man with much knowledge. They were taken to Portugal, and after questioning, Prince Henry obtained valuable information. But it was not until 1443 that the first African slaves arrived in Lagos, Algarve in the south of Portugal, brought in also by Antão Gonçalves.
Some could be considered white and handsome, others swarthy and still others quite black. [68] Zurara, a contemporary chronicler and eye witness of the first European episode of the African slave trade, wrote the painful glimpse. He insisted, however, that they were treated with kindness, and no difference was made between them and the free-born servants of Portugal. [69]
There was a regular commercial maritime between Venice and Morocco, in the 15th century to transport and deal with commercial goods and slaves. [70]
During the 1450's an average of 700 to 800 slaves yearly entered Europe through the Algarve and Lisbon. The coast of Guinea proved a better slave market than any land reached previously visited by the Portuguese
While some captives came as a result of direct incursions inland by the Portuguese most of them were regularly purchased from Muslim traders and the *Negros* themselves. Slaves could be exchanged for cloth or other merchandise, which the

Portuguese often acquired from Morocco, again, by legal trade. From Portugal a great number, the majority perhaps, were then profitably sold to Castille, Aragon and other European countries, only a part being employed in the sugar plantations (as well as other agricultural or domestic jobs) of Madeira.[71]

Writers of the 15th and 16th century exaggerated the number of slaves in Portugal. The number in Lisbon never exceeded 5,000. [72] The Portuguese could obtain slaves on the Moroccan coast, but it was dangerous. The Moors were excellent fighters and had an efficient military organization that stopped the attempts of slavery. *It would be necessary for the Portuguese to control vast portions of the hinterland, which they were never able to accomplish.*[73]

1471 - Conquest of Arzila and the Jewish Slaves - In the 1400's there were approximately 30,000 Jews in Portugal which doubled when the Spanish Catholic Kings expelled them, and in turn they sought refuge in Portugal, others parts of Europe and North Africa. Many that could not pay for their passage were reduced to slavery. [74] Isaac Abrabanel, a well known Jewish leader worked with his father for the King Afonso V and in 1471, when the Portuguese conquered Arzila, 250 Moroccan Jews were captured and brought in as slaves. Abrabanel traveled to the countryside to redeem these North-African Jews. [75] His father was the treasurer for Prince Fernando, who died in Fez, Morocco, as a captive of the Moors.

1492 - Blacks in the Americas - African immigration to the Americas may have begun before European exploration of the region. Blacks sailed with Christopher Columbus even on his first voyage in 1492, and the earliest Spanish and Portuguese explorers were likewise accompanied by blacks – Africans who had been born and reared in Ibéria. In the following four centuries millions of immigrants from sub-Africa were brought to the New World as slaves.

Most of the earliest black immigrants to the Americas were natives of Spain and Portugal, men such as Pedro Alonso Niño, a navigator who accompanied Columbus on his first voyage, and the black colonists who helped Nicolás de Ovando form the first Spanish settlement on Hispaniola or Española (Haiti) in 1502.

1498 - When the Portuguese arrived in India, slavery was everywhere, more predominant in the Islamic north. The slavery had several origins: by birth, by insolvency and in payment of debt, captive in war, some times selling themselves and their family in case of extreme necessity, etc. [76]

1501 - Spain introduced African slaves in Hispaniola or Española (Haiti). The first importation of blacks to the New World.

1505 - Portuguese King Manuel I in 1505, in answer to a request made by the people of Madeira, ordered all slaves from the Canaries to be expelled, except the ones skilled in the sugar industry, which declined after that. [77]

1518 - By 1518, the demand for slaves in the Spanish New World was so great that King Charles I of Spain sanctioned the direct transport of slaves from Africa to the American colonies. The slave trade was controlled by the crown, which sold the right to import slaves (*asiento*) to entrepreneurs.

Black slaves in Spain (about 50,000) were considered a deluxe status for the well-off families, and very few worked the fields or production. Their condition was not the worst. They worked mostly in domestic chores. The Moorish slaves in Spain, after conversion to Catholicism, worked in the fields, constituting cheap and competent labor but hated by the old Christians, as they suspected complicity with the Berbers. [78] As an example of non discriminatory practices against blacks, in 1518 Portuguese King Manuel I requests the pope to elevate the Congo Prince D. Henrique to Bishop of Utica. He becomes the first black Christian bishop.

1562 - Sir John Hawkins was considered to be the father of the English slave trade. He had been to the coast of Guinea, where he bought and kidnapped a cargo of slaves. [79] In 1562-63, John Hawkins' first slave-trading voyage, on behalf of a syndicate of London merchants, was so profitable that a more prestigious group, including Queen Elizabeth I, provided the money for a second expedition. Soon Drake joined up with his kinsmen, the Hawkinses of Plymouth, ship owners and seamen. In the late 1560's Drake accompanied John Hawkins as he ranged the West African coast gathering slaves to take across the Atlantic. [80] English Admiral John Hawkins led trading ventures that often began with a stop on the coast of Guinea (West Africa) to capture *negro* slaves. Hawkins embarked on his second voyage to the West Indies in 1564. After exchanging his cargo of slaves for the rich produce of the islands he went on to explore the Florida coast. [81]

1565 - Pedro Menéndez de Aviles of Spain was given the right to import 500 Negro slaves into Florida.

1606 - In India a law was passed in 1606 to forbid the importation of female slaves or other less than 16 years old. Also, it was said that Moors from India, were very intelligent, and with very lively eyes.

1619-1620 - Counselors called an Assembly of Burgess, who, being elected by the people, met the governor and council at Jamestown and stated: ... *About this time the Dutch brought over some negro slaves for sale, who are now wonderfully increased; besides the constant supplies of them imported yearly.* [82]

1663 - Permanent settlement of Carolina began in the mid-seventeenth century, and by 1663 it is possible that the Virginians brought a few slaves with them. Meanwhile events in England assured that North Carolina would become a slave colony. [83]

1761 - A law was passed in Portugal to consider all Indians from Brazil free. It abolished slavery within continental Portugal and also gave equal rights to people from India.

1788 - A bill designed to restrict the number of slaves carried by each ship, based on the ship's tonnage, was enacted by parliament on June 17, 1788.

1792 - Denmark abolished slave trade.

1808 - Finally, in 1807, the British Parliament passed an act prohibiting British subjects from engaging in the slave trade after March 1, 1808.

1811 - Slave trading was declared a felony punishable by transportation (exile to a penal colony) for all British subjects or foreigners caught trading in British possessions. Britain then assumed most of the responsibility for abolishing the transatlantic slave trade, partly to protect its sugar colonies.

1815 - Treaty of Vienna between Portugal and England abolished slavery north of the equator and Portugal restricted the slave trade to Brazil

1817 - Spain abandoned trade with Cuba, Puerto Rico and Santo Domingo.

1818 - Holland and France abolished the trade

1831 - Brazil agreed to abolish slavery, but trafficking continued until 1851.

1836 - In Portugal, a law was passed December 10, 1836 to abolish slavery south of the equator.

1848 - The French emancipated their slaves.

1861 - Abraham Lincoln was elected President, and the U.S. Civil War began in April. It was fought partly over the issue of slavery. It caused almost 900,000 deaths, and suffering for many more. Eventually the slaves of the Confederacy were declared free by Lincoln in 1863.

1864 - The Brazilian Emperor D. Pedro II emancipated the slaves that formed part of his daughter's dowry and committed the government to end slavery.

1865 - Slavery was constitutionally abolished in the United States with the passing of the 13th amendment.

1888 - In Brazil, on May 13, 1888, Isabel, daughter of the Brazilian Emperor D. Pedro II, signed a law to abolish slavery. When she did, someone told her that she redeemed a race but lost the throne.

Notes

[1] The Discoverers by Daniel J. Boorstin, p.9
[2] Luso-Americano, February 1996
[3] Except as noted, Peoples Chronologies by James Trager, Dicionario de Portugal Vol. I-VI, Historia de Portugal em Datas by Antonio Simões Rodrigues, The Portuguese in America by Manoel da Silveira Cardozo as well as others were used.
[4] Historia de Portugal by Oliveira Marques, V.I, p.15
[5] Azores Islands, A History by James H. Guill, Vol.5-93
[6] The True Antilles by Dr. Manuel Luciano da Silva, p.5
[7] Atlantic Islanders by Francis M. Rogers, 1979
[8] The Palm Beach Post, June 24/1995,p.2A, Luso-Americano,7/26/95
[9] The True Antilles by Dr. Manuel Luciano da Silva, p.11
[10] Colombo em Portugal, Marinha Portuguesa, p.7
[11] Ibid, p.14
[12] Historia de Portugal - Oliveira Marques, p.5,Vol. II.
[13] Portugal nos Mares, Oliveira Martins, p.37
[14] Historia da Civilização Ibérica by Oliveira Martins, p. 83
[15] The True Antilles by Dr. Manuel Luciano da Silva, p.11
[16] Set Fair for Roanoke by David Quinn
[17] Portugal nos Mares by Oliveira Martins, p. 317
[18] Columbus by Mascarenhas Barreto, p.28
[19] Portugal nos Mares by Oliveira Martins, p. 316
[20] Historia de Portugal by Oliveira Martins, p. 340-1
[21] Dicionario da Historia de Portugal by Joel Serrão,, Vol. I, p.184
[22] National Geographic Magazine, Joseph Judge, March 1988
[23] Ibid, March 1988
[24] The Portuguese-Americans by Leo Pap, p.7
[25] Set Fair for Roanoke by David Quinn, p.12
[26] Hernando de Soto Commission by John R. Swanson, p.4
[27] National Geographic Magazine, Joseph Judge, March 1988
[28] Set Fair for Roanoke by David Quinn, p.22
[29] Ibid, p.28
[30] Harvard Classics, Vol. 33, p.237
[31] Set Fair for Roanoke by David Quinn, p.350
[32] Present State of Virginia by Hugh Jones, p. 67
[33] The Present State of Virginia by Hugh Jones, p. 64
[34] Encyclopedia Britannica
[35] Early Travels in the Tennessee Country by Samuel Cole Williams, 28-29
[36] de Soto Commission by John R. Swanson, p.4
[37] Letter by Evelyn Orr of the Melungeon Research Committee
[38] Ruth Woods Dayton, Greenbriar Pioneers, Charleston, WV Pub.1942, 16
[39] Pioneer Recollections of SW Virginia by Elihu Jasper Sutherland, pp. 167-9

Notes (Cont.)

[40] The Melungeons by Jean Patterson Bible p.24
[41] Ibid, p.25
[42] Ibid
[43] Letter by Evelyn Orr of the Melungeon Research Committee
[44] History, Myths, and Sacred Formulas of the Cherokees by James Mooney, p. 22
[45] The History of Baxter County, Arkansas, (Mountain Home AR, 1972), pp. 5-6
[46] Letter by Evelyn Orr of the Melungeon Research Committee
[47] History of Tennessee and the Tennesseans by Hale & Merritt, p. 182
[48] The History of Baxter County, Arkansas, (Mountain Home AR, 1972), pp. 5-6
[49] Ibid
[50] The Melungeons by Jean Bible, History of East Tennessee, p.871
[51] History, Myths, and Sacred Formulas of the Cherokees by James Mooney, p. 22
[52] Notes on the Melungeons by Swan M. Burnett, Vol. II, p.347, American Anthropologist
[53] The Arena, Vol. 3, March, pp. 470-479.
[54] The Melungeons by Jean Patterson Bible, p.16.
[55] Letter by Evelyn Orr of the Melungeon Research Committee
[56] Ibid
[57] The Melungeons by Jean Patterson Bible, p. 12
[58] The Mystery of the Melungeons by Louise Davis, p. 11 (Nashville Tennesseean 9/29/1963)
[59] Life Magazine, June 26/1970, p.23
[60] Stinson, Byron, The Melungeons, American History Illustrated, Nov.1973
[61] By Norm Isaac for Tennessee Historical Society, Prinit Press, Box 65, Dublin IN 47335 (E.Orr)
[62] The Portuguese Seaborne empire by Charles R. Boxer, p. xxv
[63] Jews in Cape Verde and Guinea Coast by Richard Lobban, p.6
[64] King Zumbi... by T.B. Irving, p. 408 (Amer. J. Islamic S.Sciences, 9:3 Fall 1992)
[65] Contributed by: Franklin W. Knight Clayborne Carson
[66] Studies in Slavery by Jackson Warner, p. 67
[67] Infante D. Henrique e sua época, Mario Domingues, p.201
[68] Ibid, p.266-7
[69] The Discoverers by Daniel J. Boorstin, p. 167
[70] Infante D. Henrique e sua época by Mario Domingues, p.134
[71] History of Portugal by Oliveira Marques, Vol. I, p. 158-9
[72] Ibid, p. 289, V. I
[73] History of Portugal by Oliveira Marques, Vol. I, p.274
[74] Historia da Origem e... Inquisição by Alexandre Herculano, pp. 67-69
[75] The Jews of Spain by Jane Gerber, p. xxi
[76] Economia Mundial by Vitorino Magalhães Godinho, p. 547
[77] Dicionario da Historia de Portugal by Joel Serrao, Vol. II, p. 421

Notes (Cont.)

[78] Historia de España, Historia 16, p.502
[79] Pioneers of France in the New World by Francis Parkman, p. 90
[80] National Geographic Magazine, Drake by Allan Villiers, p. 224
[81] Annals of America by Clements R. Markham, Vol. 1, p.6
[82] The Presente State of Virginia by Hugh Jones, pp. 63-64
[83] History of African Americans in North Carolina by
J.Crow, P.Escott, F.Hatley, p. I

Appendix C

Portuguese Navigators, Explorers and Missionaries
Not directly involved with North-America of the 15th, 16th and 17th Century
In Alphabetical order by Last Name

Name	Surname	Date	Activity
Antonio de	Abreu	1611	Sumatra with Francisco Serrão
Lopo	Abreu	1504	India
André	Afonso	1526	Captain, Sierra Leoa
Diogo	Afonso	1461	Cape Verde Islands
Mestre Martins	Afonso	1565	Far East voyage by land and sea
Estevão	Afonso	1445	Madeira, East Africa
João	Afonso	1550	Pilot, Cape Verde
Jorge de	Aguiar	1508	India, Tristão da Cunha
Pedro Afonso de	Aguiar	1524	Brasil
Lopo Soares de	Albergaria	1515	India
Fernão Soares de	Albergaria	1552	Navigator to India
Francisco de	Albuquerque	1503	India
Afonso de	Albuquerque	1505	Africa, Brazil to India, and Vice-Roy
Pero d'	Alenquer	1470	West Africa and Guinea
Francisco de	Almeida	1509	India
Fernão Martins de	Almeida	1503	India
Lourenço de	Almeida	1502	Maldives Islands, India
Francisco	Álvares	1540	Abyssinia
Jorge	Álvares	1513	Southern China
Gonçalo	Álvares	1505	India
Diogo	Álvares	1511	Brazil and Caramuru
Padre. José	Anchieta	1560	Brazil
Pedro de	Andaia	1505	West Africa
Simão Peres de	Andrade	1500	Brazil
Anselmo de	Andrade	1560	First European to enter Tibet
Fernão Peres de	Andrade	1517	China, Canton
Martins	André	1539	Explorer, New Mexico
Pero	Anes	1470	West Africa, Diogo Cão Pilot
Pero de	Astuniga	1486	West Africa
Luis de	Ataíde	1569	India
Pero de	Ataide	1500	Brazil, India
Vasco de	Ataide	1500	Brazil, also with Bartolomeu Dias
João Afonso de	Aveiro	1486	East Africa
Diogo de	Azambuja	1451	East Africa
Simão de	Azevedo	1500	India
Fernando Roiz	Badacas	1502	India
Afonso Gonçalves	Baldaia	1436	North East Africa
Duarte	Barbosa	1500	Commercial Guide, Orient, 1500's
Diogo	Barbosa	1501	Santa Helena Island
Francisco	Barreto	1570	East Africa
Manuel de Campos	Bicudo	1600	Brazil
Simão Afonso	Bisagudo	1521	Far East
Pero Vaz	Bisagudo	1488	West Africa
Gaspar	Bocarro	1606	West Africa
Jorge	Botelho	1515	Malaca
Diogo	Botelho	1535	India
Rui de	Brito	1513	Malaca
Manuel Teles de	Brito	1504	India

Name	Surname	Date	Activity
Pedro Álvares (Gouveia)	Cabral	1500	Official discoverer of Brazil.
Gonçalo Velho	Cabral	1432	Azores
Fernando Álvares	Cabral	1432	Tangier, grandfather of Pedro Álvares Cabral
Luis Alvise	Cadamosto	1445	Genovese, northeast Africa for Portugal
João	Caetano	1555	Possible discoverer of Hawaii
Vasco Rodrigues	Caldas	1561	Brazil
Rui Gonçalves da	Câmara	1474	Azores
Pero Vaz de	Caminha	1500	Brazil
Afonso de	Campos	1601	Northwest Africa
Antonio do	Campo	1502	India
Diogo	Cão	1482	West Africa
Tomás de	Carmona	1502	India
Joao	Carvalho	1519	Pilot with Estevão Gomes
Fernão Alves de	Castanheda	1528	India, historian
Álvaro de	Castro	1547	India
Fernando de	Castro	1424	The Canaries and West Africa
Filipe de	Castro	1504	India
João de	Castro	1546	India, noticed compass magnetic deviation
Nufro de	Chaves	1560	Brazil
Gaspar	Colaço	1550	Merchant in Bolivia
Gonçalo	Coelho	1504	Brazil
Nicolau	Coelho	1500	Brazil, also with Vasco da Gama
Duarte	Coelho	1535	Brazil
João de	Coimbra	1498	With the Vasco da Gama fleet to India
Frei Henrique de	Coimbra	1500	Brazil
Gaspar	Colaço	1550	Bolivia
Aires	Correia	1500	Also with Vasco da Gama to India
Diogo Fernandes	Correia	1550	India
Gonçalo da	Costa	1541	Paraguay, South America with Cabeza de Vaca
Afonso Lopes da	Costa	1504	India
Soeiro da	Costa	1478	East Africa
Vasco	Coutinho	1540	Brazil
Leonel	Coutinho	1504	India
Pero da	Covilhã	1487	West Africa
Gaspar de	Cruz	1556	Missionary in China, Hormuz
Brás	Cubas	1550	Brazil
Tristão da	Cunha	1506	S. Atlantic Island that bears his name
Nuno Leitão da	Cunha	1500	India
Francisco	Cunha	1502	India
Rui Nunes da	Cunha	1511	Far East
Bartolomeu	Dias	1488	Round Cape of Good Hope, S. Africa
João	Dias	1520	Magellan's pilot
Dinis	Dias	1439	Northwest Africa, Cape Verde
Diogo	Dias	1506	Madagascar, São Lourenço Island, Brazil
Diogo	Dias	1525	First hospital in Mexico City
Lopo	Dias	1502	India
Pedro	Dias	1500	East Africa, Red Sea
Fernão Vaz	Dourado	1560	Cartographer born in India
Gil	Eanes	1434	Northeast Africa
Heliodoro	Eboanos	1568	Brazil
João	Escobar	1500	Brazil
Pedro	Escobar	1470	West Africa, also with Vasco da Gama
Martim	Esteves	1470	West Africa

Name	Surname	Date	Activity
Antonio de	Faria	1550	India
Gil	Fernandes	1500	India
João	Fernandes	1445	Northeast Africa
Simão	Fernandes	1580	North America
Álvaro	Fernandes	1446	Northwest Africa
Diniz	Fernandes	1450	Northwest Africa
Duarte	Fernandes	1511	Far East
Antonio	Fernandes	1514	East Africa
Gonçalo	Ferreira	1460	Guinea, West Africa
Manuel Pereira	Forjaz	1590	Tried Angola-Mozambique by land
Álvaro de	Freitas	1448	West Africa
Antonio	Galvão	1536	Captain and governor in the Moluccas
Cristovão da	Gama	1541	Somalia, son of Vasco da Gama
Paulo da	Gama	1500	India, brother of Vasco da Gama
Estevão da	Gama	1524	India, son of Vasco da Gama
Vasco da	Gama	1498	Discovered sea route to India
João da	Gama	1589	Sailed across the Pacific
Paulo da	Gama	1498	With Vasco da Gama fleet (Captain) India
Henrique	Garcês	1558	Discovers mercury in Peru
Diogo	Garcia	1506	Indian Ocean island, bears his name
Aleixo	Garcia	1521	Explores South America continent
Álvaro	Gaspar	1540	Explorer, New Mexico
Diogo	Gil	1447	Sea land to Arabia
Frei Bento de	Goes	1603	Mongolia
Pero de	Gois	1536	Brazil
Diogo	Gomes	1447	West Africa
Fernão	Gomes	1455	Guinea, West Africa
Estevão	Gomes	1524	From Newfoundland to Virginia
João	Gomes	1510	North West Africa
Amador	Gonçalves	1543	Bermudas
André	Gonçalves	1502	Brazil with Americo Vespucci
Antão	Gonçalves	1441	Northeast Africa
Gaspar	Gonçalves	1585	India, pilot
Lopo	Gonçalves	1472	East Africa
Jorge	Gonçalves	1448	East Africa
Manuel	Gonçalves	1585	India, master
Diogo	Homem	1500	Cartographer, worked for England, 1500's
Manuel Godinho de	Heredia	1596	Claim discovery of Australia in 1600
Manuel Rodrigues	Homem	1572	East Africa
Álvaro Martins	Homem	1474	Azores
Garcia	Homem	1445	Navigator, East Africa
Lopo	Homem	1500	Cartographer, worked for France, 1500's
Joao	Infante	1487	West Africa
Lançarote de	Lagos	1448	West Africa
Rui de	Lasteneda	1502	India
Jerónimo	Leitão	1585	Brazil
Gaspar de	Lemos	1488	Cape of Good Hope, with Dias
João de	Lisboa	1512	Brazil
Paulo de	Lima	1587	Malacca
Pero	Lobo	1532	Brazil
Padre. Jerónimo	Lobo	1625	East Africa, Abyssinia (Ethiopia)
Duarte	Lopes	1578	Angola, West Africa
Frei Fernando	Lopes	1487	Voyage to the land of Prestes João

Name	Surname	Date	Activity
João	Machado	1500	India
Fernão de	Magalhães	1519	Traveled with Vasco da Gama
Nuno	Manuel	1514	Exploreed Rio de La Plata in South America
Padre. Luis	Mariano	1624	Discovered Nile water falls, Marchinson
Sebastião	Marinho	1582	Brazil
Lourenço	Marques	1542	East Africa, Mozambique
João	Martins	1585	Possible north passage to India
André S.	Martins	1520	Pilot with Magellan
Jorge	Mascarenhas	1517	Discovered the Liew Islands
João de	Mascarenhas	1546	Diu, India
Pedro de	Mascarenhas	1528	India
Gil	Matoso	1502	India
David	Melgueiro	1660	North passage to India for the Dutch
Duarte de	Melo	1518	India
Fernão de	Melo	1499	S. Tomé Island off West Africa
Manuel Afonso de	Melo	1526	India
Fernão de	Mendonça	1585	Admiral, India
Cristovão de	Mendonça	1524	Possible early voyage to Australia
Pero de	Mendonça	1503	India
Duarte de	Meneses	1522	India
Pedro de	Meneses	1415	Ceuta, Morocco
Henrique de	Meneses	1524	India
Jorge de	Meneses	1525	Far East
Álvaro de	Mesquita	1519	Pilots with Estevão Gomes
Antonio de	Miranda	1517	Ambassador to Sião
Antonio	Moniz	1560	India
Belchior Dias	Moreira	1591	Brazil
Antonio de	Mota	1542	Discovers Japan
Luis de	Moura	1500	India
Bernardo	Nasci	1551	Navigator to India
Father Manuel da	Nobrega	1560	Brazil
Antonio de	Noli (Nola)	1456	Cape Verde
Antão de	Noronha	1552	India
Garcia de	Noronha	1511	Brazil
Fernando de (Fernão)	Noronha	1502	Discovered island that bears his name
João da	Nova	1501	Discovered Ascension Island
Francisco de	Novais	1501	India
Paulo Dias	Novais	1575	Kingdom of Angola
Gonçalo	Nunes	1498	With Vasco da Gama fleet to India
João	Nunes	1498	Portuguese Jew, first to set foot in India
Manuel	Nuno	1514	Explored Rio de la Plata
João	Ornelas	1446	Canary Islands
Nicolau	Orta	1507	India to Portugal by land
Padre Pero	Paes, Paez	1617	Discovered Nile river source
Afonso	Paiva	1495	Northwest Africa
Antonio	Peixoto	1506	Far East and Japan
Diogo	Pereira	1541	Far East with Saint Francis Xavier
Duarte Pacheco	Pereira	1498	North coast of Brazil
Diogo	Pereira	1535	Voyage on an 11 feet Boat, India-Portugal
Bartolomeu	Perestrelo	1423	Madeira Islands
João Lopes	Perestrelo	1502	India
Lançarote	Pessanha	1490	Far East
Luis de	Pina	1500	India

Name	Surname	Date	Activity
Simão de	Pina	1488	Cape of Good Hope, South Africa, with Dias
Fernão Mendes	Pinto	1534	Far East
Tomé	Pires	1517	China, apothecary
Diogo	Pires	1502	India
Bernardo	Pires	1524	Brazil
Gomes	Pires	1448	East Africa, Sahara region
Luis	Pires	1500	Brazil
Fernando	Pó	1472	East Africa
Francisco	Proença	1596	Brazil
Pedro Fernandes de	Queiroz	1596	New Guinea, Far East, New Hebrides, 1774
Pero	Rafael	1502	India
João	Ramalho	1522	Brazil
Rodrigues	Ravasco	1504	India
Rodrigo	Rebelo	1486	West Africa
Pero, Pedro	Reinel	1486	West Africa
Jorge	Reinel	1500	Cartographer, worked for Spain
Diogo	Ribeiro	1500	Cartographer, worked for Spain
Afonso	Ribeiro	1512	Brazil
Master	Rodrigo	1480	Physicist, astrolabe, worked royal court
Mem	Rodrigues	1486	West Africa
Fernão	Rodrigues	1503	India
Francisco	Rodrigues	1524	Navigator to Moluccas
Jeronimo Barreto	Rolim	1565	Navigator, India
Salvador Correia de	Sá	1514	Governor Rio de Janeiro, lived 101 years
Mem de	Sá	1560	Brazil
Afonso	Saldanha	1599	Brazil
Antonio	Saldanha	1540	India
Lopo Vaz de	Sampaio	1528	India
João de	Santarem	1470	East Africa
Pêro Fernão de	Sardinha	1547	India
Pantaleão de Sá	Sepulveda	1542	East Africa
Manuel de Sousa	Sepulveda	1560	India and West Africa, captain
Diogo Lopes de	Sequeira	1505	Far East, Malacca
Gomes de	Sequeira	1523	Far East
Rui de	Sequeira	1474	West Africa
João	Serrão	1520	Part of Magellan's crew
Francisco	Serrão	1511	Sumatra with Antonio de Abreu
Aires Gomes da	Silva	1500	Cape of Good Hope
Gonçalo da	Silveira	1500	Southeast Africa
João de	Silveira	1516	Far East
Antonio da	Silveira	1538	India, Diu
Diogo de	Silves	1420	Possible sighting of the Azores Islands
Gonçalo de	Sintra	1444	East Africa
Pero de (Pedro)	Sintra	1461	Northeast Africa
Fernão	Soares	1551	Navigator to India
Brás	Sodré	1502	India
Vicente	Sodré	1502	West Africa with Estevão Gomes
Bras Dias de	Solis	1512	Brazil
Diogo Lopes de	Sousa	1551	Navigator to India
Gonçalo de	Sousa	1490	West Africa
Gabriel Soares de	Sousa	1587	Indians of the Brazilian coast
Pedro Lopes de	Sousa	1532	Brazil
Tomé de	Sousa	1549	Brazil

Name	Surname	Date	Activity
Martins Afonso de	Sousa	1541	India
João Coelho de	Sousa	1580	Brazil
Francisco de	Sousa	1580	Brazil
Belchior de Sousa	Tavares	1529	Explored Rivers Euphrates, Tigris
Diogo de	Teive	1455	West Africa
Pedro	Teixeira	1600	Far East, via Central America
Tristão Vaz	Teixeira	1423	Madeira Islands
Aires	Tinoco	1446	West Africa
João Vaz de	Torres	1606	Far East
Sancho de	Tovar	1501	West Africa, Brazil
Nuno	Tristão	1443	Northeast Africa
Luis Mendes de	Vasconcelos	1502	India
Álvaro	Vasques	1446	Northeast Africa
André	Vaz	1550	India
Pero Vaz da	Veiga	1503	India
Bartolomeu	Velho	1561	Cartographer, worked for France
Gonçalo	Velho	1500	Brazil
Diogo	Veloso	1593	Cambodian ambassador to Philippines
Americo	Vespucci	1502	Genovese, coast of Brazil for Portugal
Padre Antonio	Vieira	1640	Brazil
Master José	Vizinho	1485	Physicist, astrolabe, pupil of Zacuto
Saint Francis	Xavier	1540	Born in Navarra, Spain, Lisbon and India
Abraham Ben Samuel	Zacuto	1480	Astronomer, solar tables used by Columbus
João Coutinho	Zamiro	1502	India
João Gonçalo	Zarco	1423	Madeira Islands
Francisco	Zeimoto	1542	Japan

List of 1529 Weddings of Portuguese Men and Native Women [1]

Native Wife	Portuguese Man	Wife Origin
Caterina Álvares	AfonsoÁlvares	Guzerate
Felipa Fernandes	Afonso Galego	Malabar
Luzia Fernandes	Afonso de Morales	Moor
Biatriz Nunes	Afonso de Motta	Moor
Caterina Tonso	Afonso Fernandes	Moor
Biatriz Vaz	Afonso Paes	Malabar
Felipa Morena	Afonso Rodrigues	Canarim
Caterina Afonso	Álvaro Pirez	?
Antonia Lopes	Antonio do Rego	Moor
Maria Morena	Antonio Folgado	Moor
Inês Gomes	Bastiam Gomes	Moor
Lucrecia Borges	Bras Gonçalves	Canarim
Lianor Arganosa	Bras Lopes	Malabar
Izabel da Silva	Diogo Correia	Malabar
Cristina Fernandes	Diogo de Laniz	Moor
Maria Lopes	Diogo Lopes	Moor
Margarida Vaz	Domingos Gonçalves	Burma
Vyolante Vaz	Estevão Chaves	Java
Caterina Gonçalves	Fernão Lopes	Moor
Lianor Nunes	Fernão Nunes	Malabar
Cristina de Saa	Francisco de Saa	Moor
Johana Gonçalves	Francisco Fernandes	Jaoa
Isabel Fernandes	Francisco Fernandes	Moor
Isabel Morena	Francisco Tinoco	Canarim
Biatriz Morena	Gonçalo Moreno	Nayra
Felipa Fernandes	Gregorio Fernandes	Moor
Cristina Fernandes	João Carvalho	Malabar
Justa Fernandes	João Fernandes	Moor
Caterina Fernandes	Joham Alvarez	Moor
Joana Diaz	Joham Diaz	Canarim
Maria Fernandes	Joham Gonçalves	Nayra
Branca Gonçalves	Joham Gonçalves	Socotorina
Biatriz Fernandes	Joham Gonçalves	Nayra
Biatriz Lopes	Joham Lopes	Malabar
Izabel Marques	Joham Marquez	Malabar
Maria Fernandes	Joham Nunes	Moor
Caterina Vaz	Joham Nunes Trombeta	Socotorina

[1] Historia da Lingua Portuguesa by Serafim da Silva Neto, p. 534-536

Native Wife	Portuguese Man	Wife Origin
Antonia Fernandes	Joham Vaz	Moor
Lianor Rodrigues	Jorge de Sezimbra	Moor
Caterina de Alboquerque	Jorge Nunes	Moor
Beatriz Fereyra	Lopo Afonso	Moor
Caterina Fernandes	Lourenço Saldanha	Moor
Antonia d'Albuquerque	Manuel Gonçalves	Malabar
Maria da Sylva	Manuel Gonçalves	Moor
Joana de Araujo	Nemo Vaz	Malabar
Marta Diaz	Pero d'Evora	Canarim
Inês de França	Pero de França	Moor
Izabel Fernandes	Pero Fernandes	Malabar
Isabel da Costa	Pero Mendes	Burma
Caterina Vaz	Pero Petro	Moor
Felipa Fernandes	Richarte	Moor
Guiomar Gonçalves	Rodrigo Esturiano	Moor
Filipa Fernandes	Salvador Afonso	Malabar
Briola Vaz	Simão Vaz	Nayra

List of weddings of Far-East native Women with Portuguese Men

The Classification of Moor is generic. It applies mostly to Muslims, except the Turks, which the Portuguese called Rumes. Also, to most of the India area natives, including the Mollucas, Indonesia, etc.

List of Portuguese Shipwrecked Caravels to 1550

M	D	Y	Captain/Pilot	Vessel	Shipwreck Area
7	8	1497	Gonçalo Nunes	Supply ship	Cape of Good Hope
7	8	1497	Paulo da Gama (2)	S. Rafael (1)	Off East Africa
3	9	1500	Aires Gomes da Silva		Cape of Good Hope
3	9	1500	Bartolomeu Dias		Cape of Good Hope
3	9	1500	Pêro de Ataíde		Near Mozambique
3	9	1500	Pêro Dias		Red Sea
3	9	1500	Sancho de Tovar	Rei	All survived
3	9	1500	Simão de Pina		Site unknown
3	9	1500	Vasco de Ataíde		Site unknown
2	10	1502	Antonio do Campo		Angediva *
2	10	1502	Antonio Fernandes		Sofala
2	10	1502	Brás Sodré	Leitoa a Velha	Curia Maria
2	10	1502	Diogo Fernandes Correia	Borreco	Angediva *
2	10	1502	Pêro de Ataíde		East Africa
2	10	1502	Vicente Sodré	Esmeralda	Curia Maria
4	14	1503	Francisco de Albuquerque	Rainha	Site unknown
4	14	1503	Nicolau Coelho	Faial	Site unknown
4	14	1503	Pero de Ataide	Bate Cabelo ?	Banks of S. Lazaro ?
4	14	1503	Pêro Vaz da Veiga		Cape of Good Hope
4	22	1504	Pero de Mendonça		Near S. Brás
3	21	1505	Lopo Sanches	Nau	Site unknown
3	21	1505	Pêro de Ataíde	Caravel	Outside Lisbon
3	21	1505	Pêro Ferreira Fogaça	Bela	Mozambique
5	18	1505	Francisco de Anaia	S. João	Site unknown
5	18	1505	Pêro Barreto Magalhães	Galega	Bay of Quiloa
3	6	1506	Job Queimado	Job	French captured
3	6	1506	Leonel Coutinho	Leitoa a Velha	Mozambique
3	6	1506	Rui Pereira Coutinho	S. Vicente	Natal
4	13	1507	Fernão Soares	S. Antonio	Site unknown
4	20	1507	João Chanoca	Caravela	Rio Sanagá
4	15	1507	Jorge de Castro	Rumesa	Nazareth
4	13	1507	Rui Cunha	S. João	Site unknown
4	20	1507	Vasco Gomes de Abreu	S. Romão	Santiago
4	11	1508	Jeronimo Teixeira	S. Clara	Polvoreira
4	9	1508	Jorge de Aguiar	S. João	Tristão da Cunha
		1508	Gonçalo de Sousa		Site unknown
3	12	1509	Francisco Sá	S. Vicente	Cananor
3	12	1509	Sebastião de Sousa Elvas	S. Jorge	Cananor
3	16	1510	Manuel da Cunha	S. Roque	Mozambique

M	D	Y	Captain/Pilot	Vessel	Shipwreck Area
3	25	1512	Francisco Nogueira	S. Julião	Angoche
3	14	1513	Francisco Correia	S. Antonio	S. Lázaro Island
3	22	1516	Antonio de Lima	S. Simão	Banks of S. Lazaro
3	22	1516	Francisco Sousa Mancias	N. Sra. da Luz	Banks of S. Lazaro
4	23	1519	Francisco Cunha	S. Antonio	Quiloa
4	23	1519	Luis Gusmão, Castelhano		Brazil
4	23	1519	Manuel de Sousa	S. Antonio	Quiloa
4	5	1521	Duarte de Meneses	S. Jorge	Ilha Terceira
4	23	1522	Pedro de Castelo Branco	Nazaré	Bay of Goa
4	6	1523	Aires da Cunha	S. Miguel	Mozambique
4	9	1524	Cristovão Rosado	Caravela Rosa	Site unknown
4	9	1524	Fernando Monroy	S. Jorge	Melinde Banks
4	9	1524	Francisco Brito	Barbosa	East Africa
4	9	1524	G. Pereira Macherquim	Garça	Site unknown
4	15	1525	Diogo de Melo	Paraiso	Cachopos
4	15	1525	Filipe de Castro	Corpo Santo	Cape Rosalgate
4	8	1526	Francisco de Anaia	N. S. Victoria	Near Lisbon
4	8	1526	Vicente Gil	S. Leão	Returned to port
3	26	1527	Aleixo de Abreu	Bastiana	East Africa
3	26	1527	Manuel de Larcerda	Conceição	East Africa
4	18	1528	Afonso Vaz Zambujo	Ship	Near Mozambique
4	18	1528	Bernardim da Silveira	Galeão	Sofala, East Africa
4	18	1528	João de Freitas	Nau	Canary Islands
4	18	1528	Nuno da Cunha	Rosa	Near Mozambique
		1529	João de Freitas		Cape Verde
4	20	1531	Manuel Macedo	Esperança	Calicut
		1532	Felipe de Castro	Corpo Santo	Cachopo, Barra
		1532	João de Melo e Silva	Conceição	Site unknown
3	4	1533	Francisco de Noronha	S. João	Cape of Good Hope
3	25	1536	Duarte Barreto	S. Miguel	Site unknown
4	6	1538	Bernadim Silveira	Galega	Site unknown
3	24	1539	Pero Lopes de Sousa	S. Cruz	Site unknown
4	7	1541	Martim Afonso Sousa	S. Tiago	Baçaim, R. Cabras
4	7	1541	Martim Afonso Sousa	S. Tiago	Baçaim, R. Cabras
4	4	1542	Baltasar George	Grifo	Terceira, Azores
4	4	1542	Vicente Gil	N. S. da Graça	Melinde
4	19	1544	Simão de Melo	N. S. da Graça	Near Mozambique
3	28	1547	Pedro da Silva	S. Tomé	Angoche
3	3	1549	João Figueira	Burgalesa	Site unknown
5	3	1550	Álvaro de Ataide	S. João	Cape of Good Hope
5	3	1550	Diogo de Noronha	Frol de la Mar	Mazagão
3	20	1551	Jorge de Meneses	Barrileira	Site unknown

M	D	Y	Captain/Pilot	Vessel	Shipwreck Area
3	10	1551	Lopo de Sousa	Biscainha	Site unknown
3	24	1552	Antonio Dias Figueiredo	S. Tiago	Islands unknown
3	24	1552	Antonio Moniz Barreto	Zambuco	Near Goa
3	24	1553	Fernão Álvares Cabral	S. Bento	East Africa, Natal
4	2	1554	Belchior de Sousa	S. Cruz	Site unknown
4	2	1554	Francisco de Gouveia	S. Francisco	Terceira, Azores
4	2	1554	Pedro de Mascarenhas	S. Boaventura	Goa coast
		1555	Francisco Nobre	Algaravia Nova	Pêro de Banhos
		1555	Jacome de Melo	Algaravia Velha	Terceira, Azores
4	30	1557	João Rodrigues Carvalho	Aguia	Mombaça
4	20	1557	Luis Fernandes	S. Maria Barca	East Africa
3	28	1559	D. Constantino	Garça	Site unknown
		1592		Madre de Deus	English Captured

List of Portuguese shipwrecks

The above chart has been compiled from several sources. Portuguese Navy Commander Encarnação Gomes has been instrumental in obtaining most of the information which he has been doing for many years in his series *Subsidios para o Estudo da Carreira das Indias* of the *Anais of the Clube Militar* in Lisbon. Other sources consulted were: Portuguese National Archives *Torre do Tombo*; *Livro da Fazenda* de Luis Figueiredo Falcão; *Livro das Armadas*; Portuguese National Library *Biblioteca Nacional,* and others.

Due to the variety of sources some of the details may not be correct and sometimes are contradictory. Further research is required to complete the chart, which should be done, at least covering the whole 16th century, not just the Indian route but also Brazil and Africa. This part of the Portuguese history is still to be completed and there is plenty of information out there.

Influence of the Portuguese Language on Japan and the World

Monsignor Sebastião Rodolfo Dalgado compiled no less than 47 Oriental languages with words of Portuguese origin: Concanim, 815; Malaise, 361; Japanese, 78, to name just a few. [1] At a much earlier date, in 1514, Afonso de Albuquerque, the viceroy, wrote to King Manuel I that in Cochin 29 students were registered in school to learn the Portuguese language. [2] Between 500 and 1,000 Portuguese words passed to Oriental cultures, [3] and the opposite also. E.g., *Chá* in Portuguese is the same in Chinese, and is pronounced like *shah* as it was used in Persia. Just a small example, in Malai... the following words have Portuguese roots, in the order presented: English and Portuguese, Malai: Coast - Costa - Kósta; Potatoes - Batata - Battatas; Wheat - Trigo -Trigu; Lizard - Lagarto - Lagarti; Head - Cabeça - Kembesa; Father - Pay - Pai; Mother - Mai - Mãe; Jeweler - Ourives - Orivis, and so on.[4]

Unfortunately, not enough resources have been provided for a deep study of the Portuguese language. When this is done, then many similarities will be discovered, not only in current use but also by natives many years ago.

As a point of interest, the Portuguese language also had an influence on the Japanese language.

The following are just some of the words compiled by Armando Martins Janeira in his book *O Impacto Português sobre a Civilização Japonesa.*

Japanese	Portuguese	English
Amendo	Amendoa	Almond
Amen	Amen	Amen
Anjo	Anjo	Angel
Barsan	Bálsamo	Balm
Baputesuma	Baptismo	Baptism
Kontasu	Contas	Beads of Rosary
Banku	Banco	Bench
Bisukoto	Biscoito	Biscuit
Pan	Pão	Bread
Iruman	Irmão	Brother
Manteka	Manteiga	Butter
Butan	Botão	Button
Kompra	Compra	Buy
Boru	Bolo	Cake
Kappa	Capa	Cape
Katoritu	Católico	Catholic
Karisu	Cálix	Chalice
Kirishtan	Cristão	Christian
Ekirinji	Igreja	Church
Koreijo	Colégio	College

Japanese	Portuguese	English
Kapitan	Capitão	Captain
Kataru	Catarro	Cararrh
Katana	Catana	Catan
Confeto	Confeito	Comfit
Kompasu	Compasso	Compass
Kohismo	Confissão	Confession
Kirismo	Crisma	Confirmation
Karusu	Cruz	Cross
Koppu	Copo	Cup (glass)
Jejun	Jejum	Fasting
Furasuko	Frasco	Flask
Zenerasu	General	General
Jiban	Gibão	Gerkin (short jacket)
Biirodo	Vidro	Glass
Uru	Ouro	Gold
Gomu	Goma	Gum
Abito	Habito	Habit
Inferno	Inferno	Hell
Osuhitari	Hospital	Hospital
Ostiya	Hóstia	Host (religion)
Jaketsu	Jaqueta	Jacket
Zesusu (Zesu)	Jesus	Jesus
Rabirinto	Labirinto	Labyrinth
Reguwa	Légua	League
Karuta	Carta	Letter
Manto	Manto	Mantle
Maruchiru	Mártir	Martyr
Sinnyoro	Senhor	Mister
Banzai	Banzé	Noise
Kurusan	Calção	Pants (gibão)
Paraizo	Paraíso	Paradise
Pisturu	Pistola	Pistol
Pappu	Papa	Pope (pap)
Byôbu	Biombo	Portable partition
Orashyo	Oração	Prayer
Bateren	Padre	Priest
Rõsa	Rosa	Rose
Seito	Santo	Saint
Tentasan	Tentação	Temptation
Arigato	Obrigado	Thank you
Tabako	Tabaco	Tobacco
Taifu	Tufão	Typhoon

Japanese	Portuguese	English
Birodo	Veludo	Velvet
Saya	Saya	Skirt
Shabon	Sabão	Soap
Ranbiki	Alambique	Still

Portuguese and Japanese Words.

There are many more. Naturally, some words are the same as other European languages. But since the Portuguese were the first Europeans, they brought with them to Japan and the Orient their language. [5] Also other words used throughtout the world, such as Guiné, Guinea; pagode, pagoda; moeda de ouro, moidore; varanda, verandah; cobra, etc.

Influence of the Japanese Language in Portugal

The Portuguese language has also been influenced by Japanese and other Asian languages. The following are just a few examples of the Japanese.

Japanese	Portuguese	English
Banzai	Banzé	Noise
Byôbu	Biombo	Portable partition
Katana	Catana	Catan

Influence of the Portuguese Language in the U.S.

There are at least 38 English words derived from the Portuguese language; the following are just some of them: [6, 7, 8]

English	Portuguese	English	Portuguese	English	Portuguese
Albatross	Albatroz	Firm	Firma	Picaninny [9]	Pequenino
Albino	Albino	Flamingo	Flamengo		
Apricot	Albricoque	Lingo	Lingua	Stagnant	Estagnado
Bagasse	Bagaço [10]	Madeira	Vinho	Tank	Tanque
Caste	Casta	Marmalade	Marmelada	Typhoon	Tufão
Corvette	Corveta	Molasses	Melaço	Yam	Inhame
Fetish	Fetiche	Parasol	Para-sol		

* * *

Notes

[1] A Lingua Portuguesa no Mundo by Jorge Morais Barbosa, pp. 148-155
[2] Historia da Lingua Portuguesa by Serafim da Silva Neto, p. 542
[3] Luso-Americano, 4-24-1996
[4] Lingua Portuguesa no Mundo by Jorge Morais e Silva, p. 151
[5] O Impacto Português sobre a civilização Japonesa by Pedro Canavarro
[6] Encyclopedia of English by Arthus Zeiger, p.435, Arco (1959)
[7] Michaels, Dicionario Ilustrado, 27 Edition, (1981)
[8] Lingua Portuguesa no Mundo by Jorge Morais Barbosa, p. 161
[9] Hawaiian for small child
[10] Pulp of sugar cane or grapes

The Celebrated Melungeon Case in 1872 by Judge Shepherd

* * *

The following is a reprint from the book written by Jean Patterson Bible, *The Melungeons, Yesterday and Today*, still in print. We thank the author for her permission to use it. Since it endorses some of theories about the Melungeons, it is appropriate to present it to readers.

* * *

It was in 1872 that a fledgling Chattanooga, Tennessee, lawyer based his case and won a lawsuit on the hitherto almost unheard-of theory that Melungeons were of Carthaginian or Phoenician origin. From this auspicious beginning, the young attorney Lewis Shepherd went on to become a judge and a leading member of the Chattanooga bar.

In 1915 Judge Shepherd published a collection of reminiscences of his legal experiences, entitled *Memoirs of Judge Lewis Shepherd*, which included the "Romantic Account of the Celebrated 'Melungeon' Case." In it, the judge recounts many of the details of the build-up, trial and resolution of the lawsuit that has sometimes been dubbed the "Chattanooga Story" by those who sympathized with the plight of the Melungeons.

During the era in which it took place, the case was probably one of the most publicized of its kind where a decision was rendered favoring a minority group over a white prosecutor. The outcome, the awarding of an inheritance to the daughter of a Melungeon mother and a white father, hinged on Shepherd's successfully establishing his claim that his client was not of Negro blood but was descended from the early Carthaginians. Had she been proved to have Negro blood, according to the then Tennessee law of miscegenation (Judge Shepherd defined it as the marriage of a white person with one of Negro blood to the sixth degree), the marriage of her parents would have been illegal, leaving her with no claim to her father's property.

The background of the strange true story that reads more like a romantic novel goes back to the early settlement of the Chattanooga area. A wealthy man from Virginia bought a large tract of land in Moccasin Bend, where today the Tennessee River winds its way around Chattanooga, and moved in with his family and slaves. The fertile, river-bottom land soon became a rich and productive farm, so that by the time of the owner's death, he was able to leave each of his three sons a good farm piece. Two of the brothers never married and, on their death, the surviving one inherited their estates. He rented the land, hired out his slaves and went into business in Chattanooga.

In the meantime, his widowed mother remarried and had three daughters by her second husband. Several years later, the surviving brother was stricken with a mental illness that left him temporarily deranged. By 1848, however, he was able to resume his normal schedule, including the management of his extensive holdings. One of the tenants was an elderly Melungeon named Bolton who had served in the War of 1812, joining the army in South Carolina, where he was living at the time. Bolton had a daughter "famed for her beauty, her grace of manner and modesty. She was a dark brunette. She had a suit of black hair, which was coveted by all the girls who knew her. Her form was petite and yet, withal, was so plump and so well developed as to make her an irresistibly charming young woman. She was most beautiful of face, and had a rich black eye, in whose depths the sunbeams seemed to gather. When she loosed her locks they fell, almost reaching the ground, and shone in the sunlight, or quivered like the glamour which the full moon throws on the placid water..."

The young man fell in love with her, and the attraction was mutual. They planned to get married but, when the news reached his mother and half-sister they strenuously opposed the union, knowing that if it took place, they stood to lose all chance of becoming heirs to the property he had inherited. They notified the licensing clerk that if he issued the two a marriage license, they would file suit against him, claiming not only that the young man was mentally incompetent but that the girl had Negro blood and such a marriage would be illegal. The alarmed clerk was so impressed by their threats that he refused to grant the Groom-to-be a license when he applied for one several days later.

Not to be outwitted, the young man persuaded two of his friends, Ab Carroll and John Cummings, to accompany him and the girl across the river to Dade County, Georgia, to serve as witnesses. The marriage license was purchased in Trenton, the Dade County seat, duly registered, and the ceremony was performed June 14, 1856, by a local squire at his Dade County Home.

The couple returned to the groom's plantation and set up housekeeping. Their first child, a son, died in infancy, and the second, a daughter, was born in the latter part of 1858. When the mother died in childbirth eight days later the bereaved husband was thrown into such a state of shock he never fully recovered. His mental condition was such that a guardian was appointed to look after him and manage his affairs.

In the meantime, the mother and half-sisters had not been idle. They either coerced or bribed "Aunt Betsy," the child's maternal aunt, into taking her far away and promising never to return. A little later, the aunt took the child, along with the family Bible containing the birth and marriage records, to a small place in Illinois, 75 miles from Cairo. As the time went on, the sad story was almost forgotten by the public. The insane man's guardian continued to manage his various properties until he had built up a fund of many thousand dollars for the estate. But one person had not forgotten. A friend, Samuel Williams, had kept up with the child from the beginning by a secret arrangement with her aunt Betsy to keep him informed as to her welfare.

The historic lawsuit was instituted in 1872 when the man's two surviving half-sisters and the children of the deceased half-sister brought suit in the chancery court, attempting to surcharge and falsify the settlements of the guardianship by the guardian, Mr. Foust. He was charged with mismanagement of the estate, wasting its assets, lending large sums of money to poor people, taking inadequate security from them. In addition, they sought to make him account for assets supposed to be on hand.

The second feature of the suit was that Mr. Foust's ward was an incurable lunatic, and that the complainants were heirs apparent who would certainly inherit the estate. They asked that the present guardianship be revoked and that the ward and his estate be turned over to them, promising to give bond an security that they would provide for his needs. Finally, they asked a decree adjudging them to be heirs apparent. And, for good measure, they also sued Mr. Williams and Col. John Divine, sureties on Mr. Foust's bond as guardian, in order to make good the hoped-for decree.

Now the time had come for Mr. Williams to produce the rightful heir to the estate and to protect her rights. Seeking a trustworthy and competent lawyer, he found that all the experienced ones were already involved in the suit on one side or the other. On the advice of a friend, he consulted Lewis Shepherd, a young attorney just starting out in his profession. Shepherd agreed to take the case, with Mr. Williams acting in the capacity of best friend of the young girl.

The suit they filed for the child came like a bolt out of the blue. They asked that she be adjudged the child and heir apparent of the deranged father, that she be supported and educated out of his estate. The dismayed opposition promptly labeled the whole thing a "tissue of falsehoods and slanders... a fabrication of old man Williams, and that the girl was an impostor. They even denied her identity as the child of the crazed man, and also denied that he had ever been married to his alleged wife, and claimed that if he had gone through the form of marriage it was void for numerous reasons, and the issue of such marriage was illegitimate." At that time, young Shepherd produced his trump card, the daughter in person, then nearly 15 years old. He had previously sent Mr. Williams to Illinois to bring her back to Chattanooga, along with the family Bible containing the birth and marriage records.

Proof of the marriage was not difficult to obtain as the magistrate who performed the ceremony and the two witnesses to it were still living. When asked how he remembered the exact date so well, one witness said that it was impressed on his mind because his wife had given birth to a baby girl that same evening, and the date and name were in the family Bible.

The record in the Bible carried to Illinois by aunt Betsy verified the birth of the daughter and the date. As to the father's sanity, the judge ruled that a marriage which was voidable could not be questioned by anyone except one of the parties to the contract and could not be charged collaterally.

But the issue at stake on which the real battle lines were drawn was the allegation that the marriage was void because the mother in the case had sufficient Negro blood that the ceremony could not be legally recognized because of the then Tennessee law against miscegenation.

The opposition brought in a number of old-time Negroes who testified under oath that the Boltons were kinky-headed Negroes, that "the whole bunch of them had kinky hair", just like a Mulatto Negro. They also swore that aunt Betsy and the girl's mother had kinky hair, not knowing that the young girl was at that moment actually in Chattanooga.

The "kinky head" question was settled once and for all with a deposition taken from the girl at Mr. Williams' home. Asked to cut off a lock of her hair, and pin it to the deposition, "she reached up to her topknot and pulled out her old-fashioned tucking comb, and a monstrous mass of coal black hair, as straight as the hair of a horse's tail, fell down to the floor. It was about four feet long, and perfectly free of a kink or a tendency to curl. She exhibited with her depositions a fair sample of her magnificent suit of hair, which completely destroyed the depositions of the Negroes taken on the other side to prove that the Bolton people were Negroes."

By way of additional proof, Shepherd went back to the Melungeon tradition of Carthaginian ancestry, in an exceedingly eloquent plea even in that period of old-fashioned oratory. In his account in the memoirs of how he developed his defense based on the theory of Carthaginian descent, he says it was satisfactorily established in the proof that the family of this woman was in no way allied to, or connected with, the Negro race; that there was not a feature of herself or ancestry that was at all similar to the distinguishing characteristics or features of the Negro, except that they were of dark color, about the color of a Mulatto. They had high foreheads; long, straight, black hair; high cheek bones, thin lips, small feet with high insteps and prominent Roman noses, while the features of the Negro and Mulatto were exactly the reverse of these.

In truth, these people belonged to a peculiar race, which settled in East Tennessee at an early day and, in the vernacular of the country, they were known as "Melungeons," and were not even remotely allied to Negroes. It was proven by tradition amongst these people that they were descendants of the ancient Carthaginians (sic); they were Phoenicians who, after Carthage was conquered by the Romans and became a Roman province, emigrated across the Straits of Gibraltar and settled in Portugal. They lived for many years and became quite numerous on the southern coast of Portugal, and from thence came the distinguished Venetian general Othello, whom Shakespeare made immortal in his celebrated play "The Moor of Venice." These were the same people who fought the Romans so bravely and heroically in the Punic Wars, and whose women sacrificed their long black hair to the state to be plaited and twisted into cables with which to fasten their galleys and ships of war to the shore. About the time of our Revolutionary War, a considerable body of these people crossed the Atlantic and settled on the coast of South Carolina, near the North Carolina line, and they lived amongst the people of Carolina for a number of years. At length, the people of Carolina began to suspect that they were Mulattos of free Negroes, and denied them the privileges usually accorded to white people. They refused to associate with them on equal terms and would not allow them to send their children to school with white children, and would only admit them to join their churches on the footing of Negroes.

South Carolina had a law taxing free Negroes so much per capita, and a determined effort was made to collect this tax off them. But it was shown in evidence in the trial of this case that they always successfully resisted payment of this tax, as they proved they were not Negroes.

Because of their treatment, they left South Carolina at an early day and wandered across the mountains to Hancock County, East Tennessee... A few families of them drifted away from Hancock into the other counties of East Tennessee, and now and then into the mountainous section of Middle Tennessee.

As proof that Bolton had been consistently regarded as white since his arrival in Hamilton County, it was cited that the old man had been allowed to vote in all elections at a time when Negroes were not, and also to testify in court when a Negro would have been regarded as incompetent to do so. Moreover, Shepherd added that since the grandfather received a pension for serving in the War of 1812, he was legally considered white, because at the time he enlisted, neither Negroes nor Mulattos were looked on as soldiers and could serve only as teamsters or cooks.

Other evidence included the relating of an incident in the grandfather's life when a white man killed one of his grandchildren. Bolton prosecuted him, but the defendant filed a plea in abatement saying that since Bolton was a Negro, he had no right to prosecute. The jury found the plea not true, that Bolton was not a Negro. The defendant was convicted and sent to the penitentiary.

The chancellor allowed both sides a great deal of time and leeway in arguing the case but, when the final verdict was rendered, it was in favor of the girl. The court judged that she was the heir apparent of her father, entitled to be supported and educated out of his estate, and to inherit it on his death. Her guardian was instructed to pay for her education and maintenance, and to pay the young lawyer 5,000 dollars for his services (a munificent sum for that time, especially for a beginner in law practice).

The true story of the young Melungeon girl not only had a storybook beginning, it also had a "lived happily ever afterward" ending. When Mr. Williams brought the girl back to Chattanooga, he had promised aunt Betsy that he would bring her back to Chattanooga as soon as she could dispose of her belongings, a promise he carried out. In his memoirs, Judge Shepherd gives a summary of events following the trial.

When Mr. Williams got back to Chattanooga, the girl was nearly 15 years old. She knew nothing about the ways of the world. She was totally ignorant of the prevailing fashions of dress; she did not know what a corset was or how it was worn, whether over or under the dress. She had spent most of her life in the forests along the banks of the Mississippi, where she and her aunt had made their living by cultivating a small patch with hoes, and by cutting cordwood and selling it to the steamboats which plied up and down the river, and which used wood for fuel. She knew nothing whatever of the arts of fashionable women in making themselves attractive forms and figures by skillful lacing — she was simply an uncouth, an unsophisticated, unmadeup, natural girl from the backwoods; a girl, withal, possessed of a strikingly beautiful face, and a figure which, by proper development and dress, was capable of being molded into a form that would please the most fastidious. She was very much like her mother, and possessed all the charms and grace she did, but they were undeveloped.

Mr. Williams took her to a milliner and had her provided with a wardrobe suitable to her changed surroundings. She very readily adapted herself to her new surroundings and her new life, out in the midst of civilization. She was kept at the Williams home and sent to school from there for about two years.

She had to be started at the very beginning, but, being ambitious to get education, she studied hard and learned very rapidly, and in the short time of her schooldays got a very fair and practical education. She afterwards married her teacher, who was a splendid young man and became one of the leading men in the community, and managed his wife's affairs very successfully and added considerably to her fortune. At the time of his death, which occurred about 20 years ago, he was a prominent official in the county. The echoes of the outcome of the "Celebrated Melungeon Case" reverberated throughout most of the Melungeon settlements in the Southeast. Undoubtedly it furnished a legal guidepost which affected decisions concerning Melungeons for many years afterward. [1]

Notes

[1] The Melungeons Yesterday and Today by Jean Patterson Bible, p.61

Rulers of Portugal from 1580 to 1910 *

Dynasty of Habsburgs, United Crowns, Portugal & Spain
Filipe I   1580-1598
Filipe II   1598-1621
Filipe III   1621-1640

Dynasty of Bragança
João IV   1640-1656
Afonso VI   1656-1683
Pedro II   1683-1706
João V   1706-1750
José I   1750-1777
Maria I and Pedro III   1777-1786
Maria I   1786-1792
João VI (Regent)   1792-1807
João VI (Brazil)   1807-1821
João VI (Portugal)   1821-1826
Pedro IV (Emperor of Brazil)   1822-1831
Pedro IV (Portugal)   1826-1826
Maria II   1826-1853
Isabel Maria (Regent)   1826-1828
Miguel I   1828-1834
Fernando II (Regent)   1853-1855
Pedro V   1853-1861
Luis I   1861-1889
Carlos I   1889-1908
Manuel II   1908-1910

End of Monarchy   October 5th., 1910

*   See Page 185 for Rulers of Portugal to 1580

Portuguese who contributed in one form or other to
the making of America, prior to the 20th century.

* * *

These are some of the forgotten Portuguese,
shown in alphabetical order by last name, activities & details:

* * *

Frances Affonsa; Cook; 1858; President Lincoln's cook.

Isaac Abrabanel; Jewish Leader; 1471; worked with his father for the Portuguese King Afonso V, redeemed 250 Moroccan Jews.

Carlos Pedro Diogo Andrade; Pioneer; 1825; Amador County, East Sacramento, California.

Laurinda C. Andrade; teacher; 1889; Born in Terceira.

João Areias; Sailor; 1492; member of Columbus' crew on first trip, native of Tavira, Algarve.

Mary Astor; Actress; 1890; Born in Illinois of Madeiran Immigrants.

Duarte Barbosa; Navigator; 1519; Member of Magellan (Magalhães) crew.

Pedro Barcelos; Navigator; 1494; Rediscovered Newfoundland, Greenland.

Bernard Baruch; Politician; U.S. President advisor.

Francisco L. Borges; politician; Connecticut State treasurer.

Family Bettencourt; Soldiers; 1835; fought for freedom of Texas.

Catherine of Braganza; Queen of England; 1640; Borough of Queens, N.Y., married Charles II of England

Manuel Silvestre Brazil; settled in New Mexico 1871,County Commission; Texas, 1908-1914, involved with Billy the Kid.

João Rodrigues (Cabrillo) Cabrilho; Navigator; 1500; discover of California, born in Pamela, "Freguesia de" Cabril, Montalegre, Trás-os-Montes

Benjamin J. Caetano; Politician; Lt. governor Hawaii .

André do Campo Soldier; 1541; Coronado's expedition into Grand Canyon, Texas, Arkansas, Oklahoma, Kansas.

Aaron Nunes Cardozo Amsterdam; 1752; married daughter of Moses Mendes Seixas; parents of Benjamin Cardozo.

Benjamin N. Cardozo; Judge; 1870; U.S. Supreme Court Justice.

S. N. Carvalho; artist.

Colonel John C. Freemont, photographer; exploration of the west.

Maria Anastasia Chaves; wife; married Judge Roy Bean, promoted laws for law and order.

Luis de Carvalhal; Explorer; 1579; Texas, married Guiomar Alvares de Rivera, a Jewess native of Lisbon.

João Lopes de Carvalho; Navigator; 1519; Member of Magellan's (Magalhães) crew.

João Elliot de Castro; Pioneer; 1814; early arrival in Mimai, personal physician of King Kamehamea I.

Family Chaves; Soldiers; 1835; fought for freedom of Texas.

João Coelho; Navigator; 1475; possible voyage to West Indies with Frois.

João Cordeiro; Explorer; 1540; with the Hernando de Soto expedition.

Antonio Correia; Shipmaster; 1500; Member of the Cabrilho expedition in California.

João Vaz Corte Real; Navigator; 1474; Possible arrival in North America.

Corte Real; Navigator; 1500; Dighton, Massachussets, first arrival.

Gaspar Corte Real; Navigator; 1500; Colonies of New England, Carolinas 1501-03, from Terceira, Azores.

Miguel Corte Real; Navigator; 1500; Colonies of New England, Carolinas 1501-03, from Terceira, Azores.

Family Cunha (Wager); Fisherman; 1850; Fall River, from Azores.

Estevão Dias; Navigator; 1519; Member of Magellan's (Magalhães) crew.

José Dias; Soldier; 1776; Revolutionary War, settled in Martha's Vineyard, died 1781.

João Estaço; Missionary; 1552; Native of Terceira, Azores, was named bishop of Puebla in Mexico.

Fernão Dualmo/Dulmo; Navigator; 1487; May have discovered the Antilles in 1487, British historian A. Davies.

João Afonso Estreito; Navigator; 1486; May have been in Newfoundland with Dulmo.

Brothers Faleiro; Navigator; 1519; Member of Magellan's (Magalhães) crew.

João Alvares Fagundes; Navigator; 1520; Explored Newfoundland and US East Coast in 1520, from Viana do Castelo.

Bento Fernandes; Explorer;1540; with the Hernando de Soto expedition.

Álvaro Fernandes; Explorer/writer; 1540; Gentleman of Elvas, wrote the first book about the Southeast, traveled with Hernando de Soto.

Simão Fernandes; Navigator; 1560; Explored U.S. east coast and later was the pilot under Sir William Raleigh.

Bartolomeu Ferrelo; Explorer; 1542; Chief pilot with Cabrilho, discoverer of California.

Mathias Figueira; Doctor; 1853; Founder of American College of Surgeons, born in Madeira.

Peter Francisco; Soldier; 1776; Fought in American Revolution with George Washington.

Estevão Frois; Navigator; 1475; Possible voyage to West Indies with Coelho.

Luis de Góis; Jesuit; 1545;First to take tobacco to Europe from America.

Bento de Góis; Soldier - Missionary; 1580; Born in Vila Franca do Campo, São Miguel Island, Azores.

Estevão Gomes; Navigator; 1525; US East Coast, Virginia also previously with Magellan (Magalhães).

Lewis Gomes; Portuguese Jew; 1707; Sloop Flying Horse.

Marcelino Manuel Graça (Grace); Bishop; 1882; Born in Cape Verde, founder of a large Protestant congregation.

Horta; Explorer; 1540; Southwest U.S.

Portuguese Joe Soldier; 1812; Hero captain fought in the successful Battle of Lake Erie.

João Fernandes Lavrador; Navigator; 1474; Discovered Greenland, Labrador; From Terceira, Azores.

Afonso Gonçalves; Pilot; 1519; Member of Magellan's (Magalhães) crew.

Emma Lazarus; Poet; 1800; Statue of Liberty inscription.

Benjamin Levy; Merchant; 1773; Co-founder of the first Portuguese Jewish settlement in Maryland.

Henrique Lopes; Merchant; 1500; Merchant in caravel captured by English privateers, see Irene Wright's book.

Aaron Lopes; Merchant; 1750; Baptized Catholic, fled Portugal 1740's, Newport R.I., founder of Touro Synagogue.

James Lucena; Manufacturer; Begins the manufacture of Castile soap in Rhode Island.

Jacob Lumbrozo; Physician; 1656; Portuguese Jew, settled in Maryland in 1656, died in 1666.

Abraham de Lyon; Vintner; 1737; Began growing grapes in Georgia in 1737

David Mendes Machado; Rabbi; 1734; Spanish-Portuguese congregation in New York City.

José Manuel Machado; Soldier; 1769;Commander of the Presidio in San Diego, California.

Fernão de Magalhães; Navigator; 1500; Circumnavigation of the world, crossed into the Pacific Ocean from the Atlantic.

Martim de Magalhães; Navigator; 1519; Member of Magellan's crew

Isaac Marques; Portuguese Jew; 1707; Sloop *Flying Horse*

Luis R. Medeiros; School Teacher; 1894; Honolulu, Hawaii, captain national guard.

Gracia Mendes; Diplomat; 15??; Jewess born in Lisbon, became famous in the Ottoman Empire where she fled to after the Inquisition.

Antonio Mendes; Captain, whaler; 1600; Born Terceira, Azores, first to navigate the Sacramento river.

H. Pereira Mendes; Rabbi; 1724; Shearith Israel.

Tom Mix; Cowboy; 1890; Born in Portugal as Antonio Nunes Pinguelo. ⅄

Benjamim Nunes; Soldier, Officer; 1770; Washington's staff served with ⅄ General Pulaski.

Joseph Nunes; Portuguese Jew; 1707; Sloop *Flying Horse.*

Pedro Nunes; Cosmographer; 1537;Tables and the "Tratado da Esfera"

Samuel Ribeiro Nunes; Physician; 1733; Portuguese Jew arrived in Georgia in 1733.

Pedro Fernandes de Queiroz; Navigator; 1596; West Indies, Central America to India.

Moses Pacheco; Portuguese Jew; 1658; Arrived from Amsterdam, Newport R.I.

Fernão Pais; Explorer; 1540; Southwest U.S.

John dos Passos, Journalist, poet, novelist of USA Trilogy.

Jacinto (Jason) Pereira (Perry); Consul agent; 1826; Faial, Azores, Hawaii,

John Philips; Hero US West; 1800; Manuel Filipe Cardoso, Pico, Azores.

Isaac Pinto; Economist; Far East explorer.

Jacob & Solomon Pinto; Emigrants; 1724; Residents of New Haven, CT, in
    1724.

Gonçalo Rico Navigator; 1545; Chief pilot with Ruy Lopez de Villalobos,
    sailed from Mexico to New Guinea.

Hill Portuguese Ridgmanites; Soldiers; 1776; Revolutionary war, known by the
    English colonists.

John Freitas Raposo; Merchant, postmaster; 1882; Island of Kauai, Hawaii.
    recruited labor in Madeira.

José Vieira Ramos; Settler; 1830; settled in Virginia, one of the first to receive
    American citizenship.

José Antonio Rocha; Settler; 1815; first owner of Los Angeles City Hall, son of
    a judge in Balboa, California;1868-1873.

Nicola Rodrigo; Sailor; 1586; Captured by Thomas Cavendish off the coast of
    Mexico.

Family Rodrigues; Portuguese Jew; 1624; Virginia 1624.

Gonçalo Rodrigues, Blacksmith; 1519; Member of Magellan's (Magalhães)
    crew

Francis Salvador; Politician, soldier; 1770; active in South Carolina during the
    American Revolution.

Afonso Sanches Navigator; 1452; Possible voyage to West Indies.

Antonio Martins Segurado; Explorer; 1539; with the Hernando de Soto
    expedition.

Isaac Mendes Seixas; Supporter; 1776; American Revolution, married Rachel
    Levy; Merchant vessels.

Gershom Seixas; Rabbi; 1770; Shearith Israel, for 50 years, supported the cause
    from the pulpit.

Abraham Seixas; Patriot; 1800; Colonel Georgia brigade.

Moses Seixas; Cashier; 1809; Bank of R.I., grand master of the Order of RI.

Abade José Correia da Serra Diplomat; 1801Represented Portugal after the U.S.
    Independence, Ambassador to Pres. Thomas Jefferson.

Sebastião Rodrigues Seremenho; Navigator; 1595; Surveyed the
                    California coast.

Francisco José da Silva; Whaler; 1826; Pico Azores; settled in San Francisco.

M. A. Silva; Editor; 1884; Madeira; Portuguese newspaper editor
    in Hilo, Hawaii.

Hattie Bence Silvia; Teacher; 1899; First woman teacher of
                    Portuguese descent in Fall River.

Ottis Skinner; Actor; 1858; Son of Azorean Immigrants.

João Dias Sollis; Navigator, Spain; 1500; Possible voyage to
    Central America and Brazil
Matias de Sousa; Settler, emigrant; 1634; Arrived in Maryland,
    possibly of Jewish descent.
Mae de Sousa; Opera Singer; 1800 Daughter of John de Souza,
    descendant of Jacksonville pioneers.
John Philip de Sousa; Musician; 1800; Musician, the march king
Antone S. Sylvia; Whaler; 1855; Born Azores, arrived in New
    Bedford, MA at 15, died a millionaire
Antone Ferreira Tavares; House representative; 1898;Lawyer,
    politician.
Diogo de Teive; Navigator; 1452; Azores and possible voyage to
    West Indies.
Pedro Teixeira; Navigator;1600; West Indies, Central America to
    India, discovered Tahiti in 1602.
Lucas Thomas; Politician; 1890; Elected for the territory's
    legislature.
Luis Vaz de Torres; Navigator; 1605; Discovered Torres Straits
    between Australia and New Guinea.
André de Vasconcelos; Explorer; 1540; With the Hernando de
    Soto expedition.
William Madison Wood; Textile industry; 1858; Son of
    Portuguese immigrants, mills, mansions and mergers.

Indian Tribes that may be connected with
Portuguese early settlers

Tribe	Location
Black-Waters	East Tennessee
Black-Dutch	
Black-Irish, Brown People	
Blue-Skin	Kentucky, Melungeons
Brass Ankles, Red Legs	Indians w/Portuguese surnames , named because of metal bracelets and jewelry they wore.
Bushwhackers	New England
Carmels	Ohio and Kentucky
Cajans and Creoles	Alabama and Louisiana
Cherokees	North Carolina
Croatans	Virginia, North Carolina
Cubans	North Carolina
Dead Lake	Dead Lake People, Florida Panhandle
Dominickers, Free Jack	
Guineas	West Virginia
Haliwa	Warren and Halifax Counties, Northeast NC
Jackson Whites	New York and New Jersey
Keating Mountain	New York
Lumbees or Rivers	Indians w/Portuguese surnames , Virginia Valleys
Issues	Virginia
Jackson Whites	Morris and Passaic Counties in New Jersey and Orange and Rockland Counties in New York
Mashpee	Cape Cod, Indians w/Portuguese surnames, Nunes,
Gomes, Pereira, Macedo.	
Moors	Maryland and New Jersey
Nanticokes	Sussex County in Delaware and Bridgeton in Cumberland County, New Jersey
Pool Tribe	Pennsylvania
Portugee	
Powatans	Virginia North Carolina
Ramps	Virginia
Redbones	Florida panhandle, Wewahtchka-Blownstown, Louisiana.

Tribe	Location
Ridgemanites	East Tennessee
Slaughters	New England
Turks	Sumter County
Wesorts	Maryland
Yuchi (Chisca)	Children of the Sun, Appalachian Highlands.

The above information was the result of researching many books, magazines, documents and newspapers mentioned in the Bibliography section.

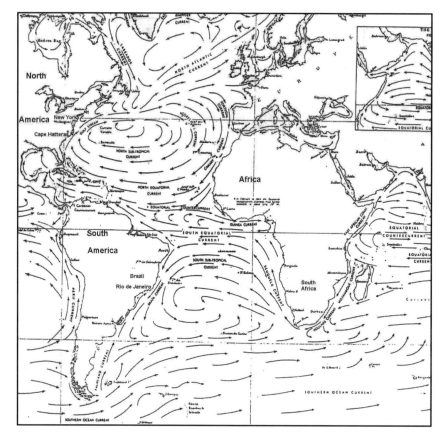

Fig. 105 - General circulation of the surface currents in the south Atlantic.

On Chapter IX, it was shown how a sailing vessel could wind up in the east coast of the North American Continent. The illustration above, shows in more detail the winds and currents of the South Atlantic.

At the last IV Portuguese Navy Academy Symposium, on November 1996, Commander Malhão Pereira made a conference about Vasco da Gama and sailing navigation. In this conference, he made it very clear how a caravel, if not properly navigated could wind up in the Caribbean or on the U.S. east coast.

This is the most logic explanation, how some of the many Portuguese ships lost or shipwrecked, could bring Portuguese and their families to America, either from Portugal or from the Far East, including natives from that region.

José Manuel Malhão Pereira is a well experienced high seas navigator, and is "Comandante de Mar e Guerra" of the Portuguese Navy. He is also the author of a book about sailing with the title *Manobrar é Preciso*, published in Portugal.

Commander Pereira, participated in the 1992 ocean *Regata,* commanding the Portuguese Navy school ship *Sagres* along with major nations, and their tall ships.

Adams, James Truslow. *Dictionary of American History.* Vol. 3. Scribners, NY (ICGP 1141), 1940.

Afonso, John Correia. *Christian and Spices, The Portuguese in India.* Unesco Courier, Paris, France, April issue, 1989.

Aguiar, João. *A Voz dos Deuses, (Memorias de Viriato).* Perspectivas e Realidades, Lisboa, 1984.

Albornoz, Michael. *De Soto, Knight of the Americas.* Franklin Watts, N.Y., 1986.

Albuquerque, Luis de. *The Courier and the Portuguese Voyages of Discovery.* Unesco, Paris, France, April issue, 1989.

Albuquerque, Luis de. *Alguns casos da India Portuguesa, D. João de Castro.* Alfa, Lisboa, 1989.

Albuquerque, Luis de. *Dicionario de Historia dos Descobrimentos Portugueses.* Circulo de Leitores, Lisboa, 1994.

Albuquerque, Luis de. *Rutters of India of D. João de Castro.* Inapa, Lisboa, 1988.

Allen, W. C. Allen. *History of Halifax County.*Cornhill Co., Boston, 1918.

Almeida, Carlos de. *The Portuguese Immigrants.* União Portuguesa do Estado da California, 1992.

Amaral, Pat. *They Ploughed the Seas.*Valkyrie Pres, Inc., 1978.

Armstrong, Zella. *Who Discovered America ?* Lookout Publishing, Chattanooga, TN, 1950.

Aswell, James & others. *God Bless the Devil, Melungeon Tales.* UNC, Chapel Hill, 1944.

Baganha, Maria Ioannis Benis. *Portuguese Emigration to the United States (1820-1930.*Garland Publishing, New York, 1990.

Baião, Antonio Blanco. *Historia da Expansão Portuguesa no Mundo, Vol. II.* Atica, Lisboa, 1939.

Bailey, Philip A. *Golden Mirages, Ramona Antonio Joseph, California Prospect.* Acoma, 1971.

Baird, Charles W. DD. *History of the Huguenot Emigration to America.* Dodd, Mead & Co. NY, 1907.

Ball, Bonnie Sage. *America's Mysterious Race*, Vol. XVI, May 64-67. Pick of the Month, 1944.

Ball, Bonnie Sage. *The Melungeons Origin & Kin.* Author, 1969.

Ball, Bonnie Sage. *The Melungeons*, The Overmountain Press, Johnson City TN, 1969.

Bancroft, Hubert Howe, *The works of Hubert of ... 1882-1890, Vols. 18-21*, History Co., San Francisco. 1882.

Barbosa, Jorge Morais. *Lingua Portuguesa no Mundo.* Sociedade Geografia de Lisboa. 1968.

Barck, Oscar Theodore, Jr. *Colonial America.* MacMillan, NY. 1958.

Barr, Phyllis Cox. *The Melungeons of Newman's Ridge.* East Tennessee State University, 1965.

Barreira, Anibal. *Historia de Portugal.* Edições ASA, 1978.

Barreto, Luis Filipe. *Camões & the Portuguese Voyages*, The Courier, Unesco,

Paris, France, April issue, 1989.

Barreto, Mascarenhas, *O Português Cristovão Columbo*. Edições Referendo, Lisboa, Portugal, 1988.

Barreto, Mascarenhas. *The Portuguese Columbus*. MacMillan Press London, England, 1992.

Bell, Aubrey F.G. *Damião de Gois, Um Humanista*. Imperio, Lisboa, 1942.

Bensaude. Joaquim. *Roteiro de Flandres e D. João II*. Sociedade Astoria, Lisboa, 1945.

Berkow, Robert. *The (Diagnosis and Therapy)*, Merck Manual, Merck Sharp, Rahway, NJ, 1982.

Berry, Brewton. *Almost White*. MacMillan, NY, 1963.

Bible, Jean Patterson. *The Melungeons Yesterday and Today*. Mountain Press, Signal Mountain, TN, 1975.

Biggs, Captain Walter. *Voyages and Travels. Vol. 33*. Drakes Voyages, Harvard Classics, 1910.

Biggs-Anderson, David-Grace M. *The Future we Inherit*. McClelland & Stewart, Secretary State of Canada, 1976.

Blackmun, Ora. *W. North Carolina, Its Mountains, Its People to 1880*. Appallachian Consortium Press, Boone, NC , 1977.

Blue, Karen I. *The Lumbee Problem*. Cambridge U.P., NY, 1980.

Boland, Charles Michael. *They all discovered America*. Double Day, NY, 1961.

Bolton, Herbert E. *The Colonization of North America*. Hafner Publishing Co., NY, 1971.

Bolton, Herbert E. *Spain's Title to Georgia*. Univ. of California Press, Berkley, 1925.

Boorstin, Daniel J. *The Discoverers*. Vintage, Random House, N.Y., 1985.

Bourne, Edward Gaylord. *Narratives Hernando de Soto*. Rodrigo Rangel, Biedma ,Allerton Book Co., NY, 1922.

Bourne, Edward Gaylord. *The Northmen, Columbus and Cabot*. Barnes & Noble, 1959.

Boxer, Charles Ralph. *From Lisbon to Goa*. Variourum Reprints, London, 1984.

Boxer, Charles Ralph. *The Portuguese Seaborne Empire*. Alfred A Knopf, NY 1969.

Boxer, Charles Ralph. *The Tragic History of the Sea*. The Hakluyt Society, 1967.

Braswell, Peggy Jo Cobb. *The Roanoke Canal*. Halifax County, 1958.

Braudel, Fernand. *The Mediterranean World...* Harper & Row, NY, 1972.

Braudel, Fernand. *The Structures of Everyday Life*. The, Harper & Row, NY, 1975.

Brazão, Eduardo. *Descobrimentos Portugueses nas Historias do Canada*. Agencia Geral do Ultramar, Lisboa, 1969.

Brazão, Eduardo. *Os Cortes Reais e o Novo Mundo*. Agencia Geral do Ultramar, Lisboa, 1965.

Brebner, John B. *Explorers of North America*. 1492/1806, Mac Millan New York, 1933.

Brito/Peres, Bernardo Gomes/Damião. *Historia Tragico-Maritima, Vol. I*. Editora do Minho, Barcelos, Portugal, 1942.

Bromwell, William J. *History of Immigration to the U.S.* Arno, NY, 1969.

Brown, Alexander. *Genesis of the United States, Vol. I, p. 337.* Russel & Russel, NY, 1964.

Burks, Jacqueline Daniel, *Treatment of the Melungeons in Gen. Literature...,*Tennessee Tech, Master Thesis, 1972. ⚔

Burns, Edward McNall. *World Civilizations.* W. W. Norotn & Co., 1955.

Cabral, Adalino. *Portinglês.* Four volumes,University. Microfilms Intern., Ann Arbor, MI, 1985.

Callahan, North. *Melungeons, in Smoky Mountain Country.* Little Brown & Co. Boston, 1952. ⚔

Cambiaire Ph.D.,Celestine Pierre ,W.V. Mountain Ballads, Last American Pioneer Stand, London, Mitre Press, 1935.

Camões, Luis Vaz de. *Os Lusiadas.* Imprensa Nacional, Lisboa, 1970.

Canfield, Jack. *Chicken Soup for the Soul* (Mark Victor Hansen), Health Communications, Inc., 1995.

Canto, Ernesto do,Centenario da Descoberta da America, Tipografia Ponta Delgada, Açores, 1892.

Cardozo, Manuel da Silveira, *Portuguese in America 590 BC - 1974 Chronology.* Oceana Publications, Dobbs Ferry, NY, 1976.

Carvalho, Agostinho de. *Portugueses na India.*Tipografia Rangel, India Portuguesa, 1943.

Castanheda, Fernão Lopes de. *Historia Descobrimento Conquista India.* (M.L.Almeida),Lello & Irmão, Porto, 2 Vols. (1979), 1551.

Chagas, Manuel Pinheiro, *Portugueses em Africa, Asia, America e Oceania,* Liv. A.M.Pereira, Lisboa, 1879.

Charnwood, Lord, *Abraham Lincoln,* Pocket Books, Cardinal, 1954.

Christovich, Mary Louise. *New Orleans Architcture.* Pelican Publishing Co. LA, 1989.

Clough & Others, Sheppard B. & Others, *Ancient Times to 1715, A History of the Western Worl,* D. C. Heath and Company, Boston, 1964.

Cohen, Martin A., Sephardim in the Americas (Abraham J. Peck), University of Alabama Press, 1993.

Cool, Linda E. *Lá Muito Longe Para Alem do Mar.* Angra do Heroismo, Açores, 1994.

Coppee, Henry, *History of the Conquest of Spain by ...Moors.* Little Brown & Co., Vol. 2, 1881.

Cortesão, Armando. *Cartografia e Cartografos Portugueses, Vol. I.* Seara Nova, Lisboa, 1935.

Cortesão, Armando. *Historia da Cartografia Portuguesa, Vol. I, II,* Junta de Investigações do Ultramar, Lisboa, 1969.

Cortesão, Jaime. *Os Descobrimentos Portugueses (2 Vol.),* Arcadia, Portugal, 1958.

Cortesão, Jaime. *Os Portugueses no Descobrimento dos E.U.* Seara Nova, Lisboa, 1949.

Cortesão,Jaime. *Viagem de Diogo de Teive e Pero Vasquez...* Imprensa da Armada, Lisboa, 1933.

Cortesão/Mota. Armando/Avelino. *Portugaliae Monumenta Cartographica.* Seara Nova, Lisboa, 1960.

Coutinho, Almirante Gago. *Onde teria invernado Gomes de Sequeira em 1525.* Sociedade de Geografia, Seie 58-1/2, Lisboa, 1940.

Crocket, W. David. *Archaeological Anomalies.* Crocket, 1994, Anudsen Publishing Company, Decorah, IA, 1994.

Crow, Escott, Jeffrey J. (Hatley). *African Americans in North Carolina*, N.C. Dept. of Cultural Resources, 1992.

Cumming, William P. *The Discoveries of John Lederer.* Univ. VA Press, Charlottesville, VA, 1958.

Cunha/Fonseca, MᵃCristina-Luis Adão. *Tratado de Tordesilhas, Diplomacia Luso-Castelhana.* Inapa, Lisboa, 1991.

Dalgado, Sebastião Rodolfo. *Glossario Luso-Asiatico.* Imprensa da Universidade, Coimbra, 1919.

Dayton, Ruth Woods. *Greenbriar Pioneers and their homes.* West Virginia Publishing, 1942.

Denton, Gilian, *History of the World.* Dorling Kindersley, 1994.

Dias, Eduardo Mayone. *Coisas da Lusalandia.* Instituo Português Ensino, 1981.

Diez, Mᵃ del Carmen Galbis. *Catalogo de Passageros a Indias.* Archivo General de Indias, Sevilla, 1986.

Dimont, Max I. *The Jews in America.* Simon & Schuster, NY, 1980.

Domingues, Mario. *Camões a sua vida e a sua época.* Romano Torres, 1980.

Domingues, Mario. *Cardeal D.Henrique, o homem, o monarca.* Romano Torres, 1964.

Domingues, Mario. *Infante D. Henrique e sua época.* Romano Torres, 2ª edição, 1957.

Domingues, Mario. *João III, D. e sua época.* Romano Torres, 1960.

Domingues, Mario. Manuel I, D. e a Epopeia dos Descobrimentos. Romano Torres, 1971.

Donald, David Herbert. *Abraham Lincoln.* Simmon & Schuster, 1995.

Dor-Ner, Zvi. *Columbus and the age of discovery.* William Morrow and Co. Ny, 1991.

Duncan, David Ewing. *Hernando de Soto.* Crown Publishers, NY, 1995.

Durant, John & Alice. *Presidents of the United States (Andrew Johnson).* Gaché Publishing New York, 1970.

Dutra, Ramiro Carvalho. *Tecnologia de Alimentos no ano 2000.* Inst. Univ. de Trás-os-Montes, 1979.

Dyson, John. *Columbus, for Gold, God and Glory.* Simon & Schuster, NY, 1991.

Entwistle, W. J. *The Spanish, Portuguese, Catalan and Basque Language.* Faber and Faber, London England, 1951.

Ewen, Charles R. *The Archaeology of Spanish Colonialism in SE United States....* Society for Historical Archaeology, 1990.

Estabrook, Arthur Howard & Ivan E. /McDougle. *Mongrel Virginians.* Williams and Williams, Baltimore, 1926.

Falcão, Luis de Figueiredo. *Livro de toda a Fazenda dos Reinos de Portugal.* Imprensa Nacional (Original 1607), 1859.

Felix, John Henry. *The Portuguese in Hawaii.* Peter F. Senecal Honolulu, Author's edition, 1978.

Fell, Barry. *America B. C. , Ancient Settlers.* Demeter Press Book, 1977.

Fernandes, Alvaro. *Gentleman of Elvas, Hernando de Soto Travels.* Florida Historical Society, 1933.

Ferreira, Ana Maria Pereira. *Essencial sobre o Corso e a Pirataria.* Universidade Nova, Lisbon, 1986.

Ferreira, Ana Maria Pereira. *Importação e o Comercio Têxtil...* 1385-1481. Universidade Nova, Lisbon, 1986.

Ferreira, Ana Maria Pereira. *Problemas Maritimos entre Portugal e França, Sec. XVI.* Imprensa Nacional, Lisboa, 1983.

Ferreira, Seomara da Veiga. *Cronica esquecida d'el Rei d. João II.* Imp. Universitaria, Edit. Estampa, 1984.

Figueiredo, Fidelino de Sousa. *A Épica Portuguesa no Século XVI.* Imprensa Nacional, Lisboa (1987), 1950.

Figueiredo, Fidelino de Sousa. *Estudos de Historia Americana.* Melhoramentos de S. Paulo, S. Paulo, Brasil, 1927.

Figueiredo, José de . *Época dos Descobrimentos.* Exposição Cultural em Sevilha, Catalogo, 1929.

Fletcher, Richard. *Moorish Spain.* Henry Holt, NY, 1992.

Flores, Joaquim/José. *Ourem, Três Contributos para a sua Historia.* Câmara Municipal de Ourem, 1994.

Flores, Maria da Conceição. *Portugueses e o Sião, seculo XVI.* Universidade Nova, Lisbon, 1991.

Fonseca, Luis Adão. *Tratado de Tordesilhas.* Inapa, Lisboa, 1991.

Fontes, Manuel da Costa. *Anti-Christian Jewish Ballad.* University of California Press, 1994.

Fontes, Manuel da Costa. *Sacrificio de Isaac, Portuguese Oral Tradition.* Journal of Folklore Research, Vol. 31-1-3, 1994.

Fontes, Manuel da Costa. *Study of the Ballad.* Folklore Institute, Ind. University, 1994.

Freijeiro, Antonio Blanco. *Historia de España.* Historia 16, Informacion , 1986.

French/Hornbuckle, Laurence/Jim. *The Cherokee Perspective.* Appalachain C. Press, Boone, NC , 1981.

Freyre/Putnam, Gilberto/Samuel. *The Master and the Slaves,* (Translation). University of California Press, 1986.

Frutuoso, Gaspar. *Saudades da Terra (Livro 4, Vol. 1, Livro 2).* Inst. Cultural Ponta Delgada, Azores, 1991.

Frutuoso/Azevedo, Gaspar/Alvaro Rodrigues. *Saudades da Terra, Historia das Ilhas....* Typ. Funchalense, Funchal, Madeira, 1873.

Fuson, Robert H., *The log of Christopher Columbus.* International Marine, Camden, 1992.

Gerber, Jane S. *Jews of Spain, The Sephardic experience.* Free Press, NY, 1992.

Gilbert Jr. , William Harlen. *Easterm Cherokees.* AMS, NY, 1978.

Gilbert Jr. , William Harlen. *Peoples of India.* Smithsonian, Washington DC, 1944.

Godinho, Vitorino Magalhães. *Os Descobrimentos e a Economia Mundial Vol. II.* Arcdadia, Lisboa, 1965.

Goertz, Richard. *João Alvares Fagundes, Capitão de Terra Nova,* 1521. Canadian Ethnic Studies Vol. XXXIII, No. 2, 1991.

Gonçalves, Julio. *Portugueses e o mar das Indias.* Livraria Luso-Espanhola, 1947.

Gowan, Walter. *New Orleans, Yesterday and Today.* LA Univ. Press, 1983.

Graham, Gerald S. *The British Empire.* Thames and Hudson, 1972.

Gregorie, Anne King. *History of Sumter County, SC.* Library Board, 1954.

Griffiths, Arthur. *In Spanish Prisons:Persecution and Punishment.* Dorset Press, NY, 1991.

Guill, James H. (Ph. D.). *Azores Islands A History.* Golden Shield Inc. , 1993.

Hale & Merritt, William T. & Dixon L. *History of Tennessee and Tennesseans Vol. 1.* Lewis Publishing Co. Chicago, NY, 1913.

Haun, Mildred. *The Hawk's Done Gone, The (Melungeon Colored).* Vanderbilt University Press, 1968.

Hawke, David. *Colonial Experience.* Bobs Merrill, NY, 1966.

Herculano, Alexandre. *Historia Origem, Estabelecimento Inquisição, Portugal.* Circulo de Leitores, Lisboa, 1982.

Hodge, Frederick Webb. *Handbook of the American Indian,* 2 Vol. Greenwood Press, 1971.

Hoffman, Paul E. *A New Andalucia and a way to the Orient.* Louisiana State University, Baton Rouge, 1990.

Hoffman, Paul E. *Spain and Roanoke Voyages.* N. C. Dept. Cultural, Raleigh, 1987.

Hollingsworth, Jess Gentry. *History of Surry County,* NC. W. H. Fisher Co. (Private Printing), 1935.

Hourani, Albert. *History of the Arab people.* Warner Books, 1992.

Hroch/Skybova, Miroslav/Anna. *Ecclesia Militans: The Inquisition.* Dorset Press, NY, 1991.

Hudson, Charles. *The Forgotten Centuries.* Georgia University Press, 1994.

Hudson, Charles M. *Juan Pardo Expeditions, The 1566-1568.* Smithsonian Press, 1990.

Huhner, Leon. *Jews in America in Colonial. . Revolutionary....* Gertzs Brothers, 1959.

Huhner, Leon. *The Jews of Newport*. Gertzs Brothers, 1959.
Huhner, Leon. *The Jews of South Carolina*. Gertzs Brothers, 1959.
Huyghe, Patrick. *Columbus was last*. Hyperion, New York, 1992.
Irwin, John Rice. *Portrait of a Pioneer, Alex Stewart*. Schiffer Publishing, West Chester, PN, 1985.
Ivey, Saundra Keyes. *Oral, Printed... Popular Culture, Tradition of the Melungeons*. University Micro Films, Michigan 48106, 1976.
Iyas, Ibn (Mamluk, Egipt). *Rivalry in the Red Sea, Portugal's impact*. Unesco, Courier, Paris, April Issue, 1989.
Janeira, Armando Martins. *Portugueses no Japão*. Publicações Dom Quixote, Lisboa, 1988.
Johnson, Charles A. *Wise County VA*. Overmountain Press, 1938.
Johnson/Malone, Allen/Dumas. *Dictionary of American Biography*, V3, 190-1, 396, 7. Schribners V5-24, 5; V17-407, 8, 1959.
Jones, Hugh. *The Present State of Virginia*. VA Historical Society, UNC Press, C. Hill, 1975.
Jordan, Vern. *The Melungeons Peoples, (Cherokee Country)*. Moccasin telegraph Network, 1996.
Kayserling, Meyer. *Historia dos Judeus em Portugal* (Trad. G. B. C. Silva). Livraria Pioneira, São Paulo, Brazil (1971), 1867.
Kegley, F. B. *Virginia Frontier*. SW Virginia Historical Society, Roanoke VA, 1938.
Kennedy, N. Brent. *The Melungeons, The Ressurection of a Proud People*. Mercer University Press, 1994.
Kinross, Patrick Balfour, Lord. *The Ottoman Centuries, Rise and Fall*. Morrow Quilll Paperbacks, NY, 1977.
Lawson/Lefler, John/Hugh Talmage. *A New Voyage to Carolina, or History of Carolina*. University of NC Press, 1984.
Levenson, Jay A. *Circa 1492*. National Gallery of Art, Yale U. Press, 1991.
Levinger, Phd, Rabbi Lee J. *History of the Jews in the United States*. Union of American Hebrew Congregations, 1961.
Lewis, Charles Lee. *David Glasgow Farragut, Vol. I, II*. United States Naval Institue, 1943.
Lewis / Loomis, Clifford M. / Albert. *Spanish Jesuit Mission in Virginia*. U. of NC Press, 1953.
Lewis/Hodge, Theodore/Frederick. *Spanish Explorers of the Southern United States*, 1528-1543. Brarnes & Noble, NY, 1959.
Ley, Charles David. *Portuguese Voyages*. J. M. Dent & Sons Ltd. London, 1953.
Lobban, Richard. *Jews in Cape Verde and on the Guinea Coast*. University of Massachusetts, Dartmouth, 1996.
Lopez, Juan Perez. El Cid, *El distierro*. Burgos, Spain, 1979.
Lourenço, Eduardo. *From National Epic to Universal Myth*. Unesco, Courier, Paris, April Issue, 1989.

Colaço, Dr. J. A. St. *Francisco Xavier - his life and times.* Internet jcolaco@bahamas. net. bs, 1996.

Lucena, João de. *Historia da Vida do Padre. Francisco de Xavier.* Alfa, Lisboa, 1989.

Lyon, Eugene. *The Enterprise of Florida.* University of Floorida, Gainsville, 1976.

Machado, José Pedro. *Grande Dicionario da Lingua Portuguesa.* Amigos do Livro Editores, Portugal, 1981.

Mahan, A. T. Alfred Thayer. *Admiral Farragut.* Haskell House, NY, 1968.

Manucy, Albert C. *Calendar of the N. C. Spanish Records,* 1566-1570. N. C. State Archives, 1946.

Marcus, Jacob Rader. *Colonial American Jew,* 1492-1776 - The. Wayne State University, 1970.

Marcus, Jacob Rader. *Early American Jewry, The Jews of NY,* Lopes-Rivera. Jewish Publications Soc. Phil. , 2 Vols. , 1951.

Markham, Clements R. *The Annals of America (1878 pp. 8-64).* Encyclopedia Britannica, Vol. 1, 1976.

Marques, A. H. de Oliveira. *Historia de Portugal, V. I, II, & III.* Palas Editores, Lisboa, 1982.

Marques, A. H. de Oliveira. *History of Portugal, Vol. I & II.* Columbia University Press, 1972.

Marques, Alfredo Pinheiro. *Guia da Historia dos Descobrimentos.* Biblioteca Nacional de Lisboa, 1988.

Marques, Alfredo Pinheiro. *Japan in early Portuguese maps.* Unesco, Paris, France, April issue, 1989.

Marques, Alfredo Pinheiro. *Portugal and the Discovery of the Atlantic.* Imprensa Nacional, 1990.

Martins, Oliveira. *Fomento Rural e Emigração* 3rd. edition. Guimarães Editores, 1994.

Martins, Oliveira. *Historia da Civilização Iberica,* 11th. edition. Guimarães Editores, 1994.

Martins, Oliveira. *Historia de Portugal,* 15th. edition. Guimarães Editores, 1968.

Martins, Oliveira. *Portugal nos Mares,* V. I 3rd. edition. V. II 2nd. edition. Guimarães Editores, 1994.

Mason, A. E. W. *The Life of Francis Drake.* Hodge and Stoughton Ltd. , 1950.

Mathews, Warren. *Abraham Was Their Father.* Mercer University Press, 1981.

Matos, Artur Teodoro de. *Na Rota das Indias.* Missão de Macau, 1994.

Mattoso, José . *Historia de Portugal,* 8 Vol. Editorial Estampa, Portugal, 1994.

Maxwell, Hu. *History of Barvour County,* West VA, Guineas. McClain Printing Co. , Parson, WV, 1968.

Mayer, Henrietta Mello. *Silva Descendants : Portuguese Genealogy.* Stonington, CT, 1978.

McCary, Ben. *Indians of the 17th century Virginia.* University of VA Press,

Charlottesville, 1990.

McEvedy, Colin . *Atlas Historico-Geografico*. Difel, Lisboa, 1984.

McGlothlen, Mike. *Melungeons and other Mestee groups*. Author, Gainesville, Florida, 1994.

McLeRoy, Sherrie/William R. *Strangers in their midst, Free Blacks of Amherst Cty*. VA. Heritage Books, MD 20716, 1993.

McRae, Barbara. *Know Your County*. Franklin Press, NC, 1985.

Mehdi, Beverlee Turner. *Arabs in America*. Oceana Publications, NY, 1978.

Melvin, Richard. *New Thoughts on the DeSotoExpedition in Gerogia*. Author, 1978.

Mertz, Henriette. *Atlantis, Dwelling Place of the Gods*. Henriette Mertz, Chicago, 1976.

Messick, Mary Ann. *History of Baxter County*. Mountain Home C. C. , 1973.

Midelfort, H. C. Erik. *Witch Hunting in Southwestern Germany*, 1562-1684. Stanford University Press, 1972.

Miers, Earl Schenk. *American Story*. Channel Press, Great Nech, NY, 1956.

Miller, Russel. *The East Indiamen*. Time-Life Books, Alexandra, Virginia, 1980.

Milling, Chapman, J. *Red Carolinians*. UNC, Chapel Hill, 1940.

Mira, Manuel. *Melungeons and the Forgottten Portuguese*. Author, 1995.

Monteiro, Saturnino. *Batalhas e Combates da Marinha Portuguesa*, Vol. 1-4. Sá da Costa, Lisboa, 1990.

Moon , William Arthur. *Peter Francisco, The Portuguese Patriot*. Colonial Publishers, 1980.

Mooney, James (George Ellison). *History, Myths and Sacred Formulas of the Cherokees*. Bright Mountain Books, Asheville NC, 1992.

Moquin, Wayne. *Makers of America: The First comers, 1536-1800*. Ed Wayne Moquin, 1971.

Moreira, Antonio Joaquim. *Sentenças da Inquisição em Lisboa, Evora e Coimbra*. Imprensa Nacional, Lisboa, 1980.

Moreira, Rafael de Faria D. *Portuguese Art in the Maritime Era*. Unesco, Courier, Paris, April Issue, 1989.

Morison, Samuel Eliot. *Admiral of the Ocean Sea*. Little, Brown and Company, 1942.

Morison, Samuel Eliot. *European Discovery of North America*. Oxford University Press, NY, 1971.

Morison, Samuel Eliot. *Journals & other documents, Columbus*, . Heritage, NY, 1963.

Morison, Samuel Eliot. *The Oxford History of the American People*. Oxford University Press, NY, 1965.

Morison, Samuel Eliot. *Portuguese Voyages to America, 15th Century*. Octagon Books, New York, 1965.

Morris, Richard B. *Encyclopedia of American History*. Harper & Row, NY, 1961.

Moura, Vasco da Graça. *Luis de Camões, the eventual life and times,* Unesco. The Courier, Japan in early Portuguese maps, April 1989.

Natella, Jr. , Arthur A. *The Spanish America 1513-1974 Chronology.* Oceana Publications, NY, 1975.

Neto, Serafim da Silva. *Historia da Lingua Portuguesa.* Presença, Rio de Janeiro, 1979.

Nichols, Philips. *Sir Francis Drake Revived.* Harvard Classics, Vol. 33, 1910.

Nunes, E. Borges. *Abreviaturas Paleograficas Portuguesas.* Faculdade de Letras de Lisboa, 1981.

Nunes, E. Borges. *Paleografia Portuguesa, Album.* Faculdade de Letras de Lisboa, 1981.

Offutt, Chris. *Melungeons from Story.* Suffolk, Ma, 1996.

Oliveira, João Brás de. *Os Navios de Vasco da Gama.* Agencia Geral do Ultramar, Imprensa Nac. , 1971.

Pap, Leo. *Portuguese Americans.* Portuguese Continental Union, 1981.

Pap, Leo. *The Portuguese in the United States: A Bibliography.* Center for Migration Studies, 1976.

Pardo, João. *Index da Chancelaria de D. João III,* Proprios. L 51, F 82v, 132, 132v - L3, F74v - L12, F74, 1523.

Pardo, Juan. *Archivos General de Indias, Juan La Bandera.* N. C. State Archives NC 2-31 AI148-2-8, T. 17, 1567.

Paredes, James Anthony. *Indians of the Southeast late 20th Century.* University of Alabama Press, 1992.

Paredes, James Anthony. *Social and Cultural Identity, Eastern Creek....* Southern Anthropological Society, UGA, 1974.

Parkman, Francis. *Pioners of France in the New World.* S. J. Parkhill & Co. , Boston, 1865.

Passos, Carlos de. *Navegação Portuguesa dos Séculos XV e XVI.* Imprensa da Universidade, Coimbra, 1917.

Patterson, George, Rev. *Portuguese in North America.* Montreal, 1891.

Perdue, Theda. *Native Carolinians, The Indians of North Carolina.* N. C. Dept. of Cultural Resources, 1985.

Pereira, A. B. de Bragança. *Portugueses em Diu.* Bastora, India, Tip. Rangel, 1938.

Pereira, Duarte Pacheco. *Esmeraldo de situ orbis, livro I, Capitulo II.* Academia Portuguesa da Historia, Lisboa, 1988.

Peres, Damião. *Historia de Portugal, Vol. III.* Portucalense Editora, 1931.

Peres, Damião. *Historia dos Descobrimentos Portugueses.* Vertente, Porto, 1981.

Pericão, Maria da Graça. *O Descobrimento da Florida.* Alfa, Lisboa, 1989.

Phillips, William D. *The Worlds of Christopher Columbus.* Cambridge U. P. , NY, 1992.

Pidal, Ramon Menendez. *Historia de España, Tomo XVIII. España* - Calpe, Madrid, 1966.

Pina, Rui de. *Chronica d'El Rey D. João II* (M. Lopes de Almeida). Lello & Irmão, Porto (1977), 1497.

Pinto, Fernão Mendes. *Peregrinação, Vol. 1.* Imprensa Nacional, Lisboa (1988), 1614.

Pinto, João Rocha. *Houve Diarios de Bordo... séculos XV e XVI.* Inst. Invest. Cientifica Tropical, Lisboa, 1988.

Pinto/Águas, Fernão Mendes/Neves. *Peregrinação,* Vol. 1. Europa-America, 1989.

Powell, William S. *The North Carolina Gazetteer.* University of N. C. , Chapel Hill, 1968.

Prestage, Edgar. *Descobridores Portugueses.* Edições Gama, Portugal, 1943.

Prestage, Edgar. *Viagens Portuguesas de Descobrimento.* Livraria Portugalia, 1940.

Pretty, Francis. *Sir Francis Drake Famous Voyage Round the World.* Harvard Classics, Vol. 33, 1910.

Price, Henry R. *Melungeons, The Vanishing Colony of Newman's Ridge.* Hancock County Drama Association, 1971.

Price, Jr. , Edward Thomas. *Geographic Analysis of White-Negro-Indian Racial Mix....* Los Angeles State College, 1953.

Price, Jr. , Edward Thomas. *Melungeons, Mix Blood Strain of the S. Appalachians.* Doctoral dissertation at University of California, 1950.

Quinn, David Beers . First Colonists, Doc. the First English Settlements, The. NC Dept. of Cultural Resources, 1982.

Quinn, David Beers. *Newfoundland from Fishery to Colony.* Arno Press, NY, 1979.

Quinn, David Beers. *North America Discovery, 1000-1612.* Univ. of South Carolina Press, 1971.

Quinn, David Beers. *The Roanoke Voyages* (2 Volumes). Dover Publications, New York, 1991.

Quinn, David Beers. *Set Fair for Roanoke.* U. N. C. Press, Chapell Hill and London, 1985.

Ramsey, J. G. M. *Annals of Tennessee, end 18th century.* Walker and James, Charleston, 1853.

Rangel, Rodrigo. *Hernando de Soto, narratives by B. Smith,* E. Bourne. Allerton Book, NY, 1936.

Read, Jan. *The Moors in Spain and Portugal.* Rowman & Littlefield, Totowa NJ, 1974.

Reparaz, Gonçalo de. *Portugueses no Vice-reinado do Peru,* XVI/XVII. Inst. Alta Cultura, 1976.

Ribeiro, Antonio Silva. *Colombo em Portugal.* Marinha Portuguesa, Lisboa, 1992.

Rice, Horace Richard. *The Buffalo Ridge Cherokee.* Bowie, MD, 1995.

Richardon, W. A. R. *Portuguese Discovery of Australia.* National Library of Australia, Albury, NSW, 1989.

Rights, Douglas L. *American Indian in NC.* John F. Blair, 1957.

Ritchie, Jean. *Singing Family of the Cumberlands.* University of Kentucky Press, 1988.

Roberts, J. M. *Pelican History of the World,* The. Penguin Books, NY, 1987.

Roddy, Edward G. Mills, *Mansions and Mergers, William M. Wood,* 1858. Merrimack Valley Textile Museum, 1982.

Rodrigues, Antonio Simões. *Historia de Portugal em Datas.* Circulo de Leitores, 1994.

Rogers, Francis Millet. *Americans of Portuguese Descent.* Sage Pub. Beverley Hills, Ca, 1974.

Rogers F. M., *Portuguese Americans,* Harvard Encyclopedia of Ethnic Groups by Cambridge, MA, 1980.

Roth, Cecil. *A. History of the Marranos.* Hermon Press, NY, 1974.

Rountree, Helen C. *Pocahontas people, Powatans Indians of Virginia.* University of Oklahoma Press, 1990.

Rountree, Helen C. *Young Pocahontas in the Indian World.* University of Oklahoma Press, 1995.

Russel-Wood, A. J. R. *Men under stress, social environment carreira da India.* Inst. Investigação Cientifica, Lisboa, 1985.

Russel-Wood, A. J. R. *World on the Move, the Portuguese in Africa* Carcanet Press Limited, 1992.

Sachar, Howard. *Farewell España.* Knopf, NY, 1994.

Sale, Kirpatrick. *Columbus, Conquest of Paradise.*. Random House, 1990.

Salley, Jr., Alexander S. *Narratives of Early Carolina.* Charles Scribner's sons, 1911.

Sams, Conway Whittle. *Conquest of Virginia, First attempt (1584 Exped.).* Keyser-Doherty Norfolk, VA, 1924.

Sandburg, Carl. *Abraham Lincoln, The Prairie Years and the War Years.* Harcourt Brace Jovanovich, Inc, 1970.

Sandburg, Carl. *Abraham Lincoln, The Prairie Years, Vol. I & II.* Harcourt Brace Jovanovich, Inc, 1970.

Sandoval, John S. *Mt. Eden cradle Salt Industry in California.* Mt. Eden Historical Publishers, 1988.

Santos, Fernando dos. *The Portuguese in Hawaii.* Luso-Americano Newspaper, Newark, N. J. 07105, 1996.

Santos, José de Almeida . *As Berlengas e os Piratas.* Academia de Marinha, 1994.

Santos, Robert L. *Azoreans to California.* Alley Cass Publications, Denair CA, 1966.

Saraiva, Antonio José . *Inquisição e Cristãos-Novos,* 5ª edição. Lisbon, Estampa, 1985.

Saraiva, José Hermano. *Historia Concisa de Portugal.* Publicações Europa-America, 1981.

Sauer, Carl Ortwin. *Sixteenth Century North-America.* Univ. of California

Press, LA, CA, 1971.

Serjeant, Robert Bertram. *The Portuguese off the South Arabian Coast.* Oxford at the Clarndon Press, 1963.

Serrão, Joaquim Verissimo. *Historia de Portugal, V III* . Verbo, 1978.

Serrão, Joel. *Cronologia geral da Historia de Portugal.* Horizonte, 1973.

Shillington, V. M. (A. B. W. Chapman). *The Commercial Relations of England and Portugal.* Burt Franklin, NY (A. B. Wallis Chapman), 1976.

Silva, Antonio de Morais e. *Grande Dicionario da Lingua Portuguesa, Vol. VI.* Confluência Editora, Portugal, 1954.

Silva, Dr. Manuel Luciano da. *Christopher Columbus name and the Pope.* Author, 1994.

Silva, Dr. Manuel Luciano da. *Columbus was 100 % Portuguese.* Author, 1989.

Silva, Dr. Manuel Luciano da. *Os Pioneiros Portugueses e a Pedra de Dighton.* Brasilia Editora, 1974.

Silva, Dr. Manuel Luciano da. *Portuguese Pilgrims and Dighton Rock.* Nelson D. Martins, Bristol, RI, USA, 1971.

Silva, Dr. Manuel Luciano da. *The True Antilles and Rock of Dighton.* Author, 1987.

Simmons, Marc. *Last Conquistador, Juan de Oñate.* University of Oklahoma Press, 1991.

Simmons, Marc. *The Little Lyon of the SW - a life of.* Ohio U. Press, 1983.

Skelton, Raleigh Ashlin. *Maps, Historical Survey.* Hermon Dunlap, Chicago, 1995.

Smith, James Morton. *Seventeenth Century America.* University of North Carolina Press, 1959.

Smith, M. Estellie. *Portuguese Enclaves: The Invisible Minority.* Southern Anthropological Society, UGA, 1974.

Smith/Sparks, Captain John/Michael. *History of Virginia or True Relations* . Michael Sparkes, 1624.

Sousa, Francisco de. *Tratado das Ilhas Novas.* Typ. Archivo Açores, Ponta Delgada, 1884.

Sousa, Frei Luiz de. *Os Anais de D. João III.* Sá da Costa, Lisboa, 1938.

Sousa, Manuel Andrade e. *Catherine of Braganza.* Edições INAPA, 1994.

South, Stanley. *Discovery of Sta. Elena, Parris Island.* Univ. of S. C. , Nat. Geographic Society, 1980.

Stapleton, Michael. *Greek and Roman Mythology.* Peter Bedrick Books, Inc. New York, 1986.

Stick, David. *Graveyard of the Atlantic (Shipwrecks of NC).* University of N. C. , Chapel Hill, 1968.

Stick, David. *Roanoke Island, the Beginnings of America.* University of N. C. , Chapel Hill, 1983.

Stick, David. *The Outer Banks of North Carolina.* University of N. C. , Chapel Hill, 1958.

Stokely/Cavender, Jim/Anthony P. *Encyclopedia of East Tennessee.* Jim

Stockley, Jeff D. Johnson Oak Ridge, 1981.

Stuart, Jess. *Daughter of the Legend*. New York, McGraw Hill, 1965.

Summers, Lewis Preston. *Annals of Southwest Virginia*. Summers, Abingdon, Virginia, 1929.

Summers, Lewis Preston. *History of Southwest Virginia*. Overmountain Press, 1989.

Sutherland, Elihu. *Pioneer recollections of Southwest VA*. Mullins Printing, Rt2, Box 307, 1984.

Sutton, Jessie, *The Heritage of Macon County*. Historical Society, 1987.

Swanton, John R. *De Soto Expedition Commission Final Report*. Smithsonian Institutional Press, 1985.

Tarbel, Ida Minerva. *In the Foot Steps of Lincoln*. Harper Brother, NY, 1924.

Tavares, Maria José Pimenta F. *Os Judeus em Portugal no Século XV*. Universidade Nova, Lisbon, 1982.

Taviani, Paolo Emilio. *Columbus, The Grand Design*. Orbis, London, 1985.

Teague, Michael. *Rota dos Navegadores Portugueses*. Quetzal Editores, Lisboa, Portugal, 1988.

TePaske, John. *Report on the Spanish Records of the NC State Archives*. Duke University, Ellen Z. McGrew, 1980.

Thapar, Romila. *History of India*. Penguin Books, 1966.

Thompson, George Malcom. *Sir Francis Drake*. William Morrow and Co. NY, 1972.

Tindall, George Brown. *America, a Narrative History*. W. W. Norton & Co. , 1984.

Trager, James. *Peoples Chronology*. Henry Holt, NY, 1994.

Treen, Maria de Freitas. *The Admiral and his Lady*. Robert Speller, NY, 1989.

Trindade, Maria José Lagos. *Portuguese Emigrations to the US. .* 19th century. SHBAI, 1976.

Ulmann, Doris. *Appalachian Photographs*. Jargon Society, KY, 1971.

Urbel, Fray Justo Perez. *La España del Siglo X*. Ediciones Alonso, Madrid, 1983.

Van Sertima, Ivan. *They came before Columbus*. Random House, NY, 1976.

Velho, Alvaro. *Roteiro da 1ª viagem de Vasco da Gama*. Agencia Geral do Ultramar, Imprensa Nac. , 1969.

Vidago, João. *Epigrafia Portuguesa nas Ilhas Bermudas, 1543*. Associação dos Arqueologos Portugueses, 1964.

Vidago, João. *O Nome da América e a Cartografia Portuguesa de 1500*. Revista Ocidente, Volume LXXV, 1968.

Viegas, Valentino. *Cronologia da Revolução de 1383-1385*. Imprensa Universitaria, 1984.

Vieira, Alberto. *Escravos no Arquipelago da Madeira, Sec. XV a XVII*. Centro Est. Hist. do Atlantico, 3 Vols. , 1991.

Viera, David J. *Bibliography History of Portuguese Language, Pedagogy*. David J. Viera, 1992.

Vigneras, Louis Andre. *La Busqueda del Paraiso y las Legendarias Islas....* Museo de Colon, Univ. Valladolid, 1976.

Warner, Jackson. *Studies in Slavery.* Mnemosyne Publishing, Miami, FL, 1851.

Weber, David J. *Spanish Frontier in North America.* Yale University Press, 1992.

Wheeler, Douglas L. *History Dictionary of Portugal.* The Scarecrow Press, Inc. NJ & London, 1993.

Wicki, Joseph. *Relação das Viagens dos Jesuitas,* 1541-1598. Inst. Inv. Cient. Trop. Lisboa, 1985.

Williams, Max R. *History of Jackson County.* Jackson County Historical Association, 1987.

Williams, Neville. *Great Lives Francis Drake.* Weidenfeld and Nicholson, London, 1974.

Williams, Neville. *The Sea Dogs.* MacMillan Publishing Co. , Inc. , NY, 1975.

Williams, Samuel Cole. *Dawn of the Tennessee Valley and TN History.* Watauga Press, Johnson City, TN, 1937.

Williams, Samuel Cole. *Early Travels in the Tennessee Country.* Watauga Press, Johnson City, TN, 1928.

Wirth, Fremont P. *The Development of America.* American Book Co. , 1938.

Wise, Jr. , W. Harvey. *Andrew Jackson, Biographical Sketch.* Burt Franklin, NY, 1935.

Witt, E. Carl. *Foot Prints in Northampton.* Northampton County, 1976.

Wolff, Christopher, Brinton. *Civilization in the West.* Prentice-Hall, Inc. , New Jersey, 2nd Ed. , 1969.

Wolforth, Sandra Knight. *The Portuguese in America.* Florida Atlantic University, 1976.

Wright, Irene A. *Further English Voyages to Spanish America.* Kraus Reprint, Liechtenstein, 1967.

Wright, Louis Booker. *The Atlantic Frontier.* Cornell University Press, 1966.

Wright, Louis Booker. *The Elizabethan's Americans.* Stratford/Avon, 1965.

Wright, Louis Booker. *History & Present St. of VA ed. Robert Beverley of 1705.* University of North Carolina, 1947.

Xavier, Pde. Manuel. *Relações da Carreira da India.* Alfa, Lisboa, 1985.

Zielonka, David M. *The Eager Immigrants.* Stipes Publishing Co. Champaign, IL, 1972.

Zurara, Gomes Eanes da . *Crónica da Guiné (José de Bragança).* Biblioteca Historica - Serie Ultramarina, 1973.

Zweig, Stephan. *Magellan, Conquerer of the seas.* MacMillan co. of America, 1938.

Newspapers, Magazines and other Media

Atlanta Journal, Native Africans' bones... by Bill Hendrick, p. C7, May 11th 1997

American Heritage, Was America discovered by Columbus, Alvin M. Josephy, Jr. , 1955.

American Heritage, Feb./Mar. , First Photograph of Lincoln, Harold Holzer, 1994.

American Heritage, Feb./Mar. , Nation of Immigrants, In the News, Bernard A. Weisberger, 1994.

American History Illustrated, The Lost Roanoke Colony (May), Walter Spearman, 1993.

American History Illustrated, The Melungeons, (November) Vol. 8, No. 7, Byron Stinson , 1973.

American History Guidebook, Chronology, Bobley Publishing, 1975.

American Anthropologist, Melungeons, The - A note on (October), Swan M. Burnett & W. H. Holmes, 1889.

American Anthropologist, Physical Anthropology and Genetics..., The - Vol. 74. William Pollitzer, 1972.

American Journal of Islamic Social Sciences, King Zumbi and the Malé Movement in Brazil, T. B. Irving, 1992.

Annais do Clube Militar, No. 1 to 11. Subsidios para o Estudo da Carreira das Indias, 1989. Cte. Carlos Alberto Encarnação Gomes, 1996.

Arena, Vol. 3. March, Malungeons, The, Dromgoole, Will Allen, 1891.

Arena, Vol. 3. May, Malungeons Tree and its Four Branches, The, Dromgoole, Will Allen, 1891.

Arkansas Gazette , Strange people of East Tennessee, January 14. Eliza N. Heiskell, Little Rock, AR, 1914.

Arkansas Gazette, Oct. 19, Fleeing Jews Discovered America Before Columbus, Cyrus H. Gordon, 1970.

Atlant, Constituition, July 6. Mistery of the Melungeons, Chris Wohlwend, 1993.

Blue Ridge Country July/August, Melungeons, The, N. Brent Kennedy, 1992.

Blue Ridge Country July/August, Melungeons, The, Joan V. Schroeder, 1991.

Boletim do Instituto, Historia da Ilha Terceira, Presença de Portugal nos E. U. A. , Vol. XVI, Manoel da Silveira Cardozo, Açores, 1958.

California History, Sept., Vol. LXVI, 3. Don Antonio José Rocha, El Portugues, Eduardo Mayone Dias and David Bertão, 1987.

The North Carolinian, Orange County Tax List, NC of 1755 (Vol. 1-4. Dec.), William Perry Johnson, Editor, 1955.

Catholic Historical, Review, The (October), Sebastian Montero:Pioneer American Missionary, Michael V. Gannon (Vol. LI, No. 3), 1965.

Charlotte, Observer (August 15) , Unlocking Melungeon Ancestry, Bruce Henderson, 1993.

Chattanooga, Sunday Times Magazine, Romance of the Melungeons, A - June 21. T. A. Rogers, 1936.

Chattanooga, Times (Oct. 19), Jews Were First to find America, Assoc. Press, NY, 1970.

Chesopiean, Archaelogy, Melungeons of Eastern Tennessee, The -Vol. 9, Thurston L. Willis, 1971.

Chicago, Tribune (August 19), Melungeon Colony Fading Away, New York Times News service, 1971.

Chicago, Tribune (Nov. 11), Melungeons a Tennessee Mystery, Editorial, 1970.

Citizen , Tribune, Morristown, TN, Melungeons June 8, Editorial, 1968.

Coalfield, Progress, June 6. Melungeon connection to Turkey, Jeff Lester, 1995.

Correio da Manhã, Relações Luso-Americanas nos anos da Independencia, white skin, Victor Luis Eleuterio, Lisboa, Portugal, 1995.

Diario de Noticias, Lisboa, Dignidade e Respeito, 11 Mar. Portugal, Editorial, 1958.

East Bay Window (Dec. 22/1993), Local Historian says Portuguese built Newport Tower , James A. Merolla, Dr. Luciano da Silva, 1993.

Enciclopedia Gallega, Grande. Volume 18. Silverio Cañada, España, 1974.

Encyclopedia, Britannica. Hard Cover Edition and CD 2. 0. Chigaco, 1993.

Encyclopedia, Britannica. Turnips in the Southeast & England, Book 22. Chicago, 1963.

Encyclopedia, Judaica. Iberian Downgrade. Suffolk, MA, 1972.

Encyclopedia, Judaica. Portugal and the Sephardim. Suffolk, MA, 1972.

Eugenics, Quarterly (Vol. 4-4 Dec.), American Triracial Isolates, Calvin L. Beale, 1957.

Figueiró dos Vinhos, Municipal Tourism Office Edition, Turismo Local, 1979.

National Genealogical Society, Melungeons, The - Essay Review, June Vol. 84. 2. Virginia Easley DeMarce, PhD. , 1996.

Geographic Magazine, National, Afghanistan's Border, Along the, June, 1985.

Geographic Magazine, National, Basque Whaling in America, XVI century, July, 1985.

Geographic Magazine, National, Celts, Europe's Founders, May, 1977.

Geographic Magazine, National, Elizabethans in America, December, Blanch Nettleton Epler, M.D., 1933.

Geographic Magazine, National, Fair of the Berber Brides, Carla Hunt, January, 1980.

Geographic Magazine, National, Forgotten Centuries, Exploring-Joseph Judge, March, 1988.

Geographic Magazine, National, Francis Drake, Sir and John Hawkins, February, 1975.

Geographic Magazine, National, Long slow death of a Jewish Language, November, 1993.

Geographic Magazine, National, Moors Ruled Spain, July, 1988.
Geographic Magazine, National, New England's Little Portugal, January, O. Louis Mazzatenta, 1975.
Geographic Magazine, National, Portugal at Cross Roads, October, 1965.
Geographic Magazine, National, Portuguese Sea Route to India, November, 1992.
Geographic Magazine, National, Turkish portrait of the World in 1513. March, 1994.
Geographical Review (April No. 2), Melungeons, The, Edward T. price, 1951.
Gowen Research Foundation , News Letter, Articles by Evelyn McKinley Orr and M. Ruth Johnson, Evelyn Orr & Ruth Johnson (1989 to 1996), 1996.
Halifax County, Centennial Year Book, County Commissioners, 1958.
Halifax Heritage, Historical Sketches, Weldon High School, 1958.
Hammond, C. S. Historical Atlas. C. S. Hammond & Co. , 1957.
Hancock County, Post, July 4. Hancock County Land of Mistery (Transcript 10 pages), William P. Groshe, McClung Historical Coll. , 1968.
Historical Review, North Carolina, Vol. 16. Catawba Nation and its neighbors, The, Frank G. Speck, 1939.
Historical Review, North Carolina, Vol. 19, Acculturation of the Eastern Cherokees, The, Leonard Bloom, 1942.
Historical Review, North Carolina, Vol. 46. Spanish Discovery of North Carolina in 1566. L. A. Vigneras, 1969.
Human, Biology, Sept. Vol. 41. 3. Survey of Demography, Genetics, Melungeons, William Pollitzer & William H. Brown, 1969.
Jornal, O, New Providence, Melungeons and their claim of Portuguese, Manuel Mira, 1995.
Journal and, Tribune (July 29), Melungeons Mystery Race, Associated Press, 1923.
Journal of Medicine, Genetic (30:235-239), Hereditary anaemias in Portugal, epidemiology…, Martins, Olim, Melo, Magalhães, Rodrigues, 1993.
Journal Washington, Academy Sciences, Jan. 15. Mixed Bloods of the upper Monongahela Valley, WV, William Harlen Gilbert Jr. , Vol. 36-1. 1946.
Journal of Science, Mixed Blood Racial Strain of Carmel,., Ohio, Magoffin, KY. Ohio, Vol. 50, Edward Thomas Price Jr., 1950.
Kingsport, Times News (Nov. 26), Melungeon Line Almost Extint, John Gamble (UPI), 1964.
Kingsport, Times News (Oct. 6), Melungeon and Turks. A Key to a Mystery, Brad Lifford, 1996.
Kingsport, Times News (May 28), Melungeon Museum, Christopher Schnaars, 1996.
Kingsport, Times News (Dec. 6), Melungeons Subject of Study, Barbara Watson, 1992.
Kingsport, Times News (Sept. 5), Last of the Melungeons, The, Editorial, Focus, 1971.

Knoxville, News Sentinel (April 26), Melungeon ways are passing, Willard Yarbrough, 1972.

Knoxville, News Sentinel (Oct. 10), Mediterranean Schollar's Theory, Associated Press, 1970.

Knoxville, News Sentinel (Jan. 8), Maligned Mountain Folk, Willard Yarbrough, 1968.

Knoxville, News Sentinel (Jun 10), Olive-Skinned Hancock Countians, Willard Yarbrough, 1966.

Knoxville, News Sentinel (Nov. 26), Mysterious E-T Mountain Clan, John Gamble, 1964.

Knoxville, Register (April 19), Melungeon Drama goes on despite money problems, Editorial, 1972.

Luso, Americano (Apr. 6), Manuel Brazil, um pioneiro Português no NM e TX, Geoffrey L. Gomes, 1994.

Luso, Americano (April 10), Bermuda Portuguese and Politician Interview, Newark, NJ, 1996.

Luso, Americano (April 19), Garrafa com mensagem de NJ deu à costa em Portugal, Franklin Cruz, April 19, 17, 1996.

Luso, Americano (April 24), Presença Portuguesa na India, Fernando G. Rosa, 1996.

Luso, Americano (Jan. 13. Apr. 6), Manuel Brazil, um pioneiro Português no NM, Geoffrey L. Gomes (1993 & 1994), 1993.

Luso, Americano, Dec. 1st , Sinagoga de Tomar, Magazine, 1995.

Luso, Americano (March 15), Melungos, Chamam-se, Manuel Mira, 1995.

Luso, Americano (May 3), New York Portuguese, The First, Newark, NJ, 1996.

Luso, Americano (May 31), Livro sobre o Sudeste dos E. U. , Manuel Mira, 1995.

Luso, Americano (Nov. 22), Abade José Correia da Serra, Henrique Mano, 1996.

Luso, Americano (July 8), Various Articles in Portuguese about Columbus, A. Oliveira, Dr. Luciano da Silva, IlidioMartins, 1992.

Macon, County, Archaeological report, Industrial Park, Cherokee Village, Susan M. Collins, Dave Moore, Ruth Y. Wetmore, 1977.

Macon County Heritage. Macon Co. Historical Society, Inc. - The. Delmar Printing, 2nd printing, 1993.

Mare Liberum - Dec. 1992. N°4. Movimento da Carreira da India nos Secs. 16-18, Lopes-Frutoso-Guinote, 1992.

Mare Liberum - Mar. 1994. N°7. Instrumentos de Navegação. . época Descobrimentos, José Manuel Malhão Pereira, 1994.

Mariner's Mirror, The (April), Portuguese Roteiros by Charles Ralph Boxer, Society for Nautical Research, London, 1934.

McClung, Historical Society, Melungeons at Oakdale, The, Otho N. Walraven, 1968.

McClung, Historical Society, Melungeons, The, Historical Collection, 1968.
Melungeon Bibliography, University of Tennessee, Knox. , Reference Library, Knoxville, 1992. ⅄
Mundo Português, Various Issues, Henrique Mano, 1996.
Nashville Banner, Aug. 3. What do you know about Malungeons, Douglas Anderson, 1924.
Nashville Tennesseean, Melungeon Mistery, by Louise Davis, also the Magazine, Louise Davis - 22/29 Sep. 1963. 1963.
New Orleans, Portuguese and Associations, Public Library, 1850.
New York Times, Indian resist integration plan in NC county, Sept. 13. Ben Franklin, 1970.
New York Times, Mysterious Hill Folk Vanishing, August 10. Jon Nordheimer, 1971.
News & The Observer (Raleigh, NC), Melungeons, Author finds clues to mysterious origin, Associated Press (Nov. 15), 1995.
News & The Observer (Raleigh, NC), Mistery of Virginia's Melungeons, The (Jul. 12), Chris Wohlwend, 1993.
News & The Observer (Raleigh, NC), Turkish TV and Universities study Melungeons, Editor - 11/15/1995. 1995.
Palm Beach Post, July 10. Pocahontas tale, plagiarism, West Palm beach, FL, 1995.
Portuguese Post, May 14. Greek Presence in Tavira, Newark, NJ, 1996.
Palm Beach Community College, Center for Multicultural Affairs, West Palm beach, FL, 1989.
PBS TV, VHS Cassete Spice Islands, Ring of Fire by Lorne and Lawrence Blair, 1988.
Portuguese Around us, Melungeons TV Program w/Dr. Luciano da Silva, VHS Cassete, 1995.
Portuguese Heritage, Portuguese settlement was family oriented, William Freitas, Ph. D. , 1993.
Portuguese Historical/Cultural Society, Portuguese Pioneers in Sacramento, Lionel Holmes, Joseph D'Alessandro, 1977.
Portuguese Studies Review (ICGP), Portuguese in the US, A Bibliography, David Wheeler, David Viera, Geoffrey Gomes, 1995.
R. T. P. TV, Portugal, Melungeons TV Program, Mario Crespo, VHS Cassete, 1994.
R. T. P. TV, Portugal, Melungeons TV Program, 2nd. program, VHS Cassete, 1995.
Reader's Digest (July pp. 191-197), Our Fair Lady:The Statue of Liberty, Special Feature, 1986.
Revista de Portugal (Fev. V. 6-N° 29), Lusismos na União da Africa do Sul, Antonio Barradas, 1945.
Roanoke Rapids, Sunday Herald (Mar. 2nd.), Northampton's Portuguese go Elsewhere… Front Page, Dick Kern, 1958.

Saturday Evening Post (Oct. 18), Sons of the Legend, Terry P. Wilson, William L. Worden, 1947.

Savannah Synangogue, History of the First Savannah Synagogue, City Tourism Office, 1992.

Shepperds TV Channel, Melungeons (Satellite, G4-6), VHS Cassete, 1989.

Smithsonian Institute (Synoptic data), Survival of Indian. Part-Indian Blood E. U. S. , William Harlen Gilbert Jr. , 1947.

State, The , NC Magazine, Melungeons, The, Arthur Billy, 1994.

Tennessee, Anthropological Association. , Bibliography of Tennessee Anthropology, Donald Bruce Ball, 1976.

Tennessee, Anthropologist Association 15/1. Melungeons, Comparisons of Gene Dist. , spring, James L. Guthrie, 1990.

Tennessee, Conservationist, Mystery people of Tennessee, The - August, Swan Burnett & W. H. Holmes, 1959.

Tennessee (Spring), Historical Quarterly, Andrew Jackson, a citizen of Spain, Robert V. Remini, 1995.

Tennessee Valley , Historical Review, Mistery of the Melungeons, The (Spring issue), Louise Davis, 1972.

Terrae (Journal), Incognitae (Vol. XIV), Turks, Moors, Blacks, and Others in Drake's…, David B. Quinn, 1986.

Terrae (Journal), Incognitae (Vol. II, pp. 25/28), The Voyage of Esteban Gomez from Florida to the Baccalaos, Louis Andre Vigneras, 1976.

Terrae (Journal), Incognitae 14. pp. 23/39), Motives of Portuguese Expansion…Indonesia…16th century, John Parker, 1982.

Terrae (Journal), Incognitae 13. pp. 31/34), Original Sources…Revisionism…Historiography of Discovery, John Parker, 1981.

Times Picayune, Islenos, The - the fight for survival of a culture, John R. Kemp, 1979.

Transylvania Times, Dec. 7. p. 8B, Mysterious Culture winds through Kentucky, Bryon Crawford, 1995.

Tuscaloosa News, Alabama (Nov. 1), Historic ancestry explored, solving a folklore mystery, Dana Beyerle, 1993.

UPEC , Life (Spring), Portuguese Immigrants in Nevada, Donald Warrin, 1989.

UPEC , Life (Summer), Portuguese. . on the Western frontier, Antonio Monteiro, Geoffrey L. Gomes, 1988.

Virginian Pilot, Segregated Portuguese Children, Jan. 26-1958. Luther Carther, 1958.

Wall Street, Journal, April 14. B1-B5. Appallachian Clan Mines Web sites for Ancestral Clues, Fred R. Bleakley, 1997.

President Clinton's Message
on Portugal Day
June 10, 1997

"I'm delighted to extend warm greetings to everyone celebrating Dia de Portugal.

This special day, dedicated to the life and memory of the great Portuguese poet, Luiz Vaz de Camões, remind us of how much the people and culture of Portugal have contributed to the world over the centuries. Today, as a model of democracy among the nations of Europe, Portugal continues to to build on its noble past by looking with confidence to the future.

The Portuguese people have played a vital role in the life of our nation as well. America has been continually renewed and enriched by the many different people who choose to come here and become our fellow citizens. Each brings a part of his or her own heritage, which over time becomes part of our common heritage. As we seek to become more united people, we must not forget our roots, for they remind us of who we are and of what we have to share with others. Portuguese-Americans can be proud of their roots and of the outstanding contribuitions they have made to our national life. From business to the arts, from governmment to academia, they have strengthened our nation and enriched our cultural heritage.

As we celebrate Portugal's National Day, let is also remember to celebrate the diversity that continues to be America's greatest strenth. Best wishes to all for a wonderful day".

Bill Clinton